REASONING
ABOUT
ACTIONS & PLANS
PROCEEDINGS OF THE 1986 WORKSHOP

EDITED BY
MICHAEL P. GEORGEFF & AMY L. LANSKY
SRI INTERNATIONAL

JUNE 30—JULY 2, 1986
TIMBERLINE, OREGON

SPONSORED BY
THE AMERICAN ASSOCIATION FOR ARTIFICIAL INTELLIGENCE
and the
CENTER FOR THE STUDY OF LANGUAGE AND INFORMATION

MORGAN KAUFMANN PUBLISHERS, INC.
95 FIRST STREET
LOS ALTOS, CALIFORNIA 94022

Editor and President   *Michael B. Morgan*
Coordinating Editor   *Jennifer M. Ballentine*
Production Manager   *Mary Borchers*
Cover Designer   *Irene Imfeld*
Compositor   *Shirley Tucker*
Production Assistant   *Lisa de Beauclair*

Library of Congress Cataloging-in-Publication Data

Reasoning about actions and plans.

   ''Sponsored by the American Association for Artificial
Intelligence [and the] Center for the Study of Language and
Information.''
   Includes bibliographies and index.
   1. Artificial intelligence—Congresses.   2. Problem
solving—Congresses.   I. Georgeff, Michael P., 1946–
II. Lansky, Amy L., 1955–   .   III. American Association
for Artificial Intelligence.   IV. Stanford University.
Center for the Study of Language and Information.
Q334.R42   1987   006.3   86-27748
ISBN 0-934613-30-3 (pbk.)

MORGAN KAUFMANN PUBLISHERS, INC.
95 First St., Suite 120
Los Altos, California 94022
© 1987 by Morgan Kaufmann Publishers, Inc.
All rights reserved

CONTENTS

FOREWORD

One feature that is critical to the survival of all living creatures is their ability to act appropriately in dynamic environments. For lower life forms, it seems that sufficient capability is provided by stimulus-response and feedback mechanisms. Higher life forms, however, require more complex abilities, such as reasoning about the future and forming plans of action to achieve their goals. Reasoning about actions and plans can thus be seen as fundamental to the development of intelligent machines that are capable of dealing effectively with real-world problems. The papers in this volume discuss approaches to a number of the more challenging problems in this area.

One basic requirement for building such machines is that we have a model of actions and events capable of representing the complexity and richness of the real world. The traditional approach to this task has been to consider that, at any given moment, the world is in one of a potentially infinite number of states and that any changes in state are wrought by the occurrence of actions or events. In this type of framework, actions and events are usually modeled as mappings on world states. But such a view of action is clearly not suitable for problem domains in which, for example, actions can take place over possibly long intervals of time, or where the presence of other agents or dynamic processes allows for concurrent or simultaneous activity.

It is also necessary to develop formalisms that allow us to reason about the effects of actions in a reasonably natural and tractable fashion. This turns out to be much more difficult than it first appears; actions may influence the world in extremely complex ways. Indeed, the functions, relations, or intervals that we use to model actions often cannot be readily described in some concise yet sufficiently complete form. Furthermore, we will often have incomplete knowledge of the world, necessitating that we have some means of making reasonable assumptions about the possible occurrence of other events or the behaviors of other agents.

A second major task confronting us is the development of techniques for forming plans of action to achieve given goals. This requires not only that we be able to reason effectively about actions and events, but also that we have means for searching the space of all possible future courses of action to find one that best meets the prescribed goals. In any reasonably complex application, the potential solution space is enormous; a major part of the planning problem is thus to devise ways of narrowing this space. A planning agent must also be able to recognize potentially conflicting plans and be able to coordinate its activities with those of other agents. Often this will require the agents to communicate about their respective world beliefs and intended plans of action, or to infer these from one another's behavior.

Of course, the ability to plan is not much help unless the agent doing the planning can survive in the world in which it is embedded. This brings us to a third problem area: the design of systems that are actually *situated* in the world and that must operate effectively given the real-time constraints of their environment. To describe such agents, it is often convenient to endow them with the psychological attitudes of belief, desire, and intention. The problem that then arises is how to specify the properties we expect of these attitudes, how the latter interrelate with one another, and how they determine rational behavior.

For example, such agents need to be able to reason about their current intentions and plans, altering and modifying them in the light of possibly changing beliefs and desires. They must also be able to reflect upon their own problem-solving and reasoning activities – to choose between possibly conflicting desires, to decide when to stop planning and start acting, and to determine how long they should stay committed to any particular goal. The very survival of autonomous systems may depend on their ability to react quickly to new situations and to modify their goals and intentions accordingly.

The purpose of the Timberline Workshop was to explore some of these issues in detail and to try to provide a sound foundation upon which the design of machines capable of rational activity could be based. The papers contained herein represent an important step in this direction.

A number of individuals and organizations contributed substantially to the success of the workshop and the compilation of this proceedings. In particular, we wish to thank Margaret Olender for her invaluable organizational and secretarial support. We also wish to express our appreciation for the generous support of the American Association for Artificial Intelligence and the Center for the Study of Language and Information at Stanford University.

Michael P. Georgeff
Amy L. Lansky

ON THE SEMANTICS OF STRIPS

Vladimir Lifschitz
Computer Science Department
Stanford University
Stanford, CA 94305

Abstract

STRIPS is a problem solver which operates with world models represented by sets of formulas of first-order logic. A STRIPS system describes the effect of an action by a rule which defines how the current world model should be changed when the action is performed. The explanations of the meaning of these descriptions in the literature are very informal, and it is not obvious how to make them more precise. Moreover, it has been observed that minor and seemingly harmless modifications in standard examples of STRIPS systems cause STRIPS to produce incorrect results. In this paper we study the difficulties with interpreting STRIPS operator descriptions and define a semantics which draws a clear line between "good" and "bad" uses of the language of STRIPS.

1. Introduction

STRIPS (Fikes and Nilsson 1971) is a problem solver which operates with *world models*, represented by sets of formulas of first order-logic. A STRIPS system is defined by an *initial* world model, which describes the initial state of the world, and by a set of *operators*, which correspond to actions changing the current state. Using means-ends analysis, STRIPS attempts to find a sequence of operators transforming the initial world model into a model which satisfies a given *goal formula*.

The *description* of each operator consists of its *precondition* (the applicability condition, expressed by a first-order formula), its *add list* (the list of formulas that must be added to the current world model), and its *delete list* (the list of formulas that may no longer be true and therefore must be deleted). A resolution theorem prover is used for the verification of operator preconditions, for establishing the validity of the goal formula in the last world model, and also for directing the search.

The explanation of the meaning of operator descriptions in (Fikes and Nilsson 1971) is very brief and is almost completely reproduced in the parenthesized comments above. It is not immediately clear how to make this explanation more precise; more specifically, it turns out to be a non-trivial task to define under what conditions the delete list of an operator may be considered sufficiently complete. Moreover, some minor and seemingly harmless modifications in the main example of (Fikes and Nilsson 1971) cause STRIPS to produce incorrect results (see Sections 4 and 5 below). Alan Bundy observes that the AI literature "abounds with plausible looking formalisms, without a proper semantics. As soon as you depart from the toy examples illustrated in the paper, it becomes impossible to decide how to represent information in the formalism or whether the processes described are reasonable or what these processes are actually doing" (Bundy 1983). Is STRIPS a formalism of this sort?

In this paper we do the additional theoretical work needed to make sure that this is not the case. We study the difficulties with interpreting STRIPS operator descriptions and define a semantics which draws a clear line between "good" and "bad" uses of the language of STRIPS.

2. Operators and Plans

We start with an arbitrary first-order language L. A *world model* is any set of sentences of L. An *operator description* is a triple (P, D, A), where P is a sentence of L (the *precondition*), and D and A are sets of sentences of L (the *delete list* and the *add list*).

Consider an example from Section 3.2 of (Fikes and Nilsson 1971). In this example, the language contains some object constants and two predicate symbols, unary ATR and binary AT. Intuitively, the language is designed for describing the locations of a robot and of other objects. We think of the universe of the intended model as consisting of these objects and their possible locations. $ATR(x)$ means that the robot is at location x. $AT(x, y)$ means that the object x is at location y. Let now k, m, n be object constants of this language. The operator $push(k, m, n)$ for pushing object k from m to n is described by the triple:

Precondition: $ATR(m) \land AT(k, m)$.

Delete list: $\{ATR(m), AT(k, m)\}$.

Add list: $\{ATR(n), AT(k, n)\}$.

What we defined here is a family of operator descriptions, one for each triple of constants k, m, n. The precondition shows that the corresponding action is possible whenever the robot and object k are both at location m. The delete list tells us that these two facts should be removed from the current world model when the operator $push(k, m, n)$ is applied. The add list requires that the information about the new location of the robot and of object k, represented by the formulas $ATR(n)$ and $AT(k, n)$, be added to the model.

A *STRIPS system* Σ consists of an *initial* world model M_0, a set Op of symbols called *operators*, and a family of operator descriptions $\{(P_\alpha, D_\alpha, A_\alpha)\}_{\alpha \in Op}$.

Section 4 of (Fikes and Nilsson 1971) introduces a STRIPS system which represents the world consisting of a corridor with several rooms and doorways, a robot and a few boxes and lightswitches. The language contains, in addition to ATR and AT, some other predicate symbols, for instance:

$TYPE(x, y)$: x is an object of type y,

$CONNECTS(x, y, z)$: door x connects room y with room z,

$NEXTTO(x, y)$: object x is next to object y,

$INROOM(x, y)$: object x is in room y,

$STATUS(x, y)$: the status of lightswitch x is y.

The initial world model in this example consists mostly of ground atoms, such as

$$TYPE(DOOR1, DOOR),$$
$$CONNECTS(DOOR1, ROOM1, ROOM5),$$
$$INROOM(ROBOT, ROOM1),$$
$$STATUS(LIGHTSWITCH1, OFF).$$

It contains also one universally quantified formula,

$$\forall xyz(CONNECTS(x, y, z) \supset CONNECTS(x, z, y)). \tag{1}$$

Among the operators we find:

    *goto*1(m): robot goes to location m,

    *goto*2(m): robot goes next to item m,

    pushto(m, n): robot pushes object m next to object n,

    gothrudoor(k, l, m): robot goes through door k from room l to room m,

    turnonlight(m): robot turns on lightswitch m,

and a few others.

This system will be subsequently referred to as the "main example".

Given a STRIPS system Σ, we define a *plan* to be any finite sequence of its operators. Each plan $\overline{\alpha} = (\alpha_1, \ldots, \alpha_N)$ defines a sequence of world models $M_0, M_1, \ldots, M_N$, where M_0 is the initial world model and

$$M_i = (M_{i-1} \setminus D_{\alpha_i}) \cup A_{\alpha_i} \qquad (i = 1, \ldots, N). \tag{2}$$

We say that $\overline{\alpha}$ is *accepted* by the system if

$$M_{i-1} \vdash P_{\alpha_i} \qquad (i = 1, \ldots, N). \tag{3}$$

In this case we call M_N the *result* of executing $\overline{\alpha}$ and denote it by $R(\overline{\alpha})$.

In what terms do we want to describe the semantics of STRIPS?

We think of the world described by the language L as being, at any instant of time, in a certain *state*; we assume that one of the states, s_0, is selected as *initial*. We assume that it is defined for each state s which sentences of L are (known to be) *satisfied* in this state, and that the set of sentences satisfied in state s is closed under predicate logic. An *action* is a partial function f from states to states. If $f(s)$ is defined then we say that f is *applicable* in state s, and that $f(s)$ is the *result* of the action. We assume that an action f_α is associated with each operator α. A STRIPS system along with this additional information will be called an *interpreted* STRIPS system.

A world model M of an interpreted STRIPS system Σ is *satisfied* in a state s if every element of M is satisfied in s. For each plan $\overline{\alpha} = (\alpha_1, \ldots, \alpha_N)$ of Σ, we define $f_{\overline{\alpha}}$ to be the composite action $f_{\alpha_N} \ldots f_{\alpha_1}$.

3. Semantics: A First Attempt

Consider a fixed interpreted STRIPS system $\Sigma = (M_0, \{(P_\alpha, D_\alpha, A_\alpha)\}_{\alpha \in Op})$. Our goal is to define under what conditions Σ can be considered *sound*. We start with the most straightforward formalization of the intuition behind operator descriptions.

Definition A. An operator description (P, D, A) is *sound* relative to an action f if, for every state s such that P is satisfied in s,

(i) f is applicable in state s,

(ii) every sentence which is satisfied in s and does not belong to D is satisfied in $f(s)$,

(iii) A is satisfied in $f(s)$.

Σ is *sound* if M_0 is satisfied in the initial state s_0, and each operator description $(P_\alpha, D_\alpha, A_\alpha)$ is sound relative to f_α.

Soundness Theorem. *If Σ is sound, and a plan $\overline{\alpha}$ is accepted by Σ, then the action $f_{\overline{\alpha}}$ is applicable in the initial state s_0, and the world model $R(\overline{\alpha})$ is satisfied in the state $f_{\overline{\alpha}}(s_0)$.*

Proof. Let $\overline{\alpha} = (\alpha_1, \ldots, \alpha_N)$ be a plan accepted by Σ. Let us prove that for every $i = 0, \ldots, N$ action $f_{\alpha_i} \ldots f_{\alpha_1}$ is applicable in s_0, and M_i defined by (2) is satisfied in state $f_{\alpha_i} \ldots f_{\alpha_1}(s_0)$. The proof is by induction on i. The basis is obvious. Assume that M_{i-1} is satisfied in $f_{\alpha_{i-1}} \ldots f_{\alpha_1}(s_0)$. By (3), it follows that P_{α_i} is satisfied in this state too. Since $(P_{\alpha_i}, D_{\alpha_i}, A_{\alpha_i})$ is sound relative to f_{α_i}, we can conclude that $f_{\alpha_i} f_{\alpha_{i-1}} \ldots f_{\alpha_1}(s_0)$ is defined, and that both $M_{i-1} \setminus D_{\alpha_i}$ and A_{α_i} are satisfied in this state. By (2), it follows then that M_i is satisfied in this state too.

There is a serious problem, however, with Definition A: it eliminates all usual STRIPS systems as "unsound". Consider, for instance, the description of $push(k, m, n)$ given in Section 2. The two atoms included in its delete list are obviously not the only sentences which may become false when the corresponding action is performed. Their conjunction is another such sentence, as well as their disjunction or, say, any sentence of the form $ATR(m) \wedge F$, where F is provable in predicate logic. To make the delete list complete in the sense of Definition A, we would have to include all such sentences in it. The delete list will become infinite and perhaps even non-recursive!

The designer of a STRIPS system cannot possibly include in a delete list all arbitrarily complex formulas that may become false after the corresponding action is performed. In our main example, the delete lists of all operator descriptions contain only atomic formulas. The same can be usually found in other examples of STRIPS systems. When describing an operator, we can try to make the delete list complete in the weaker sense that all *atoms* which may become false are included. More precisely, we may be able to guarantee condition (ii) for *atomic* sentences, but it is not realistic to expect that it will hold for all sentences in the language.

It would be a mistake, however, to restrict (ii) to atoms in Definition A and make no other changes, because that would make the assertion of the Soundness Theorem false. World models may include non-atomic sentences, and the weaker form of (ii) does not guarantee that such sentences are deleted when they become false. What is the right way to exploit this "atomic completeness" of delete lists?

One possible solution is to change the definition of a world model and require that it include atomic sentences only. In this case we should also allow only atomic formulas in add lists (otherwise $R(\overline{\alpha})$ will generally include non-atomic formulas and thus will not be a world model), and there will be no need to allow anything other than atoms in delete lists. (In this "atomic STRIPS", logical connectives and quantifiers would be still allowed in preconditions and in the goal formula).

This somewhat restrictive approach gives a satisfactory interpretation of many simple STRIPS systems. In fact, the description of STRIPS in (Nilsson 1980), for ease of exposition, allows only conjunctions of ground literals in world models, which is almost equally restrictive. But let us remember that our main example contains a non-atomic formula, (1). Why does that system appear to function correctly? This question is addressed in the next section.

4. Non-Atomic Formulas in World Models

Consider the description of the operator $turnonlight(LIGHTSWITCH1)$ in the main example. Its delete list is $\{STATUS(LIGHTSWITCH1, OFF)\}$. When the operator is applied, the atomic sentence $STATUS(LIGHTSWITCH1, OFF)$ (which is a part of the initial world model) will be deleted. Now let us change the example slightly and replace this atomic sentence in the initial world model by the stronger assumption that *all* lightswitches are originally turned off:

$$\forall x(TYPE(x, LIGHTSWITCH) \supset STATUS(x, OFF)). \tag{4}$$

This formula will not be deleted wnen $turnonlight(LIGHTSWITCH1)$ is applied, which will cause STRIPS to malfunction.

Sentences (1) and (4) have the same logical complexity, and they are assumed to be both satisfied in the initial state of the world. What is wrong about including (4) in the initial world model? This example seems to confirm that "the frontier between "acceptable" and "ridiculous" (STRIPS-like) axiomatizations of the world is a very tenuous one" (Siklóssy and Roach 1975).

There is, however, an obvious difference between (1) and (4): the former is satisfied not only in the initial state, but in *every* state of the world. This difference is crucial. It is true that in the main example non-atomic formulas are never deleted from world models; but there can be no need to delete (1). This is why it is safe to include (1) in M_0.

A similar precaution should be taken with regard to including non-atomic formulas in add lists. We can extend the main example, for instance, by the operator $turnoffalllights$, with the add list consisting of one formula (4). If $turnonlight(m)$

is applied after this operator, we will have a difficulty similar to the one discussed above. A non-atomic formula may be included in an add list only if it is satisfied in every state of the world. (Of course, it can be included then in the initial world model as well.)

This discussion suggests the following modification of Definition A.

Definition B. An operator description (P, D, A) is *sound* relative to an action f if, for every state s such that P is satisfied in s,
  (i) f is applicable in state s,
 (ii) every atomic sentence which is satisfied in s and does not belong to D is satisfied in $f(s)$,
(iii) A is satisfied in $f(s)$,
 (iv) every non-atomic sentence in A is satisfied in all states of the world.

Σ is *sound* if
  (v) M_0 is satisfied in the initial state s_0,
 (vi) every non-atomic sentence in M_0 is satisfied in all states of the world,
(vii) every operator description $(P_\alpha, D_\alpha, A_\alpha)$ is sound relative to f_α.

The Soundness Theorem remains valid for the new definition.

Proof. Let $\overline{\alpha} = (\alpha_1, \ldots, \alpha_N)$ be a plan accepted by Σ. Let us prove that for every $i = 0, \ldots, N$ action $f_{\alpha_i} \ldots f_{\alpha_1}$ is applicable in s_0, M_i is satisfied in state $f_{\alpha_i} \ldots f_{\alpha_1}(s_0)$, and every non-atomic formula in M_i is satisfied in all states. The proof is by induction on i. The basis is obvious. Assume that M_{i-1} is satisfied in $f_{\alpha_{i-1}} \ldots f_{\alpha_1}(s_0)$, and all non-atomic formulas in M_{i-1} are satisfied in all states. It follows from (3) that P_{α_i} is satisfied in state $f_{\alpha_{i-1}} \ldots f_{\alpha_1}(s_0)$. Since $(P_{\alpha_i}, D_{\alpha_i}, A_{\alpha_i})$ is sound relative to f_{α_i}, we can conclude that $f_{\alpha_i} f_{\alpha_{i-1}} \ldots f_{\alpha_1}(s_0)$ is defined, that every non-atomic formula in $M_{i-1} \setminus D_{\alpha_i}$ or in A_{α_i} is satisfied in this state, and that every atomic formula in any of these two sets is satisfied in all states. By (2), it follows then that M_i is satisfied in state $f_{\alpha_i} \ldots f_{\alpha_1}(s_0)$, and that every non-atomic formula in M_i is satisfied in all states.

5. The General Semantics of STRIPS

Our work has not come to an end yet. The careful examination of the main example reveals a small detail which shows that, in spite of all our efforts, that system is *not* sound in the sense of Definition B.

This peculiarity, pointed out in (Siklóssy and Roach 1975), is connected with the delete lists of some operators which change the position of the robot: $goto1(m)$, $goto2(m)$, $pushto(m, n)$ and $gothrudoor(k, l, m)$. As can be expected, the delete lists of these operators contain ground atoms which describe the robot's current position. They include all atoms of the form $ATROBOT(\$)$, where $\$$ is any object constant. They also include the atoms $NEXTTO(ROBOT,\$)$. However, they do *not* include $NEXTTO(\$,ROBOT)$.

This non-symmetry is somewhat counterintuitive, because the authors apparently interpret $NEXTTO$ as a symmetric predicate. For instance, the delete list of $pushto(m,n)$ (the robot pushes object m next to object n) contains both $NEXTTO(\$,m)$ and $NEXTTO(m,\$)$, and its add list contains both $NEXTTO(m,n)$ and $NEXTTO(n,m)$. One may get the impression that the non-symmetric treatment of $NEXTTO$ with $ROBOT$ as one of the arguments is an oversight.

However, this is not an oversight, but rather a trick carefully planned by the authors in the process of designing the main example. They make sure that assertions of the form $NEXTTO(\$,ROBOT)$ never become elements of world models in the process of operation of the system: there are no atoms of this form in M_0 or on the add lists of any operators. For example, the add list of $goto2(m)$ contains $NEXTTO(ROBOT,m)$, but not $NEXTTO(m,ROBOT)$, even though these atomic sentences both become true and, from the point of view of Definition B, nothing prevents us from adding both of them to the current world model.

The purpose of this is obvious: storing information on the objects next to the robot in both forms would have made the operator descriptions longer and would have led to computational inefficiency. In principle, it is possible to go even further in this direction and, for instance, store facts of the form $NEXTTO(BOXi,BOXj)$ only when $i < j$.

It is easy to accomodate the systems which use tricks of this kind by slightly generalizing Definition B. Let E be a set of sentences; the formulas from E will be called *essential*. Definition B corresponds to the case when E is the set of ground atoms.

Definition C. An operator description (P, D, A) is *sound* relative to an action f if, for every state s such that P is satisfied in s,
 (i) f is applicable in state s,
 (ii) every essential sentence which is satisfied in s and does not belong to D is satisfied in $f(s)$,
(iii) A is satisfied in $f(s)$,
(iv) every sentence in A which is not essential is satisfied in all states of the world.

Σ is *sound* if
 (v) M_0 is satisfied in the initial state s_0,
 (vi) every sentence in M_0 which is not essential is satisfied in all states of the world,
(vii) every operator description $(P_\alpha, D_\alpha, A_\alpha)$ is sound relative to f_α.

It should be emphasized that Definition C defines the soundness of operator descriptions and STRIPS systems only with respect to a given class of sentences that are considered essential. The choice of this class E is an integral part of the design of a STRIPS system, along with its language, its initial model, and the set of its operators with their descriptions. When a STRIPS system is introduced, it is advisable to make the choice of E explicit; the description of the main example, for instance, will be more complete if we specify that a sentence is considered essential in this system if it is an atom and does not have the form $NEXTTO(\$, ROBOT)$. This information will help the user to avoid mistakes when the initial model is modified to reflect different assumptions about the initial state of the world, or when new operators are added to the system.

The treatment of $NEXTTO$ in the main example shows that it may be advantageous to make E a proper subset of the set of ground atoms. Sometimes it may be convenient to include some non-atomic formulas in E. For instance, we may wish to update negative information by means of adding and deleting negative literals; then E would be the set of ground literals, both positive and negative.

The proof of the Soundness Theorem given in the previous section can be easily generalized to soundness in the sense of Definition C.

Acknowledgements

This research was partially supported by DARPA under Contract N0039-82-C-0250. I would like to thank John McCarthy and Nils Nilsson for useful discussions, and Michael Gelfond for comments on an earlier draft of this paper.

References

A. Bundy, *The Computer Modelling of Mathematical Reasoning*, Academic Press, 1983.

R. E. Fikes and N. J. Nilsson, STRIPS: A new approach to the application of theorem proving to problem solving, *Artificial Intelligence* **2** (1971), 189-208.

N. J. Nilsson, *Principles of Artificial Intelligence*, Tioga Publishing Company, Palo Alto, Califormia, 1980.

L. Siklóssy and J. Roach, Model verification and improvement using DISPROVER, *Artificial Intelligence* **6** (1975), 41-52.

A THEORY OF PLANS

Zohar Manna
Stanford University
Weizmann Institute

Richard Waldinger
SRI International

ABSTRACT

Problems in commonsense and robot planning are approached by methods adapted from program synthesis research; planning is regarded as an application of automated deduction. To support this approach, we introduce a variant of situational logic, called *plan theory*, in which plans are explicit objects.

A machine-oriented deductive-tableau inference system is adapted to plan theory. Equations and equivalences of the theory are built into a unification algorithm for the system. Special attention is paid to the derivation of conditional and recursive plans. Inductive proofs of theorems for even the simplest planning problems, such as clearing a block, have been found to require challenging generalizations.

1. INTRODUCTION

For many years, the authors have been working on *program synthesis*, the automated derivation of a computer program to meet a given specification. We have settled on a deductive approach to this problem, in which program derivation is regarded as a task in theorem proving (Manna and Waldinger [80], [85a]). To construct a program, we prove a theorem that establishes the existence of an output meeting the specified conditions. The proof is restricted to be constructive, in that it must describe a computational method for finding the output. This method becomes the basis for the program we extract from the proof.

For the most part, we have focused on the synthesis of *applicative* programs, which yield an output but produce no side effects. We are now interested in adapting our deductive approach to the synthesis of *imperative* programs, which may alter data structures or produce other side effects.

Plans are closely analogous to imperative programs, in that actions may be regarded as computer instructions, tests as conditional branches, and the world as a huge data structure. This analogy suggests that techniques for the synthesis of imperative programs may carry over into the planning domain. Conversely, we may anticipate that insights we develop by looking at a relatively simple planning domain, such as the blocks world, would then carry over to program synthesis in a more complex domain, involving array assignments, destructive list operations, and other alterations of data structures.

Consider the problem of clearing a given block, where we are not told whether the block is already clear or, if not, how many blocks are above it. Assume that we are in a blocks world in which blocks are all the same size, so that only one block can fit directly on top of another, and in which the robot arm may lift only one block at a time. Then we might expect a planning system to produce the following program:

$$makeclear(a) \quad \Leftarrow \quad \begin{cases} \textit{if } clear(a) \\ \textit{then } \Lambda \\ \textit{else } makeclear(hat(a)); \\ \qquad put(hat(a), table). \end{cases}$$

In other words, to clear a given block a (the *argument*), first determine whether it is already clear. If not, clear the block that is on top of block a, and then put that block

This research was supported by the National Science Foundation under Grants DCR-82-14523 and DCR-85-12356, by the Defense Advanced Research Projects Agency under Contract N00039-84-C-0211, by the United States Air Force Office of Scientific Research under Contract AFOSR-85-0383, by the Office of Naval Research under Contract N00014-84-C-0706, by United States Army Research under Contract DAJA-45-84-C-0040, and by a contract from the International Business Machines Corporation.

A preliminary version of part of this paper was presented at the *Eighth International Conference on Automated Deduction*, Oxford, England, July 1986.

on the table. Here Λ is the empty sequence of instructions, corresponding to no action at all, and $hat(a)$ is the block directly on a, if one exists. The action $put(u, v)$ places the block u on top of the object v.

Note that the *makeclear* program requires a conditional (*if-then-else*) and a recursive call to *makeclear* itself. Planning systems have often attempted to avoid constructing plans using these constructs by dealing with completely known worlds. Had we known exactly how many blocks were to be on top of block a, for example, we could have produced a plan with no conditionals and no recursion. Once we begin to deal with an uncertain environment, we are forced to introduce some constructs for testing and for repetition.

A fundamental difficulty in applying a theorem-proving approach to plan construction is that the meaning of an expression in a plan depends on the situation, whereas in ordinary logic the meaning of an expression does not change. Thus, the block designated by $hat(a)$ or the truth-value designated by $clear(a)$ may change from one state to the next. The traditional approach to circumventing this difficulty relies on a *situational logic*, i.e., one in which we can refer explicitly to situations or states of the world.

2.   THE TROUBLE WITH SITUATIONAL LOGIC

In this section, we describe conventional situational logic and point out some of its deficiencies when applied to planning. These deficiencies motivate the introduction of our own version of situational logic, called "plan theory."

Conventional Situational Logic

Situational logic was introduced into the literature of computer science by McCarthy [63]. A variant of this logic was incorporated into the planning system QA3 (Green [69]). In the QA3 logic, function and predicate symbols whose values might change were given state arguments. Thus, rather than speaking about $hat(x)$ or $clear(x)$, we introduce the *situational function* symbol $hat'(w, x)$ and the *situational predicate* symbol $Clear(w, x)$, each of which is given an explicit state argument w; for example, $hat'(w, x)$ is the block on top of block x in state w. Actions are represented as functions that yield states; for example, $put'(w, x, y)$ is the state obtained from state w by putting block x on object y.

Facts about the world may be represented as axioms in situational logic. For example, the fact that the hat of an unclear block is on top of the block is expressed by the axiom

> *if   not Clear*(w, x)
> *then   On*$\big(w,\ hat'(w, x),\ x\big)$.

Actions can also be described by situational-logic axioms. For example, the fact that after block x has been put on the table, block x is indeed on the table is expressed by the axiom

> *if Clear(w, x)*
> *then On(put'(w, x, table), x, table).*

In a conventional situational logic, such as the QA3 logic, to construct a plan that will meet a specified condition, one proves the existence of a state in which the condition is true. More precisely, let us suppose that the condition is of the form $Q[s_0, a, z]$, where s_0 is the initial state, a the argument or input parameter, and z the final state. Then the theorem to be proved is

$$(\forall s_0)(\forall a)(\exists z)Q[s_0, a, z].$$

For example, the plan to clear a block is constructed by proving the theorem

$$(\forall s_0)(\forall a)(\exists z)\,Clear(z, a).$$

From a situational-logic proof of this theorem, using techniques for the synthesis of applicative programs, one can extract the program

$$makeclear'(s_0, a) \;\Leftarrow\; \begin{cases} \textit{if } Clear(s_0, a) \\ \textit{then } s_0 \\ \textit{else let } s_1 \textit{ be } makeclear'\big(s_0,\, hat'(s_0, a)\big) \textit{ in} \\ \quad put'\big(s_1,\, hat'(s_1, a),\, table\big). \end{cases}$$

This program closely resembles the *makeclear* program we proposed initially, except that it invokes situational operators, which contain explicit state arguments.

Executable and Nonexecutable Plans

It would seem that, by regarding plans as state-producing functions, we can treat an imperative program as a special kind of applicative program and use the same synthesis methods for both. In other words, we can perhaps extract programs from situational-logic proofs and regard these programs as plans. Unfortunately, there are some programs we can extract from proofs in this formulation of situational logic that cannot be regarded as plans.

For example, consider the problem illustrated in Figure 1. The monkey is presented with two boxes and is informed that one box contains a banana and the other a bomb, but he is not told which. His goal is to get the banana, but if he goes anywhere near the bomb it will explode. As stated, the problem should have no solution. However, if we formulate the problem in conventional situational logic, we can prove the appropriate theorem,

$$(\forall s_0)(\exists z)\,Hasbanana(z).$$

monkey

a

b

Fig. 1:   *The Monkey, the Banana, and the Bomb*

The "program" we extract from one proof of this theorem is

$$getbanana(s_0) \Leftarrow \begin{cases} if \ Hasbanana(goto'(s_0, a)) \\ then \ \ goto'(s_0, a) \\ else \ \ goto'(s_0, b) \ . \end{cases}$$

According to this plan, the monkey should ask whether, if it were to go to box a, it would get the banana? If so, it should go to box a; otherwise, it should go to box b. We cannot execute this "plan" because it allows the monkey to consider whether a given proposition *Hasbanana* is true in a hypothetical state $goto'(s_0, a)$, which is different from the current state s_0.

We would like to restrict the proofs in situational logic to be constructive, in the sense that the programs we extract should correspond to executable plans. This kind of consideration has influenced the design of our version of situational logic, called *plan theory*.

3.   PLAN THEORY

In plan theory we have two classes of expressions. The *static* (or *situational*) *expressions* denote particular objects, states, and truth-values. For example, the static expressions $hat'(s, b)$, $Clear(s, b)$, and $put'(s, b, c)$ denote a particular block, truth-value, and state, respectively (where b and c denote blocks and s denotes a state). We shall also introduce corresponding *fluent terms*, which will not denote any particular object, truth-value, or state, but which will *designate* such elements with respect to a given state. For example, the fluent terms

$$hat(d), \quad clear(d), \quad \text{and} \quad put(d, \hat{d})$$

will only designate a block, truth-value, or state, respectively, with respect to a given state (where d and $\hat{d}$ are themselves fluent terms that designate blocks).

Fluent terms themselves do not refer to any state explicitly. To see what element a fluent term e designates with respect to a given state s, we apply a *linkage operator* to s and e, obtaining a static expression. We use one of three linkage operators,

$$s{:}e, \quad s{::}e, \quad \text{or} \quad s{;}e ,$$

depending on whether e designates an object, truth-value, or state, respectively. For example, the static expressions

$$s{:}hat(d) \quad s{::}clear(d), \quad \text{and} \quad s{;}put(d, \hat{d})$$

will indeed denote a particular block, truth-value, and state, respectively.

While we shall retain static expressions as specification and proof constructs, we shall restrict our proofs to be constructive in the sense that the programs we extract from them will contain no static expressions, but only fluent terms. Because fluent terms do not refer to states explicitly, this means that the knowledge of the agent will be restricted to the implicit current state; it will be unable to tell what, say, the hat of a given block is in a hypothetical or future state. In this way, we ensure that the programs we extract may be executed as plans. Nonplans, such as the *getbanana* "program" mentioned above, will be excluded.

Now let us describe plan theory in more detail.

Elements of Plan Theory

Plan theory is a theory in first-order predicate logic that admits several sorts of terms.

- The *static (situational) terms*, or *s-terms*, denote a particular element. They include

  - *object* s-terms, which denote an object, such as a block or the table.

  - *state* s-terms, which denote a state.

For example, $hat'(s, b)$ is an object s-term and $put'(s, b, c)$ is a state s-term, if s is a state s-term and b and c are object s-terms.

- The *static (situational) sentences*, or *s-sentences*, denote a particular truth-value.

For example, $Clear(s, b)$ is an s-sentence, if s is a state s-term and b an object s-term .

- The *fluent terms*, or *f-terms*, only designate an element with respect to a given state. They include

    - *object* f-terms, which designate an object with respect to a given state.

    - *propositional* f-terms, which designate a truth-value with respect to a given state.

    - *plan* f-terms, which designate a state with respect to a given state.

For example, $hat(d)$, $clear(d)$, and $put(d, \hat{d})$ are object, propositional, and plan f-terms, respectively. The plan f-constant Λ denotes the empty plan.

Object f-terms denote *object fluents*, propositional f-terms denote *propositional fluents*, and plan f-terms denote *plans*. We may think of object fluents, propositional fluents, and plans as functions mapping states into objects, truth-values, and states, respectively. Syntactically, however, they are denoted by terms, not function symbols. To determine what elements these terms designate with respect to a given state, we invoke the *in* function ":", the *in* relation "::", and the execution function ";" .

The *in* Function ":"

If s is a state s-term and e an object f-term,

$$s{:}e$$

is an object s-term denoting the object *designated by e in state s*. For example, $s_0{:}hat(d)$ denotes the object designated by the object f-term $hat(d)$ in state s_0.

In general, we shall introduce object f-function symbols $f(u_1, \ldots, u_n)$ and object s-function symbols $f'(w, x_1, \ldots, x_n)$ together, where f takes object fluents $u_1, \ldots, u_n$ as arguments and yields an object fluent, while f' takes a state w and objects $x_1, \ldots, x_n$ as arguments and yields an object. The two symbols are linked in each case by the *object linkage* axiom

$$w{:}f(u_1, \ldots, u_n) \ = \ f'(w, \ w{:}u_1, \ \ldots, \ w{:}u_n) \qquad \text{(object linkage)}$$

(Implicitly, variables in axioms are universally quantified. For simplicity, we omit sort conditions such as $state(w)$ from the axioms.)

For example, corresponding to the object f-function $hat(u)$, which yields a block fluent, we have an object s-function $hat'(w, x)$, which yields a fixed block. The appropriate instance of the *object linkage* axiom is

$$w{:}hat(u) \ = \ hat'(w, w{:}u).$$

Thus $s{:}hat(d)$ denotes the block on top of block $s{:}d$ in state s. (This is not necessarily the same as the block on top of $s{:}d$ in some other state s'.)

The *in* Relation "::"

The *in* relation :: is analogous to the *in* function :. If s is a state s-term and e a propositional f-term,

$$s :: e$$

is a proposition denoting the truth-value *designated by e in state s*. For example, $s_0 :: clear(d)$ denotes the truth-value designated by the propositional f-term $clear(d)$ in state s_0.

In general, we shall also introduce propositional f-function symbols $r(u_1, \ldots, u_n)$ and s-predicate symbols $R(w, x_1, \ldots, x_n)$ together, with the convention that r takes object fluents $u_1, \ldots, u_n$ as arguments and yields a propositional fluent, while R takes a state w and objects $x_1, \ldots, x_n$ as arguments and yields a truth-value. The two symbols are linked in each case by the *propositional-linkage* axiom

$$w :: r(u_1, \ldots, u_n) \equiv R(w, w{:}u_1, \ldots, w{:}u_n) \qquad \text{(propositional linkage)}$$

For example, corresponding to the propositional f-function $clear(u)$, which yields a propositional fluent, we have an actual relation $Clear(w, x)$, which yields a truth-value. The instance of the *propositional-linkage* axiom that relates them is

$$w :: clear(u) \equiv Clear(w, w{:}u).$$

Thus $s :: clear(d)$ is true if the block $s{:}d$ is clear in state s.

The Execution Function ";"

If s is a state s-term and p a plan f-term,

$$s; p$$

is a state s-term denoting the state obtained by *executing plan p in state s*. For example, $s; put(d, \hat{d})$ is the state obtained by putting block d on object $\hat{d}$ in state s.

In general, we shall introduce plan f-function symbols $g(u_1, \ldots, u_n)$ and state s-function symbols $g'(w, x_1, \ldots, x_n)$ together, where g takes object fluents $u_1, \ldots, u_n$ as arguments and yields a plan, while g' takes a state w and objects $x_1, \ldots, x_n$ as arguments and yields a new state. The two symbols are linked in each case by the *plan linkage* axiom

$$w; g(u_1, \ldots, u_n) = g'(w, w{:}u_1, \ldots, w{:}u_n) \qquad \text{(plan linkage)}$$

For example, corresponding to the plan f-function $put(u, v)$, which takes object fluents u and v as arguments and produces a plan, we have a state s-function $put'(w, x, y)$, which takes a state w and the actual objects x and y as arguments and produces a new state. The appropriate instance of the *plan linkage* axiom is

$$w; put(u, v) = put'(w, w{:}u, w{:}v).$$

The empty plan Λ is taken to be a right identity under the execution function; that is,

$$w;\Lambda = w \qquad\qquad (empty\ plan)$$

for all states w.

Rigid Designator

Certain fluent constants (f-constants) are to denote the same object regardless of the state. For example, we may assume that the constants *table* and *banana* always denote the same objects. In this case, we shall identify the object fluent with the corresponding fixed object.

An object f-constant u is a *rigid designator* if

$$w{:}u \;=\; u \qquad\qquad (rigid\ designator)$$

for all states w.

For example, the fact that *table* is a rigid designator is expressed by the axiom

$$w{:}table \;{\cdot}{=}\; table$$

for all states w. In the derivation of a plan, we shall assume that our argument (or input parameter) a is a rigid designator. On the other hand, some f-constants, such as *here*, *the-highest-block*, or *the-president*, are likely not to be rigid designators.

The Composition Function ";;"

We introduce a notion of composing plans.

If p_1 and p_2 are plan f-terms, $p_1;;p_2$ is the *composition* of p_1 and p_2.

Executing $p_1;;p_2$ is the same as executing first p_1 and then p_2. This is expressed by the *plan composition* axiom

$$w;(p_1;;p_2) \;=\; (w;p_1);p_2 \qquad\qquad (plan\ composition)$$

for all states w and plans p_1 and p_2. Normally we shall ignore the distinction between the composition function ;; and the execution function ; , writing ; for both and relying on context to make the meaning clear.

Composition is assumed to be associative; that is

$$(p_1;;p_2);;p_3 \;=\; p_1;;(p_2;;p_3) \qquad\qquad (associativity)$$

for all plans p_1, p_2, and p_3. For this reason, we may write $p_1;;p_2;;p_3$ without parentheses.

The empty plan Λ is taken to be the identity under composition, that is,

$$\Lambda;;p \;=\; p;;\Lambda \;=\; p \qquad\qquad (identity)$$

for all plans p.

Specifying Facts and Actions

As in conventional situational logic, facts about the world may be expressed as plan theory axioms. For example, the principal property of the *hat* function is expressed by the *hat* axiom

$$\text{if } not\, Clear(w, y)$$
$$\text{then } On\big(w,\, hat'(w,y),\, y\big) \qquad\qquad (hat)$$

for all states w and blocks y. (As usual, for simplicity, we omit sort conditions such as $state(w)$ from the antecedent of the axiom.) In other words, if block y is not clear, its hat is directly on top of it. (If y is clear, its hat is a "nonexistent" object, not a block.) It follows, if we take y to be $w{:}v$ and apply the *propositional* and *object linkage* axioms, that

$$\text{if } not\,\big(w :: clear(v)\big)$$
$$\text{then } w :: on\big(hat(v),\, v\big).$$

for all states w and block fluents v. Other axioms are necessary for expressing other properties of the *hat* function.

The effects of actions may also be described by plan theory axioms. For example, the primary effect of putting a block on the table may be expressed by the *put-table-on* axiom

$$\text{if } Clear(w,\, x)$$
$$\text{then } On(put'(w, x, table),\, x,\, table) \qquad (put\text{-}table\text{-}on)$$

for all states w and blocks x. The axiom says that after a block has been put on the table, the block will indeed be on the table, provided that it was clear beforehand. (The effects of attempting to move an unclear block are not specified and are therefore unpredictable.) It follows, if we take x to be $w{:}u$ and apply the *linkage* axioms plus the rigidity of the designator *table*, that

$$\text{if } w :: clear(u)$$
$$\text{then } On\big(w;put(u, table),\, w{:}u,\, table\big)$$

for all states w and block fluents u.

Note that, in the consequent of the above property, we cannot conclude that

$$\big(w;put(u, table)\big) :: on(u, table),$$

that is, that after putting u on the table, u will be on the table. This is because u is a fluent and we have no way of knowing that it will designate the same block in state $w; put(u, table)$ that it did in state w. For example, if u is taken to be $hat(a)$, the property allows us to conclude that, if $s_0 :: clear\big(hat(a)\big)$, then

$$On\big(s_0;put\big(hat(a), table\big),\, s_0{:}hat(a),\, table\big).$$

In other words, the block that was on block a initially is on the table after execution of the plan step. On the other hand, we cannot conclude that

$$(s_0;put(hat(a),table)) :: on(hat(a),\ table),$$

that is, that $hat(a)$ is on the table after the plan step has been executed. In fact, in this state, a is clear and $hat(a)$ no longer designates a block.

Plan Formation

To construct a plan for achieving a condition $\mathcal{Q}[s_0, a, z]$, where s_0 is the initial state, a the input object, and z the final state, we prove the theorem

$$(\forall s_0)(\forall a)(\exists z_1)\mathcal{Q}[s_0,\ a,\ s_0;z_1].$$

Here z_1 is a plan variable. In other words, we show, for any initial state s_0 and input object a, the existence of a plan z_1 such that, if we are in state s_0 and execute plan z_1, we obtain a state in which the specified condition $\mathcal{Q}$ is true. A program producing the desired plan is extracted from the proof of this theorem. Informally, we often speak of this program as a plan itself, although in fact it computes a function that only produces a plan when it is applied to an argument.

Note that, in the QA3 version of situational logic, one proves instead the theorem

$$(\forall s_0)(\forall a)(\exists z)\mathcal{Q}[s_0,\ a,\ z].$$

The phrasing of the theorem in plan theory ensures that the final state z can indeed be obtained from s_0 by the execution of a plan z_1. For example, the plan for clearing a block is constructed by proving the theorem

$$(\forall s_0)(\forall a)(\exists z_1)\big[Clear(s_0;z_1,\ a)\big].$$

In other words, the block a is to be clear after execution of the desired plan z_1 in the initial state s_0.

In the balance of this paper, we present a machine-oriented deductive system for plan theory in which we can prove such theorems and derive the corresponding plans at the same time. We shall use the proof of the above theorem, together with the concomitant derivation of the *makeclear* plan, as a continuing example.

4.   THE PLAN-THEORY DEDUCTIVE SYSTEM

To support the synthesis of applicative programs, we developed a *deductive-tableau* theorem-proving system (Manna and Waldinger [80], [85a]), which combines nonclausal resolution, well-founded induction, and conditional term rewriting within a single framework. In this paper, we carry the system over into plan theory. Although a full introduction to the deductive-tableau system is not possible here, we describe just enough to make this paper self-contained.

Deductive Tableaux

The fundamental structure of the system, the *deductive tableau*, is a set of rows, each of which contains a plan theory sentence, either an *assertion* or a *goal*, and an optional term, the *plan entry*. We can assume that the sentences are quantifier-free. Let us forget about the plan entry for a moment.

Under a given interpretation, a tableau is *true* whenever the following condition holds:

> If all instances of each of the assertions are true,
> then some instance of at least one of the goals is true.

Thus, variables in assertions have tacit universal quantification, while variables in goals have tacit existential quantification. In a given theory, a tableau is *valid* if it is true under all models for the theory.

To prove a given sentence valid, we remove its quantifiers (by skolemization) and enter it as the initial goal in a tableau. Any other valid sentences of the theory that we are willing to assume may be entered into the tableau as assertions. The resulting tableau is valid if and only if the given sentence is valid.

The deduction rules add new rows to the tableau without altering its validity; in particular, if the new tableau is valid, so is the original tableau. The deductive process continues until we derive as a goal the propositional constant *true*, which is always true, or until we derive as an assertion the propositional constant *false*, which is always false. The tableau is then automatically valid; hence the original sentence is too.

In deriving a plan $f(a)$, we prove a theorem of form

$$(\forall s_0)(\forall a)(\exists z_1)\mathcal{Q}[s_0, a, s_0; z_1].$$

In skolemizing this, we obtain the sentence

$$\mathcal{Q}[s_0, a, s_0; z_1],$$

where s_0 and a are skolem constants and z_1 is a variable. (Since this sentence is a theorem or goal to be proved, its existentially quantified variables remain variables, while its universally quantified variables become skolem constants or functions. The intuition is that we are free to choose values for the existentially quantified variables, whereas the values for the universally quantified variables are imposed on us. The situation is precisely the opposite for axioms or assertions.)

To prove this theorem, we establish the validity of the initial tableau

assertions	goals	plan: $s_0;f(a)$
	$\mathcal{Q}[s_0,\, a,\, s_0;z_1]$	$s_0;z_1$

For example, the initial tableau for the *makeclear* derivation is

assertions	goals	plan: $s_0;makeclear(a)$
	1. $Clear(s_0;z_1,\, a)$	$s_0;z_1$

Certain valid sentences of plan theory, such as the axioms for blocks-world actions, would be included as assertions.

Plan Entry

Note that the initial tableau includes a plan entry $s_0;z_1$. The plan entry is the mechanism for extracting a plan from a proof of the given theorem. Throughout the derivation, we maintain the following *correctness* property:

> For any model of the theory, and for any goal [or assertion] in the tableau,
>   if some instance of the goal is true [assertion is false],
>   then the corresponding instance $s_0;t$ of the plan entry (if any)
>   will satisfy the *specified condition* $\mathcal{Q}[s_0,\, a,\, s_0;t]$.

In other words, executing the plan t produces a state $s_0;t$ that satisfies the specified condition. The initial goal already satisfies the property in a trivial way, since it is the same as the specified condition. Each of the deduction rules of our system preserves this correctness property, as well as the validity of the tableau.

If a goal [or assertion] has no plan entry, this means that any plan will satisfy the specified condition if some instance of that goal is true [assertion is false]. In other words, we do not care what happens in that case.

Basic Properties

It may be evident that there is a duality between assertions and goals; namely, in a given theory,

> a tableau that contains an assertion $\mathcal{A}$ is valid
>   if and only if
> the tableau that contains instead the goal (*not* $\mathcal{A}$), with the same plan entry, is valid.

On the other hand,

> a tableau that contains a goal G is valid
>> if and only if
> the tableau that contains instead the assertion ($not\,G$), with the same plan entry,
> is valid.

This means that we could shift all the goals into the assertion column simply by negating them, thereby obtaining a refutation procedure; the plan entries and the correctness properties would be unchanged. (This is done in conventional resolution theorem-proving systems.) Or we could shift all the assertions into the goal column by negating them. Nevertheless, the distinction between assertions and goals has intuitive significance, so we retain it in our exposition.

Two other properties of tableaux are useful. First, the variables of any row in the tableau are dummies and may be renamed systematically without changing the tableau's validity or correctness. Second, we may add to a tableau any instance of any of its rows, preserving the validity and correctness.

Primitive Plans

We want to restrict our proofs to be sufficiently constructive so that the plans we extract can be executed. For this purpose, we distinguish between *primitive* symbols, which we know how to execute, and *nonprimitive* symbols, which we do not. For example, we regard the function symbols : and *hat'* and the predicate symbols :: and *Clear* as nonprimitive, because we do not want to admit them into our plans. On the other hand, we regard the f-function symbols *hat* and *clear* as primitive.

In deriving a plan, we shall maintain the *primitivity* property, namely, that the final segment t of the plan entry $s_0;t$ for any assertion or goal of the tableau shall be composed entirely of primitive symbols. Otherwise the new row is discarded.

Extracting the Plan

As we have mentioned, the deductive process continues until we derive either the final goal *true* or the final assertion *false*. At this point, the proof is complete and we may extract the plan

$$f(a) \Leftarrow t,$$

where $s_0;t$ is the plan entry associated with the final row.

This is because we have maintained the correctness property that the plan entry of any goal [or assertion] must satisfy the specified condition $Q[s_0, a, s_0;t]$ when that goal [or assertion] is true [or false]. Since the truth symbol *true* is always true and the truth symbol *false* always false, the plan entry $s_0;t$ will always satisfy the specified condition.

We know also that the extracted plan will be executable, because we have maintained the primitivity property, which requires that the plan term t be expressed exclusively in terms of primitive symbols. (Should the final plan still contain variables, these may be replaced by any primitive terms.)

In the next section we begin to introduce the deduction rules of our system, emphasizing those that need to be adapted for plan theory or that play a major role in plan derivations.

5.   FORMATION OF CONDITIONALS

The resolution rule accounts for the introduction of conditionals, or tests, into the derived plan and also is important for ordinary reasoning. Because a special adaptation of the rule is necessary to form conditionals in plan theory without introducing the nonprimitive predicate symbol :: into the plan, we first consider applications of the rule that do not form conditionals.

The Resolution Rule: Ground Version

We begin by disregarding the plan entries and considering the ground version, in which there are no variables. We describe the rule in a tableau notation.

assertions	goals
$\mathcal{F}[\mathcal{P}]$	
$\mathcal{G}[\mathcal{P}]$	
$\mathcal{F}[true]$ or $\mathcal{G}[false]$	

More precisely, if our tableau contains two assertions, $\mathcal{F}[\mathcal{P}]$ and $\mathcal{G}[\mathcal{P}]$, which share a common subsentence $\mathcal{P}$, we may replace all occurrences of $\mathcal{P}$ in $\mathcal{F}[\mathcal{P}]$ with *true*, replace all occurrences of $\mathcal{P}$ in $\mathcal{G}[\mathcal{P}]$ with *false*, take the disjunction of the results, and (after propositional simplification) add it to the tableau as a new assertion.

The rationale for this rule is as follows. We suppose that $\mathcal{F}[\mathcal{P}]$ and $\mathcal{G}[\mathcal{P}]$ are true under a given model, and show that ($\mathcal{F}[true]$ or $\mathcal{G}[false]$) is then also true. We distinguish between two cases. In the case in which $\mathcal{P}$ is true, because $\mathcal{F}[\mathcal{P}]$ is true, its equivalent $\mathcal{F}[true]$ is true. On the other hand, in the case in which $\mathcal{P}$ is false, because $\mathcal{G}[\mathcal{P}]$ is true, its equivalent $\mathcal{G}[false]$ is true. In either case, the disjunction ($\mathcal{F}[true]$ or $\mathcal{G}[false]$) is true.

Note that the rule is asymmetric in its treatment of $\mathcal{F}[\mathcal{P}]$ and $\mathcal{G}[\mathcal{P}]$. In fact, it can be restricted according to the "polarity" of the occurrences of $\mathcal{P}$, the common subsentence.

We may require that some occurrence of $\mathcal{P}$ in $\mathcal{F}[\mathcal{P}]$ be of *negative polarity* (i.e., it must be within the scope of an odd number of implicit or explicit negations) and that some occurrence of $\mathcal{P}$ in $\mathcal{G}[\mathcal{P}]$ be of *positive polarity* (i.e., it must be within the scope of an even number of implicit or explicit negations). The antecedent of an implication is considered to be within the scope of an implicit negation. Thus, in applying the rule between two assertions

$$(if\ P\ then\ Q) \quad and \quad (P\ or\ R),$$

the role of $\mathcal{F}[\mathcal{P}]$ must be played by $(if\ P^-\ then\ Q)$, in which P has negative polarity, and the role of $\mathcal{G}[\mathcal{P}]$ by $(P^+\ or\ R)$, in which P has positive polarity, yielding the new assertion

$$(if\ true\ then\ Q)\ or\ (false\ or\ R),$$

that is, after propositional simplification, $(Q\ or\ R)$. Reversing the roles of the two assertions yields the trivial assertion *true*, which is of no value in the proof. This strategy has been shown by Murray [82] to retain completeness for first-order logic.

If only one of the goals has a plan entry, the new goal is given the same plan entry. (The case in which both goals have plan entries requires the introduction of a conditional plan and is treated separately.)

We have applied the rule between two assertions but, by duality, the rule can just as well be applied between two goals or between an assertion and a goal. In these cases, a new goal is introduced, which is a conjunction rather than a disjunction. In applying the polarity strategy, each goal must be considered to be within the scope of an implicit negation.

We assume that all the sentences in a tableau are subjected to full propositional simplification. Rules such as

$$\mathcal{P}\ and\ true\ \rightarrow\ \mathcal{P}$$
$$\mathcal{P}\ and\ \mathcal{P}\ \rightarrow\ \mathcal{P}$$
$$not(not\,\mathcal{P})\ \rightarrow\ \mathcal{P}$$

are applied repeatedly wherever possible before an assertion or goal is entered. Simplification is always necessary when the resolution rule is applied.

The Resolution Rule: General Version

We have up to now been considering the ground case, in which the sentences have no variables. In the general case, the rule may be expressed as follows:

assertions	goals
$\mathcal{F}[\mathcal{P}]$	
$\mathcal{G}[\mathcal{P}']$	
$\mathcal{F}\theta[true]$ or $\mathcal{G}\theta[false]$	

More precisely, let us suppose that our tableau contains two assertions $\mathcal{F}[\mathcal{P}]$ and $\mathcal{G}[\mathcal{P}']$, which have been renamed so that they have no variables in common. The subsentences $\mathcal{P}$ and $\mathcal{P}'$ are not necessarily identical, but they are unifiable, with a most-general unifier θ; thus $\mathcal{P}\theta = \mathcal{P}'\theta$. Then we may apply θ to $\mathcal{F}[\mathcal{P}]$ and $\mathcal{G}[\mathcal{P}']$, replace all occurrences of $\mathcal{P}\theta$ in $(\mathcal{G}[\mathcal{P}])\theta$ with $true$, replace all occurrences of $\mathcal{P}'\theta$ in $(\mathcal{G}[\mathcal{P}'])\theta$ with $false$, take the disjunction of the results, and (after propositional simplification) add it to our tableau as a new assertion. In other words, after applying the most-general unifier θ, we use the ground version of the rule. If exactly one of the rows has a plan entry t, the appropriate instance $t\theta$ of that entry is inherited by the new row. If it turns out that $t\theta$ contains nonprimitive symbols, the new row is discarded to maintain the primitivity property.

In general, there may be several unifiable subsentences $\mathcal{P}_1, \mathcal{P}_2, \ldots$ in $\mathcal{F}$ and several unifiable subsentences $\mathcal{P}'_1, \mathcal{P}'_2, \ldots$ in $\mathcal{G}$. The substitution θ must then be a most-general unifier for all these sentences.

Equational Unification

Typically our knowledge of the world is represented by assertions in the tableau. It is possible, however, to build certain of the equations and equivalences of a theory into an equational-unification algorithm (Fay [79]; see also Hullot [80], Martelli and Rossi [86]), so they need not be included among the assertions. Properties of plan theory may be represented in this way, including the *linkage*, *rigidity*, and *composition* axioms.

For example, consider the sentences

$$Clear(s_0;z_1, a) \quad \text{and} \quad Clear\big(put'(w, x, table), y\big).$$

Regarded as expressions in pure first-order logic, these sentences are not unifiable, because the function symbols ; and put' are distinct. Suppose we apply the substitution

$$\{y \leftarrow a, \ w \leftarrow s_0, \ x \leftarrow s_0{:}u, \ z_1 \leftarrow put(u, table)\}.$$

Then we obtain the sentences

$$Clear\big(s_0;put(u, table), a\big) \quad \text{and} \quad Clear\big(put'(s_0, s_0{:}u, table), a\big),$$

respectively. These are distinct sentences, but in plan theory we have

$$Clear\big(s_0;put(u, table), a\big) \ \equiv \ Clear\big(put'(s_0, s_0{:}u, s_0{:}table), a\big)$$

$$(\text{by the } plan \; linkage \text{ axiom})$$

$$\equiv \; Clear\big(put'(s_0, \; s_0{:}u, \; table), \; a\big)$$

$$(\text{by the rigidity of the designator } table).$$

In short, by applying the substitution we have obtained sentences equivalent in plan theory. This substitution is returned by the equational-unification algorithm. We shall say that the two sentences have been unified *invoking* the two properties cited.

Most-general equational unifiers are not unique. For example, consider the substitution

$$\{y \leftarrow a, \; w \leftarrow s_0{;}z_2, \; x \leftarrow (s_0{;}z_2){:}u, \; z_1 \leftarrow z_2{;}put(u, table)\}.$$

Applying this substitution to the same two sentences, we obtain

$$Clear\big(s_0{;}(z_2{;}put(u, table)), \; a\big)$$

and

$$Clear\big(put'(s_0{;}z_2, \; (s_0{;}z_2){:}u, \; table), \; a\big),$$

respectively. But

$$Clear\big(s_0{;}(z_2{;}put(u,table)), \; a\big) \; \equiv \; Clear\big((s_0{;}z_2){;}put(u,table), \; a\big)$$

$$(\text{by the } plan \; composition \text{ axiom})$$

$$\equiv \; Clear\big(put'\big(s_0{;}z_2, \; (s_0{;}z_2){:}u, \; (s_0{;}z_2){:}table\big), \; a\big)$$

$$(\text{by the } plan \; linkage \text{ axiom})$$

$$\equiv \; Clear\big(put'(s_0{;}z_2, \; (s_0{;}z_2){:}u, \; table), \; a\big)$$

$$(\text{by the rigidity of the designator } table).$$

In general, the equational-unification algorithm may yield an infinite stream of most-general unifiers. We obtain a different resolvent for each of these substitutions.

Examples

Let us illustrate the resolution rule with an example from the *makeclear* derivation.

Example (resolution).   Suppose our tableau contains the initial goal

assertions	goals	plan: $s_0{;}makeclear(a)$
	1. $\boxed{Clear(s_0{;}z_1, \; a)}$ $^-$	$s_0{;}z_1$

and the *put-table-clear* axiom

if $On(w, x, y)$ and $Clear(w, x)$ then $\boxed{Clear\big(put'(w, x, table), y\big)}^{+}$		

The axiom asserts that, after a block has been put on the table, the block underneath it is clear.

As we have seen above, the two boxed subsentences are equationally unifiable in the blocks-world theory. One of the most-general unifiers is

$$\{y \leftarrow a, \ w \leftarrow s_0;z_2, \ x \leftarrow (s_0;z_2){:}u, \ z_1 \leftarrow z_2;put(u, table)\}.$$

The polarity of the boxed subsentences is indicated by their annotation. (The goal is negative because goals are within the scope of an implicit negation.) Let us apply the resolution rule, taking $\mathcal{P}$ and $\mathcal{P}'$ to be the boxed subsentences and θ to be the above unifier. Recall that, according to the duality property, we can shift the assertion into the goal column by negating it. We obtain

	$true$ and $not \begin{pmatrix} if\ On\big(s_0;z_2, (s_0;z_2){:}u, a\big)\ and \\ \quad Clear(s_0;z_2, (s_0;z_2){:}u) \\ then\ false \end{pmatrix}$	$s_0;\, z_2;\, put(u, table)$

which simplifies propositionally to

	2. $On\big(s_0;z_2, (s_0;z_2){:}u, a\big)$ and $\quad Clear\big(s_0;z_2, (s_0;z_2){:}u\big)$	$s_0;\, z_2;\, put(u, table)$

In other words, if after execution of some plan z_2, some block u is on block a but is itself clear, we can achieve our specified condition by first executing plan z_2 and then putting block u on the table. ⌐

To present another step of the *makeclear* derivation, we give a further example of branch-free resolution.

Example (resolution).   The boxed subsentence of the new goal,

	2. $\boxed{On\big(s_0;z_2,\ (s_0;z_2){:}u,\ a\big)}^{\ -}$ and	$s_0;z_2;\ put(u,table)$
	$Clear\big(s_0;z_2,\ (s_0;z_2){:}u\big)$	

unifies equationally with the boxed subsentence of the *hat* axiom,

if $not\ Clear(w,y)$		
then $\boxed{On\big(w,\ hat'(w,y),\ y\big)}^{\ +}$		

with a most-general unifier

$$\{y \leftarrow a,\ u \leftarrow hat(a),\ w \leftarrow s_0;z_2\}.$$

The equational-unification algorithm here invokes the equalities

$$(s_0;z_2){:}hat(a)\ =\ hat'(s_0;z_2,\ (s_0;z_2){:}a),$$

which is an instance of the *object linkage* axiom, and

$$(s_0;z_2){:}a\ =\ a,$$

which is a consequence of the rigidity of the input parameter a. Applying the resolution rule, we obtain (after propositional simplification)

	3. $Clear\big(s_0;z_2,\ (s_0;z_2){:}hat(a)\big)$ and	$s_0;z_2;$
	$not\ Clear(s_0;z_2,\ a)$	$put\big(hat(a),table\big)$

In other words, if, after execution of some plan step z_2, the block a is not clear but the block $hat(a)$ is, we can achieve our specified condition by first executing plan z_2 and then putting $hat(a)$ on the table. ⌙

Resolution with Conditional Formation

In applying the resolution rule between two rows, both of which have plan entries, we must generate a conditional plan entry. If we applied the ordinary resolution rule in such a case, we would be forced to introduce tests that contain the predicate symbol :: . We would have no way of executing the resulting nonprimitive plans. To avoid introducing nonprimitives into the plan entry, we employ the following resolution rule. We present the ground version of the rule as it applies to two goals:

assertions	goals	plan: $s_0;f(a)$
	$\mathcal{F}[s::p]$	$s;e_1$
	$\mathcal{G}[s::p]$	$s;e_2$
	$\mathcal{F}[true]$ and $\mathcal{G}[false]$	$s;\begin{pmatrix} if\ p \\ then\ e_1 \\ else\ e_2 \end{pmatrix}$

In other words, suppose our tableau contains two goals, both of which refer to the truth of the same propositional fluent p in a common state s. Suppose further that s is an initial segment of the plan entries for each of the two goals. Then we can introduce the same new goal as the previous branch-free version of the rule. The plan entry associated with this goal has as its initial segment the common state s of the given plan entries. Its final segment is a conditional whose test is the matching propositional fluent p and whose *then*-clause and *else*-clause are the final segments e_1 and e_2, respectively, of the given plans.

The rationale for this plan entry is as follows. We suppose that the new goal $(\mathcal{F}[true]$ and $\mathcal{G}[false])$ is true and show that the associated plan entry satisfies the specified condition.

We distinguish between two cases. In the case in which $s::p$ is true, because the conjunct $\mathcal{F}[true]$ is true, the given goal $\mathcal{F}[s::p]$ is also true, and hence the associated plan entry $s;e_1$ satisfies the specified condition. In this case, the conditional plan

$$s\,;(if\ p\ then\ e_1\ else\ e_2)$$

will also satisfy the condition because, when executed in state s, the result of the test of p will be true.

Similarly, in the case in which $s::p$ is false, the given goal $\mathcal{G}[s::p]$ is true, the associated plan entry $s;e_2$ satisfies the specified condition, and the conditional plan will also satisfy the condition. Thus, in either case the conditional plan satisfies the specified condition.

Of course, the rule applies to assertions as well as to goals. The polarity strategy may be imposed as before. We have given the ground version of the rule; in the general version, in which the rows may have variables, we first apply a most-general unifier of the subsentences $s::p$ and $s'::p'$, after renaming as necessary; we then use the ground version of the rule.

We illustrate this with an example.

Example (resolution with conditional formation). Suppose our tableau contains the two goals

	goals	plan: $s_0; makeclear(a)$
	$\boxed{(s_0;z_1)::clear(a)}$ $^-$	$s_0;z_1$
	$not \boxed{(s_0;\Lambda)::clear(a)}$ $^+$	$s_0;\Lambda; makeclear\big(hat(a)\big);$ $put\big(hat(a), table\big)$

The boxed subsentences are unifiable, with a most-general unifier $\{z_1 \leftarrow \Lambda\}$. The unified subsentences both refer to the truth of the same propositional fluent $clear(a)$ in a common state, the state $s_0;\Lambda$. The state s_0 is an initial segment for the plan entries of each of the given goals. Therefore we can apply the resolution rule to obtain (after propositional simplification)

	$true$	$s_0;\Lambda; \begin{pmatrix} if\ clear(a) \\ then\ \Lambda \\ else\ makeclear\big(hat(a)\big); \\ \quad put\big(hat(a), table\big) \end{pmatrix}$

Using equational unification, we can take advantage of properties of plan theory in applying the resolution rule. For instance, we could apply the rule in this example if our two goals were

$$Clear(s_0;z_1,\ a)$$

and

$$not\ \big(s_0 :: clear(a)\big)$$

to obtain the same result. (The first is our goal 1.) This could be the final step of a *makeclear* derivation. ◢

Let us remark that we could formulate a resolution rule without the restriction that the common state be an initial segment of the plan entries. If these entries were s_1' and s_2', the plan entry for the derived goal could be taken to be

$$if\ s::p\ then\ s_1'\ else\ s_2'.$$

The unrestricted rule does preserve the validity and correctness of the tableau. However, because the new plan entry contains the nonprimitive symbol $::$, the row would have to be discarded immediately. This is why we are forced to restrict the rule.

Resolution with Equality Matching

Sometimes in an attempt to apply the resolution rule, two subsentences will fail to unify completely but will "nearly" unify; that is, all but certain pairs of subterms will unify. In such cases, instead of abandoning the attempt altogether, it may be advantageous to go ahead and apply the rule but impose certain conditions upon the conclusion. This is the effect of applying the *resolution rule with equality matching.*

In its simplest (ground) version, the rule may be expressed as follows:

assertions	goals
	$\mathcal{F}[\mathcal{P}\langle s\rangle]$
	$\mathcal{G}[\mathcal{P}\langle t\rangle]$
	$s = t$ *and* $\mathcal{F}[true]$ *and* $\mathcal{G}[false]$

Here $\mathcal{P}\langle s\rangle$ and $\mathcal{P}\langle t\rangle$ are identical except that certain occurrences of s in $\mathcal{P}\langle s\rangle$ are replaced by t in $\mathcal{P}\langle t\rangle$. If they were completely identical, we could apply the ordinary resolution rule to obtain the new goal ($\mathcal{F}[true]$ *and* $\mathcal{G}[false]$). Instead, we obtain this goal with the additional conjunct $s = t$. The treatment of the plan entry is analogous to that for the original resolution rule.

Our rule is a nonclausal version of the E-resolution rule (Morris [69]) or the RUE-resolution rule (Digricoli and Harrison [86]). In Manna and Waldinger [86], we generalize the rule to allow more than one pair of mismatched terms and to employ reflexive binary relations other than equality, but we shall not require these extensions here.

In the nonground version, in which the sentences may contain variables, we apply a substitution to the given rows and then apply the ground version of the rule to the results. The substitution is the outcome of an abortive attempt to unify the subsentences. We shall see that, for a given pair of sentences, the substitution we employ and the pair of mismatched subterms we obtain are not necessarily unique. Some of the strategic aspects of choosing the substitution and term pair are discussed by Digricoli and Harrison [86].

Example (resolution with equality matching).   Suppose our tableau contains the goal

	$\boxed{Clear(s_0;z_2,\ (s_0;z_2):hat(a))}$ $^{-}$ *and* $Q(z_2)$	$s_0;\ z_2;$ $put(hat(a),table)$

and the assertion

if $R(w,u)$ *then* $\boxed{Clear(w;makeclear(u),\ w:u)}$ $^{+}$			

The two boxed subsentences are not unifiable. However, if we apply the substitution

$$\{u \leftarrow hat(a),\ w \leftarrow s_0;z_2\},$$

we obtain the sentences

$$Clear\big(s_0;z_2,\ (s_0;z_2):hat(a)\big)$$

and

$$Clear\big((s_0;z_2);makeclear(hat(a)),\ (s_0;z_2):hat(a)\big).$$

Our mismatched terms are then

$$s_0;z_2 \quad \text{and} \quad (s_0;z_2);makeclear(hat(a)).$$

The conclusion of the rule is then (before simplification)

$s_0;z_2 = (s_0;z_2);makeclear(hat(a))$ *and* *true and* $Q(z_2)$ *and* *not* $\big(if\ R(s_0;z_2,\ hat(a))\ then\ false\big)$	$s_0;\ z_2;$ $\qquad put(hat(a),\ table)$

On the other hand, if we apply the substitution

$$\{w \leftarrow s_0,\ z_2 \leftarrow makeclear(u)\},$$

the boxed subsentences become

$$Clear\big(s_0;makeclear(u),\ (s_0;makeclear(u)):\ hat(a)\big)$$

and

$$Clear\big(s_0;makeclear(u),\ s_0:u\big).$$

Our mismatched terms are then

$$(s_0;makeclear(u)):hat(a) \quad \text{and} \quad s_0:u,$$

and the conclusion of the rule (after simplification this time) is then

$(s_0;makeclear(u)):hat(a) = s_0:u$ *and* $Q(makeclear(u))$ *and* $R(s_0,u)$	$s_0;\ makeclear(u);$ $\qquad put(hat(a),table)$

In applying resolution with equality matching, we have altered an ordinary unification algorithm to return mismatched terms instead of failing. If we alter instead an equational-unification algorithm, we can invoke properties of our plan theory in our search for near-unifiers.

6.   FORMATION OF RECURSION

The mathematical-induction rule accounts for the introduction of the basic repetitive construct — recursion — into the plan being derived. We employ well-founded induction, i.e., induction over a well-founded relation; this is a single, very general rule that applies to many subject domains.

The Mathematical-Induction Rule

A well-founded relation $\prec_\alpha$ is one that admits no infinite decreasing sequences, i.e., sequences $x_1, x_2, x_3, \ldots$ such that

$$x_1 \succ_\alpha x_2 \quad \text{and} \quad x_2 \succ_\alpha x_3 \quad \text{and} \quad \ldots.$$

For instance the less-than relation $<$ is well-founded in the theory of nonnegative integers but not in the theory of real numbers. A well-founded relation need not be transitive.

The instance of the *well-founded induction rule* we require can be expressed as follows (the general rule is notationally more complex):

Suppose that our initial tableau is

assertions	goals	plan: $s_0; f(a)$
	$\mathcal{Q}[s_0,\, a,\, s_0; z_1]$	$s_0; z_1$

In other words, we are trying to construct a program f that, for a given input a, yields a plan $f(a) = z_1$ satisfying our condition $\mathcal{Q}[s_0,\, a,\, s_0; z_1]$. According to the well-founded induction rule, we may prove this under the induction hypothesis that, for a given state w and input u, the program f will yield a plan $f(u)$ satisfying the condition $\mathcal{Q}[w,\, w{:}u,\, w; f(u)]$, provided that the input $w{:}u$ is less than the original input $s_0{:}a$, that is, a, with respect to some well-founded relation. More precisely, we may add to our tableau, as a new assertion, the induction hypothesis

if $\langle w,\, w{:}u \rangle \prec_\alpha \langle s_0,\, a \rangle$ *then* $\mathcal{Q}[w,\, w{:}u,\, w; f(u)]$		

Here w and u are both variables, and $\prec_\alpha$ is actually a well-founded relation on pairs of states and objects. The relation $\prec_\alpha$ is arbitrary; its selection may be deferred until later in the proof.

Example (*well-founded induction rule*).   The initial tableau in the *makeclear* derivation is

assertions	goals	plan: $s_0;makeclear(a)$
	1. $Clear(s_0;z_1, a)$	$s_0;z_1$

By application of the well-founded induction rule, we may add to our tableau the new assertion

if $\langle w, w{:}u \rangle \prec_\alpha \langle s_0, a \rangle$ *then* $Clear(w;makeclear(u), w{:}u)$		

In other words, we may assume inductively that the *makeclear* program will yield a plan *makeclear(u)* that satisfies the specified condition for any input u in any state w, provided that the state-block pair $\langle w, w{:}u \rangle$ is less than the pair $\langle s_0, a \rangle$ with respect to some well-founded relation $\prec_\alpha$. ⬛

Use of the induction hypothesis in the proof may account for the introduction of a recursive call into the derived program.

Example (formation of recursive calls). In the *makeclear* derivation, we have obtained the goal

	3. $\boxed{Clear\left(s_0;z_2, (s_0;z_2){:}hat(a)\right)}^{-}$ *and*
	    $not\ Clear(s_0;z_2, a)$
		$s_0; z_2;$
		    $put\left(hat(a), table\right)$

The boxed subsentence "nearly" unifies with the boxed subsentence of our induction hypothesis,

if $\langle w, w{:}u \rangle \prec_\alpha \langle s_0, a \rangle$ *then* $\boxed{Clear\left(w;makeclear(u), w{:}u\right)}^{+}$		

If we take the substitution to be

$$\{w \leftarrow s_0,\ z_2 \leftarrow makeclear(u)\},$$

the mismatched subterms are

$$\left(s_0;makeclear(u)\right){:}hat(a) \quad \text{and} \quad s_0{:}u.$$

We obtain the new goal

4. $(s_0;makeclear(u)){:}hat(a) \;=\; s_0{:}u$ and $not\,Clear(s_0;makeclear(u),\,a)$ and $\langle s_0,\; s_0{:}u \rangle \prec_\alpha \langle s_0,\; a \rangle$	$s_0;\,makeclear(u);$ $\quad put\big(hat(a),table\big)$

Other substitutions are possible, resulting in other new goals. ⌐

Note that, at this stage of the derivation, a recursive call $makeclear(u)$ has been introduced into the plan entry for the new goal 4. The condition $\langle s_0,\, s_0{:}u \rangle \prec_\alpha \langle s_0,\, a \rangle$ in the goal ensures that this recursive call will not contribute to nontermination. Any nonterminating computation involves an infinite sequence of nested recursive calls $makeclear(a)$, $makeclear(u)$, $makeclear(u')$, ... From any such sequence we can construct an infinite decreasing sequence of pairs $\langle s_0,\, a \rangle$, $\langle s_0,\, s_0{:}u \rangle$, $\langle s_0,\, s_0{:}u' \rangle$, ..., which is contrary to the well-foundedness of $\prec_\alpha$.

The Choice of a Well-founded Relation

Although the well-founded induction principle is the same from one theory to the next, each theory has its own well-founded relations. We actually take well-founded relations to be objects in each theory and regard the expression $x \prec_\alpha y$ as a notation for a three-place relation $\prec(\alpha, x, y)$, where α is a variable that ranges over well-founded relations.

For the blocks-world theory, one relation of particular importance is the *on* relation, which holds if one block is directly on top of another. In a given state, this relation is well-founded because we assume that towers of blocks cannot be infinite. More precisely, for each state w, we define the well-founded relation $\prec_{on_w}$ by the following *on-relation* axiom:

$$x \prec_{on_w} y \;\equiv\; On(w, x, y) \qquad\qquad (on\ relation)$$

(Note that for each state w we obtain a different relation $\prec_{on_w}$.) This relation has the *hat* property

$(*)$ $\qquad$ *if* $not\,(w :: clear(v))$
$\qquad$ *then* $w{:}hat(v) \prec_{on_w} w{:}v.$

The *on* relation $\prec_{on_w}$ applies to blocks, but the desired relation $\prec_\alpha$ in goal 4 applies to state-block pairs. However, for any well-founded relation $\prec_\beta$, there exists a corresponding well-founded *second-projection* relation $\prec_{\pi_2(\beta)}$ on pairs, defined by the following *second-projection* axiom:

$$\langle x_1,\, x_2 \rangle \prec_{\pi_2(\beta)} \langle y_1,\, y_2 \rangle \;\equiv\; x_2 \prec_\beta y_2 \qquad\qquad (second\ projection)$$

In other words, two pairs are related by the *second-projection* relation $\prec_{\pi_2(\beta)}$ if their second components are related by $\prec_\beta$. As usual we omit the sort conditions, but here β

is a variable that ranges over well-founded relations. (Of course, there is a *first-projection* axiom also, but the second projection is the one we shall use.)

By applying rules of the system to the above properties, we may reduce our most recent goal

	4.	$(s_0;makeclear(u)){:}hat(a) = s_0{:}u$ and $not\,Clear(s_0;makeclear(u),\,a)$ and $\langle s_0,\,s_0{:}u \rangle \prec_\alpha \langle s_0,\,a \rangle$	$s_0;makeclear(u);$ $put(hat(a),table)$

to obtain, by the *second-projection* axiom, taking α to be $\pi_2(\beta)$,

	5.	$(s_0;makeclear(u)){:}hat(a) = s_0{:}u$ and $not\,Clear(s_0;makeclear(u),\,a)$ and $s_0{:}u \prec_\beta a$	$s_0;makeclear(u);$ $put(hat(a),table)$

and then, by the above *hat* property $(*)$, taking β to be on_{s_0},

	6.	$(s_0;makeclear(hat(a))){:}hat(a)$ $= s_0{:}hat(a)$ and $not\,Clear(s_0;makeclear(hat(a)),\,a)$ and $not\,(s_0 {::} clear(a))$	$s_0;makeclear(hat(a));$ $put(hat(a),table)$

Through these steps, the well-founded relation $\prec_\alpha$ on state-block pairs is chosen to be $\prec_{\pi_2(on_{s_0})}$, the second projection of the *on* relation in the initial state s_0.

At this stage, we have completed the derivation of the entire *else*-branch of the *makeclear* program.

The Need for Generalization

One might believe that the derivation is nearly complete; all that remains is to dispense with the first two conjuncts of our goal 6,

$(\dagger)$ $\qquad (s_0;makeclear(hat(a))){:}hat(a) = s_0{:}hat(a)$

and

$(\ddagger)$ $\qquad not\,Clear(s_0;makeclear(hat(a)),\,a).$

(The third conjunct, $not(s_0 {::} clear(a))$, will then be eliminated by resolution with the initial goal 1, resulting in the introduction of the conditional construct into the final plan.) In fact, closer examination of the above two conditions indicates that they are not so straightforward.

The first condition (†) requires that, after $hat(a)$ has been cleared, the value of $hat(a)$ should be the same as it was before. In other words, we must show that the *makeclear* program we are constructing will not move $hat(a)$ in the process of clearing it. In fact, the program does not move $hat(a)$, but nothing in its specification forces it to be so well-behaved. If *makeclear* were trying to be economical with table space, it might clear $hat(a)$ by putting underneath it all the blocks that were previously on top of it, as illustrated below:

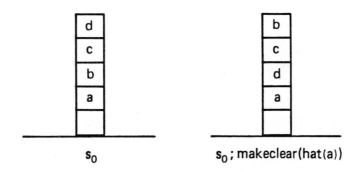

Here a hypothetical *makeclear* program has cleared $hat(a)$, that is, b, by putting c and d underneath b. The subsequent value of $hat(a)$ is d, not b, which is contrary to the condition. An attempt to put $hat(a)$ on the table will then lead to unpredictable results because d is not clear.

The second condition (‡) of the goal requires that, in the process of clearing $hat(a)$, we do not inadvertently clear a. Again the program we are constructing will not do this, but there is nothing in the specification that prevents an over ambitious *makeclear* program from clearing a or any other block when it was asked only to clear $hat(a)$, as illustrated below:

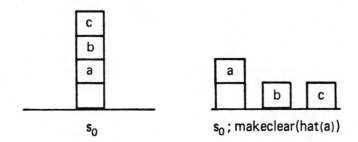

Attempting to move $hat(a)$ will then lead to unpredictable results because $hat(a)$ is not a block.

The only knowledge we have about *makeclear* is that given in our induction hypothesis, which depends in turn on what is required by our specification. We have not specified what $makeclear(a)$ does to blocks underneath its input parameter a or elsewhere on the table. Thus it is actually impossible to prove the two conditions.

In proving a given theorem by induction, it is often necessary to prove a stronger, more general theorem, so as to have the benefit of a stronger induction hypothesis. Such strengthening is mentioned by Polya [57] (see also Manna and Waldinger [85b]) and is done automatically by the system of Boyer and Moore [79]. By analogy, in constructing a program to meet a given specification, it is often necessary to impose a stronger specification, so as to have the benefit of more powerful recursive calls.

This turns out to be the case with the $makeclear$ problem; the program must be constructed to meet not the given specification, but the following stronger one:

$$(\forall s_0)(\forall a)(\exists z_1) \begin{bmatrix} Clear(s_0;z_1, a) \ \ and \\ (\forall g) \begin{bmatrix} if \ Over(s_0, a, g) \\ then \ \ not \ Clear(s_0;z_1, g) \ \ and \\ \qquad hat'(s_0;z_1, g) = hat'(s_0, g) \end{bmatrix} \end{bmatrix}$$

(Here $Over(w, x, y)$ holds if block x is directly or indirectly supported by object y in state w.) In other words, in clearing block a, we do not clear any block g that is underneath a, nor do we change the hat of any such block g. In short, the relative positions of all the blocks underneath a remain unchanged. This theorem gives us an induction hypothesis strong enough to show that, in clearing $hat(a)$, or $hat(hat(a))$, or $hat(hat(hat(a)))$, or ..., we do not move $hat(a)$ itself. The induction hypothesis is also strong enough to enable us to prove the new condition in the theorem.

With human intuition, it may not be difficult to formulate such strengthened theorems. But the strengthening required by this problem seems to be beyond the capabilities of the Boyer-Moore system or other current theorem provers.

Although we do not know exactly how the condition could be strengthened automatically, let us suppose that it can be done. In this case, we must "edit" the derivation by adding the new condition as a conjunct in the initial goal, to obtain

	goals	plan: $s_0;makeclear(a)$
	1*. $\boxed{Clear(s_0;z_1, a)}^{-}$ and $\begin{bmatrix} if \ Over(s_0, a, g'(z_1)) \\ then \ \ not \ Clear(s_0;z_1, g'(z_1)) \\ and \ hat'(s_0;z_1, g'(z_1)) \\ = hat'(s_0, g'(z_1)) \end{bmatrix}$	$s_0;z_1$

Here $g'(z_1)$ is a skolem function obtained by removing the quantifier $(\forall g)$ from the given goal. In presenting the derivation, we shall drop the argument of this function and write

g throughout.

We attempt to mimic the original derivation, applying the same sequence of rules to the altered goals.

For example, in the original derivation we applied the resolution rule to goal 1 and the *put-table-clear* axiom

if $On(w,x,y)$ and $Clear(w,x)$ then $\boxed{Clear\big(put'(w,x,table),\ y\big)}$ +		

In the altered derivation, we apply the resolution rule to the altered goal 1* and this axiom, to obtain

	2*. $On\big(s_0;z_2,\ (s_0;z_2){:}u,\ a\big)$ and $Clear\big(s_0;z_2,\ (s_0;z_2){:}u\big)$ and $\begin{bmatrix} if\ Over(s_0,\ a,\ g) \\ then\ \ not\ Clear\big(s_0;z_2;put(u,table),\ g\big) \\ and\ hat'\big(s_0;z_2;put(u,table),\ g\big) \\ = hat'(s_0,\ g) \end{bmatrix}$	$s_0;\,z_2;$ $put(u,table)$

This goal is the same as goal 2 except for the addition of a third conjunct.

We proceed by mimicking the remaining steps of the original derivation. We allow ourselves to interpose additional steps as necessary. Although the induction hypothesis is now strong enough to establish the two troublesome conditions in our original derivation, additional deductive steps must be introduced to handle the new conjunct in our goal. These steps do not affect the final program.

Ultimately we derive the goal

	$not\big(s_0 :: clear(a)\big)$	$s_0;makeclear\big(hat(a)\big);$ $put\big(hat(a),\ table\big)$

As we have seen, we can apply the resolution rule to our initial goal 1 and this one, to obtain the final goal

	$true$	$s_0;\ \begin{pmatrix} if\ clear(a) \\ then\ \Lambda \\ else\ makeclear\big(hat(a)\big); \\ put\big(hat(a),\ table\big) \end{pmatrix}$

From this goal we extract the plan

$$
makeclear(a) \;\Leftarrow\;
\begin{cases}
\textit{if } clear(a) \\
\textit{then } \Lambda \\
\textit{else } makeclear(hat(a)); \\
\qquad put(hat(a),\, table).
\end{cases}
$$

7.   DISCUSSION

In this section we touch on some matters we have not treated in this paper.

Comparison with Human Planning

The reader may have been struck by the complexity of the reasoning required by the *makeclear* derivation, as contrasted with the apparent simplicity of the original planning problem. In fact the most difficult parts of the proof are involved not with generating the plan itself, but with proving that it meets the specified conditions successfully. We might speculate that human beings never completely prove the correctness of the plans they develop, relying instead on their ability to draw plausible inferences and to replan at any time if trouble arises. By a process of successive debugging, the HACKER system of Sussman [73] developed a plan similar to our *makeclear* plan, but it never demonstrated the plan's correctness. (It also relied on somewhat higher-level knowledge.) While imprecise inference may be necessary for planning applications, fully rigorous theorem proving seems better-suited to more conventional program synthesis.

The Problem of Strategic Control

Many people believe that a theorem-proving approach is inadequate for planning because a general-purpose theorem prover will never be able to compete with a system whose strategies are designed especially for problem solving. Although we have not yet dealt with the strategic question, we propose to overlay a general-purpose theorem prover with a special strategic component for planning. For example, the WARPLAN system (Warren [74]) might be regarded as a situational-logic theorem prover equipped with a strategy that enables it to imitate the STRIPS planning system (Fikes and Nilsson [71]). We speculate that, in the same way, a theorem prover could be induced to mimic any dedicated planning system, given the requisite strategic component.

ACKNOWLEDGMENTS

The authors would like to thank Martin Abadi, Tom Henzinger, Peter Ladkin, Vladimir Lifschitz, John McCarthy, and Jonathan Traugott for reading this manuscript, discussing its content, and suggesting improvements. Thanks also to Dag Mellgren and Mark Stickel, for assistance in applying their implementations of two equational-unification algorithms, and to Evelyn Eldridge-Diaz, for her patience in TEXing many versions of the manuscript.

REFERENCES

Boyer and Moore [79]
R. S. Boyer and J S. Moore, *A Computational Logic*, Academic Press, Orlando, Fla., 1979.

Digricoli and Harrison [86]
V. J. Digricoli and M. C. Harrison, Equality-based binary resolution, *Journal of the ACM*, Vol. 33, No. 2, April 1986, pp. 253–289.

Fay [79]
M. Fay, First-order unification in an equational theory, *Proceedings of the Fourth Workshop on Automated Deduction*, Austin, Texas, Feb. 1979, pp. 161–167.

Fikes and Nilsson [71]
R. E. Fikes and N. J. Nilsson, STRIPS: A new approach to the application of theorem proving to problem solving, *Artificial Intelligence*, Vol. 2, No. 3–4, Winter 1971, pp. 189–208.

Green [69]
C. C. Green, Application of theorem proving to problem solving, *Proceedings of the International Joint Conference on Artificial Intelligence*, Washington, D.C., May 1969, pp. 219–239.

Hullot [80]
J.-M. Hullot, Canonical forms and unification, *Proceedings of the Fifth Conference on Automated Deduction*, Les Arcs, France, July 1980, pp. 318–334.

Kowalski [79]
R. Kowalski, *Logic for Problem Solving*, North-Holland, New York, N.Y., 1979.

Lifschitz [85]
V. Lifschitz, Circumscription in the blocks world, unpublished report, Stanford University, Stanford, Calif., Dec. 1985.

McCarthy [63]
J. McCarthy, Situations, actions, and causal laws, technical report, Stanford University, Stanford, Calif., 1963. Reprinted in *Semantic Information Processing* (Marvin Minsky, editor), MIT Press, Cambridge, Mass., 1968, pp. 410–417.

McCarthy and Hayes [69]
J. McCarthy and P. Hayes, Some philosophical problems from the standpoint of artificial intelligence, *Machine Intelligence 4* (B. Meltzer and D. Michie, editors), American Elsevier, New York, N.Y., 1969, pp. 463–502.

Manna and Waldinger [80]
Z. Manna and R. Waldinger, A deductive approach to program synthesis, *ACM Transactions on Programming Languages and Systems*, Vol. 2, No. 1, Jan. 1980, pp. 90–121.

Manna and Waldinger [85a]
Z. Manna and R. Waldinger, The origin of the binary-search paradigm, *Proceedings of the Ninth International Joint Conference on Artificial Intelligence*, Los Angeles, Calif., Aug. 1985, pp. 222–224. Also in *Science of Computer Programming* (to appear).

Manna and Waldinger [85b]
Z. Manna and R. Waldinger, *The Logical Basis for Computer Programming*, Vol. 1: *Deductive Reasoning*, Addison-Wesley, Reading, Mass., 1985.

Manna and Waldinger [86]
Z. Manna and R. Waldinger, Special relations in automated deduction, *Journal of the ACM*, Vol. 33, No. 1, Jan. 1986, pp. 1–60.

Martelli and Rossi [86]
A. Martelli and G. Rossi, An algorithm for unification in equational theories, *Proceedings of the Third Symposium on Logic Programming*, Salt Lake City, Utah, Sept. 1986.

Morris [69]
J. B. Morris, E-resolution: Extension of resolution to include the equality relation, *Proceedings of the International Joint Conference on Artificial Intelligence*, Washington, D.C., May 1969, pp. 287–294.

Murray [82]
N. V. Murray, Completely nonclausal theorem proving, *Artificial Intelligence*, Vol. 18, No. 1, 1982, pp. 67–85.

Polya [57]
G. Polya, *How to Solve It*, Doubleday and Company, Garden City, N.Y., 1957.

Stickel [85]
M. E. Stickel, Automated deduction by theory resolution, *Journal of Automated Reasoning*, Vol. 1, No. 4, 1985, pp. 333–355.

Sussman [73]
G. J. Sussman, *A Computational Model of Skill Acquisition*, Ph.D. thesis, MIT, Cambridge, Mass., 1973.

Waldinger and Lee [69]
> R. J. Waldinger and R. C. T. Lee, PROW: A step toward automatic program writing, *Proceedings of the International Joint Conference on Artificial Intelligence*, Washington, D.C., May 1969, pp. 241–252.

Warren [74]
> D. H. D. Warren, WARPLAN: A system for generating plans, technical report, University of Edinburgh, Edinburgh, Scotland, 1974.

FORMULATING MULTIAGENT, DYNAMIC-WORLD PROBLEMS
IN THE CLASSICAL PLANNING FRAMEWORK

Edwin P.D. Pednault*
Aritificial Intelligence Center
SRI International
333 Ravenswood Avenue
Menlo Park, CA 94025

ABSTRACT

This paper demonstrates how some multiagent, dynamic-world planning problems may be formulated as single-agent, static-world problems, thereby permitting them to be solved with techniques originally intended for the latter. This approach to formulating such problems requires that dynamic worlds be modeled in the same manner as their static couterparts, and that simultaneous actions be modeled as sequential actions. The former is accomplished by introducing time as a parameter in the description of dynamic worlds. To model simultaneous actions as sequential ones, the idea of a *boundary condition* is introduced. A boundary condition exists at a point in time and determines the future course of events, up to the next boundary condition. The effect of simultaneous actions is then modeled by modifying boundary conditions sequentially. To provide concrete examples, a new language is introduced for the purpose of describing actions and their effects. This language, called ADL, combines the the notational convenience of the STRIPS operator language with the semantics and expressive power of the situation calculus. ADL thus has the same facilities as the STRIPS language for coping with the frame problem, but it is a more expressive language in that it permits actions to be described whose effects change according to the circumstances underwhich they are performed. In addition, ADL overcomes the semantic pitfalls of the STRIPS language that are discussed by Lifschitz.

*Current address: AT&T Bell Laboratories, Crawfords Corner Road, Holmdel, New Jersey 07733.

1. INTRODUCTION

Until recently, virtually all work in automatic planning has been concerned with ways of representing and solving what might be called the *classical planning problems*. In this type of problem, the world is regarded as being in one of a potentially infinite number of states. Performing an action causes the world to pass from one state to the next. In the specification of a problem, we are given a set of goals, a set of allowable actions, and a description of the world's initial state. We are then asked to find a sequence of actions that will transform the world from any state satisfying the initial-state description to one that satisfies the goal description. This framework has typically been used to model real-world problems that involve a single agent (e.g., a robot) operating in an environment that changes only as the result of the agent's action, and otherwise remains static.

Much contemporary research, on the other hand, is concerned with broader classes of planning problems, particularly those that involve multiple agents operating in dynamic worlds; for example, two children playing on a seesaw. To model such problems, appropriate representations for simultaneous actions and continuous processes are required, along with mechanisms for solving problems by using such representations. Hendrix [15] was one of the first to address these representational issues, having developed a system for simulating the effects of simultaneous actions in a dynamic world. More recent contributions have been made by Allen [2], Georgeff [9–12], Lansky [16, 17], and McDermott [21, 23], each of whom has used a different approach to the problem of representing actions and processes: Allen advocates a logic of time intervals, Georgeff employs a modified state-based approach, Lansky uses an event-based logic, while McDermott prefers a logic that combines states with continuous time lines. Stuart [29, 30] has examined the problem of synchronizing plans executed by different agents to avoid undesirable interactions among plans. Cheeseman [4], Dean [6], Tate [5, 33], Vere [35, 36], and Vilain [37] have concentrated primarily on representing and reasoning about the time and duration of events.

At this stage in the game, the primary objective is to develop epistemologically adequate [20] formalisms for representing and reasoning about simultaneous actions and continuous processes. The next step is to construct planning techniques that utilize these formalisms. Some work has already been done in this direction, notably by Allen and Kooman [1], Cheeseman [4], Georgeff and Lansky [10], Lansky [16], and McDermott [22]. However, these techniques are still in their infancy. The purpose of this paper is to help further these efforts by showing how some multiagent, dynamic-world problems may be formulated and solved in the classical planning framework. It is hoped that, by looking at the classical planning framework in this new light, it may be possible to discern how solution techniques developed for the classical problems can be transferred to frameworks that are more suitable for solving multiagent, dynamic-world problems.

This paper focuses primarily on ways of formulating multiagent, dynamic-world problems as classical planning problems. As part of our exposition, a new language, called ADL, will be introduced for the purpose of describing actions and their effects. ADL differs from its predecessors in that it combines the notational convenience of the STRIPS operator language [7] with the semantics and expressive power of the situation calculus [20] and first-order dynamic logic [13]. From the point of view of syntax, descriptions in ADL resemble STRIPS operators with conditional add and delete lists. This syntax permits actions to be described whose effects are highly state-dependent. At the same time, it allows the frame problem [14] to be circumvented to the extent that one need only specify what changes are made when an action is performed, not what remains unaltered. However, the semantics of ADL is drastically different from that of STRIPS. Whereas STRIPS operators define transformations on state descriptions, ADL schemas define transformations on the states themselves. In this respect, the semantics of ADL is similar to that of the situation calculus and first-order dynamic logic. Furthermore, by adopting a different semantics, ADL avoids the pitfalls of the STRIPS language that are discussed by Lifschitz [18].

As we shall see, ADL is well suited to the multiagent, dynamic-world problems that are presented. Once a problem is formulated with ADL, it can be solved by means of the techniques described in my thesis [25] and in a earlier technical report [24]. An explicative review of these techniques, however, is beyond the scope of this paper.

2. DEFINING THE CLASSICAL PLANNING PROBLEMS

To make clear the issues involved in formulating multiagent, dynamic-world problems as classical planning problems, the latter will now be defined mathematically. This definition is set-theoretic in nature and is based on ideas borrowed from first-order dynamic logic [13].

As previously stated, the world is regarded, in classical planning problems, as being in any one of a potentially infinite number of states. The effect of an action is to cause the world to jump from one state to another. This permits an action to be characterized as a set of current-state/next-state pairs, summarizing the possible state transitions that could occur when the action is performed. Stated mathematically, an action is a set a of ordered pairs of the form $\langle s, t \rangle$, where s and t are states, s being the "current state" and t being the "next state."

In many situations, there is no uncertainty as to how the world will change when an action is performed. In such cases, performing an action will cause the world to jump from one state to a unique next state. Mathematically speaking, an action a has this property if and only if for every state s there is at most one state t such that $\langle s, t \rangle \in a$ (i.e., such that the ordered pair $\langle s, t \rangle$ appears in a). Hence, performing action a when the world is in state s will always cause the world to jump to state t.

In other situations, the effect of an action might be unpredictable. In such cases, there will be a collection of states that the world could jump to when the action is performed, but the exact state would not be known beforehand. In mathematical terms, the effect of performing action a in state s will be uncertain if and only if there is more than one state t such that $\langle s, t \rangle \in a$. For example, if performing action a in state s will cause the world to jump to one of the states $t_1, \ldots, t_n$, but it is not known beforehand which it will be, then this is modeled by having each of the ordered pairs $\langle s, t_1 \rangle, \ldots, \langle s, t_n \rangle$ appear in the set a.

Although some actions can be performed under any circumstances, most actions can occur only when the world is in one of a limited number of states. For example, to walk through a doorway, the door must be open. If the world is in a state in which the door is closed, the action of walking through the doorway becomes impossible. In our mathematical framework, an action a may be executed in a state s if and only if there is some state t such that $\langle s, t \rangle \in a$. The set of states in which a may take place is given by

$$\mathrm{dom}(a) = \{s \mid \langle s, t \rangle \in a \text{ for some state } t\}$$

The function dom is borrowed from set theory [27, 31], where $\mathrm{dom}(a)$ is called the *domain* of the set of ordered pairs a.

In the statement of a classical planning problem, we are given a set of allowable actions, a set of possible initial states, and a set of acceptable goal states. Told that the world is currently in one of the possible initial states, we are then asked to find a sequence of allowable actions that, when executed, will leave the world in one of the acceptable goal states. A classical planning problem can therefore be viewed as an encoding of this information:

Definition 2.1. A *classical planning problem* is a quadruple of the form $\langle \mathcal{W}, \mathcal{A}, \mathcal{I}, \mathcal{G} \rangle$, where
  (1) $\mathcal{W}$ is the set of all possible states of the world
  (2) $\mathcal{A}$ is the set of allowable actions
  (3) $\mathcal{I}$ is the set of possible initial states
  (4) $\mathcal{G}$ is the set of acceptable goal states.

A solution to a classical planning problem is a sequence of actions $a_1 a_2 \cdots a_n$ that will transform the world from any of the possible initial states into one of the acceptable goal states. To guarantee this result, a number of conditions must be satisfied. First, it must be possible to execute each of the actions in the given order. This requires that it be possible to first perform a_1 in any of the possible initial states, then a_2 in any state that could result from performing a_1, then a_3 in any state that could result from performing a_2, etc. If these conditions hold, the sequence is said to be *executable*. Finally, for the sequence to be a solution, the world must necessarily be in one of the goal states once all the actions have been carried out.

To express these conditions mathematically, the following notation is introduced.

  (1) Let ϵ denote the empty sequence; that is, the sequence containing no actions. "Executing" ϵ therefore leaves the world undisturbed.

  (2) If σ and γ are two sequences of actions, then $\sigma\gamma$ is the sequence obtained by appending γ to the end of σ. For example, if $\sigma = a_1 a_2$ and $\gamma = a_3 a_4 a_5$, then $\sigma\gamma = a_1 a_2 a_3 a_4 a_5$. Note that $\sigma\epsilon = \epsilon\sigma = \sigma$.

  (3) If there exists a sequence γ such that $\sigma\gamma = \theta$, then σ is said to be a *prefix* of θ. For example, the prefixes of the sequence $a_1 a_2 a_3 a_4 a_5$ are ϵ, a_1, $a_1 a_2$, $a_1 a_2 a_3$, $a_1 a_2 a_3 a_4$, and $a_1 a_2 a_3 a_4 a_5$.

The concept of a prefix permits us to express the executability conditions for a sequence as follows: a sequence θ is executable if and only if, for every prefix σa of θ, where a is an action, a can be performed in every state that could result from the execution of σ. The set of states that could result when σ is executed is given by the function $\text{Result}(\sigma, I)$, which is defined recursively as follows:

$$\text{Result}(\epsilon, I) = I \tag{2.2a}$$

$$\text{Result}(\gamma a, I) = \{t \mid \langle s, t \rangle \in a \text{ for some } s \in \text{Result}(\gamma, I)\} \tag{2.2b}$$

Thus, if no actions task place, the set of possible resulting states is merely the set of possible initial states. If one or more actions are performed, the set of resulting states is obtained by considering every state transition that could possibly occur when the sequence is executed. Thus, an action a can be performed in every state that could result from the sequence σ if and only if $\text{Result}(\sigma, I) \subset \text{dom}(a)$ (i.e., every state in $\text{Result}(\sigma, I)$ also appears in $\text{dom}(a)$). This permits the following definitions to be formulated:

Definition 2.3. A sequence of actions θ is said to be *executable* with respect to a set of possible initial states I if and only if $\text{Result}(\sigma, I) \subset \text{dom}(a)$ for every prefix σa of θ such that a is an action.

Definition 2.4. A *solution* to a classical planning problem $\langle \mathcal{W}, \mathcal{A}, I, \mathcal{G} \rangle$ is a sequence of actions θ drawn from $\mathcal{A}$ such that θ is executable with respect to I and $\text{Result}(\theta, I) \subset \mathcal{G}$.

3. THE ONTOLOGY OF ACTIONS IN CLASSICAL PLANNING

When a formalism is proposed for describing some aspect of the real world, two questions naturally arise: in what sense does the formalism reflect reality, and to what degree? This section is intended to at least partially answer these questions with respect to the classical planning problems. Specifically, we shall consider how various kinds of real-world planning problems may be modeled as classical planning problems, particularly those problems involving dynamic environments and multiple agents. In each case, our primary emphasis will be on establishing a correspondence between actions in the real world and the formal notion of an action used in classical planning problems. Our goal, however, is not to understand the true nature of actions in the real world, but rather to determine how a particular mathematical construct may be used to model problems of interest.

Historically, the formal notion of an action developed in Section 2 was used to model problems that involve a single agent operating in an environment that remains essentially static, except while the agent is performing an action. To illustrate, imagine a robot in a closed room that contains a table on which a number of wooden blocks of equal size are stacked. The robot may be commanded (say, by radio) to move the blocks one at a time, either placing them elsewhere on the table or stacking them on top of other blocks. When issued a command, the robot will reach for the block to be moved, pick it up, position it over the desired location, and deposit it. Once the block has been deposited, the robot will stand motionless until the next command is received. Thus, except for those periods when the robot is carrying out a order, the robot and the blocks remain static (i.e., their respective positions remain fixed).

Imagine further that our goal is to have the robot arrange the blocks in a particular configuration. To determine an appropriate sequence of commands, all we need to know about each command are its net effects–that is, what the final respective positions of the robot and the blocks would be once the command has been carried out. The exact motion of the robot and the blocks during execution is unimportant. This leads us directly to the classical planning framework: First we can define a state to be a particular arrangement of the robot and blocks. Then we can catalogue the effects of a command by means of a set of current-state/next-state pairs specifying what the final disposition of the robot and blocks would be for each possible arrangement at the moment a command is invoked. This way of formalizing the problem ignores the details of the robot's motion while retaining all of the information relevant to planning a sequence of commands. It should be noted, however, that this formalization is possible only because the robot and the blocks remain stationary between the completion of one task and the start of the next.

In many real-world situations, though, the world is not static but is in continuous state of flux. For example, suppose that our robot is trying to land a spacecraft on the moon. At any point in time, the robot may change the vehicle's flight path by adjusting the attitude of the vehicle and/or its thrust. Unlike the blocks in the previous example, however, the vehicle is in continuous motion until it lands (safely, we hope) on the lunar surface.

Single-agent, dynamic-world problems, such as the one just described, can be formulated in the classical planning framework by assigning new interpretations to the mathematical notions of state and state transition. In the static case, the world does not change between the end of one action and the beginning of the next. This permits a state to represent everything that is true of the world at a given point in time between one action and the next. In a dynamic situation, however, this is not sufficient, since the world may be continually changing of its own accord from one moment to the next. Hence, what may be true at one point in time might not be true an instant later. How, then, is it possible to model actions in a dynamic environment as sets of current-state/next-state pairs? The key is to use states not for cataloguing what is true of the world at given instants in time, but rather for cataloguing what is true at each individual point in time, for all such points. To use McDermott's terminology [21, 23], a state according to this new interpretation is a *chronicle* of all that is true, was true, and will be true of the world, from the beginning of time through to the end of time.

Since we are interpreting states as chronicles, how should we interpret state transitions? The most sensible answer is to interpret a state transition as the initiation of an action or course of action at a particular point in time. Under this interpretation, when a state transition is made from one chronicle to the next, the past with respect to the new chronicle must be identical to the past with respect to the preceding chronicle. This reflects the commonsense intuition that the past is inaccessible and therefore cannot be changed. The future portion of the new chronicle, however, may be different. That portion must catalogue everything that would be true henceforth, *provided that no further actions are initiated*. In particular, it would record the events that take place as a result of executing the action whose initiation the state transition represents. If a new action is initiated, it must obviously follow all prior initiations. This corresponds to the commonsense intuition that time always moves forward, never backward.

This new way of interpreting states and state descriptions is illustrated in the figure below. States (i.e., chronicles) are shown as time lines, while state transitions are depicted as jumps from one time line to another that has the same past.

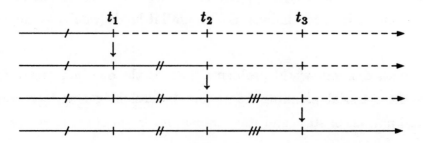

As an example, consider again the problem of landing a spacecraft on the moon, where the allowable actions are to adjust the attitude of the vehicle and the thrust. For a given adjustment, the future course of events will be dictated by the physics of the situation and will not change unless further adjustments are made. Each new adjustment places the spacecraft on a new trajectory, do that a new chronicle of events comes into force. Each new chronicle has the same past as the preceding one, since the previous history of the vehicle does not change; only the future is changed.

It is interesting to note that the ontology of time and action presented above is identical, within isomorphism, to the ontology put forth by McDermott [21, 23]. This isomorphism becomes evident from the fact that each of McDermott's forward-branching trees can be expanded into a set individual chronicles and a set of transitions from one chronicle to the next. Furthermore, a set of chronicles, together with a set of transitions between chronicles that share the same past, can be collapsed into a forward-branching tree. This isomorphism is significant, since it reinforces our earlier conjecture that it may be possible to transfer techniques for solving classical planning problems to frameworks that are better suited to the modeling of simultaneous actions and dynamic processes. A first step toward effecting this transfer is to establish such an isomorphism.

Thus far, we have considered problems involving a single agent acting in a world that may be static or dynamic. In some real-world situation, though, there may be several agents capable of performing tasks simultaneously. To maximize productivity, as many agents as possible should be working at any given time. Therefore, we would like to construct plans that coordinate the simultaneous execution of actions by these agents. In attempting to formulate such problems in the classical planning framework, though, we are faced with a major incongruity—i.e., that actions in the classical planning framework may be performed only sequentially whereas multiple agents tend to act simultaneously. In some situation, however, the effect of executing actions simultaneously is the same as doing them sequentially, regardless of the order of execution. This happens, for example, when the actions affect independent parts of the world and so do not interact. If such is the case, we can solve the problem by assuming that actions are to be carried out sequentially, and then transform the resulting sequential plan into a parallel plan for coordinating their simultaneous execution. This parallel plan could be in the form of a partial ordering of actions that specifies which actions may be performed simultaneously, which sequentially.

Such a partial order may be constructed in the following manner. First, to each action in the sequence we assign a unique symbol that identifies that action and its position in the sequence. Next, we construct a binary relation $\prec$ on these identifiers that will be used to define the partial order. The binary relation itself is defined as follows: We start by writting $x \prec y$ as shorthand for $\langle x, y \rangle \in \prec$. Then, for any pair of identifiers x and y, we define $x \prec y$ to be true if and only if the action corresponding to x precedes the action corresponding to y in the sequential plan and these two actions cannot be performed simultaneously. The desired partial order is then given by the *transitive closure* [27, 31] of $\prec$, which we write as $\prec^*$. Mathematically speaking, $\prec^*$ is the smallest binary relation such that

(1) If $x \prec y$ then $x \prec^* y$

(2) If $x \prec^* y$ and $y \prec^* z$ then $x \prec^* z$.

The relation $\prec^*$ specifies in the following way which actions may be performed simultaneously and which sequentially. If $x \prec^* y$, the action corresponding to x must be carried out before the action corresponding to y. On the other hand, if neither $x \prec^* y$ nor $y \prec^* x$, then the actions corresponding to x and y may be executed simultaneously.

It should be emphasized that the procedure just outlined works correctly if and only if the effect of performing actions simultaneously is the same as performing them sequentially. However, not all actions behave this way. Some actions have synergistic effects when performed simultaneously. As a result, their effects are different when performed simultaneously as compared with their sequential execution. For example, consider the effect when two agents lift opposite ends of a table upon which various objects have been placed. If the ends of the table are raised sequentially, the objects on the table might slide around and perhaps even fall off. On the other hand, if the ends are lifted simultaneously and with equal force, the objects on the table will remain more or less fixed. Chapman [3] gives a similar example involving the assembly of LEGO™ blocks. In his example, two agents are pressing down on opposite ends of a LEGO™ block that is resting on top of another LEGO™ block. If the agents apply equal force simultaneously, the first block will mate with the bottom block. On the other hand, if unequal force is applied or if equal force is applied sequentially, the first block will merely pivot and jam.

On the surface, it would appear that synergistic simultaneous actions cannot be dealt with in the classical planning framework, since the latter requires that actions be performed sequentially. Nevertheless, by choosing the appropriate representation, some synergistic simultaneous actions can be made to look like sequential actions, thereby permitting their formulation in the classical planning framework. In the table illustration given above and in Chapman's LEGO^{TM} example, this property can be achieved by modeling the forces that are acting upon on the objects. The overall motion of the objects is determined by the sum of the applied forces and the physical constraints. The primary effect of an action is to apply a force. Since the individual forces acting upon an object can be combined in any order to determine the net force, the actions of applying force can be considered sequentially. This allows the actions to be formulated as sets of current-state/next-state pairs, where each state is a chronicle of all that is true, was true, and will be true of the world, and where each state transition represents the effect of adding or subtracting a force vector at a particular instant. When a transition occurs, not only is the future portion of the chronicle modified, but a record is made noting the force that was added or deleted, along with the time at which this occurred. In this way, the net effect of simultaneously adding or subtracting forces can be determined through a sequence of state transitions.

This approach to determining the net effect of synergistic simultaneous actions can be generalized in the following way. The primary effect of an action is to establish a boundary condition at the point in time at which the action is initiated. The future course of events is then determined by these boundary conditions. In the table example and in Chapman's LEGO^{TM} example, the boundary conditions are the forces applied to the objects. When actions are performed simultaneously, they add to and modify one another's boundary conditions. The resulting boundary conditions then determine the net effect of the actions. Furthermore, the boundary conditions is are modified in a way that enables the actions and their contributions to the boundary conditions to be considered sequentially and in any order. In this way, synergistic simultaneous actions can be made to resemble sequential actions, thus permitting the problem to be formulated in the classical planning framework.

A concrete example of this technique is presented in Section 5. First, however, suitable languages need to be established for representing states and actions.

4. DESCRIBING STATES AND ACTIONS

When solving complex problems, it is often impossible to deal with states and state transitions explicitly, since the number of possible states of the world may be infinite—or at least so large as to make it impractical to enumerate them all. In such cases, states and actions must be dealt with implicitly by creating languages that can express facts about states and actions. The problem would then be specifed and solved by using these languages. Facts in the languages would relate not just to individual states/actions, but to groups thereof. This is necessary so that an infinite number of states and state transitions can be described by a finite number of facts. For example, the lunar landing problem of Section 3 involves uncountably many states; nevertheless, only a page or two of mathematical formulas will suffice to define the problem precisely. Languages for describing states and actions can also be useful when solving problems that involve only a small number of states, as it may be more convenient to present the problems in terms of facts about states and actions than in terms of the states and actions themselves.

The principal requirement of languages for describing states and actions is unambiguousness. Descriptions are intended to represent facts, which are by definition not subject to interpretation. Hence, there can be no ambiguity as to whether or not a given state or action satisfies a given description. Therefore, a description must either be true with respect to a state or an action, or it must be false. Additionally, a description need not be complete: certain details might be left out, either because they are not known or because they are thought to be unimportant. Moreover, if a description is incomplete, there will be a multiplicity of states or actions that satisfy it.

Provided the above conditions are met, literally any language could be used to express facts about states and/or actions. For the purposes of this paper, two particular lanuages will be used. In keeping with much of the previous work in automatic planning, formulas of first-order logic [27, 34] will be used to express facts about states. To describe actions, a new language called ADL will be introduced. ADL has an advantage over its predecessors in that it can be used to define actions whose effects change depending on the circumstances in which they are performed. This feature is necessary to illustrate how multiagent, dynamic-world problems may be formulated in the classical planning framework.

ADL relies on a nonstandard semantics for first-order logic derived from the semantics of first-order dynamic logic [13]. It is also similar to the semantics of first-order logic as presented by Manna and Waldinger [19]. Since a nonstandard semantics is being used, let us examine it in detail.

4.1 STATE DESCRIPTIONS AND FIRST-ORDER LOGIC

Since formulas shall be used to express facts about states, a given state will either satisfy a given formulas or it will not. To express this relationship symbolically, we shall write

$$s \models \varphi$$

to mean that state s satisfies the formula φ (or, equivalently, that φ is true when the world is in state s). Similarly,

$$s \not\models \varphi$$

means that state s does not satisfy the formula φ (or, equivalently, that φ is false when the world is in state s). One use of this notation is to define the set of initial states I and the set of goal states $\mathcal{G}$ for a planning problem in terms of state descriptions. Specifically, if Γ is a formula that describes the initial state of the world, and if G is a formula that describes the goals to be achieved, then

$$I = \{s \mid s \models \Gamma\}$$
$$\mathcal{G} = \{s \mid s \models G\}$$

The concept in first-order logic that most closely satisfies the above relationship between states and formulas is that of an *algebraic structure*. An algebraic structure M is a tuple of the form

$$M = \langle D; r_1, \ldots, r_n; f_1, \ldots, f_m; d_1, \ldots, d_k \rangle .$$

where

(1) D is a nonempty set of objects called the *domain* of the structure
(2) $r_1, \ldots, r_n$ are relations on D
(3) $f_1, \ldots, f_m$ are functions on D
(4) $d_1, \ldots, d_k$ are distinguished elements of D.

As in set theory [31], relation r_i holds among elements $x_1, \ldots, x_n$ of D if and only if $\langle x_1, \ldots, x_n \rangle \in r_i$, and $f_i(x_1, \ldots, x_n) = y$ if and only if $\langle x_1, \ldots, x_n, y \rangle \in f_i$ (note that, in set theory, a function is just a special kind of relation). Also, the functions that appear in an algebraic structure must be defined everywhere; that is, if f_i is a function of n variables, then, for every combination of n elements $x_1, \ldots, x_n$ of D, there must exist an element y of D such that $\langle x_1, \ldots, x_n, y \rangle \in f_i$. In this way, an algebraic structure completely specifies which relations and functions hold among the elements of D, and which do not. Borrowing the terminology of set theory, we shall call a function of n variables an *n-ary* function (i.e., *unary*, *binary*, *ternary*, etc.) and a relation among n elements an *n-ary* relation.

Algebraic structures are used to model a situation in the real world by choosing an appropriate set of objects for the domain of the structure, together with an appropriate collection of relations, functions, and distinguished elements for cataloguing the relevant information about the situation. For example, suppose we have a world that consists of a $TABLE$ and three blocks A, B, and C, where blocks A and B are resting on the $TABLE$ and block C is stacked on top of block A. This arrangement of blocks can be described by a single binary relation ON such that $\langle x, y \rangle \in ON$ if and only if x is on top of y. Thus, we can use the algebraic structure BLK given below to represent this state of affairs:

$$BLK = \langle D_{BLK}; ON_{BLK}; ; A, B, C, TABLE \rangle \, .$$

where

$$D_{BLK} = \{A, B, C, TABLE\}$$

and

$$ON_{BLK} = \{\langle C, A \rangle, \langle A, TABLE \rangle, \langle B, TABLE \rangle\} \, .$$

In this algebraic structure, A, B, C, and $TABLE$ have all been identified as distinguished elements. The double semicolon indicates that there are no functions in the structure.

Formulas of a first-order language are used to describe facts about algebraic structures. In a first-order language, each relation, function, and distinguished element of an algebraic structure has a corresponding symbol in the language: the symbols corresponding to relations are called relation symbols, for functions they are called function symbols, and for distinguished elements they are called constant symbols. These symbols are commonly referred to as the *nonlogical symbols* and are defined by the user of the logic. For example, we might use the symbol On to stand for the ON relation discussed above, and the symbols A, B, C, and $TABLE$ to stand for the distinguished elements $\mathcal{A}$, $\mathcal{B}$, $\mathcal{C}$, and $\mathcal{TABLE}$ respectively. For notational purposes, we shall write $M(Y)$ to mean the component of the algebraic structure M that corresponds to the nonlogical symbol Y. Thus, for the algebraic structure BLK defined above,

$$BLK(\text{On}) = \{\langle \mathcal{C}, \mathcal{A}\rangle, \langle \mathcal{A}, \mathcal{TABLE}\rangle, \langle \mathcal{B}, \mathcal{TABLE}\rangle\}$$
$$BLK(A) = \mathcal{A}$$
$$BLK(B) = \mathcal{B}$$
$$BLK(C) = \mathcal{C} \tag{4.1}$$
$$BLK(TABLE) = \mathcal{TABLE}$$

We shall often refer to $M(Y)$ as the *interpretation* of symbol Y in structure M.

In addition to the nonlogical symbols supplied by the user, a first-order language has a second group of symbols, called the *logical symbols*, that are built in. They are used to connect nonlogical symbols together to produce formulas. This group consists of variable symbols (e.g., $x_1, x_2, \ldots$) that range over objects in the domain of an algebraic structure, the symbols $TRUE$ and $FALSE$, the equality symbol "=", the universal quantifier "$\forall$" (meaning *for all*), the existential quantifier "$\exists$" (meaning *there exists*), and the logical connectives "$\wedge$", "$\vee$", "$\neg$", "$\rightarrow$", and "$\leftrightarrow$" (corresponding in meaning, respectively, to *and, or, not, implies,* and *if and only if*).

To show how the logical symbols are used to construct formulas in a first-order language, we need to introduce the notion of a *term*. Terms are syntactic constructs that denote objects in the domain of an algebraic structure. For example, in Equation 4.1, the constant symbol A is a term that denotes the object $\mathcal{A}$ in the algebraic structure BLK. Terms are constructed from constant symbols, function symbols, and variables according to the following rules:

(1) Every constant symbol and every variable symbol is a term.

(2) If $t_1, \ldots, t_n$ are terms and F is an n-ary function symbol, then $F(t_1, \ldots, t_n)$ is a term.

(3) Nothing else is a term.

Using the notion of a term, the syntax for formulas of a first-order language is defined as follows:

(1) *TRUE* and *FALSE* are formulas.

(2) If t_1 and t_2 are terms, then $(t_1 = t_2)$ is a formula.

(3) If $t_1, \ldots, t_n$ are terms and R is an n-ary relation symbol, then $R(t_1, \ldots, t_n)$ is a formula.

(4) If φ and ψ are formulas, then $\neg\varphi$, $(\varphi \wedge \psi)$, $(\varphi \vee \psi)$, $(\varphi \rightarrow \psi)$, and $(\varphi \leftrightarrow \psi)$ are formulas.

(5) If φ is a formula and x is a variable, then $\forall x \, \varphi$ and $\exists x \, \varphi$ are formulas.

(6) Nothing else is a formula.

To make formulas more readable, parentheses will be omitted whenever possible as long as this omission does not render the reading of the formula ambiguous. Also, formulas of the form $\neg(t_1 = t_2)$ will be written as $t_1 \neq t_2$ and sequences of quantifiers of the same type will be simplified by grouping the variables involved under one quantifier. For example, the formula

$$\forall x_1 \forall x_2 \forall x_3 \left(\left(\left(\mathrm{On}(x_1, x_3) \wedge \mathrm{On}(x_2, x_3) \right) \wedge \neg(x_3 = \mathit{TABLE}) \right) \rightarrow (x_1 = x_2) \right)$$

may be written as

$$\forall x_1 \, x_2 \, x_3 \left(\left(\mathrm{On}(x_1, x_3) \wedge \mathrm{On}(x_2, x_3) \wedge x_3 \neq \mathit{TABLE} \right) \rightarrow x_1 = x_2 \right).$$

This particular formula is true if and only if all blocks are stacked so that at most one block is on top of another.

In the usual semantics of first-order logic, algebraic structures are used to assign truth-values to *closed formulas* (i.e., formulas in which all variables are associated with quantifiers). The formula given above is an example of a closed formula, since the variables x_1, x_2, and x_3 are all associated with the universal quantifier $\forall$. Given an algebraic structure, a closed formula will either be true or false with respect to the structure. The formula given above, for example, is true with respect to the algebraic structure BLK defined earlier. The relationship between algebraic structures and closed formulas is therefore identical to the relationship we desire between states and formulas. However, formulas that contain *free variables* (i.e., variables not associated with any quantifier) do not necessarily have unique truth values with respect to algebraic structures. For example, the formula $\neg\text{On}(x, A)$ would be true with respect to the algebraic structure BLK if x had the value A, B, or $TABLE$; however, if x had the value C, the formula would be false. What is usually done with free variables is to view them as being universally quantified. The formula $\neg\text{On}(x, A)$ would then be equivalent to the formula $\forall x \neg\text{On}(x, A)$.

When constructing plans, however, it is often convenient to use free variables as placeholders for terms yet to be chosen [1–6, 16, 25, 26, 28, 33, 35, 36, 38], or as parameters in a generalized plan [8]. Consequently, if the same free variable appears in more than one formula, we want that free variable to represent the same object in each of the formulas. This use, however, is inconsistent with the usual interpretation of free variables as being universally quantified. What is required is that free variables be assigned interpretations in a manner similar to constant symbols. This can be accomplished by defining states as follows:

Definition 4.2. A state is a pair of the form $\langle M, V \rangle$, where M is an algebraic structure and V is a function that maps variable symbols to elements of the domain of M.

The function V serves to assign interpretations to free variables. For notational convenience, we shall define $s(Y)$ to mean the interpretation of the symbol Y in state s; that is, if $s = \langle M, V \rangle$, then

$$s(Y) = \begin{cases} M(Y), & \text{if } Y \text{ is a relation, function, or constant symbol} \\ V(Y), & \text{if } Y \text{ is a variable symbol} \end{cases}$$

Also, we will refer to the domain of the algebraic structure of a state as the domain of the state.

Given a state s as defined above, and a formula φ, either φ will be true with respect to s or it will be false. To define this relation precisely, we first need to define a *denotation function* for terms. Terms refer to objects; hence, for a particular state, each term will denote a particular object in the domain of that state. Let $[\![\tau]\!]_s$ be the denotation of term τ in state s. Then $[\![\tau]\!]_s$ can be defined recursively as follows:

(1) $[\![C]\!]_s = s(C)$ for any constant symbol C

(2) $[\![x]\!]_s = s(x)$ for any variable x

$$(3) \quad \llbracket F(\tau_1, \ldots, \tau_n) \rrbracket_s = s(F) \left(\llbracket \tau_1 \rrbracket_s, \ldots, \llbracket \tau_n \rrbracket_s \right) ,$$

where F is a function symbol, $\tau_1, \ldots, \tau_n$ are terms, and $s(F) \left(\llbracket \tau_1 \rrbracket_s, \ldots, \llbracket \tau_n \rrbracket_s \right)$ is the result of applying the function denoted by F in state s to the denotations of the terms $\tau_1, \ldots, \tau_n$ in s.

To define the truth value of a quantified formula, an additional bit of notation is required. We shall write $s[x \mapsto d]$ to mean the state obtained by changing the interpretation of variable x to d in state s. Thus, the interpretation of a symbol Y in $s[x \mapsto d]$ is given by

$$s[x \mapsto d](Y) = \begin{cases} s(Y) & \text{if } Y \text{ is not the variable } x \\ d & \text{if } Y \text{ is the variable } x \end{cases}$$

The above notation permits the satisfaction relation $s \models \varphi$ between a state s and a formula φ to be defined recursively as follows:

(1) $s \models \textit{TRUE}$

(2) $s \not\models \textit{FALSE}$

(3) $s \models (\tau_1 = \tau_2)$ if and only if $\llbracket \tau_1 \rrbracket_s = \llbracket \tau_2 \rrbracket_s$

(4) $s \models R(\tau_1, \ldots, \tau_n)$ if and only if $\langle \llbracket \tau_1 \rrbracket_s, \ldots, \llbracket \tau_n \rrbracket_s \rangle \in s(R)$

(5) $s \models (\varphi \wedge \psi)$ if and only if $s \models \varphi$ and $s \models \psi$

(6) $s \models (\varphi \vee \psi)$ if and only if $s \models \varphi$ or $s \models \psi$, or both

(7) $s \models \neg\varphi$ if and only if $s \not\models \varphi$

(8) $s \models (\varphi \rightarrow \psi)$ if and only if $s \not\models \varphi$ or $s \models \psi$, or both

(9) $s \models (\varphi \leftrightarrow \psi)$ if and only if $s \models \varphi$ and $s \models \psi$, or $s \not\models \varphi$ and $s \not\models \psi$

(10) $s \models \forall x\, \varphi$ if and only if $s[x \mapsto d] \models \varphi$ for every element d in the domain of s

(11) $s \models \exists x\, \varphi$ if and only if $s[x \mapsto d] \models \varphi$ for some d in the domain of s.

4.2 ADL: A LANGUAGE FOR DESCRIBING ACTIONS

Let us now consider a language for describing actions. This language, called ADL for Action Description Language, has the interesting property that it is syntactically similar to the STRIPS operator language of Fikes and Nilsson [7], yet it has relatively the same expressive power as the situation calculus of McCarthy and Hayes [20]. In fact, any classical planning problem that can be formulated in the situation calculus can also be formulated with ADL, and vice versa (a formal proof of the equivalence appears elsewhere [25], but is beyond the scope of the current paper). As a result, ADL can be used to describe actions whose effects are highly dependent upon the state of the world in which the action is performed. However, the syntactic properties of ADL enable the frame problem of the situation calculus to be circumvented—at least to the extent that one has only to specify the changes that take place when an action is performed, not what remains the same. The latter is provided implicitly by the language. Consequently, ADL has an advantage over other languages in that it is powerful yet convenient to use. The version of ADL presented here is an extension of a similar language introduced in an earlier technical report [24].

ADL is intended to be a practical language for describing actions. To arrive at this language, certain constraints were imposed on the kinds of actions that could be described in ADL. The first constraint is that the set of states in which an action can be performed must be representable as a well-formed formula. In other words, for an action a to be describable in ADL, there must exist a formula π^a such that

$$\mathrm{dom}(a) = \{s \mid s \models \pi^a\}.$$

This formula is called the *precondition* of the action. Note that this is a standard requirement incorporated into all planning systems to date.

The second constraint is that an action should not alter the domain of a state. That is, for any action a that can be described in ADL, and for any pair of states $\langle s, t \rangle \in a$, the domains of s and t must be identical. This requirement is of concern only when we wish to describe actions that create or destroy objects in the world. An example of such an action would be the GENSYM function in LISP, which creates new LISP atoms. Because actions are required to preserve the domain of a state, the effect of creating or destroying objects must be simulated by introducing a unary relation, say U, where $U(x)$ is true if and only if object x "actually" exists. Objects would then be "created" or "destroyed" by modifying the interpretation of U. Of course, this would require that the domain of a state include all objects that could possibly exist. Note that this is precisely the way in which GENSYM is implemented in a real computer: GENSYM does not create LISP atoms "out of thin air," but rather locates an area of unused memory and claims it for use as a new atom.

The third constraint is that an action must preserve the interpretations of free variables; that is, for any action a that can be described in ADL, and for any pair of states $\langle s, t \rangle \in a$, it must be the case that $s(x) = t(x)$ for every variable symbol x. The reason for this is that we shall want to use free variables as parameters in a plan. Consequently, a free variable that appears at more than one point in a plan should represent the same object at each of those points. Hence, we must require that actions preserve the interpretations of free variables.

The fourth constraint is that actions described in ADL be deterministic; that is, for any state $s \in \operatorname{dom}(a)$, there is a unique state t such that $\langle s, t \rangle \in a$. The rationale for this constraint is that it allows an action to be decomposed into a collection of functions—one for each relation symbol, function symbol, and constant symbol. Each function in the collection is a mapping from states to interpretations of the corresponding symbol in the succedent states. Thus, if f_Y is the function corresponding to symbol Y for action a, and if $\langle s, t \rangle \in a$, then $t(Y) = f_Y(s)$.

To provide a way of specifying these functions, we shall introduce our fifth and final constraint, which is that each function be representable as a formula. That is, each function f_Y corresponding to a symbol Y is then defined by a formula φ_Y, such that

(1) For each n-ary relation symbol R, $R(x_1, \ldots, x_n)$ is true in the succedent state if and only if $\varphi_R(x_1, \ldots, x_n)$ was true previously (where $x_1, \ldots, x_n$ are the free variables of φ_R).

(2) For each n-ary function symbol F, $F(x_1, \ldots, x_n) = w$ is true in the succedent state if and only if $\varphi_F(x_1, \ldots, x_n, w)$ was true previously.

(3) For each constant symbol C, $C = w$ is true in the succedent state if and only if $\varphi_C(w)$ was true previously.

Stated mathematically, for every pair of states $\langle s, t \rangle \in a$, and for every n-ary relation symbol R, every n-ary function symbol F, and every constant symbol C, there must exist formulas $\varphi_R(x_1, \ldots, x_n)$, $\varphi_F(x_1, \ldots, x_n, w)$, and $\varphi_C(w)$, such that

(1) $t(R) = \{\langle d_1, \ldots, d_n \rangle \mid s[x_i \mapsto d_i] \models \varphi_R(x_1, \ldots, x_n)\}$

(2) $t(F) = \{\langle d_1, \ldots, d_n, e \rangle \mid s[x_i \mapsto d_i][w \mapsto e] \models \varphi_F(x_1, \ldots, x_n, w)\}$

(3) $t(C) = d$ such that $s[w \mapsto d] \models \varphi_C(w)$.

For example, suppose we have an action for placing block B on top of block C. After this action is applied, block B is situated atop block C and every block except B remains where it was. Therefore, $\mathrm{On}(x, y)$ is true following the action if and only if

$$(x = B \wedge y = C) \vee (x \neq B \wedge \mathrm{On}(x, y))$$

was true just prior to execution. In other words, if the action is performed in state s, the interpretation of On in the succedent state is the set of ordered pairs $\langle d, e \rangle$, such that

$$s[x \mapsto d][y \mapsto e] \models (x = B \wedge y = C) \vee (x \neq B \wedge \mathrm{On}(x, y)) \ .$$

If this action were performed with the blocks stacked as described in Section 4.1, where the interpretation of On was $\{\langle B, \mathcal{TABLE} \rangle, \langle C, \mathcal{A} \rangle, \langle \mathcal{A}, \mathcal{TABLE} \rangle\}$, then the resulting interpretation of On would be $\{\langle B, C \rangle, \langle C, \mathcal{A} \rangle, \langle \mathcal{A}, \mathcal{TABLE} \rangle\}$.

When solving a planning problem, it is important to know exactly what modifications an action induces in a state before the appropriate actions for achieving the intended goals can be selected. Therefore, we shall express the above-defined φ_R's, φ_F's and φ_C's in terms of other formulas that make the modifications explicit, and then deal exclusively with these other formulas. For relation symbols, this means expressing each φ_R associated with an action a in terms of two other formulas, α_R and δ_R, which, respectively, describe the additions to and the deletions from the interpretation of R. In other words, if action a is performed in state s, the interpretation of R in the succedent state is given by

$$t(R) = (s(R) - D_R) \cup A_R \ ,$$

where $s(R)$ is the interpretation of R in state s, D_R the set of tuples to be deleted from $s(R)$, and A_R the set of tuples to be added to $s(R)$, and where A_R and D_R are given by

$$A_R = \{\langle d_1, \ldots, d_n \rangle \mid s[x_i \mapsto d_i] \models \alpha_R(x_1, \ldots, x_n)\}$$
$$D_R = \{\langle d_1, \ldots, d_n \rangle \mid s[x_i \mapsto d_i] \models \delta_R(x_1, \ldots, x_n)\} \, .$$

We shall further require that A_R and D_R be nonoverlapping (i.e., $A_R \cap D_R = \emptyset$), so that additions and deletions may be done in any order. Consequently,

$$(s(R) - D_R) \cup A_R = (s(R) \cup A_R) - D_R$$

This requires that, for every state $s \in \mathrm{dom}(a)$,

$$s \models \neg \exists x_1 \cdots x_n \, (\alpha_R(x_1, \ldots, x_n) \wedge \delta_R(x_1, \ldots, x_n))$$

Given formulas α_R and δ_R, as defined above, formula φ_R is expressed by

$$\alpha_R(x_1, \ldots, x_n) \vee (\neg \delta_R(x_1, \ldots, x_n)) \wedge R(x_1, \ldots, x_n) \tag{4.3}$$

To paraphrase, $R(x_1, \ldots, x_n)$ is true after performing action a if and only if action a made it true, or it was true beforehand and action a did not make it false. Note that it is possible to find appropriate formulas α_R and δ_R for any given formula φ_R; for example, we can let $\alpha_R(x_1, \ldots, x_n)$ be the formula $\varphi_R(x_1, \ldots, x_n)$ and $\delta_R(x_1, \ldots, x_n)$ be $\neg \varphi_R(x_1, \ldots, x_n)$. For efficient problem solving, though, α_R and δ_R should be chosen to reflect the minimal modifications required in the interpretation of R. For example, for the block-stacking action described previously, a suitable $\alpha_{\mathrm{On}}(x, y)$ would be $(x = B \wedge y = C)$ and a suitable $\delta_{\mathrm{On}}(x, y)$ would be $(x = B \wedge y \neq C)$. Note that $\delta_{\mathrm{On}}(x, y)$ cannot be $(x = B)$, since $\alpha_{\mathrm{On}}(x, y)$ and $\delta_{\mathrm{On}}(x, y)$ are constrained from being true simultaneously.

The formulas defining the interpretations of the function symbols in the succedent state can be restructured in much the same way as the formulas for relation symbols. In the case of functions, however, we can take advantage of the fact that a function must be defined everywhere, as required by the definition of an algebraic structure. Consequently, $F(x_1, \ldots, x_n) = w$ is true after an action has been performed if and only if the action changed the value of $F(x_1, \ldots, x_n)$ to w, or the action preserved the value of $F(x_1, \ldots, x_n)$ and $F(x_1, \ldots, x_n) = w$ was true previously. These modifications can be described by a single formula $\mu_F(x_1, \ldots, x_n, w)$ that is true if and only if the value of $F(x_1, \ldots, x_n)$ is to be changed to w when the action is applied. Since functions have unique values, μ_F

must have the property that, for any instantiation of $x_1, \ldots, x_n$, either there is a unique w for which $\mu_F(x_1, \ldots, x_n, w)$ is true or there are no w's for which $\mu_F(x_1, \ldots, x_n, w)$ is true. Given such a μ_F, the formula φ_F defining the interpretation of F in the succedent state is expressed by

$$\mu_F(x_1, \ldots, x_n, w) \vee (\neg \exists w \, [\mu_F(x_1, \ldots, x_n, w)] \wedge F(x_1, \ldots x_n) = w) \; . \qquad (4.4a)$$

As with α_R and δ_R, an appropriate μ_F can be found given any formula φ_F; for example, we can let $\mu_F(x_1, \ldots, x_n, w)$ be $\varphi_F(x_1, \ldots, x_n, w)$. However, for efficient problem solving, μ_F should be chosen to reflect the minimal modifications required in the interpretation of F. As an example, suppose that we wish to model the assignment statement $U \leftarrow V$, where U and V are program variables. To do so, we could have a function Val that maps program variables to their values, plus an action that updates $\text{Val}(U)$ to be the value of $\text{Val}(V)$. An appropriate update condition $\mu_{\text{Val}}(x, w)$ for this action would then be $(x = U \wedge w = \text{Val}(V))$.

Constant symbols are handled in exactly the same way as function symbols, since the former may be thought of as functions without arguments. Therefore, φ_C is given by

$$\mu_C(w) \vee (\neg \exists w \, [\mu_C(w)] \wedge C = w) \qquad (4.4b)$$

Note that Formula (4.4b) is simply a special case of Formula (4.4a) in which $n = 0$.

The syntax of ADL is designed to provide a convenient means of specifying the α, δ, μ, and π formulas that define an action. To illustrate the syntax of ADL, consider the following two actions described in ADL:

> $\text{Put}(p, q)$
> > PRECOND: $p \neq q$, $p \neq TABLE$, $\forall z \neg \text{On}(z, p)$,
> > > $[q = TABLE \vee \forall z \neg \text{On}(z, q)]$
> > ADD: $\text{On}(p, q)$
> > DELETE: $\text{On}(p, z)$ for all z such that $z \neq q$

> $\text{Assign}(u, v)$
> > UPDATE: $\text{Val}(u) \leftarrow \text{Val}(v)$

The first action, Put(p, q), is a block-stacking action for placing a block p on top of an object q, where q may be either another block or the table. The second action, Assign(u, v), simulates a statement that might appear in a programming language for assigning to variable u the value of variable v.

As the examples illustrate, a description in ADL consists of a name, an optional parameter list, and four optional groups of clauses labeled PRECOND, ADD, DELETE, and UPDATE. The PRECOND group consists of a list of formulas that define the set of states in which an action may be performed. Every formula in the list must be true when the action is performed; hence, the precondition π for the action is the conjunction of these formulas. If the list is empty, π is taken to be the formula *TRUE*, meaning that the action may be performed in every state. Thus, the precondition of Assign(u, v) is the formula *TRUE*, whereas the precondition of Put(p, q) is the formula

$$p \neq q \wedge p \neq \textit{TABLE} \wedge \forall z \neg \text{On}(z, p) \wedge [q = \textit{TABLE} \vee \forall z \neg \text{On}(z, q)]$$

The α and δ formulas for an action are specified by the ADD and DELETE groups, respectively. Each group consists of a set of clauses of the following forms:

(1) $R(t_1, \ldots, t_n)$
(2) $R(t_1, \ldots, t_n)$ if ψ
(3) $R(t_1, \ldots, t_n)$ for all $z_1, \ldots, z_k$
(4) $R(t_1, \ldots, t_n)$ for all $z_1, \ldots, z_k$ such that ψ ,

where R is a relation symbol, $t_1, \ldots, t_n$ are terms, ψ is a formula, and $z_1, \ldots, z_k$ are variable symbols that appear in terms $t_1, \ldots, t_n$ but not in the parameter list. Each of the clauses in an ADD group corresponds to an *add condition*, $\hat{\alpha}_R$, for some relation symbol R. The formula α_R that defines the set of tuples to be added to the interpretation of R is obtained by taking the conjunction of each of the add conditions for R defined in the group. If no add conditions are specified for symbol R, α_R is taken to be the formula *FALSE*, meaning that no tuples are to be added to the interpretation of R. The semantics of the DELETE group is similar to the ADD group except that, in this case, each clause corresponds to a *delete condition*, $\hat{\delta}_R$, for some relation symbol R. The conjunction of the delete conditions for R defines the formula δ_R. If no delete conditions are specified for R, δ_R is taken to be the formula *FALSE*, meaning that no tuples are to be deleted from the interpretation of R. The add/delete conditions that correspond to each of the four types of clauses are listed in the table below:

Clause	$\hat{\alpha}_R(x_1, \ldots, x_n)/\hat{\delta}_R(x_1, \ldots, x_n)$
$R(t_1, \ldots, t_n)$	$(x_1 = t_1 \wedge \cdots \wedge x_n = t_n)$
$R(t_1, \ldots, t_n)$ if ψ	$(x_1 = t_1 \wedge \cdots \wedge x_n = t_n \wedge \psi)$
$R(t_1, \ldots, t_n)$ for all $z_1, \ldots, z_k$	$\exists z_1 \cdots z_n \, (x_1 = t_1 \wedge \cdots \wedge x_n = t_n)$
$R(t_1, \ldots, t_n)$ for all $z_1, \ldots, z_k$ such that ψ	$\exists z_1 \cdots z_n \, (x_1 = t_1 \wedge \cdots \wedge x_n = t_n \wedge \psi)$

Thus, $\alpha_{\mathrm{On}}(x, y)$ for $\mathrm{Put}(p, q)$ is given by

$$\alpha_{\mathrm{On}}(x, y) \equiv (x = p \wedge y = q) \,.$$

Similarily, $\delta_{\mathrm{On}}(x, y)$ is given by

$$\delta_{\mathrm{On}}(x, y) \equiv \exists z \, (x = p \wedge y = z \wedge z \neq q) \,,$$

which simplifies to

$$\delta_{\mathrm{On}}(x, y) \equiv (x = p \wedge y \neq q) \,.$$

In the above equations, the symbol "$\equiv$" is used to denote equality between formulas. A separate symbol is used so as to avoid possible confusion with the logical symbol "$=$".

The UPDATE group is used to specify the μ-formulas that define the interpretations of the function symbols in the succedent state. The UPDATE group consists of a set of clauses of the following forms:

(1) $C \leftarrow t$

(2) $C \leftarrow t$ if ψ

(3) $C \leftarrow t$ for all $z_1, \ldots, z_k$

(4) $C \leftarrow t$ for all $z_1, \ldots, z_k$ such that ψ

(5) $F(t_1, \ldots, t_n) \leftarrow t$

(6) $F(t_1, \ldots, t_n) \leftarrow t$ if ψ

(7) $F(t_1, \ldots, t_n) \leftarrow t$ for all $z_1, \ldots, z_k$

(8) $F(t_1, \ldots, t_n) \leftarrow t$ for all $z_1, \ldots, z_k$ such that ψ ,

where C is a constant symbol, F is a function symbol, $t_1, \ldots, t_n, t$ are terms, ψ is a formula, and $z_1, \ldots, z_k$ are variable symbols that appear in terms $t_1, \ldots, t_n, t$ but not in the parameter list. Each clause in an UPDATE group corresponds to an *update condition*, $\hat{\mu}_F$, for some function symbol F, or to an update condition, $\hat{\mu}_C$, for some constant symbol C. The formula μ_F that defines the modifications in the interpretation of F is obtained by taking the conjunction of each of the update conditions $\hat{\mu}_F$ defined in the group. Likewise for the formula μ_C. If no update conditions are specified for a function/constant symbol F/C, μ_F/μ_C is taken to be the formula *FALSE*, meaning that no modifications are made in the interpretation of F/C. The update conditions that correspond to each of the eight types of clauses are listed below:

Clause	$\hat{\mu}_C(w)/\hat{\mu}_F(x_1, \ldots, x_n, w)$
$C \leftarrow t$	$(w = t)$
$C \leftarrow t$ if ψ	$(w = t \wedge \psi)$
$C \leftarrow t$ for all $z_1, \ldots, z_k$	$\exists z_1, \ldots, z_k \, (w = t)$
$C \leftarrow t$ for all $z_1, \ldots, z_k$ such that ψ	$\exists z_1, \ldots, z_k \, (w = t \wedge \psi)$
$F(t_1, \ldots, t_n) \leftarrow t$	$(x_1 = t_1 \wedge \cdots \wedge x_n = t_n \wedge w = t)$
$F(t_1, \ldots, t_n) \leftarrow t$ if ψ	$(x_1 = t_1 \wedge \cdots \wedge x_n = t_n \wedge w = t \wedge \psi)$
$F(t_1, \ldots, t_n) \leftarrow t$ for all $z_1, \ldots, z_k$	$\exists z_1 \cdots z_n \, (x_1 = t_1 \wedge \cdots \wedge x_n = t_n \wedge w = t)$
$F(t_1, \ldots, t_n) \leftarrow t$ for all $z_1, \ldots, z_k$ such that ψ	$\exists z_1 \cdots z_n \, (x_1 = t_1 \wedge \cdots \wedge x_n = t_n \wedge w = t \wedge \psi)$

For example, for the $\mathrm{Put}(p, q)$ action defined earlier,

$$\mu_A(w) \equiv FALSE \qquad\qquad \mu_C(w) \equiv FALSE$$
$$\mu_B(w) \equiv FALSE \qquad\qquad \mu_{TABLE}(w) \equiv FALSE$$

and, for the $\mathrm{Assign}(u, v)$ action,

$$\mu_{\mathrm{Val}}(x, w) \equiv (x = u \wedge w = \mathrm{Val}(v)) \, .$$

As the forgoing discussion demonstrates, ADL has a well-defined semantics. Actions are defined by providing the appropriate add, delete, and update conditions for the appropriate symbols. As long as these formulas obey the constraints imposed earlier, the descriptions in ADL will define a unique set of current-state/next-state pairs. To summarize these constraints, $\alpha_R^a(x_1, \ldots, x_n)$ and $\delta_R^a(x_1, \ldots, x_n)$ must be mutually exclusive for every n-ary relation symbol R, and $\mu_F^a(x_1, \ldots, x_n, w)$ must define a partial function mapping $x_1, \ldots, x_n$ to w for every n-ary function symbol (constant symbol) F. Because actions are described directly in terms of their effects on the state of the world, and not in terms of the formulas they make true/false, ADL avoids the semantic pitfalls of the STRIPS operator language that are discussed by Lifschitz [18].

To reason about what formulas are made true/false by actions described in ADL, *regression operators* [38] are first constructed for these actions. A regression operator for an action described in ADL is a function mapping formulas to formulas that defines the necessary and sufficient conditions that must hold before an action is performed for some condition to be true afterward. Regression operators enable us to determine whether some formula φ holds at a point p in a plan by providing us with a formula ψ that would have to be true in the initial state for φ to be true at point p. The formula ψ can then be compared with the initial state to ascertain the truth of φ at point p. The construction of regression operators from ADL descriptions and their use in plan synthesis are described elsewhere [24, 25].

5. EXAMPLES

In this section, we shall present a number of examples illustrating how multiagent, dynamic-world problems can be formulated and solved as classical planning problems. Let us first consider a specific multiagent, static-world problem. Suppose we have a world consisting of four blocks, A, B, C and D, stacked on a table, A initially on top of B, C atop D, and both B and D resting on the table. Let us suppose further that our goal is to have A on top of D and C on top of B. However, instead of having only a single robot to control, we now have two robots, R_1 and R_2. They may be commanded to both pick up and deposit blocks. But these particular robots are unable to carry more than one block at a time. Their actions can be described in ADL as follows:

PickUp (rbt, blk)

  PRECOND: Robot(rbt), $blk \neq TABLE$, $\forall z \, \neg$Holding(rbt, z),

  $\forall z \, \neg$Holding(z, blk), $\forall z \, \neg$On(z, blk)

  ADD: Holding(rbt, blk)

  DELETE: On(blk, z) for all z

PutDown (rbt, obj)

  PRECOND: Robot(rbt), $obj = TABLE \vee \forall z \, \neg$On$(z, obj)$

  ADD: On(z, obj) for all z such that Holding(rbt, z)

  DELETE: Holding(rbt, z) for all z

Both actions require the parameter rbt to designate one of the robot, R_1 or R_2. The PickUp action corresponds to the command that causes robot rbt to pick up object blk. For the robot to do so, blk cannot be the table, the robot cannot be holding any other object, no other robot can be holding blk, and nothing can be on top of blk. After robot rbt performs this action, it will be holding block blk, and block blk will be removed from its prior resting place. The PutDown action corresponds to the command that causes robot rbt to put whatever it is holding on top of object obj. To do so, either obj must be the table or there must be nothing on top of obj. When this action is executed, all objects held by robot rbt are placed on top of obj, with rbt releasing its hold on these objects.

Using the planning technique described in an earlier paper [24], we can obtain the following plan for placing block A atop block D, and block C atop block B:

$$\text{PickUp}\,(R_1, A) \;\rightarrow\; \text{PickUp}\,(R_2, C) \;\rightarrow\; \text{PutDown}\,(R_1, D) \;\rightarrow\; \text{PutDown}\,(R_2, B)$$

To construct a parallel plan, we note that PickUp (R_1, A) and PickUp (R_2, C) can be performed simultaneously by the robots, as can PutDown (R_1, D) and PutDown (R_2, B). However, neither PickUp (R_1, A) nor PickUp (R_2, C) can be executed at the same time as PutDown (R_1, D) or PutDown (R_2, B). Thus, the parallel plan would be to allow PickUp (R_1, A) and PickUp (R_2, C) to be performed simultaneously, after which actions PutDown (R_1, D) and PutDown (R_2, B) could also be concurrent.

Let us now consider a single-agent, dynamic-world problem: specifically, the lunar-landing problem described in Section 3. In this example, the thrust and attitude of the vehicle are adjusted simultaneously by a single robot. We shall assume a two-dimensional version of the problem in which the controls can be set at any point in time to provide a desired acceleration at a desired angular orientation. Once set, the acceleration and orientation are maintained until the next adjustment. If we disregard the possibility of running out of fuel or crashing into the moon, the effect of setting the controls can be formulated in ADL as follows:

Adjust(a, θ, t')

> PRECOND: $t_0 \leq t'$, $min \leq a \leq max$
>
> UPDATE: $a_0 \leftarrow a$, $\theta_0 \leftarrow \theta$, $t_0 \leftarrow t'$
>
> $x(t) \leftarrow \frac{1}{2} a \sin \theta \, (t - t')^2 + v_x(t')(t - t') + x(t')$ fa t st $t \geq t'$
>
> $y(t) \leftarrow \frac{1}{2} (g - a \cos \theta)(t - t')^2 + v_y(t')(t - t') + x(t')$ fa t st $t \geq t'$
>
> $v_x(t) \leftarrow a \sin \theta \, (t - t') + v_x(t')$ fa t st $t \geq t'$
>
> $v_y(t) \leftarrow (g - a \cos \theta)(t - t') + v_y(t')$ fa t st $t \geq t'$

where a is the net acceleration, θ the angular orientation, and t' the time at which the controls are adjusted, and where "fa" is shorthand for "for all", and "st" shorthand for "such that". The constants a_0, θ_0, and t_0 denote the acceleration, orientation, and time of the most recent adjustment, respectively. The functions $x(t)$ and $y(t)$ define the x and y coordinates of the vehicle as functions of time, while $v_x(t)$ and $v_y(t)$ define the component velocities of the vehicle along the x and y axes. Since t_0 is the time of the most recent adjustment, Adjust(a, θ, t') has the precondition that t' be greater than or equal to t_0. Adjust(a, θ, t') also has the precondition that the net acceleration lie within certain bounds, reflecting the limitations of the vehicle's engine. When an adjustment is made, the future is thereby altered, placing the vehicle on a new trajectory. The history of the vehicle's travel, however, is preserved.

The goal of a lunar-landing problem is to land safely within a certain distance of some targeted point. To ensure a safe landing, the x and y velocities must be sufficiently small and the attitude of the vehicle must be sufficiently close to vertical. This goal can be expressed as follows:

$$\exists t\,[\, y(t) = 0 \wedge \; -d_x \leq x(t) \leq d_x \; \wedge \quad 0 \leq v_y(t) \leq d_{v_y}$$
$$\wedge -d_{v_x} \leq v_x(t) \leq d_{v_x} \wedge -d_\theta \leq \quad \theta_0 \quad \leq d_\theta \,]$$

In the initial state, t_0 would represent the time at which control of the vehicle is turned over to the planner, a_0 would represent the net acceleration at that time, and θ_0 would represent the angular orientation. The functions $x(t)$, $y(t)$, $v_x(t)$, and $v_y(t)$ would have to be defined accordingly, and would have to reflect the position and velocity of the craft at time t_0. In addition, the arithmetic and trigonometric functions would have to be defined. With the appropriate formulas selected for initial-state description, the problem could then be solved by using the techniques presented elsewhere [25].

To give an example of a multiagent, dynamic-world problem, let us again consider a lunar-landing situation, but this time with the thrust and attitude adjusted independently by different robots. Although this is not the most representative of multiagent problems, it does serve to illustrate how the concept of boundary conditions can be used to handle the problem of synergistic simultaneous actions. As discussed in Section 3, by applying this notion, synergistic simultaneous actions can be made to resemble sequential actions. In the case of the lunar-landing problem, we can use acceleration and angular orientation as boundary conditions. This permits us to define the actions for setting the thrust and attitude as follows:

Thrust(a, t')

PRECOND: $t_0 \leq t'$, $min \leq a \leq max$

UPDATE: $a_0 \leftarrow a$, $t_0 \leftarrow t'$

$x(t) \leftarrow \frac{1}{2} a \sin \theta_0 \, (t - t')^2 + v_x(t')(t - t') + x(t')$ fa t st $t \geq t'$

$y(t) \leftarrow \frac{1}{2}(g - a \cos \theta_0)(t - t')^2 + v_y(t')(t - t') + x(t')$ fa t st $t \geq t'$

$v_x(t) \leftarrow a \sin \theta_0 \, (t - t') + v_x(t')$ fa t st $t \geq t'$

$v_y(t) \leftarrow (g - a \cos \theta_0)(t - t') + v_y(t')$ fa t st $t \geq t'$

Angle(θ, t')

> **PRECOND:** $t_0 \leq t'$

> **UPDATE:** $\theta_0 \leftarrow \theta, \ t_0 \leftarrow t'$
>
> $x(t) \leftarrow \frac{1}{2}a_0 \sin\theta \, (t - t')^2 + v_x(t')(t - t') + x(t')$ fa t st $t \geq t'$
>
> $y(t) \leftarrow \frac{1}{2}(g - a_0 \cos\theta)(t - t')^2 + v_y(t')(t - t') + x(t')$ fa t st $t \geq t'$
>
> $v_x(t) \leftarrow a_0 \sin\theta \, (t - t') + v_x(t')$ fa t st $t \geq t'$
>
> $v_y(t) \leftarrow (g - a_0 \cos\theta)(t - t') + v_y(t')$ fa t st $t \geq t'$

Adjusting the thrust does not affect the attitude of the vehicle; hence, the effect of this action is to update the acceleration boundary condition and thus to adjust the vehicle's future trajectory in accordance with the new acceleration and the previous angular orientation. Similarly, adjusting the attitude does not affect the thrust; hence, the effect of this action is to update the angular-orientation boundary condition and to adjust the vehicle's future trajectory in accordance with the new angular orientation and the previous acceleration. By defining the above actions in this manner, we obtain the desired property that performing $\text{Thrust}(a_1, t_1)$ followed by $\text{Angle}(\theta_1, t_1)$ has the same effect as performing $\text{Angle}(\theta_1, t_1)$ followed by $\text{Thrust}(a_1, t_1)$. Furthermore, their combined effect is the same effect as $\text{Adjust}(a_1, \theta_1, t_1)$. Thus, by using acceleration and angular orientation as boundary conditions, we have effectively made synergistic simultaneous actions resemble sequential actions. A problem involving these actions can therefore be solved by first constructing a sequential plan and then transforming it into a parallel plan as described in Section 3.

Technically speaking, the position and velocity of the vehicle at the time an adjustment is made should also be considered as boundary conditions, since the future motion of the vehicle depends on them. However, it is the thrust and attitude that are being modified directly by the actions; the position and velocity at the time of adjustment are not modified, but instead serve as continuity constraints. This suggests that, when the concept of boundary conditions is applied, it is important to distinguish between those conditions that are modified by an action directly and those that play the role of continuity constraints.

6. SUMMARY

We have shown how some multiagent, dynamic-world problems may be formulated in the classical planning framework, thereby enabling them to be solved using classical planning techniques. The two main obstacles to formulating such problems this way is representing simultaneous actions and representing continuous processes. As was explained, continuous processes can be represented in the classical planning framework by interpreting (1) a state as a chronicle of all that is true, was true, and will be true of the world at every point in time, and (2) a state transition as the initiation of an action or course of action. It was also shown that the classical framework is adequate for handling some simultaneous actions in spite of the fact that actions in that must be performed sequentially. By representing a problem in the appropriate manner, some simultaneous actions can be made to look like sequential ones, permitting their formulation in the classical planning framework. A general approach to representing actions, based on the concept of boundary conditions, was introduced to accomplish this objective. Whether this approach can be applied in all cases is left to subsequent research. In any event, the fact that some simultaneous actions can be represented in the classical planning framework suggests the feasibility of transferring techniques for solving classical planning problems to other frameworks that are specifically designed for modeling simultaneous actions and dynamic processes.

As part of the presentation, ADL, a new language for describing actions and their effects, was introduced. Because it combines the best features of the STRIPS operator language [7] and the situation calculus [20], ADL offers the advantage of both expressive power and notational convenience. Furthermore, ADL avoids the semantic pitfalls of the STRIPS operator language that are discussed by Lifschitz [18]. This is done by describing the effects of actions directly in terms of state transformations, as opposed to transformations on descriptions of states.

Acknowledgments

The research reported herein was conducted at SRI International and was supported by the Office of Naval Research under Contract N00014-85-C-0251. The views and conclusions expressed in this document are those of the author and should not be interpreted as necessarily representing the official policies or endorsements, either expressed or implied, of the Office of Naval Research or the U.S. Government. The author wishes also to thank AT&T Bell Laboratories for providing the facilities to complete the final draft of this report.

References

[1] Allen, J.F. and J.A. Kooman, "Planning Using a Temporal World Model," *Proc. IJCAI-83*, Karlsruhe, West Germany, pp 741–747 (August 1983).

[2] Allen, J.F., "Towards a General Theory of Action and Time," *Artificial Intelligence*, Vol. 23, pp 123–154 (1984).

[3] Chapman, D., "Planning for Conjunctive Goals," Technical Report 802, Artificial Intelligence Laboratory, Massachusetts Institute of Technology, Cambridge, Massachusetts (November, 1985).

[4] Cheeseman, P., "A Representation of Time for Automatic Planning," *Proc. IEEE Int. Conf. on Robotics*, Atlanta, Georgia (March 1984).

[5] Currie, K. and A. Tate, "O-Plan: Control in the Open Planning Architecture," Report AIAI-TR-12, Artificial Intelligence Applications Institute, University of Edinburgh, Edinburgh, Scotland (1985).

[6] Dean, T., "Temporal Imagery: An Approach to Reasoning about Time for Planning and Problem Solving," Research Report 433, Computer Science Department, Yale University, New Haven, Connecticut (October 1985).

[7] Fikes, R.E. and N.J. Nilsson, "STRIPS: A New Approach to the Application of Theorem Proving to Problem Solving," *Artificial Intelligence*, Vol 2, pp 189–208 (1971).

[8] Fikes, R.E., Hart, P. and N.J. Nilsson, "Learning and Executing Generalized Robot Plans," *Artificial Intelligence*, Vol. 3, No. 4, pp 251–288 (1972).

[9] Georgeff, M.P., "A Theory of Action for Multiagent Planning," *Proc. AAAI-84*, Austin, Texas, pp 121–125 (August, 1984).

[10] Georgeff, M.P. and A.L. Lansky, "A System for Reasoning in Dynamic Domains: Fault Diagnosis on the Space Shuttle," Technical Note 375, Artificial Intelligence Center, SRI International, Menlo Park, California (January 1986).

[11] Georgeff, M.P., "Actions, Processes, and Causality," in M.P. Georgeff and A.L. Lansky (eds.), *Reasoning about Actions and Plans: Proceedings of the 1986 Workshop* (Morgan Kaufmann, Los Altos, California, 1987).

[12] Georgeff, M.P., "The Representation of Events in Multiagent Domains," *Proc. AAAI-86*, Philadelphia, Pennsylvania, pp 70–75 (August 1986).

[13] Harel, D., "First-Order Dynamic Logic," *Lecture Notes in Computer Science*, Vol. 68, G. Goos and J. Hartmanis eds. (Springer-Verlag, New York, New York, 1979).

[14] Hayes, P., "The Frame Problem and Related Problems in Artificial Intelligence," in *Artificial and Human Thinking*, A. Elithorn, and D. Jones eds., pp 45–59 (Jossey-Bass, 1973).

[15] Hendrix, G.G., "Modeling Simultaneous Actions and Continuous Processes," *Artificial Intelligence*, Vol. 4, pp 145–180 (1973).

[16] Lansky, A.L., "Behavioral Specification and Planning for Multiagent Domains," Technical Note 360, Artificial Intelligence Center, SRI International, Menlo Park, California (1985).

[17] Lansky, A.L., "A Representation of Parallel Activity Based on Events, Structure, and Causality," in M.P. Georgeff and A.L. Lansky (eds.), *Reasoning about Actions and Plans: Proceedings of the 1986 Workshop* (Morgan Kaufmann, Los Altos, California, 1987).

[18] Lifschitz, V., "On the Semantics of STRIPS," in M.P. Georgeff and A.L. Lansky (eds.), *Reasoning about Actions and Plans: Proceedings of the 1986 Workshop* (Morgan Kaufmann, Los Altos, California, 1987).

[19] Manna, Z., and R. Waldinger, *The Logical Basis for Computer Programming, Volume I: Deductive Reasoning* (Addison-Wesley, Reading, Massachusetts, 1985).

[20] McCarthy, J. and P. Hayes, "Some Philosophical Problems from the Standpoint of Artificial Intelligence," in *Machine Intelligence 4*, B. Meltzer and D. Michie eds., pp 463–502 (Edinburgh University Press, Edinburgh, Scotland, 1969).

[21] McDermott, D., "A Temporal Logic for Reasoning about Processes and Plans," *Cognitive Science*, Vol. 6, pp 101–155 (1982).

[22] McDermott, D., "Generalizing Problem Reduction: A Logical Analysis," *Proc. IJCAI-83*, Karlsruhe, West Germany, pp 302–308 (August 1983).

[23] McDermott, D., "Reasoning about Plans," in *Formal Theories of the Commonsense World*, Hobbs, J.R. and R.C. Moore eds., pp 269–317 (Ablex Publishing, Norwood, New Jersey, 1985).

[24] Pednault, E.P.D., "Preliminary Report on a Theory of Plan Synthesis," Technical Report 358, Artificial Intelligence Center, SRI International, Menlo Park, California (August 1985).

[25] Pednault, E.P.D., *Toward a Mathematical Theory of Plan Synthesis*, Ph.D. thesis, Department of Electrical Engineering, Stanford University, Stanford, California.

[26] Sacerdoti, E.D., "A Stricture for Plans and Behavior," Technical Note 109, Artificial Intelligence Center, SRI International, Menlo Park, California (August 1975).

[27] Shoenfield, J.R., *Mathematical Logic* (Addison-Wesley, Reading, Massachusetts, 1967).

[28] Stefik, M., "Planning With Constraints (MOLGEN: Part 1)," *Artificial Intelligence*, Vol. 16, No. 2, pp 111–140 (May 1981).

[29] Stuart, C, "An Implementation of a Multi-Agent Plan Synchronizer," *Proc. IJCAI-85*, University of California at Los Angeles, Los Angeles, California, pp 1031–1033 (August 1985).

[30] Stuart, C, "A New View of Parallel Activity for Conflict Resolution," in M.P. Georgeff and A.L. Lansky (eds.), *Reasoning about Actions and Plans: Proceedings of the 1986 Workshop* (Morgan Kaufmann, Los Altos, California, 1987).

[31] Suppes, P., *Axiomatic Set Theory* (Dover, New York, New York, 1972).

[32] Sussman, G.J., "A Computational Model of Skill Aquisition," Report AI TR-297, Artificial Intelligence Laboratory, Massachusetts Institute of Technology, Cambridge, Massachusetts (August 1973).

[33] Tate, A., "Goal Structure, Holding Periods and Clouds," in M.P. Georgeff and A.L. Lansky (eds.), *Reasoning about Actions and Plans: Proceedings of the 1986 Workshop* (Morgan Kaufmann, Los Altos, California, 1987).

[34] Van Dalen, D., *Logic and Structure* (Springer-Verlag, Berlin, Germany, 1980).

[35] Vere, S., "Planning in Time: Windows and Durations for Activities and Goals," *IEEE Trans. on Pattern Analysis and Machine Intelligence*, Vol 5., No. 3, pp 246–267 (May 1983).

[36] Vere, S., "Temporal Scope of Assertions and Window Cutoff," *Proc. IJCAI-85*, University of California at Los Angeles, Los Angeles, California, pp 1055–1059 (August 1985).

[37] Vilain, M.B., "A System for Reasoning about Time," *Proc. AAAI-82*, Pittsburgh, Pennsylvania, pp 197–201 (August 1982).

[38] Waldinger, R., "Achieving Several Goals Simultaneously," in, *Machine Intelligence 8*, E. Elcock and D. Michie eds., pp 94–136 (Ellis Horwood, Edinburgh, Scotland, 1977).

What is the frame problem?

Yoav Shoham

Yale University
Computer Science Department

Abstract

Ever since its introduction by McCarthy and Hayes in 1969, the so-called *frame problem* has been the object of much fascination and debate. Although it was defined in the narrow context of the *situation calculus*, a specific temporal formalism, it was clear from the start that it is in fact a manifestation of some fundamental problem in temporal reasoning. Despite its apparent universal nature, however, we know of no attempt to define the problem in its most general form. This is precisely our aim here. We argue that the frame problem arises from the conflicting desires to reason both rigorously and efficiently about the future. This conflict does not depend on the particular underlying temporal formalism. In particular, we identify two formalism-indepedent problems, called the *qualification problem* and the *extended prediction problem*, which subsume the frame problem. To illustrate the fact that these problems are indeed inherent to the prediction task and not to a particular formalism, we show that they arise in two distinct frameworks: classical mechanics, and Hayes' *histories* notation.

Ever since its introduction by McCarthy and Hayes in 1969 [3], the so-called *frame problem* has been the object of much fascination and debate. Although it was defined in the narrow context of the *situation calculus*, a specific temporal formalism, it was clear from the start that it is in fact a manifestation of some fundamental problem in temporal reasoning. Despite its apparent universal nature, however, I know of no attempt to define the problem in its most general form. As one respected researcher once said to me, "I can't tell you what the frame problem is, but I recognize it when I see it." I believe that if we want to solve the frame problem then we will benefit from defining it first, which is what I will try to do here.

I argue that the frame problem arises from the conflicting desires to reason both rigorously and efficiently about the future. This conflict does not depend on the particular underlying temporal formalism. In particular, I will identify two formalism-indepedent problems, called the *qualification problem* and the *extended prediction problem*, which subsume the frame problem.

Since the problems under discussion arise in the context of the prediction task, let me introduce them in that context. The first section describes a simple case of predicting the future, and brings up problems that arise if one tries to use either classical mechanics or the *histories* formalism due to Hayes. The second section abstracts away from these two particular frameworks, and offers a general characterization of the problems.

1   A specific prediction task

To see what problems are involved in predicting the future, let us consider a simple case of predicting the behavior of physical objects. Imagine an intelligent robot watching friends play a game of billiards. We join him when there are exactly two balls left on the pool table, and together with robot we watch them roll towards a collision point as shown in Figure 1.[1] We know exactly what is about to happen: the two balls will collide and bounce off appropriately, as shown in Figure 2. The question is whether the robot can be expected to know that too, and if so how. How does the robot represent what he sees on the pool table, and what physics does he employ to predict the outcome?

---

[1] John McCarthy has prepared me for the wrath of some who might be offended by my terminology. It seems that in the following I have confused the vulgar game of billiards with the noble activity of shooting pool, or was it the other way around.

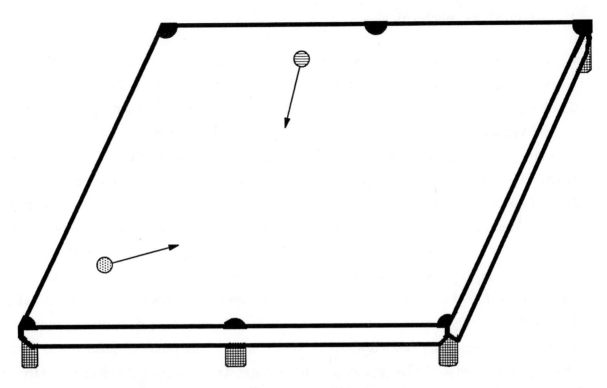

Figure 1: First part of the billiards scenario

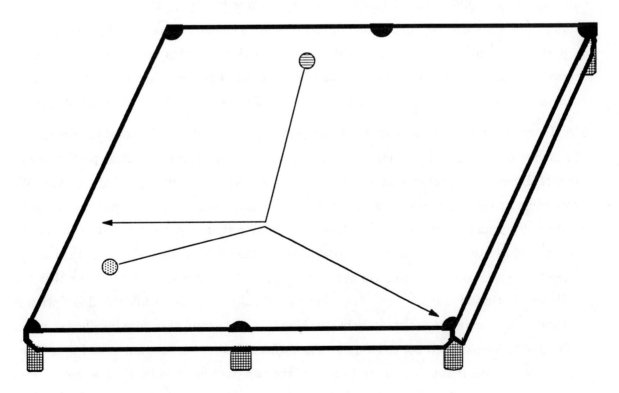

Figure 2: The complete billiards scenario

1.1   Classical mechanics

Let us first examine what happens if the robot uses classical, or Newtonian, mechanics. Newtonian mechanics keeps track of the values of *quantities*, which are functions on time. These quantities are represented by variables whose values range over some interval of the reals. Examples of quantities are force $f(t)$, acceleration $a(t)$ and mass $m(t)$. The latter is, of course, a constant function in classical mechanics. Typically, the time argument to the functions is omitted, so one writes simply f, a and m. The actual formulation of the physical laws comes in the form of *equations*, which are constraints on values the quantities may assume simultaneously. An example of an equation is $f = m \times a$, which is really shorthand for $\forall t\ f(t) = m(t) \times a(t)$. Two special quantities are spatial location $x(t), y(t), z(t)$ and time itself t, in both cases of which the laws of physics refer only to relative value. The way this is enforced is by using differentials. Time and space appear *only* as differentials, as in $v \mathrm{d}t = \mathrm{d}x$. By convention the formulations include only time derivatives, reflecting the intuition that what physics is about is keeping track of the values of quantities as they change in time, and so the last equation appears as $v = \mathrm{d}x/\mathrm{d}t$, or (since the only derivatives are time derivatives) simply as $v = x'$. One finds also equations in which time *seems* to appear as an undifferentiated quantity (as in $v = a \times t$), but in these cases the t really stands for "elapsed time," or interval duration, and the equations can be viewed simply as a particular solution of the original differential equations (in this case, $a = \mathrm{d}v/\mathrm{d}t$), given certain boundary conditions (in this case, $v_0 = 0$ and the fact that the acceleration is constant.) The same applies to equations that seem to mention absolute spatial values.

To summarize, then, the way Newtonian mechanics talk about temporal information is by having functions of time be their subject matter. These functions of time participate in sets of differential equations, in which all derivatives are taken with respect to time. We now come to the question of how one specifies the initial conditions in a physics problem, and what permits one to predict from this specification that, say, the two balls will collide. One would *like* to say that the initial conditions are the position and velocity of the balls at some time prior to the collision (in order to simplify the analysis, we can assume that the balls are elastic and that they are of equal mass and size). However, while this description is sufficient for humans, it is not, strictly speaking, complete, and therefore insufficient when subjected to formal inference techniques. The problem is that we have not stated that there are no *other* balls that affect the trajectory of the two particular balls. Even worse, it does not explicitly state that there are no holes in the table through which balls might drop, no strong winds that affect the trajetories of balls, and so on. What then constitutes a correct description of the scenario?

In [5], Montague offers a formal analysis of Newtonian mechanics. Actually, he talks of *particle mechanics* and *celestial mechanics*. Particle mechanics consist of Newton's three laws. Celestial mechanics is the specialization of it which specifies that the force between any two particles is given by the law of gravitation. Montague's interest lies in testing whether the formal theories have any of several formally defined properties such as that of being deterministic. For us what is interesting is the actual encoding of the theory of particle mechanics (p. 311-318) (adding the gravitational axiom is a straightforward specialization of the theory that doesn't concern us immediately.) Of that, much is devoted to axiomatizing the properties of the real numbers and of the integers (p. 312-316). These don't concern us here directly either since we assume those are well understood (in fact, even with Montague's axioms we are still left with "nonstandard" models of numbers, and he conditions subsequent theorems on assuming the standard model). What is important is Montague's encoding of Newton's laws, which relies on viewing the world as an *n-particle system*. In other words, the objects in the domain of discourse are exactly n particles, where n is some fixed integer. The initial conditions are exactly those envisioned by Laplace[2]: the mass, position and velocity of all the balls at some time prior to the collision. In general, one must have a finite number of quantites one is interested in, and the initial conditions are a complete listing of their values at some time point. In our domain, this translates to fixing the number of balls, and giving their individual positions and velocities at some point as the initial conditions.

There are some problems with this framework. First, all the initial conditions must refer to the exact same time point. That excludes questions of the form "If city A is 100 miles away from city B, train 1 leave city A towards city B at 1:00 travelling at 20 mph, and train 2 leaves city B towards city A at 2:00 travelling at 15 mph, when will the two trains meet?," which are so common in textbooks. Second, it seems a little perverse to have to talk about scenarios with different number of balls as if they are unrelated. Is there no way to factor the number of balls out of the formulation? Furthermore, what if there are an infinite number of balls? In that case Montague's formulation does not apply, and for a good reason, as we shall see below when we discuss his encoding of the Newton's second law. Finally, even restricting ourselves to a single situation with a finite number of balls,

---

[2]The assertion due to Laplace is that the positions and momenta of all particles in the universe at one time completely determine their positions and momenta at all other times.

what if there are very many of them? Do we really have to talk about millions of balls that are millions of miles away? In celestial mechanics these have an effect on the two balls under consideration (though a negligible one), but in the case of billiard balls they only do if they collide with one of the balls. While not a *logical* problem, it certainly poses a practical one.

I will return to these problems shortly, but for the moment let us proceed under the conditions that satisfy Montague's formulation, namely a finite number of balls whose initial conditions are given. In our example, suppose there are exactly five balls (including the two colliding balls), whose position, mass and velocity at some time instant prior to the collision is given. Our remaining task is to justify a modest version of Laplace's claim: given the description of all the balls at the initial time instant, deduce the collision and new trajectories of the two particular balls. To do that, we need to assign precise meaning to the laws of physics. Consider Newton's second law, $f = m \times a$, whose intended meaning is that at any given instant in time, the net force on an object is equal to the product of its mass and acceleration (since we assume uniform mass, we can assume the law $f = a$ and the appropriate adjustment of units.) The meaning of the phrase *net force* is the summation of all individual forces acting on the object, and this is where the assumption of a fixed finite number of balls is critical. If there are n balls, the number of individual forces on each ball is $n - 1$, one for each other ball. (Actually, Montague would say that there are n forces, thus allowing for "external" forces.) This assumption can only be made if we have fixed in advance the number of balls. Furthermore, it is easy to make sense of the notion of summation if there are a finite number of elements that are being summed. Montague's encoding in logic of the summation operator strongly relies on this finiteness. Things are less obvious if we allow infinite summation, and in fact it's not clear what it means for an infinite number of balls to collide. Of course, it makes perfect sense to speak of an infinite number of balls, only a finite number of which collide at any moment, but that too is outside the scope of Montague's formulation. Anyway, since we're making Montague-like assumptions, all that remains for us is to specify the individual forces that the balls exert on one another. In Montague's case that force is the law of gravitation. In our case it is the law of conservation of momentum. Given the law of conservation of momentum, we can define the force between any two particles as follows.

1. Two balls exert force on each other *only* if they touch.

2. In this case the magnitude of this force is the appropriate function of their individ-

ual velocities, positions and directions at the time of the collision, and the law of conservation of momentum.

Given these assumptions, the laws of physics actually make the right prediction: they constrain the two balls to collide and bounce off appropriately. This "prediction," however, is purely model theoretic. No attention was paid to the problem of actually *computing* the point of collision. In fact, it is very unclear how to perform the computation, since all axioms refer to time *points*. Somehow we must identify the "interesting" points in time or space, and interpolate between them by integrating differentials over time. The problem seems a little circular, though, since the identity of the interesting points *depends* on the integration. For example, understanding where the two balls are heading logically precedes the identification of the collision: if we don't know that the two balls are rolling towards each other, there is no reason to expect something interesting at the actual collision point.

How do people solve such physics problems? The inevitable answer seems to be that they "visualize" the problem, identify a solution in some mysterious ("analog") way, and only then *validate* the solution through physics. Much of what goes on in the industry of so-called *qualitative physics* can be viewed as at attempt to lift that shroud of mystery and emulate the visualization process on a computer [1]. The solution offered in qualitative physics is related to another issue addressed by it and which was ignored here, the fact that precise numerical information (such as the precise distance between two billiard balls) is unnecessary and unavailable. In qualitative physics it is replaced by qualitative information (such as that whether the distance between the two balls is zero or nonzero, and whether it is increasing, constant or decreasing). A set of such qualititive values gives rise to a qualitative *state*, and, given one such state, one uses the "envisionment" procedure to determine the next state (or set of possible next states.)

The details of qualitative physics are not crucial here; all I needed was the principal idea behind the process of envisionment. The envisionment in the billiards domain is simple: it embodies the rule, which is a simple derivative of the physics, that a ball's velocity and travel direction is unchanged during an interval in which it collides with no other ball. But if in our domain the heuristic for identifying interesting points is simple, in richer domains it is more complex. When we throw a rock we know that the next interesting time point is when its parabolic trajectory is interrupted by our neighbor's window, and when we fix our car's tire we know that the next interesting point is when we next drive over a sharp object. In general it can be arbitrarily hard to identify interesting points from the physics.

Beside making the claim that classical physics is awkward on pragmatic grounds, I am in fact willing to stick my neck out and make a psychological claim, namely that instant-based physics, while a parsimonious encoding of physical knowledge that is most appropriate as a scientific formulation, is not the basis of human understanding of physical situations. I contend that a baby knows that pushing the hanging toy results in its swinging back and forth and displaying magnificent colors before he "knows" that applying force to objects results in their infinitesimal movement. I realize that it can be argued that we have special purpose but subconscious apparatus for encoding the instantaneous information and for performing the integration across time. I don't think the issue can be resolved until such an apparatus is actually produced; certainly introspection is useless. One relevant piece of evidence points against it, though, and it is the fact that people find it natural to think about intervals of motions (and change in general), and that intervals of motion surface in language at a very early age, whereas the mathematical abstraction of infinitesimal change is not learned until high school and for most people remains a slightly puzzling concept throughout their lives. At any rate, let us note that we know for certain that computers do not have such special apparatus, and until one is invented for them we must provide them with the means of identifying interesting points.

To summarize the discussion of classical physics, I have said that if we start out with the complete description of the balls at some point in time, stipulate that those are the only balls that exist, assume that no other potentially influential events take place (no other objects touch the balls, there are no holes in the table, no ball is about to explode, etcetera), adopt a Montague-like description of Newton's kinematic equations, and formulate a dynamic rule about the force exerted between any two balls, then classical physics captures the future behavior of the balls. The most serious drawbacks associated with this approach are:

1. The initial conditions must be refer to a unique instant of time. Furthermore, we must give a *complete* description of the initial conditions, which unless abbreviated is too costly. So far we have no way of saying "this is all the information that is relevant to the problem."

2. The physics specify which predictions are warranted by the initial conditions, but not how to make them. This information must be supplied from outside the physics.

3. The rules of physics are constraints on the simultaneous values of quantities. This instantaneous flavor of the rules, which makes the formulation elegant and parsimonious, is not only the reason that prediction is hard but also the reason that physics

rules seem so different from the knowledge that underlies human understanding of physical situations.

These shortcomings are actually manifestations of very general problems, ones that transcend the particular framework of classical physics. Before I explicate these general problems, though, let me first give a better feel for them by showing how they are manifested in a different setting, Pat Hayes' *histories* framework.

1.2   Histories

In [2] Pat Hayes suggested a new way of discussing physical scenarios: *histories*. A history is a contiguous chunk of spacetime with which we associate a *type*. Intuitively, the type corresponds to period during which the behavior of the physical object is qualitatively the same. Hayes applied the theory to reasoning about the behavior of liquids. A piece of liquid can exhibit one of several behaviors: free falling, spreading on a surface, being contained in an upward-concave rigid object, entering a container, leaving it, and so on. Each of those is a history-type, and we can write axioms constraining the co-existence of several histories having various types. For example, no two histories may overlap in spacetime. Or, as another example, if there is an entering-history along the rim of a full container then there must also be a leaving (conservation of matter), and so on. The hope is that by creating a rich enough vocabulary of history-types and writing enough restrictions on them we will be able to capture the behavior of the physical objects.

Let us try to reason about our billiards scenario in the histories framework. In our domain of billiards we may want to speak about various kinds of histories: rolling histories, falling histories, parabolic-flight histories, collision histories, strong-wind histories, and probably many others. Let us not worry too much about the precise taxonomy, since the problem will not be lack of expressiveness but rather difficulty of reasoning. For the sake of discussion let us assume two types of histories: ROLLING histories and COLLISION histories, where ROLLING histories describe the rolling of a billiard ball along a straight line. Thus we can represent the scenario involving the two balls by four ROLLING histories, two for each ball, as shown in Figure 3: H11 denotes the history of the first ball until the collision and H12 denotes the history of the same ball after the collision, and similarly H21 and H22 denote the histories of the second ball before and after the collision, respectively. We could now write axioms describing the relation between H11, H12, H21 and H22. I won't do that; let us agree that such axioms could be written. The question we are interested in is,

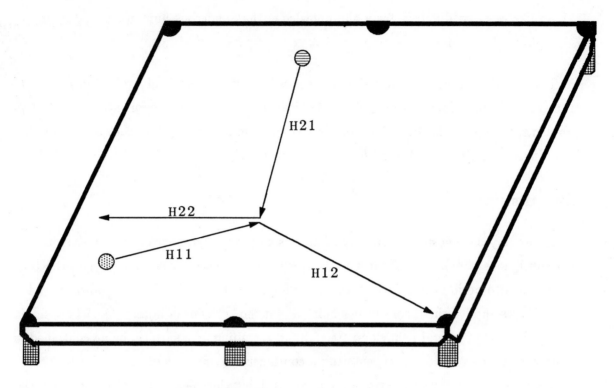

Figure 3: Four ROLLING histories

again, how to represent the initial conditions and from this representation deduce the rest
of the scenario.

A natural representation of the initial conditions is by two histories, one for each ball.
Those may be respective prefixes of H11 and H21, or the initial *slices* of those two histories.
(A slice is the projection of a history onto a point in time. This option requires that we
be able to speak about the *velocity* of a history.) Let us consider the first case, shown
graphically in Figure 4, in which the initial conditions are prefixes of H11 and H21, say
H11' and H21' (the other case would behave similarly.) We would need axiom(s) that
guarantee that the two balls continue rolling. In other words, we need to predict two new
ROLLING histories. What should those two new histories look like? What should be their
spatio-temporal extent? Surely neither can extend beyond the collision point. Should the
two new histories end exactly at the collision point? If the answer is *no*, then clearly we are
in trouble, since we can iterate this process indefinitely. We now have two new histories,
say H11" and H21". From those we need to conclude yet two more histories, and so on
(see Figure 5). It follows that the two new ROLLING histories H11" and H21" must end
exactly at the collision. What set of axioms could guarantee this property? Furthermore,

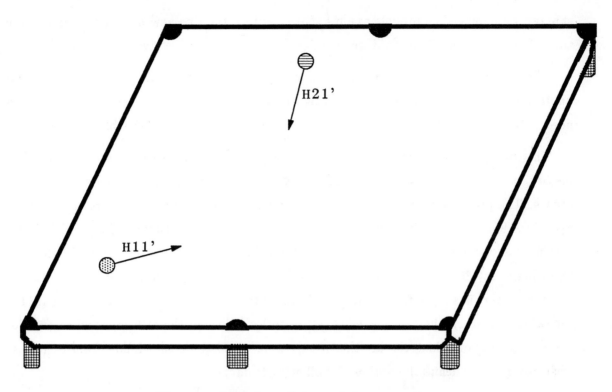

Figure 4: Initial conditions of the scenario

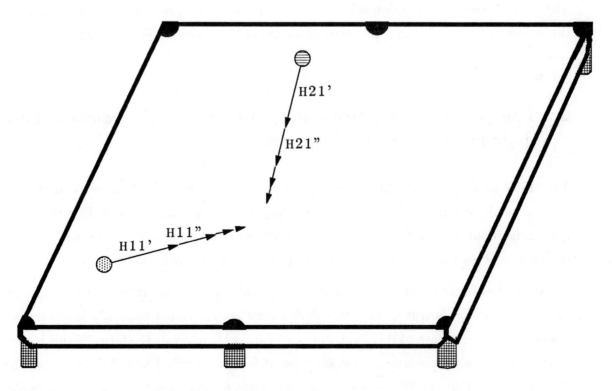

Figure 5: An infinite number of histories?

suppose we managed to provide axioms that constrain the two new histories to end at the time of the collision. How could we effectively *compute* this time given the axioms?

The key property of each of the two new histories is that it will persist *until it meets another history in spacetime*, which in this case happens to be the other new history. We need to somehow capture the property of persisting "for as long as possible".

This brings us to another problem. One may say that since we have only one other history, it is trivial to determine when and where the first intersection between histories occurs. The problem with that is that we have not explicitly said that there are no other histories. For example, we have not explicitly ruled out the existence of a third ball deflecting one of the two original balls before the collision with the other original ball. It is tempting to say "ok, the *only* two histories are the ones I told you about, H11' and H21'." That, however, is simply false, since beside those two histories we have H11" and H21", the collision history, the two new ROLLING histories following the collision, and so on. Nor can we say "the only histories are the two given ones and those that follow from them," at least not until we define the notion of "following from".

These problems with using the histories framework are closely related to the problems with using classical mechanics, which were discusses in the previous subsection, and to the infamous frame problem. The general nature of the problems is discussed in the next section.

2   The problems of *qualification* and *extended prediction*, and their relation to the *frame problem*

The problems that arise in either classical mechanics or the histories framework are symptomatic of all systems for reasoning about change. The general problem is how to reason *efficiently* about what is true over extended periods of time, and it has to do with certain tradeoffs between risk-taking and economy in the process of prediction.

Any rules-of-change (or physics) must support inferences of the form "if *this* is true at this time then *that* is true at that time." Since we are interested primarily in predicting the future, a special case of this form will be of particular interest, the form "if this is true at this time then that is true at that *later* (or at least *no earlier*) time." The crux of the first problem is that the "if" part might get too large to be of practical use. For example, if one wishes to be careful about her predictions, in order to infer that a ball rolling in a certain direction will continue doing so she must verify that there are no strong winds, that no one is about to pick up the ball, that the ball does not consist of condensed explosives that are about to go off in the next instant of time, and we can continue this list, getting arbitrarily ridiculous. Or, to use another example, when one pulls the trigger of a loaded gun one would like to predict that a loud noise will follow, but strictly speaking there are a whole lot of other factors that need to be verified: that the gun has a firing pin, that the bullets are made out of lead and not marshmallows, that there is air to carry the sound, and so on.

The alternative is to be less conservative and base the predictions on only very partial information, hoping that those factors which have been ignored will not get in the way. This means that from time to time one must be prepared to make mistakes in her predictions (after all, the ball *might* turn out to be a miniature hand grenade whose fuse has just run out, and someone *might* have tampered with the gun), and be able to recover from them when she does.

I will call this the *qualification problem*.[3] To summarize, it is the problem of trading off the amount of knowledge that is required in order to make inferences on the one hand, and the accuracy of those inferences on the other hand. In the particular context of predicting the future, it is the problem of making sound predictions about the future without taking into account everything about the past. Notice that the problem would disappear if we were willing to dramatically idealize the world: we could take it as a fact that noise always follows the firing of a loaded gun, and simply assume that guns always have firing pins, that there are never vacuum conditions, and so on. The premise, however, is that such an overidealization is a nonsolution, since the whole point is for our robots to be able to function in a realistically complex environment.

Severe as it is, the qualification problem is not the only problem that exists, and even if we solved it we would still be in trouble. Briefly, although we would be able to make individual inferences fairly easily, we might be forced to make very many of them. Since we are interested in the prediction task, let me explain the problem in the particular context of predicting the future.

---

[3]In [6] I called it the *intra-frame problem*. I then regretted that term, and in [7] I renamed it the *initiation* problem. Later I found that term too inappropriate, and since Matt Ginsberg pointed out the similarity between "my" problem and the problem John McCarthy called the *qualification problem*, I decided to adopt the latter term. Although McCarthy's notion might have been broader than the one presented here, I don't think I'm misusing the terminology too badly.

The problem now has to do with the length of time intervals in the future to which the predictions refer (regardless of how much information about the past we require in order to make the predictions), or with the "then" part of the "if-then" inference mentioned earlier. Again, it involves a tradeoff between efficiency and reliability. The most conservative prediction refers to a very short interval of time, in fact an instantaneous one, but that makes it very hard to reason about more lengthy future periods. For example, if on the basis of observing a ball rolling we predict that it will roll just a little bit further, in order to predict that it will roll a long distance we must iterate this process many times (in fact, an infinite number of times). I will call this the *extended prediction* problem.[4]

We have seen the problem arise in classical physics: given (e.g.) the force f at time t, you can only deduce the velocity in the infinitesimal time period following t. In order to deduce the velocity after a finite amount of time you must perform integration over the appropriate interval, but you do not know which interval it is.

The disadvantages of the conservative prediction which refers to only a short time period suggest making predictions about more lengthy intervals. For example, when you hit a billiard ball you predict that it will roll in a straight line until hitting the edge of the table, and when you throw a ball into the air you predict that it will have a parabolic trajectory. The problem with these more ambitious predictions is again that they are defeasible, since, for example, a neighbor's window might prevent the ball from completing the parabola. Indeed, this is exactly the problem we encountered in the histories framework: we had no coherent criterion for determining the duration of the predicted ROLLING histories.

To summarize, the general extended prediction problem is that although we might be able to make predictions about short future intervals, we might have to make a whole lot of them before we can predict anything about a substantial part of the future. A special case of this is the *persistence* problem, which is predicting on the basis of the past that a fact will remain unchanged throughout a lengthy future interval (as opposed to the general problem of inferring arbitrary things about such an interval). For example, when we take

---

[4](More naming history.) In [6] I called this the *inter-frame* problem. I then regretted that name and, borrowing from Drew McDermott, renamed it the *persistence problem* in [7]. Finally, I realized that persistence was a special case of the general problem, that of predicting occurrences over extended periods of time, and hence the final name.

the billiard ball out of the pocket and place it on a chosen spot on the table, we would like to predict that it will remain in that spot until we hit it.[5]

This problem was noticed a long time ago in the particular context of the *situation calculus*, the formalism introduced by John McCarthy and Pat Hayes in 1969 [3]. The situation calculus takes as basic the notion of *situations*, which are snapshots of the world at a given moment in time. The result of performing an *action* is the transition from one situation to another.[6] For example, if the action *PAINT(HOUSE17,RED)* is taken in any situation s_1, the result is a situation s_2 in which the color of *HOUSE17* is red. But now consider taking the action *REARRANGE-FURNITURE* in s_2, which results in a new situation s_3. What is the color of *HOUSE17* in s_3? One would like to say that it is still red, since rearranging the furniture does not affect the color of the house, but unfortunately the formalism does not say that. We could add to the formalism the fact that after you rearrange the furniture the color of the house remains unchanged, and this would be what McCarthy and Hayes call a *frame axiom*. The problem is that you'd need many such axioms: rearranging the furniture doesn't clean the floors, doesn't change the president of the United States, and the list can be continued infinitely.

(Notice that the problem becomes even worse if one allows concurrent actions, which the situation calculus did not. In this case the frame axioms are simply wrong: someone *might* paint your house while you are busy rearranging your furniture. So we must add an exception to the rule: rearranging furniture results in no change in the color of the house, unless in the meanwhile someone paints the house a different color. But even this isn't quite right, since although someone might paint your house, he might be using a paint that fades away immediately. Therefore we must state an exception to the exception, and so on.)

McCarthy and Hayes called this the *frame problem*. I have had mixed success persuading colleagues that the persistence problem and the frame problem coincide. Since the frame problem was never defined in more detail or generality than it was two paragraphs ago, it

---

[5](A philosophical aside.) In [4] Drew McDermott notes that most facts in the world are persistent, and luckily so, because otherwise the world would appear very chaotic and unpredictable to us (or, to quote his reinterpretation of the well-known phrase, the world would become a "blooming buzz"). It seems to me that an alternative view is possible, which relies on a cognitive version of Heisenberg's uncertainty principle. According to this view much of the world is indeed in a state of unfathomable flux, perhaps most of it, and we latch onto the (possibly scarce) time invariants simply because that is all we are capable of doing. The objects and properties of which we talk and think are exactly those out of which we can construct meaningful assertions that are not invalid by the time they are constructed.

[6]For those familiar with dynamic logic, this is precisely the view of the world in a dynamic logic with only deterministic atomic programs and only the composition operator.

seems that the argument is somewhat futile. Certainly philosophers have read into the frame problem even more than the general extended prediction problem (see, e.g., a forthcoming book edited by Z. Pylyshyn). At any rate, these terminological quibbles are not crucial. What is important is to understand the problems.

3   Summary

I have defined two problems that arise when one tries to predict the future both reliably and efficiently, the *qualification problem* and the *extended prediction problem*. In contrast with the frame problem, these two problems do not depend on any particular underlying formalism. I have not offered a solution to either problem here. A partial solution appears in [7], and a full one will appear in my dissertation [8].

Bibliography

[1] D. G. Bobrow (Ed.), *Special Volume on Qualitative Reasoning and Physical Systems,* Artificial Intelligence, 24/1-3 December (1984).

[2] P. J. Hayes, Naive Physics 1 - Ontology for Liquids, in J. R. Hobbs and R. C. Moore eds., *Formal Theories of the Commonsense World,* Ablex, Norwood, New Jersey, 1984.

[3] J. M. McCarthy and P. J. Hayes, Some Philosophical Problems From the Standpoint of Artificial Intelligence, *Readings in Artificial Intelligence,* Tioga Publishing Co., Palo Alto, CA, 1981, pages 431–450.

[4] D. V. McDermott, *A Temporal Logic for Reasoning about Processes and Plans,* Cognitive Science, 6 (1982), pp. 101–155.

[5] R. Montague, Deterministic Theories, in R. H. Thomason ed., *Formal Philosophy: selected papers of Richard Montague,* Yale University Press, 1974.

[6] Y. Shoham, *Ten Requirements for a Theory of Change,* New Generation Computing, 3/4 (1985).

[7] Y. Shoham, Chronological Ignorance: Time, Nonmonotonicity and Necessity, *Proc. AAAI,* Philadelphia, PA, August 1986.

[8] Y. Shoham, *Reasoning about Change: Time and Causation from the Standpoint of Artificial Intelligence,* Ph.D. Thesis, Yale University, Computer Science Department, 1986.

ACTIONS, PROCESSES, AND CAUSALITY

Michael P. Georgeff

Artificial Intelligence Center, SRI International
and
Center for the Study of Language and Information

ABSTRACT

The purpose of this paper is to construct a model of actions and events that facilitates reasoning about dynamic domains involving multiple agents. Unlike traditional approaches, the proposed model allows for the simultaneous performance of actions, rather than use an interleaving approximation. A generalized situation calculus is constructed for describing and reasoning about actions in multiagent settings. Notions of *independence* and *correctness* are introduced, and it is shown how they can be used to determine the persistence of facts over time and whether or not actions can be performed concurrently. Unlike most previous formalisms in both single- and multiagent domains, the proposed law of persistence is *monotonic* and thus has a well-defined model-theoretic semantics. It is shown how the concept of *causality* can be employed to simplify the description of actions and to model arbitrarily complex machines and physical devices. Furthermore, it is shown how sets of causally interrelated actions can be grouped together in *processes* and how this structuring of problem domains can substantially reduce combinatorial complexity. Finally, it is indicated how the law of persistence, together with the notion of causality, makes it possible to retain a simple model of action while avoiding most of the difficulties associated with the frame problem.

This research has been made possible by a gift from the System Development Foundation, by the Office of Naval Research under Contract N00014-85-C-0251, and by the National Aeronautics and Space Administration, Ames Research Center, under Contract NAS2-12521.

Introduction

In developing automatic systems for planning and reasoning about actions, it is essential to have epistemologically adequate models of events, actions, and plans. Most early work in action planning assumed the presence of a single agent acting in a static world. In the formulation of these problems, the world was considered to be in one of a potentially infinite number of states and actions were viewed as mappings between these states [4,16,18,22]. However, the formalisms developed did not allow for simultaneous action, and as such are inadequate for dealing effectively with most real-world problems that involve other agents and dynamically changing environments.

Some attempts have recently been made to provide a better underlying theory of action. McDermott [20] considers an action (or event) to be a set of sequences of states and describes a temporal logic for reasoning about such actions. Allen [1] adopts a similar view and specifies an action by giving the relationships among the intervals over which the action's conditions and effects are assumed to hold. Related formalisms have been developed by Dean [3], Pelavin [24] and Shoham [29].

A quite different and potentially powerful approach has recently been proposed by Lansky [14]. Instead of modeling actions and events in terms of world states, she regards events as primitive and defines states derivatively.

In this paper, we shall examine some of the problems that arise in the representation of events, actions, and plans in multiagent domains, and describe a model of events and actions that overcomes most of these problems.

Actions and Events

We consider that, at any given instant, the world is in a particular *world state*. Each world state consists of a number of *objects* from a given domain, together with various *relations* and *functions* over those objects. A sequence of world states is called a *world history*.

A given world state has no duration; the only way the passage of time can be observed is through some change of state. The world changes its state by the occurrence of *events* or *actions*.[1] An *event type* is a set of state sequences, representing all possible occurrences of the event *in all possible situations* [1,20]. Except where the distinction is important, we shall call event types simply events.

We shall restrict our attention herein to *atomic events*. An atomic event is one in which each state sequence comprising the event contains exactly two elements; it can thus be modeled as a transition relation on world states. The transition relation of a given event must comprise all possible state transitions, *including those in which other events occur simultaneously with the given event*. Consequently, the transition relation of an atomic event places restrictions

---

[1]From a technical standpoint, we shall use these terms synonymously.

on those world relations that are directly affected by the event, but leaves most others to vary freely (depending upon what else is happening in the world). This is in contrast to the classical approach, which views an event as changing some world relations but leaving most of them unaltered.

For example, consider a domain consisting of blocks A and B at possible locations 0 and 1. Assume a world relation that represents the location of each of the blocks, denoted loc. Consider two events, $move(A, 1)$, which has the effect of moving block A to location 1, and $move(B, 1)$, which has a similar effect on block B. According to the classical approach [22], these events would be modeled as follows:

$$move(A, 1) \;\;=\;\; \{\langle loc(A, 0), loc(B, 1)\rangle \to \langle loc(A, 1), loc(B, 1)\rangle$$
$$\langle loc(A, 0), loc(B, 0)\rangle \to \langle loc(A, 1), loc(B, 0)\rangle\}$$

and similarly for $move(B, 1)$.

Every instance (transition) of $move(A, 1)$ leaves the location of B unchanged, and similarly every instance of $move(B, 1)$ leaves the location of A unchanged. Consequently, it is impossible to compose these two events to form one that represents the simultaneous performance of both $move(A, 1)$ and $move(B, 1)$, except by using some interleaving approximation [23].

In contrast, our model of these events is

$$move(A, 1) \;\;=\;\; \{\langle loc(A, 0), loc(B, 1)\rangle \to \langle loc(A, 1), loc(B, 1)\rangle$$
$$\langle loc(A, 0), loc(B, 1)\rangle \to \langle loc(A, 1), loc(B, 0)\rangle$$
$$\langle loc(A, 0), loc(B, 0)\rangle \to \langle loc(A, 1), loc(B, 1)\rangle$$
$$\langle loc(A, 0), loc(B, 0)\rangle \to \langle loc(A, 1), loc(B, 0)\rangle\}$$

and similarly for $move(B, 1)$.

This model represents all possible occurrences of these events, including their simultaneous execution with other events. For example, if $move(A, 1)$ and $move(B, 1)$ are performed simultaneously, the resulting event will be the intersection of their possible behaviors:

$$move(A, 1) \| move(B, 1) \;\;=\;\; move(A, 1) \cap move(B, 1)$$
$$=\;\; \{\langle loc(A, 0), loc(B, 0)\rangle \to \langle loc(A, 1), loc(B, 1)\rangle\}$$

Thus, to say that an event has taken place is simply to place constraints on some world relations, while leaving most of them to vary freely.

Of course, to specify events by listing all the possible transitions explicitly would, in any interesting case, be infeasible. We therefore need some formalism for describing events and world histories. The one we use here is a generalization of the situation calculus [18], although most of our remarks would apply equally to other logic-based formalisms.

We first introduce the notion of a *fluent* [18], which is a function defined on world states. If we are using predicate calculus, the values of these fluents will range over the relations, functions, and objects of the domain. For example, the location of a given block A is a fluent whose value in a given state is the location of block A in that state. If, in a state s, the location of A is 1, we shall write this as $holds(loc(A,1),s)$. Expressions denoting fluents that range over objects are often called *designators*, with a distinction drawn between those whose denotations are constant over all states (so-called *rigid* designators) and those whose denotations may vary (*nonrigid* designators).

As in the single-agent case, the well-formed formulas of this situation calculus may contain logical connectives and quantifiers; they can thus express general assertions about world histories. However, we do not use a "result" function to specify the state resulting from an event (or action). The reason is that, in our formalism, events are not functions on states but rather relations on states, and the occurrence of an event in a given state need not uniquely determine the resulting state. Therefore, for a given world history w containing state s, we let $succ(s,w)$ be the successor of s, and use a predicate $occurs(e,s)$ to mean that event e occurs in state s. This formulation, in addition to allowing a wider class of events than in the standard situation calculus, also enables us to state arbitrary temporal constraints on world histories [24].

In reasoning about actions and events, one of the most important things we need to know is how they affect the world – that is, we must be able to specify the effects of actions and events when performed in given situations. We can do this as follows.

Let ϕ and ψ be relational fluents. Then we can describe the effects of an event e with axioms of the following form:[2]

$$\forall w,s \, . \, holds(\phi,s) \wedge occurs(e,s) \supset holds(\psi, succ(s,w)) \tag{1}$$

This statement is intended to mean that, if ϕ is true when event e occurs, ψ will be true in the resulting state. It has essentially the same meaning as $\phi \supset [e]\psi$ in dynamic logic [11].

With axioms such as these, we can determine the strongest [provable] postconditions and weakest [provable] preconditions of arbitrary events and actions. These can then be used to form plans of action to accomplish given goals under prescribed initial conditions [17,26].

It is important to note that axioms of the above form cannot characterize the transition relation of any given event completely, no matter how many are provided. For example, with such axioms alone, it is not possible to prove for any two actions that they can be performed concurrently (nor that a plan containing concurrent actions is executable). We shall have more to say about this later.

---

[2]We have simplified the notation in two ways. First, without stating so explicitly, we assume throughout that s and $succ(s,w)$ are elements of w. Second, we shall often use event *types* to stand for an event *instance* of the given type. Thus, axiom 1 should be viewed as shorthand for the following axiom, where ι is an event instance:

$\forall w,s,\iota \, . \, element(s,w) \wedge element(succ(s,w),w) \wedge type(\iota,e) \wedge holds(\phi,s) \wedge occurs(\iota,s) \supset holds(\psi, succ(s,w)) \, .$

Of course, we are often able to make stronger statements about actions and events than given above. For example, the event $move(A, 1)$ satisfies

$$\forall w, s \, . \, occurs(move(A, 1), s) \equiv holds(loc(A, 0), s) \wedge holds(loc(A, 1), succ(s, w))$$

This specification characterizes the event $move(A, 1)$ completely – there is nothing more that can be said about the event or, more accurately, about its associated transition relation. (The importance of this distinction will be made clear when we consider causal relationships among events.)

Thus, *at this point in the story,* the frame problem [12,18] does not arise. Because events, per se, need not place any restrictions on the majority of world relations, we do not require a large number of frame axioms stating what relations are left unchanged by the performance of an event (indeed, such statements would usually be false). In contrast to the classical approach, we therefore do not have to introduce any *frame rule* [12] or STRIPS-like assumption [4] regarding the *specification* of events.

Independence

We have been regarding atomic actions or events as imposing certain constraints on the way the world changes while leaving other aspects of the situation free to vary as the environment chooses. That is, each action's transition relation describes all the potential changes of world state that could take place during the performance of the action. Which transition actually occurs in a given situation depends, in part, on the actions and events that take place in the environment. However, unless we can reason about what happens when some subset of all possible actions and events occurs – for example, when the only relevant actions being performed are those of the agent of interest – we could predict very little about the future and any useful planning would be impossible.

To handle this problem, we first introduce the concept of *independence*. We define a predicate $indep(p, e, s)$, which we take to mean that the fluent p is independent of (i.e., not directly affected by) event e in situation s. Unlike classical models of actions and events, this does not mean that, if we are in a state s in which p holds, p will also hold in the resulting state. Rather, if p is independent of e in some state s, the transition relation associated with e will include transitions to states in which p does not hold, as well as ones in which p holds, while not constraining the values of any other fluents in the resulting state.[3] In the general case, we have to specify independence for all three types of fluents: the relation-valued, function-valued, and object-valued.

---

[3]Independence can be defined as follows. Let $tr(e, s, s')$ denote that $\langle s, s' \rangle$ is an element of the transition relation associated with event e. Then we have that p is independent of e in state s if and only if, for all ϕ such that ϕ is consistent with both p and $\neg p$, $(\exists s' \, . \, tr(e, s, s') \wedge holds(p \wedge \phi, s')) \equiv (\exists s' \, . \, tr(e, s, s') \wedge holds(\neg p \wedge \phi, s'))$. This, of course, is not computable. Note also that an event transition relation may include states that cannot occur (because of some domain constraint) in any world history.

For example, we might have

$$\forall s, x, y \,.\, holds(x \neq A, s) \supset indep(loc(x,y), move(A,1), s) \,.$$

This axiom states that, for all x and y, $loc(x,y)$ will be independent of event $move(A,1)$, provided that x is not block A.

In our ontology, a world state can change only through the occurrence of events. Furthermore, in keeping with our intuitive notion of independence, events that are independent of some property cannot influence that property. We therefore have

$$\forall w, s, \phi \,.\, holds(\phi, s) \land \neg holds(\phi, succ(s,w)) \supset \exists e \,.\, (occurs(e,s) \land \neg indep(\phi, e, s)) \quad (2)$$

From this we can directly deduce the following *law of persistence*:

$$\forall w, s, \phi \,.\, holds(\phi, s) \land \forall e \,.\, (occurs(e,s) \supset indep(\phi, e, s)) \supset holds(\phi, succ(s,w)) \quad (3)$$

This rule states that, if we are in a state s where some condition ϕ holds, and if all events that occur in state s are independent of ϕ, then ϕ will also hold in the next (resulting) state. For example, we could use this rule to infer that, if $move(A,1)$ were the only event to occur in some state s, the location of B would be the same in the resulting state as it was in s.

Unlike many other approaches to persistence [3,10,12,20,25,29], the foregoing law is *monotonic*; that is, the law does not involve any nonmonotonic operators or depend on any consistency arguments. Nor is it some fortuitous property of the world in which we live. Rather, it is a *direct consequence* of our notions of event and independence. What makes planning useful for survival is the fact that we can structure the world in a way that keeps most properties and events independent of one another, thus allowing us to reason about the future without complete knowledge of all the events that could possibly be occurring.

At first glance, however, it appears as though we would encounter considerable difficulty in specifying independence, simply on the grounds that it should be ascertainable for each possible fluent/event pair. Indeed, this is hardly surprising, as the foregoing law of persistence is little different in this respect from the original formalisms that gave rise to the frame problem [18].

There are two ways we could deal with this difficulty. One is to remain monotonic and rely on general axioms regarding independence to reduce combinatorial complexity. The other is to apply some nonmonotonic rule or minimization criterion that would allow independence to be specified more succinctly. I discuss the nonmonotonic approach elsewhere [8]; herein, I want to examine briefly the monotonic specification of independence, so as to show that such an approach is – in some cases – a practical alternative.

One way in which the combinatorics can be substantially reduced is by explicitly specifying *all* the events that could possibly affect each fluent.[4] For example, for a given fluent p, we

---

[4]This is essentially what Lansky does when she defines state predicates in terms of events [14].

might have axioms such as the following:

$$\forall s, e \, . \, \neg indep(p, e, s) \supset ((e = e_1) \vee (e = e_2) \vee \ldots)$$

or, in its contrapositive form

$$\forall s, e \, . \, \neg((e = e_1) \vee (e = e_2) \vee \ldots) \supset indep(p, e, s)$$

As one would expect that, out of all possible events, there will be relatively few that affect a given fluent, such specifications can reduce considerably the combinatorics of providing separate independence axioms for each fluent/event pair. A minor complication is that, because we allow composite events (such as $e_1 \| e_2$, and that combined with, say, e_3, and so forth), the axioms for independence cannot be quite so simple as given above. However, this presents no serious difficulty.

A more substantial problem, however, is that this approach requires one to know the effects of *all* actions and events that could possibly occur. That is, such axioms do not allow for the possibility that *unspecified* events could affect the fluents of interest. This approach would therefore seem too strong for many real-world applications, though may be useful in less general contexts.

There are other ways to specify independence, however, that manage to avoid the combinatorial problem, yet do so without banishing unspecified events from the scene and without introducing nonmonotonicity. In particular, it may be possible to provide axioms describing the extent to which various actions and events exert their influence. For example, it may be that events outside a particular region R cannot affect properties inside that region:

$$\forall s, e, \phi \, . \, internal_f(\phi, R, s) \wedge external_e(e, R, s) \supset indep(\phi, e, s)$$

In this way, a single axiom can specify independence for an entire class of fluent/event pairs. In large real-world domains this will invariably lead to a substantial reduction in the combinatorics of the problem. In small blocks worlds, on the other hand, it will not – but writing down all the independence axioms in such a case is not much of a problem either.

Interference

If we are interested in constructing plans of action, one of the more important considerations is whether or not the actions constituting such plans are indeed performable. In single-agent planning, this question is quite easily handled by means of explicitly specifying preconditions that guarantee action performability. As we shall see, however, it is much more complex in multiagent domains.

The source of the problem in multiagent planning is that it is not possible to state simple preconditions for each individual action, the satisfaction of which would ensure its performability. In multiagent domains, whether or not an action can be performed will depend not only on the fulfillment of such preconditions, but also on which events or actions may (or are required to) occur simultaneously with the given action; it is, after all, of little use to form a plan that calls for the simultaneous or concurrent performance of actions that are inherently precluded from coexisting.

This problem is far more crucial than it may first appear. In particular, we are not concerned merely with issues of deadlock avoidance. In planning and other forms of practical reasoning, the failure of an action does not necessarily mean that the agent or device performing the action will thereafter be unable to proceed. Rather, such failure is usually taken to mean that the *desired* or *intended* effects of the action have not been achieved. Thus, though true deadlock may occur quite rarely, actions often fail to produce their intended effects because of interference with other, often unanticipated events.

Moreover, much of human planning revolves around the *coordination* of plans of action. Some of this is concerned with synchronizing the activities of agents so that tasks involving more that one agent can be carried out successfully. Such synchronization can be accomplished by specifying explicitly what temporal relations should hold among the activities of the various agents [14,31]. The more difficult problem is to identify interactions among potentially conflicting actions. Indeed, the recognition of possible plan conflicts is considered by some philosophers to be at the heart of rational behavior [2].

One way to specify such constraints on actions and events is to provide explicit axioms stating which events should occur simultaneously and which should not. For example, we could have the axiom

$$\forall s . \neg(occurs(e_1, s) \wedge occurs(e_2, s))$$

to mean that event e_1 could not occur simultaneously with event e_2. This is exactly the approach employed by Lansky [14] and Pelavin [24]. However, while it seems that the synchronization of actions for cooperative tasks is most naturally expressed directly (that is, by explicitly specifying the required temporal relations between specific actions), it seems unreasonable to require that all possible action *conflicts* also be so specified. For most real-world domains, it is more natural to specify just the effects of actions and to *deduce*, as the need arises, whether or not any two actions will interfere with each another. Furthermore, for domains of any complexity, there are potentially a very large number of actions and events that could interfere with one another. In such cases, the explicit specification of interference would entail severe combinatorial difficulties, although *appropriate* structuring of the problem domain [14] could substantially reduce the combinatorics.

It is desirable, therefore, to be able to determine freedom from conflict for any specified events, given simply a description of the effects of these events upon the world. To do this, we need to prove that the intersection of the transition relations corresponding to the events of interest is nonempty.

At first glance, it appears as if axioms about the effects of events are *all* we really need for determining the possibility or not of event simultaneity. For example, let us assume we have the following axioms describing events e_1 and e_2:

$$\forall w, s \;.\; holds(p, s) \wedge occurs(e_1, s) \supset holds(q_1, succ(s, w))$$

$$\forall w, s \;.\; holds(p, s) \wedge occurs(e_2, s) \supset holds(q_2, succ(s, w))$$

From this we can infer that

$$\forall w, s \;.\; holds(p, s) \wedge occurs(e_1 \| e_2, s) \supset holds(q_1 \wedge q_2, succ(s, w))$$

Nevertheless, it would be unwise to take these axioms as the basis of a plan to achieve $q_1 \wedge q_2$. The reason is that, given these axioms alone (or any others of the same form), it is simply not possible to *prove* that events e_1 and e_2 can occur simultaneously. Nor is it possible to use consistency arguments to justify the assertion that these events can so occur; indeed, whether or not these events can take place simultaneously depends on how they affect other world properties. For example, simultaneity would be impossible if e_1, say, always resulted in r being true while e_2 always resulted in r being false. (Of course, given *sufficient* axioms about the effects of e_1 and e_2, we could, in this case, prove that they *could not* occur together.)

Even if we are given necessary and sufficient conditions for the occurrence of events [1], we are still not out of the woods. For example, consider that events e_1 and e_2 satisfy the following axioms:

$$\forall w, s \;.\; occurs(e_1, s) \equiv holds(p, s) \wedge holds(q_1, succ(s, w))$$

$$\forall w, s \;.\; occurs(e_2, s) \equiv holds(p, s) \wedge holds(q_2, succ(s, w))$$

That is, a necessary and sufficient condition for e_1 having occurred is that p holds at its inception and q_1 holds at its completion; for e_2, q_2 must hold at its completion. But, even in this case, the best we can do is to try to prove that it is *consistent* for these events to occur simultaneously. This is clearly unsatisfactory from a computational standpoint. Furthermore, such reasoning is essentially nonmonotonic; the addition of further axioms may render previously consistent formulas inconsistent and any previous conclusions about possible event simultaneity may have to be withdrawn.

Another alternative is to determine interference by checking mutual independence for every fluent in the domain [7]. The major problem with such an approach is that this determination has to be made for every possible fluent, *including unspecified ones*. For example, despite the fact that two events may be mutually independent with respect to every specified fluent in the domain, there may exist some unspecified fluent for which they are not mutually independent. We are thus required to assume that the explicitly denoted fluents are the *only* ones relevant to the determination of interference.

Just as we wanted to avoid introducing any nonmonotonic operator or consistency criterion into our law of persistence, here also we want to avoid any form of nonmonotonicity. The solution we propose is based on being able to specify conditions under which we can guarantee performability of a given action or event. Such a condition will be called a *correctness condition* and, for a given event e, condition p, and state s, will be denoted $cc(p, e, s)$. The intended meaning of this statement is that any event that does not interfere with (affect) condition p will not interfere with (prevent) the occurrence of event e.[5] In addition, of course, we would need appropriate axioms defining the preconditions for the performance of e, but this is easily handled in the standard manner.

We now introduce the notion of freedom from interference. We shall say that events e_1 and e_2 are *interference-free* in a state s if the following condition holds:

$$\exists \phi, \psi \; . \; cc(\phi, e_1, s) \wedge cc(\psi, e_2, s) \wedge indep(\phi, e_2, s) \wedge indep(\psi, e1, s)$$

This condition will hold if, in state s, events e_1 and e_2 have no direct effect on the same properties of the domain. For example, consider the events $move(A, 1)$ and $move(B, 1)$ described earlier. We have the following:[6]

$$\forall s, x, y, X \; . \; holds(x \neq X, s) \supset indep(loc(x, y), move(X, 1), s)$$

$$\forall s, X \; . \; cc(loc(X, 1), move(X, 1), s)$$

If A and B are assumed to denote different objects, it is easy to see that $move(A, 1)$ and $move(B, 1)$ are interference-free. Note that we have assumed that both A and B can occupy the same location at the same time. If this were not the case, the correctness conditions for $move(A, 1)$ and $move(B, 1)$ would have to be altered to include this additional constraint. The events would then not be interference-free.

It immediately follows that two events will be able to occur simultaneously in a state s if

1. The preconditions of each event are satisfied in s, and

2. The events are interference-free in s.

It should be noted that, if we wish to show that two events can proceed concurrently (which not only includes simultaneity but also allows either event to precede the other), we also need to prove that the preconditions of each event are independent of the other event. This can be done in the same way as for the correctness conditions. One might, in

---

[5]Correctness conditions can be defined as follows. Let $tr(e, s, s')$ denote that $\langle s, s' \rangle$ is an element of the transition relation associated with event e. Then we have that p is a correctness condition for an event e if and only if, for all ϕ such that both ϕ and $\neg \phi$ are consistent with p, $(\exists s' \; . \; tr(e, s, s')) \wedge holds(p \wedge \phi, s')) \equiv (\exists s' \; . \; tr(e, s, s') \wedge holds(p \wedge \neg \phi, s'))$. As with the definition of independence, this is not computable.

[6]We assume x and y are rigid designators; see reference [17] for a discussion of this issue.

such circumstances, reserve the term "interference-free" for events that affect neither each other's correctness conditions nor preconditions [6]. Actions $move(A, 1)$ and $move(B, 1)$ are also interference-free in this stronger sense, as neither action affects the preconditions of the other.

In case two events do affect the same fluents (and thus do not satisfy the condition of interference freedom given above), it might yet be that the fluents are affected in the same way. If this is so, we say that the events are *compatible*. Compatible events can occur simultaneously, and in this sense are also interference-free.

Causality

One problem that we have not properly addressed is the apparent complexity of the axioms of independence and correctness. For example, while it might seem reasonable to state that the location of block B is independent of the movement of block A, as everyone knows, this is simply untrue in most interesting worlds. Whether or not the location of B is independent of the movement of A will depend on a whole host of conditions, such as whether B is in front of A, on top of A, on top of A but tied to a door, and so on. Indeed, it is often this apparent endless complexity rather than the combinatorial factors that many people have in mind when they refer to the frame problem.

One way to solve this problem is by introducing a notion of *causality*. We allow two kinds of causation, one in which an event causes the simultaneous occurrence of another event, and the other in which an event causes the occurrence of a consecutive event. We denote these two causal relations by $causes_s(\phi, e_1, e_2)$ and $causes_n(\phi, e_1, e_2)$, respectively, where ϕ is the condition under which event e_1 causes event e_2. These two kinds of causality are sufficient to describe the behavior of any procedure, process, or device that is based on discrete (rather than continuous) events.

The axioms expressing the effects of causation are

$$\forall w, s, \phi, e_1, e_2 . \; causes_s(\phi, e_1, e_2) \land holds(\phi, s) \land occurs(e_1, s) \supset occurs(e_2, s)$$

$$\forall w, s, \phi, e_1, e_2 . \; causes_n(\phi, e_1, e_2) \land holds(\phi, s) \land occurs(e_1, s) \supset occurs(e_2, succ(s, w))$$

For example, we might have a causal law to express the fact that, whenever a block x is moved, any block on top of x and not somehow restrained (e.g., by a string tied to a door) will also move. We could write this as

$$\forall x, y, l . \; causes_s((on(y, x) \land \neg restrained(y)), move(x, l), (move(y, l))$$

If this axiom holds, the movement of x will *cause* the simultaneous movement of y whenever y is on top of x and is not restrained.

We use the notion of causality in a purely technical sense and, while it has many similarities to commonsense usage, we are not proposing it as a fully-fledged theory of causality.

Location:

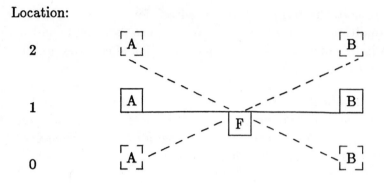

Figure 1: Possible Seesaw States After Moving F

Essentially, we view causation as a relation between atomic events that is conditional on the state of the world. We also relate causation to the temporal ordering of events, and assume that an event cannot cause another event that precedes it. However, as stated above, we do allow an event to cause another that occurs simultaneously. This differs from most other formal models of causality [14,20,29], although Allen [1] also allows simultaneous causation.

We can also use causality to maintain invariants over world states and to simplify the specification of actions and events. Consider, for example, a seesaw, with ends A and B and fulcrum F (Figure 1). Assume that A, F, and B are initially at location 0, and consider an event $move_F$ that moves F to location 1. Because of the squareness of the fulcrum and the constraint that A, F, and B must always remain collinear, $move_F$ also results in the movement of A and B to location 1.

We could model $move_F$ by a somewhat complex event that, in and of itself, would affect not only the location of F, but also the locations of A and B. Using this model, the locations of F, A, and B *would not* be independent of $move_F$. However, an alternative view would be to consider that the only property affected by $move_F$ is the location of the fulcrum F, and to let $move_F$ *cause* the simultaneous movement of A and B.

For example, we might have the following causal laws:

$causes_s(true, move_F, move(A, 1))$

$causes_s(true, move_F, move(B, 1))$

The intended meaning of these causal laws is that, if we perform the event $move_F$, both $move(A, 1)$ and $move(B, 1)$ are caused to occur simultaneously with $move_F$.

With this axiomatization, the locations of A and B *will* be independent of $move_F$. Of course, because $move_F$ always causes the movement of A and B, their locations will always be *indirectly* affected by the movement of F; however, from a technical standpoint, we consider the locations of A and B independent of $move_F$ itself (though not of the composite event that consists of the simultaneous movements of F, A, and B). The axioms of independence (and, similarly, correctness) can thus be considerably simplified, but at the cost of introducing more complex causal laws. The advantage of doing things this way is that the complexity is thereby shifted to reasoning about relationships among events, but away from reasoning about the relationships between events and fluents.

There are a number of things to be observed about this approach. First, provided that we add a domain constraint requiring that A, F, and B always remain collinear, we could simplify the above causal laws so that, for example, we require only that $move(A, 1)$ be caused by $move_F$. Using the collinearity constraint, together with the law of persistence, we can then infer that there must exist yet another event that occurs in state s and that brings about the simultaneous movement of B.

In many cases, therefore, we do not need to include causal laws to maintain invariant world conditions; we can instead make use of the constraints on world state to infer the existence of the appropriate events. However, if we do adopt this approach, we shall have to find some way of inferring (either monotonically or nonmonotonically) which of all the potentially appropriate events is the intended one (for example, did the event move B alone, or did it have other effects on the world as well?).

Second, causal laws can be quite complex, and may depend on whether *or not* other events take place as well as on conditions that hold in the world. As a consequence, the application of causal laws need not yield a unique set of caused events. For example, one causal law could require that an event e_1 occur if e_2 does not, whereas another could require that e_2 occur as long as e_1 does not. Given only this knowledge of the world, the most we could infer would be that just one of the events has occurred – but *which* one would be unknown.

Third, for planning possible future courses of action, the extent of causality must somehow be limited. Unless we have either first-order axioms or some nonmonotonic rule to limit causation, any given event could conceivably cause the occurrence of any other event. Clearly, with the possibility of so many events occurring, any useful planning about the future becomes impossible. This is not a difficult problem, but some care must be taken in addressing it [8].

It is interesting to note that the "deductive operators" used in SIPE [32] are very much like the causal laws described herein. Furthermore, SIPE limits the extent of causation by use of an implicit closed-world assumption so that, if causation between any two events cannot be proved, it is assumed that no such relation exists. This yields precisely those events that are *causally necessary*.

Finally, some predicates are better considered as *defined*, which avoids overpopulating the world with causal laws. For example, the distance between two objects may be considered a defined predicate. Instead of introducing various causal laws stating how this relation is altered by various move events, we can simply work with the basic entities of the problem domain and infer the value of the predicate from its definiens when needed.

Events as Behaviors

So far, we have identified actions and events with the sets of all their possible behaviors. However, at this point we encounter a serious deficiency in this approach, as well as all others that model actions and events in this way [1,3,20,24,28]. Let us return to the example of the seesaw described in the previous section. Again assume that A, F, and B are initially at location 0, and consider two actions, $move_F$ and $move'_F$, both of which move F to location 1 (see Figure 1). We require that both events also allow all possible movements of A and B, depending on what other events are occurring at the same time (such as someone lifting B). Of course, the objects must always remain collinear. However, $move_F$ and $move'_F$ differ in that, *when performed in isolation*, $move_F$ results in the simultaneous movement of A and B to location 1, whereas $move'_F$ leaves the location of A unchanged while moving B to location 2.

Because both $move_F$ and $move'_F$ exhibit exactly the same class of possible behaviors, the transition relations associated with each of these events will be identical. From a purely behavioral point of view, this is how things should be. To an external observer, it would appear that $move_F$, say, sometimes changed the location of A and not B (when some simultaneous event occurred that raised A to location 2), sometimes changed the location of B and not A (when some simultaneous event raised B), and sometimes changed the locations of both A and B. (Of course, $move_F$ would always change the location of F). As there is no *observation* that could allow the observer to detect whether or not another event was occurring simultaneously, there is no way $move_F$ could be distinguished from $move'_F$ or any other event that had the same transition relation.

On the other hand, it is very convenient to be able to make such distinctions; humans seem to have no trouble reasoning about events of this kind, and it would be unwise to exclude them from our theory. For example, $move_F$ and $move'_F$ may correspond to two different ways of moving F. On the surface, these events would appear to allow the same class of behaviors but, because of unobserved differences in the ways that they are performed, could exhibit different behaviors in specific situations. In other cases, while an event like $move_F$ might be appropriate to seesaws, an event isomorphic to $move'_F$ might be necessary for describing the movement of objects in other contexts. For example, consider the case in which, instead of being components of a seesaw, A is a source of light and B is F's shadow.

Thus, if we wish to be able to distinguish events such as $move_F$ and $move'_F$, we have to allow events with identical transition relations to have differing effects on the world, depending on what other events are, or are not, occurring at the same time. Unfortunately, our current model of events simply leaves us no way to represent this. We cannot restrict the transition relation of $move_F$, say, so that it will always yield the state in which A, F, and B are all at location 1, because that would prevent A or B from being moved simultaneously to other locations. Similarly, we cannot restrict the transition relation of $move'_F$ to allow only the movement of B. Nor can we use any general default rule or minimality criteria to determine the intended effects of an event when performed in any specific context (because that would yield identical models for both $move_F$ and $move'_F$). Indeed, in the situation in which $move_F$ is performed in isolation, note that we do *not* minimize the changes in world relations or maximize their persistence: *both A and B* change location along with F.

We therefore consider events to be objects of the domain that have an associated transition relation, but do not require that events with the same transition relation be deemed equivalent. Events having the same transition relation may differ in other properties; in particular, they may play different causal roles in a theory of the world.[7]

For example, in the case of the seesaw, we might have the following axiom for $move_F$:

$$causes_s(p, move_F, move(A, 1))$$

where $p \equiv \lambda(s)(\forall e \, . \, occurs(e, s) \supset \; int\text{-}free(e, move(A, 1), s))$.

The intended meaning of this causal law is that the movement of F will cause the movement of A to location 1, provided no event occurs that interferes with the movement of A. If desired, one could use a similar causal law to describe the movement of B.

On the other hand, $move'_F$ would cause the movement of B to location 2 when performed in isolation:

$$causes_s(q, move'_F, move(B, 2))$$

where $q \equiv \lambda(s)(\forall e \, . \, occurs(e, s) \supset \; int\text{-}free(e, move(B, 2), s))$.

It is important to note that this view of events (and any view that, in one way or another, associates an event with the set of all its possible behaviors [1,3,20,24,28]) requires that the event transition relation include *all* possible transitions under all possible situations, *including* the simultaneous occurrence of other events. For example, if we wish to allow for two pushing events opposed to one another to exert sufficient frictional force on a block to enable it to be lifted, this composite event must be one of the permissible transitions in each of the individual push events. Thus, two events cannot be combined to yield, synergistically, an event that is not part of the actions themselves. It follows that, in the specification of an event, we can only state what is true of *all* possible occurrences of the event. In the case of the push event, it would be a mistake to write an axiom stating that the effect of a push event on a block is to move the block. While this may be true if there is but a single event affecting the block in question, it is clearly false when two or more such events are acting upon the block simultaneously.

What *is* true of all push events (and hence can be stated as an axiom) is that they exert a force on the object being pushed. Other axioms could then be used to specify under what

---

[7]In a previous paper [7] I identified events with transition relations and let actions alone assume different causal roles independently of their associated transition relation. Considering the vast literature that already exists on events and actions, and which, if anything, makes a somewhat different distinction, I now believe this to have been a bad idea.

conditions opposing forces generate sufficient frictional force to lift objects, while a third group of axioms could describe how the resultant forces on an object cause it to move. Depending on the desired level of description, this axiomatization could be either simplified or elaborated.

Processes

It is often convenient to be able to reason about groups of causally interrelated events as single entities. For example, we might want to amalgamate the actions and events that constitute the internal workings of a robot, or those that pertain to each component in a complex physical system. Such groupings of events, together with the causal laws that relate them to one another, will be called *processes*.

We assume that we have a set of processes and can classify various events and fluents as being either internal or external with respect to these processes. Let $internal_f(\phi, P, s)$ and $external_f(\phi, P, s)$ denote these relationships as they hold between a fluent ϕ and process P in state s, and let $internal_e(e, P, s)$ and $external_e(e, P, s)$ denote these relationships between an event e and process P in state s.

We place a number of constraints on the internal and external fluents and events of a process. First, we require that, for both fluents and events, those classified as internal be mutually exclusive of those classified as external. Second, we require that, in all situations, each internal event have a correctness condition that is dependent only on internal fluents. This property can be expressed as follows:

$$\forall e, s, P . internal_e(e, P, s) \supset \exists \phi . internal_f(\phi, P, s) \wedge cc(\phi, e, s)$$

We impose a similar constraint on the preconditions of internal events. Next, we require that internal fluents be independent of all events except internal ones:

$$\forall e, s, \phi, P . internal_f(\phi, P, s) \wedge \neg internal_e(e, P, s) \supset indep(\phi, e, s)$$

External events and fluents are required to obey similar constraints. It is then not difficult to prove that, if the above axioms are satisfied, the internal events and external events of a given process are interference-free.

Finally, we require that there be no *direct* causal relationship between internal and external events. Thus, the only way the internal events of a given process can influence the external events of the process (or vice versa) is through indirect causation by an event that belongs to neither category. Within concurrency theory, these intermediary events (more accurately, event types) are often called *ports*. Processes thus impose causal boundaries and independence properties on a problem domain, and can thereby substantially reduce cominatorial complexity. Lansky's notion of a *group* [14] is quite similar to our notion of process.

The ease with which processes can be identified will depend strongly on the problem domain. In standard programming systems (at least those that are well structured), processes can be used to represent scope rules and are fairly straightforward to specify. On NASA's proposed space station, most of the properties of one subsystem (such as the attitude control system) will be independent of the majority of actions performed by other subsystems (such as the environmental and life support system), and thus these subsystems naturally correspond to processes as defined here. Lansky [14] gives other examples in which processes are readily specified.

In other situations, the specification of processes might be more complicated. For example, we might know that interference at a distance can occur only as a result of electromagnetic or gravitational phenomena, and so utilize this knowledge to impose causal boundaries whenever electromagnetic emissions are shielded and gravitational forces are negligible. Moreover, in many real-world situations, dependencies will vary as the spheres of influence and the potential for interaction change over time. For example, consider how many actions in real life are taken solely for the purpose of limiting or enhancing interference with other systems (such as closing a door for privacy, camouflaging military equipment, or making a phone call).

If we are to exploit the notion of process effectively, it is important to define various composition operators and to show how properties of the behaviors of the composite processes can be determined from the behaviors of the individual processes. For example, we should be able to write down descriptions of the behaviors of individual agents, and from these descriptions deduce properties of groups of agents acting together (concurrently). We should *not* have to consider the internal behaviors of each of these agents to determine how the group as a whole behaves. In contrast, all the so-called hierarchical planning systems (e.g., NOAH [27] and SIPE [32]) analyze interaction down to the atomic level (as was noticed early by Rosenschein [26]).

The existing literature on concurrency theory [13,21] provides a number of useful composition operators. Some examples are given below. They can all be defined in terms of the causal relations introduced earlier, although we need to introduce a special "no-op" or "wait" event to prevent forcing the processes to operate in lockstep with one another.

Prefixing (:)

The process $e : P$ is one that can begin by performing the event (strictly speaking, event *type*) e, after which it behaves exactly like P.

Sequencing (;)

The process P ; Q behaves first like P and, if that concludes successfully, behaves next like Q.

Ambiguity (+)

The process $P + Q$ can behave like either P or Q. For example, if

$$R = (b : P) + (c : Q) \quad ,$$

then R can either perform b and evolve into P or perform c and evolve into Q.

Parallelism (&)

The process $P \& Q$ is one in which both P and Q run concurrently. Events that are designated as synchronous must occur simultaneously, whereas other events can choose to occur simultaneously with one another or be arbitrarily interleaved.

We must, of course, provide various axioms about these operators so that they will be useful. For example, it is not difficult to show that any [temporal] property that holds of the behaviors of a process P (or Q) will also hold for the composite process $P \& Q$.

Such axioms may not appear to be very useful, as the properties that hold of each process will, in general, depend on what other events could occur in the environment. However, to the extent that the properties of a process's behaviors are specified in terms of its internal events and fluents, they will be independent of the context in which the process is embedded. For example, consider the two very simple processes P and Q given below:

$P = a : b : P$, and

$Q = c : d : Q$.

Strictly speaking, we have to provide a fixed-point operator to define these processes [13], but the intended meaning should be clear. Now, if the event types a and b are mutually exclusive and are internal with respect to process P, all behaviors of P will be such that the number of events of type a, denoted $\#a$, and the number of events of type b, $\#b$, obey the constraint: $\#a - 1 \leq \#b \leq \#a$. This would *not* be the case if a and b were not internal events of process P, as any other process could then choose to perform an arbitrary number of events of type a or b concurrently with process P.

Now let's assume that c and d are internal events of process Q, and thus obey a law similar to that given for P. Furthermore, let us assume that events of type b and d are always constrained to be simultaneous with some interface event e, and vice versa. Using the fact that the behaviors of the composite process $P \& Q$ will satisfy the same constraints as the component processes, it is not difficult to prove that $\#a - 1 \leq \#c \leq \#a + 1$.

Despite the triviality of the example, the important point is that, in proving the above result, we have not had to examine the internal workings of either process P or Q. For example, had the internal structure of these processes been entirely different, this result would have remained valid (provided, of course, that the processes had still imposed the same constraints on the number of occurrences of events a, b, c, and d). Furthermore, in determining the properties of the individual behaviors of P and Q we have not had to consider the external environment in which they are embedded; the relationship between the number or occurrences of events a and b in process P is independent of external happenings, and similarly for events c and d in process Q.

There are a number of complexities in the specification of processes that require some care. For example, a process may *fail* at any time (because some precondition has not been or cannot be met, or some correctness condition has been violated, etc.). Thus, the behaviors generated by a process will include both failed and successful behaviors, where each failed behavior is a prefix of some successful behavior. Indeed, the notion of a process generating both successful and failed behaviors is essential to planning in real-world domains – we frequently select a plan of action according to how it can *fail* rather than how it succeeds. Amy Lansky and I have discussed this question in more detail elsewhere [9].

Nondeterministic processes present another problem that has to be addressed with caution. Such processes can differ from one another despite the fact that they generate identical behaviors (both successful and failed). The reason for this is that nondetermistic processes can behave differently in different environments even though their sets of potential behaviors are identical. This issue is explored at length in the literature on concurrency and various means of handling the problem have been developed [13,21].

In summary, the notion of process allows us to structure problem domains and thus avoid considering how every event affects every other event or fluent. It can therefore lead to a substantial reduction in the combinatorics of the problem. Furthermore, we can describe complex domains in a compositional way – that is, we can specify properties of individual processes independently of other processes, and then determine the behavior of the combined processes from knowledge of the behaviors of the component processes.

The Frame Problem

The frame problem, as Hayes [12] describes it, is concerned with providing, in a reasonably natural and tractable way, appropriate "laws of motion." Our approach to this problem has been to provide a proper model-theoretic account of actions and events, and to formulate first-order axioms and rules that allow the effects of actions and events to be determined monotonically. Furthermore, by introducing the notions of independence and correctness, we obviate the necessity of using nonmonotonic operators or consistency arguments to obtain useful results regarding persistence and interference.

Of course, we are left with the problem of *specifying* independence and correctness. There are essentially two problems here: (1) the apparent combinatorial difficulties in expressing all the required independence and correctness axioms; and (2) the complexity to be expected of many, if not most, of these axioms in real-world applications.

The first of these problems is probably overstated in much of the literature on the frame problem. Thus, just as in the axiomatization of any large or infinite domain, the number of axioms required to specify independence (and correctness) can be substantially reduced by the use of general axioms that allow specific instances of independence to be deduced as needed. This can substantially reduce the combinatorial problem and has the advantage of remaining within the bounds of first-order logic.

Where desired, some simple closed-world assumption or minimality criterion could additionally be used to ease specification of the independence relation for the basic fluents of the domain. This can be quite straightforward, although some care has to be taken with the situation variable [8,10].

The second problem is handled by introducing causal laws that describe how actions and events bring about (cause) others. Indeed, without such causal laws, the specification of independence would become as problematic as is the specification of persistence in the standard formalisms. Of course, the causal laws can themselves be complex (just as is the physics of the real world), but the representation and specification of actions and events are thereby kept simple.

Some researchers take a more general view of the frame problem, seeing it as the problem of reasoning about the effects of actions and events with *incomplete information* about what other events or processes (causally related or otherwise) may also be occurring. Unfortunately, this problem is often confused with that of providing an adequate *model* of events, with the result that there is usually no clear model-theoretic semantics for the representation.

For example, one of the major problems in reasoning about actions and plans is to determine which events can possibly occur at any given moment. Based on the relative infrequency of "relevant" events (or that one would "know about" these if they occurred), it has been common to use various default rules [25], nonmonotonic operators [3,20], or minimal models [15,19,29] to constrain the set of possible event occurrences. However, there are many cases in which this is unnecessary – where we can *prove*, on the basis of general axioms about independence and correctness, that no events (or effects) of interest could possibly occur. We may even have axioms that allow one to avoid considering whole classes of events, such as when one knows that certain events are external with respect to a given process. Thus, in many cases, there may be no need to use default rules or minimality principles – reasoning about plans and actions does not have to be nonmonotonic.

When we *do* need to make assumptions about event occurrences, default rules and circumscription can be very useful. For example, by minimizing the extensions of the *occurs* and *causes* predicates, we can obtain a theory in which the only event occurrences are those that are *causally necessary* [8]. This kind of reasoning seems to correspond closely to much of commonsense planning. However, in making reasonable assumptions about a given domain, we do not have to limit ourselves to such default rules or minimality criteria. In some cases, it may be preferable to use, for example, domain-specific rules defining what assumptions are appropriate or, alternatively, a more complicated information-theoretic approach based on quantitative probabilities of event occurrences.

To take a familiar example [1], it seems reasonable, at first, to assume that my car is still where I left it this morning, unless I have information that is inconsistent with that assumption. However, this premise gets less and less reasonable as hours turn into days, weeks, months, years, and centuries – even if it is quite *consistent* to make such a premise. This puts the problem where it should be – namely, in the area of making reasonable assumptions, not in the area of *defining* the effects of actions [4,12,25], the persistency of facts [3,20], or causal laws [29].

Of course, most of the axioms we might state about the real world are subject to *qualification* [18]. Our aim has not been to solve this problem, although the notion of causality helps to some extent. Furthermore, because our approach has a well-defined semantics and can be formalized in first-order logic, we provide a sound base on top of which can be built various meta-theories regarding the handling of qualifications and other kinds of assumptions. I address some of these issues elsewhere [8].

Conclusions

We have constructed a model of actions and events suited to reasoning about domains that involve multiple agents or dynamic environments. The proposed model provides for simultaneous actions, and a generalized situation calculus is used to describe the effects of actions in multiagent settings. Notions of *independence* and *correctness* were introduced and it was shown how they can be used to determine the persistence of facts over time and whether or not actions can be performed concurrently. Both these notions I consider critical to reasoning *effectively* about multiagent domains. Furthermore, unlike most previous formalisms in both single and multiagent domains, the proposed law of persistence is *monotonic* and therefore has a well-defined model-theoretic semantics.

We have also demonstrated how the concept of *causality* can be used to simplify the description of actions and to model arbitrarily complex machines and physical devices. It was also shown how sets of causally interrelated actions can be grouped together in *processes* and how this structuring of a problem domain can substantially reduce combinatorial complexity. The notion of structuring the problem domain by using general axioms about independence and causal influence appears to be essential for solving complex multiagent problems. The only existing work I know of that incorporates such an idea is the planning system being developed by Lansky [14].

Although we did not consider implementation issues directly, the concepts and laws introduced by us were aimed at providing a sound basis for practical planning and reasoning systems. For example, one of the most efficient action representations so far employed in AI planning systems – the STRIPS representation [4,16] – is essentially the special case in which (1) the effects of an action can be represented by a conjunction of either positive or negative literals, called the *add list*; (2) the action is independent of all properties except those given in (or deducible from) the *delete list* of the action; (3) a single precondition determines performabilty of the action; and (4) no actions ever occur simultaneously with any other. The approach used by Pednault [22] can also be considered the special case in which there are no simultaneous actions.

Furthermore, the work here indicates how the STRIPS representation could be extended to the multiagent domain. For example, one possibility would be to stay with the single-agent representation, adding to it the requirement that the correctness conditions of an action be represented by the same conjunction of literals given in the add list of the action. Causal laws could be introduced in the manner of the deductive operators of SIPE [32], thereby increasing the expressive power of the approach without introducing the problems usually associated with extending the STRIPS assumption [25]. In this way, some of the traditional planning systems may be able to be modified to handle multiagent domains. Alternatively, the approach of Manna and Waldinger [17] could be applied to these domains by employing the generalized situation calculus we introduced here. Finally, our approach has shown how we can deduce constraints on the occurrence of actions and events from relatively simple axioms about their effects and influence. These constraints can then be used by event-based planners [5,14,31] to form synchronized plans involving the cooperation of multiple agents in dynamically changing environments.

Acknowledgments

I wish especially to thank Amy Lansky and Ed Pednault, both of whom helped greatly in clarifying many of the ideas presented in this paper. I am also indebted to Vladimir Lifschitz for some very enlightening discussions, and to Richard Waldinger who criticized an earlier draft of this paper.

References

[1] Allen, J. F., "Towards a General Theory of Action and Time," *Artificial Intelligence*, 23, pp. 123-154 (1984).

[2] Bratman, M., *Intention, Plans, and Practical Reason*, Harvard University Press, Cambridge, Massachusetts, forthcoming.

[3] Dean, T., "Planning and Temporal Reasoning under Uncertainty," *Proceedings of the IEEE Workshop on Knowledge Based Systems*, Denver, Colorado (1984).

[4] Fikes, R. E., and Nilsson, N. J., "STRIPS: A New Approach to the Application of Theorem Proving to Problem Solving," *Artificial Intelligence*, 2, pp. 189 – 208 (1971).

[5] Georgeff, M. P. "Communication and Interaction in Mulitagent Planning," *Proceedings of the Third National Conference on Artificial Intelligence*, Washington, D.C. (1983).

[6] Georgeff, M. P., "A Theory of Action tor Multiagent Planning," *Proceedings of the Fourth National Conference on Artificial Intelligence*, Austin, Texas (1984).

[7] Georgeff, M. P., "A Representation of Events in Multiagent Domains," *Proceedings of the Fifth National Conference on Artificial Intelligence*, Philadelphia, Pennsylvania (1987).

[8] Georgeff, M. P., "Many Agents are Better than One," Forthcoming SRI Technical Note, Artificial Intelligence Center, SRI International, Menlo Park, California. (1987).

[9] Georgeff, M. P., and Lansky, A. L., "Procedural Knowledge," *Proc. IEEE*, Special Issue on Knowledge Representation (1986).

[10] Hanks, S., and McDermott, D., "Default Reasoning, Nonmonotonic Logics, and the Frame Problem," *Proceedings of the Fifth National Conference on Artificial Intelligence*, Philadelphia, Pennsylvania (1986).

[11] Harel, D. *First Order Dynamic Logic*, Lecture Notes in Computer Science, 68, Springer-Verlag (1979).

[12] Hayes, P. J., "The Frame Problem and Related Problems in Artificial Intelligence," in *Artificial and Human Thinking*, A. Elithorn and D. Jones (eds.), Jossey-Bass (1973).

[13] Hoare, C. A. R., *Communicating Sequential Processes*, Series in Computer Science, C. A. R. Hoare (ed.), Prentice Hall, Englewood Cliffs, New Jersey (1985).

[14] Lansky, A. L., "A Representation of Parallel Activity Based on Events, Structure, and Causality," *Proceedings of the 1986 Workshop on Reasoning about Actions and Plans*, Timberline Lodge, Timberline, Oregon (1987).

[15] Lifschitz, V. "Circumscription in the Blocks World," Computer Science Working Memo, Stanford University, Stanford, California (1985).

[16] Lifschitz, V. "On the Semantics of STRIPS," *Proceedings of the 1986 Workshop on Reasoning about Actions and Plans*, Timberline Lodge, Timberline, Oregon (1987).

[17] Manna, Z., and Waldinger, R. W., "A Theory of Plans," *Proceedings of the 1986 Workshop on Reasoning about Actions and Plans*, Timberline Lodge, Timberline, Oregon (1987).

[18] McCarthy, J., and Hayes, P. J., "Some Philosophical Problems from the Standpoint of Artificial Intelligence, in *Machine Intelligence 4*, pp. 463 – 502 (1969).

[19] McCarthy, J. "Applications of Circumscription to Formalizing Commonsense Knowledge," *Proceedings of the Nonmonotonic Reasoning Workshop*, AAAI, Menlo Park, California (1984).

[20] McDermott, D., "A Temporal Logic for Reasoning about Processes and Plans," *Cognitive Science*, 6, pp. 101-155 (1982).

[21] Milner, R., *A Calculus of Communicating Systems*, Lecture Notes in Computer Science 92, Springer Verlag, New York (1980).

[22] Pednault, E. P. D., "Toward a Mathematical Theory of Plan Synthesis," Ph.D. thesis, Department of Electrical Engineering, Stanford University, Stanford, California (1986).

[23] Pednault, E. P. D., "Solving Multiagent Dynamic World Problems in the Classical Planning Framework," *Proceedings of the 1986 Workshop on Reasoning about Actions and Plans*, Timberline Lodge, Timberline, Oregon (1987).

[24] Pelavin, R., "A Formal Logic for Planning with a Partial Description of the Future," Ph.D. Thesis, Department of Computer Science, University of Rochester, Rochester, New York (1986).

[25] Reiter, R., "A Logic for Default Reasoning," *Artificial Intelligence*, 13, pp. 81 – 132 (1980).

[26] Rosenschein, S. J., "Plan Synthesis: A Logical Perspective," *Proceedings of the Seventh International Joint Conference on Artificial Intelligence*, Vancouver, British Columbia (1981).

[27] Sacerdoti, E.D., *A Structure for Plans and Behavior*, Elsevier, North Holland Publishing Company, New York, New York (1977).

[28] Shoham, Y. and Dean, T., "Temporal Notation and Causal Terminology," Working Paper, Department of Computer Science, Yale University, New Haven, Connecticut (1985).

[29] Shoham, Y. "Chronological Ignorance: Time, Nonmonotonicity, Necessity and Causal Theories," *Proceedings of the Fifth National Conference on Artificial Intelligence*, Philadelphia, Pennsylvania (1986).

[30] Shoham, Y. "What is the Frame Problem," *Proceedings of the 1986 Workshop on Reasoning about Actions and Plans*, Timberline Lodge, Timberline, Oregon (1987).

[31] Stuart, C. J., "An Implementation of a Multi-Agent Plan Synchronizer Using a Temporal Logic Theorem Prover," *Proceedings of the Ninth International Joint Conference on Artificial Intelligence*, Los Angeles, California (1985).

[32] Wilkins, D. E., "Domain-Independent Planning: Representation and Plan Generation," *Artificial Intelligence*, 22, pp. 269-302 (1984).

A REPRESENTATION OF PARALLEL ACTIVITY
BASED ON
EVENTS, STRUCTURE, AND CAUSALITY

Amy L. Lansky

Artificial Intelligence Center, SRI International
and
Center for the Study of Language and Information

ABSTRACT

Most AI domain representations have been based on state-oriented world models. In this paper we present an event-based model that focuses on domain events (both atomic and nonatomic) and on the causal and temporal relationships among them. Emphasis is also placed on representing *locations* of activity and using them to structure the domain representation. Our model is based on first-order temporal logic, which has a well-understood semantics and has been employed extensively in concurrency theory. We show how temporal-logic constraints on *event histories* (records of past activity) can facilitate the description of many of the complex synchronization properties of parallel, multiagent domains.

This research has been made possible by the Office of Naval Research, under Contract N00014-85-C-0251, and by the National Science Foundation, under Grant IST-8511167. The views and conclusions contained in this paper are those of the author and should not be interpreted as representative of the official policies, either expressed or implied, of the Office of Naval Research, NSF, or the United States government.

Introduction

The duality between events and states is a well-known phenomenon. In a state-based representation, the world is viewed as a series of states or "snapshots" that are altered by events. Events are modeled solely in terms of their state-changing function. Alternatively, the dual, event-based approach represents the world in terms of a set of interrelated events. In this context, the "state" of the world at any particular point in time is represented in terms of the set of events that have occurred up to that moment (see Figure 1).

Most AI domain representations have relied on state-based models. In this paper we explore the dual view and examine its impact on the representation of multiagent domains — domains in which parallel activity is inherent and vital. As with most dualities, the choice of one representation over another may not affect any essential capability for expression; after all, one dual representation can usually be converted into the other. However, the mere form of a representation may make certain kinds of properties more natural to express and reason about. We believe that an event-based approach holds this advantage with respect to many of the complicated properties of multiagent worlds.

The representation described in this paper is based on the GEM concurrency model [16,17,18,19]. As advocated by philosophers such as Davidson [6] and as manifested in several AI representations such as Allen's and Georgeff's [1,9], GEM reifies events and explicitly represents their causal and temporal interrelationships. However, unlike previous AI representations, events are the *primary* elements of our world model and state is defined strictly in terms of past event activity. Thus, the work described in this paper explores the use of events and event relationships in way that is more general than previous work on knowledge representation and reasoning.

Another important aspect of the GEM representation is an explicit emphasis on *location* of activity. Specific mechanisms are provided for structuring events into logical locations of occurrence as well as for grouping those locations together in various ways. These event structures help organize the way a domain is described – for instance, particular domain constraints can be scoped within a given context or subset of events. Structural contexts can also be used to actually represent properties of the domain. For example, particular event sets can be used to represent locations of forced sequential activity, scopes of potential causal effect, or the boundaries of localized forms of knowledge. In this way, domain structure helps to attack aspects of the frame problem. Domain structure can also be utilized as a heuristic in guiding computation; for example, it can serve as a guideline for the decomposition of planning tasks.

Within an event-based model, such as the one we are proposing, a notion of "state" is most naturally defined in terms of past activity: the state of the world at any point in time is merely a record of the events that have occurred and their interrelationships (once again, see Figure 1). *State descriptions* can be used to characterize sets of states, just as in a state-based model. These descriptions are typically formulas that describe patterns of past activity – for

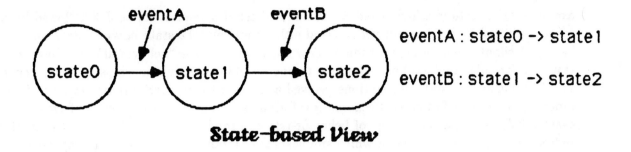

eventA : state0 -> state1

eventB : state1 -> state2

State-based View

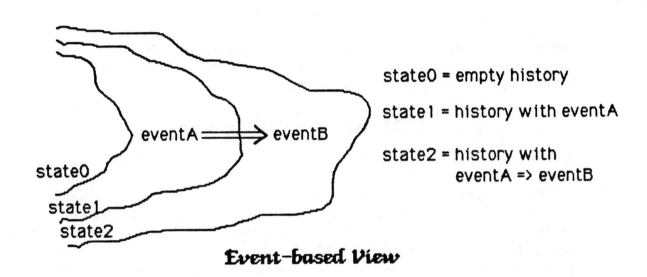

state0 = empty history

state1 = history with eventA

state2 = history with
            eventA => eventB

Event-based View

Figure 1: State/Event Duality

example, "the state in which a red robot has registered a request for tool X followed by a request for tool Y, but has not yet received either tool" or "the state in which Jack and Jill have just simultaneously begun running down the hill." These "behavioral" descriptions of state are formulas that explicitly describe temporal and causal relationships *between events*. In GEM, behavioral state descriptions (as well as all domain constraints) are stated as first-order temporal-logic formulas. Because these formulas are cast directly in terms of events and event relationships, a wide range of behavior-related properties can be described succinctly. Indeed, descriptions of states in which simultaneous activity has occurred are impossible to formulate in many state-based representations. As we will show, more conventional state descriptions based on state predicates can also be utilized in our event-based framework.

The primary aim of this paper is to convey the expressive power behind a world model based on structured, interrelated events. We begin by motivating our underlying approach and relating it to other work. The next section provides a more formal description of the GEM world model and presents a semantics for our domain descriptions. The power behind this representation is then more fully illustrated through construction of a complex domain description. Finally, we focus on the modeling of nonatomic events, on building state descriptions, and on the frame problem. We conclude with a brief discussion of our current work on building a planner based on this event-oriented framework.

Motivation and Background

A Scenario

One of the primary goals behind any representational mechanism is to capture the properties of a domain in a useful and coherent way. Consider the following scenario. Three sets of friends decide to meet for dinner at an elegant restaurant. Each person must find his or her own mode of transport to the restaurant (personal car or taxi) and the first person from each party to arrive must book a reservation for his or her group. The maitre d' at the restaurant, Felix, happens to be a somewhat mercenary fellow who gives preference to parties that bribe him. In fact, everyone knows that a $50 bribe will guarantee eventual seating. However, he does have some scruples; he will seat a party only if a table of the correct size is available and if the entire party has arrived (members of a party must be seated simultaneously). All other things being equal, he will then seat parties on a first-come-first-served basis. After being seated, guests may then choose, order, and eat their meals.

This scenario, though somewhat complex, is really fairly typical of situations we confront in our day-to-day lives. To describe it requires representation of several interlocking synchronization constraints (all of Felix's seating rules) as well as multiple ways of achieving particular goals (traveling to the restaurant by car or taxi). It also manifests some naturally emerging forms of structure: the individuals are grouped into parties; certain locations of activity may be viewed as resources at which only limited forms of activity may occur (the tables at the restaurant, the attention of Felix); knowledge is partitioned (some of Felix's actions and habits are known by all, whereas others may not be). These kinds of properties are typical of many domains, including factory management and scheduling, robotics, and organizational coordination.

When planning for a domain such as this, it is clear that some activities are loosely coupled and can be planned separately (each person's plan for getting to the restaurant), while others must be tightly coordinated (the seating of the three parties). In addition, the expansion of some nonatomic actions will preserve a sense of locality and maintain constraints that may have been solved at a higher level of abstraction (for example, each person's menu selection plan). In other cases, however, nonatomic-event expansion will result in activity that spans across locations accessible to others, and may thus require rechecking after expansion (possible contention for the use of a limited number of taxis).

Later on we shall illustrate our GEM-based representational approach by building a specification of this scenario. In the conclusions we also outline a planner currently under construction that is based on GEM and that explicitly uses domain structure to guide the planning process. First, however, we take a brief look at other common forms of domain specification and the ways in which they might tackle the restaurant problem.

Other Approaches

Most traditional AI domain representations model the world as a sequence of states, and actions or events as relations between sets of states [8,22,26].[1] States descriptions are typically constructed in terms of a set of state predicates, and actions are defined in terms of preconditions and postconditions on state. This is the basic descriptive framework underlying classical planning systems such as STRIPS [8], NOAH [27], and other planners [31,32,33]. Some of these representations require that all events be totally ordered in time [8,22]. In others, events are ostensibly partially ordered, but it is still assumed that potentially interacting events occur in some total order that conforms to the partial order [27]. For instance, this premise underlies use of the STRIPS assumption [8]. While the STRIPS assumption can be used to determine the effect of individual events on world state, it cannot be used to determine the combined effect of simultaneous events. Since parallel, multiagent domains may sometimes even *require* that events occur at the same time (for example, two robots picking a heavy block up together), this is a definite limitation.[2]

Another disadvantage of traditional state-based frameworks is that they spread the representation of some kinds of properties across several action descriptions. For example, to encode the restaurant scenario's seating rules, several state predicates would have to be main-

---

[1]Although they are often viewed as distinct in the philosophical literature, we shall use the terms "action" and "event" interchangeably.

[2]Recent work by Georgeff [9] has made progress in extending the situation-calculus framework to accommodate simultaneous events. A model-based approach is used, along with a semantic (rather than syntactic) frame rule. However, properties that involve particular relationships between events (such as simultaneity) must still be described in Georgeff's framework by using what is essentially event-based description. Thus, although his model is state based, explicit relationships between events are used.

tained to encode the "synchronization state" of the reservation desk: who is waiting, in what order they arrived, who gave the biggest bribe, how large the parties are, what tables are available, etc. The preconditions and postconditions of reservation and seating-related actions would involve complex manipulation of and interactions among these predicates. Each of the seating constraints is essentially spread out among the descriptions of the actions that are involved. Changes in the constraints may therefore entail fairly complex and nonobvious changes in action descriptions. Clearly, it would be simpler if each of Felix's rules were encoded as a separate, succinct constraint on the relationship among domain actions.

More recent approaches to domain representation have been based on *state intervals*. Events (actions) and/or predicates are modeled as state sequences occurring over an interval of time, and domain properties are described in terms of interval-ordering constraints [1,7,12,23,28]. This form of representation has the benefit of allowing the state of the world *during* an event to be modeled explicitly and reasoned about. Event intervals can be temporally related in all possible ways (for example, they can be interleaved or simultaneous). Most interval-based models also explicitly utilize relationships between events (although sometimes only relationships between types or classes of events are allowed). However, events themselves are not considered the primary objects of the world model.

Unfortunately, many of these interval-based approaches do not capture the semantics of concurrent activity in a clear manner. For example, merely equating an event type with a set of state intervals (typically, the intervals which represent successful event occurrences) gives no clue as to how events are *achieved* or *composed* – e.g., what can or cannot be done by an agent.[3] This hampers reasoning about interactions and relationships between events, as well as about how events may fail. Georgeff's recent paper elaborates this point [9].

Some interval-based models (in particular, McDermott's [23]) also do not adequately capture existing or potential relationships between event instances. It is useful to be able to reason about specific causal event-pairs, or the particular events composing a nonatomic event, not just causal and composite relationships between classes of events. For example, in the restaurant scenario, it is important to know precisely which reservation events correspond to which seating events. Otherwise, Felix's seating rules could not be enforced. In addition, most interval-based representations employ a notion of causality that implies eventuality – i.e., if a class of events A has a causal relationship with a class of events B, then, if an event of type A occurs, an event of type B must too. It is therefore difficult to talk about situations in which an event has occurred but has not yet caused (and perhaps never will cause) its corresponding effect. For example, one might view a party's entering a restaurant and making a reservation as causing the party to be subsequently seated. However, such a seating need not necessarily materialize.[4]

---

[3]However, Allen and Koomen [2] do utilize a simple form of event decomposition similar to NOAH operators.

[4]While it is nonstandard, we have found it advantageous to view causality as a phenomenon more akin to *enablement*. To say that class A causes class B means that any event of type B must have been "enabled by" an event of type A. However, an occurrence of an event of type A does not guarantee that it will cause an event of type B. If, however, such a relationship *does* exist, it is perfectly reasonable to say that it is causal. If an eventuality requirement is also desired, it must be stated explicitly.

Finally, none of these domain representations utilize event location (i.e. structural relationships between events) in any complex way.[5] These kinds of relationships are important if we want to capture those aspects of a domain that are truly affected by locality – for example, forced sequentiality within certain regions, or boundaries of causal effect.

As we shall illustrate, an ontology based on structured, interrelated events has a distinctly different flavor from the interval-based approaches, although it shares with them many of the advantages over more traditional representations. Information about event relationships is captured explicitly. We can easily talk about particular event instances and their various temporal, causal, and simultaneity interrelationships, as well as how particular events constitute a specific nonatomic event. Event intervals and interval relationships can also be utilized. Complex structural relationships among events (i.e. various kind of event locations and groupings of locations) are also represented. The temporal logic underlying our model has a well-understood semantics and has been used extensively in concurrency theory [25,19]. Our use of temporal-logic constraints over *history sequences* (sequences of accumulating records of past behavior) is distinct from most previous approaches (although Stuart uses a similar idea [30]). Because histories include all information about previous events and their interrelationhips, they facilitate use of complex information about the past.

GEM: An Informal View

Because our approach is somewhat unconventional, it is useful to begin with an informal description of the GEM world model. This discussion will be formalized later.

Our event-oriented representation is based on the view that the world can be modeled as a myriad of interrelated events occurring at locations (see Figure 2). The most basic events are *atomic*; they are not observably decomposable. Nonatomic events are then composed of these atomic events. Three partial relations may hold between events: a causal relation $\leadsto$, a temporal order $\Longrightarrow$, and a relation that embodies required simultaneity $\rightleftharpoons$. Structural relationships are also used to describe event locations as well as nonatomic event composition.

A useful way of understanding our world model is as a two-tiered structure. The upper tier is based on partially ordered sets of events related by $\leadsto$, $\Longrightarrow$, and $\rightleftharpoons$ as well as by structural relationships. We call a particular set of interrelated events a *world plan*. The lower tier of our world model consists of the set of executions *admitted by* a world plan. It is this lower tier that is usually identified as the "world model" in most state-based representations. Because each world plan may allow many possibly executions, branching state models are conventionally used to represent this execution-level view of the world. However, we have found it easier to reason about the world primarily in terms of world plans (the upper tier). These structures are definitely a more compact representation than branching state models – in fact, they correspond directly to the usual notion of a "plan."

---

[5]Of course, many models do associate events with their performing agent. Nonetheless, this is a very limited form of event structure.

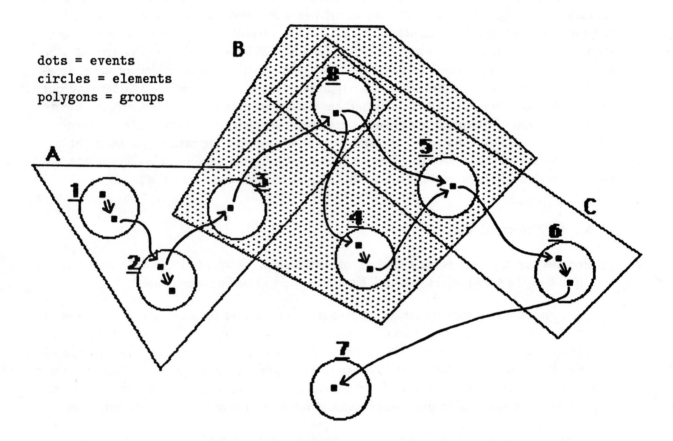

dots = events
circles = elements
polygons = groups

Figure 2: Events, Elements, and Groups

A world plan also more clearly represents what is actually "knowable" about a domain — i.e., it models the *observable* and *necessary* qualities of a domain. For example, if $\Longrightarrow (e1, e2)$ is true of a world plan, $e1$ must occur before $e2$ in every domain execution. However, if two events are observably unrelated temporally (they are unrelated by $\Longrightarrow$ in the world plan), in some world executions they may occur in a particular order, while in others they may be simultaneous. (In fact, any two events that are unrelated by $\Longrightarrow$ are *potentially* simultaneous.) In contrast, if $\rightleftharpoons (e1, e2)$ is true of a world plan, $e1$ and $e2$ must occur simultaneously in every world execution. The distinction between known relations and the executions admitted by them is especially useful when dealing with parallel domains. For example, people can usually perceive the known temporal order of specific world processes (and thereby can reason easily about them), but find it difficult to know exactly how these processes are interleaved (the actual world executions). World plans are thus a much more intuitive way of viewing the world than are world executions.

Because GEM's causal relation is nonstandard in some ways, it merits some additional clarification. As mentioned earlier, our causal relation $\rightsquigarrow$ is weaker than in other representations (for example, McDermott's [23]) in that it decouples causality from eventuality. A class of events (say *Reservations*) may hold a causal relationship to another class of events (*Seating* events), but the mere occurrence of an event of the first class does not necessarily entail that it *will inevitably* cause an event of second type. Once an event *does* cause another event, however, this relationship is represented explicitly. Of course, if an eventuality requirement is also desired, it can be specified by using a temporal logic constraint (i.e., we could say, "Every reservation must eventually cause a seating").

Our causal relation also necessarily implies an ordering in time (if $e1$ causes $e2$, it must also occur before $e2$). Therefore, we distinguish between causality and *identification* of events (for example, the identification of a light-switch-flipping event with the event of turning on the light). However, our use of the simultaneity relation $\rightleftharpoons$ enables modeling of event identification and other forms of required simultaneous activity. As in most representations using causality, GEM's causal relation is irreducible and must be induced from outside the logic.

As mentioned earlier, events in a world plan are also clustered into locations. The most basic type of location is a locus of forced sequential activity; that is, all events belonging to such a location must be totally ordered within the temporal order $\Longrightarrow$. We call these sequential locations *elements* and they are depicted in Figure 2 as circles.

Elements (and the events composing them) may also be grouped into larger regions of activity. We call these locations *groups*, depicted in Figure 2 as polygonal areas. When forms of activity logically occur at the same "location," but are not necessarily sequential, it is natural to model the location as a group consisting of many elements. For example, one might model a robot arm as a group consisting of many sequential elements. As illustrated in Figure 2, groups can be composed hierarchically or overlap.

Group structure is used by GEM to impose constraints on the causal relationships among events. In essence, the group boundaries may be considered just that – boundaries of causal access. Thus, groups A and C in Figure 2 might each be used to represent locations of activity within a robot (perhaps different segments of an arm) that can be causally related only through activity in group B (a joint). In contrast, the activity at element 7 is accessible to all locations (can be caused by activity at all locations – i.e., it is *global*). The activity at element 8 is not only accessible to activity within groups A, B, and C, but, because it is part of groups A, B, and C, it can affect or cause activity at all locations (it could perhaps represent the robot's brain). A group may also be associated with *ports* or access holes that serve as causal interfaces between the group and the events outside it.

The "state" of the world at any particular moment is modeled in GEM as the sum of past activity that has occurred. States embody not only what is true at particular moments, but also what has occurred in the past; we therefore call them *histories* or *pasts*. This view of state as an event history actually conforms quite naturally to what humans know about the world. If we allow events that model *observations*, then what can possibly be known at any particular moment (i.e. the known state of the world) will be derivable from the events that have occurred (i.e., past observations and actions). If we further categorize past activity into those sets of events occurring at, or observable from, particular sets of locations – say, those associated with the particular group modeling a robot – we can then model the "beliefs" of that robot as its localized view of past activity.

GEM's entire representational capability is built upon the basic framework we have just described. A GEM *specification* describes a particular domain by delineating the kinds of events and event structures found in the domain and then imposing constraints on the set of possible world plans (and therefore on the set of possible world executions). In the GEM specification language, constraints on actions and their interrelationships are formulated in first-order temporal logic over sequences of histories (world executions). These constraints may be scoped or applied within locations of activity. All of these capabilities are formalized and illustrated in the next two sections.

Domain Model

As stated in the preceding section, the GEM model may be viewed as two-tiered: the upper tier models the world in terms of *world plans* (sets of interrelated events, elements, and groups); the lower tier models the actual physical executions allowed by world plans. Each world plan is composed of a set of unique objects, called *events*, that are related by a temporal ordering $\Longrightarrow$, a causal relation $\rightsquigarrow$, and a simultaneity relation $\rightleftharpoons$. Events are also grouped into *elements* which may further belong to *groups* (groups may also belong to surrounding groups).

$$W \; = \; < E, EL, G, \Longrightarrow, \leadsto, \rightleftharpoons, \varepsilon >$$

- $E =$ A set of event objects
- $EL =$ A set of element objects
- $G =$ A set of group objects
- $\Longrightarrow : (E \times E)$ The temporal ordering
- $\leadsto : (E \times E)$ The causal relation
- $\rightleftharpoons : (E \times E)$ The simultaneity relation
- $\varepsilon : (E \times (EL \cup G)) \cup ((EL \cup G) \times G)$ A subset relation between events and elements or groups in which they are contained, as well as between elements and groups and the surrounding groups in which they are contained.

For now we assume that all events are atomic. Thus, each event in a world plan models an atomic event that has occurred in the world domain, each relation or ordering relationship models an actual relationship between domain events, and each element or group models a logical location of activity. Later on in this paper we shall extend this basic model to accommodate nonatomic events. Note that our assumption of event atomicity does not imply that events are totally ordered; they *may* happen simultaneously. From an intuitive standpoint, it might be useful for the reader to view each atomic event as the endpoint of some logical world action.

Every event in a world plan must be distinct; it may be viewed as a unique token. Events may be parameterized and may also be organized into types, each of which represents some class of world events. For example, *Paint(Object, Color)* could represent the class of world events, each of which paints an object a certain color. A specific instance of this type would be *paint(ladder, red)*. Lowercase tokens are used to denote specific event instances, while uppercase is used for event classes or types. A similar convention is used for parameter values and types, as well as for group and element instances and types.

As described earlier, events are related by three kinds of partial relationships, $\Longrightarrow$, $\leadsto$, and $\rightleftharpoons$. The temporal order $\Longrightarrow$ is an irreflexive, antisymmetric, transitive relationship that models event ordering in time.[6] The causal relation $\leadsto$ is irreflexive and antisymmetric, but *not* transitive – it represents "direct" causality between events. Every domain is, by default, associated with a constraint that requires causally related events to also be temporally related ($\leadsto$(e1,e2) $\supset$ $\Longrightarrow$(e1,e2)), but the reverse is not true; just because two events may be forced to occur in some sequence does not mean that they are causally related. Finally,

---

[6]Note that we make no use of explicit time values. In multiagent domains, it is actually disadvantageous to rely on such values for purposes of synchronizaton; the use of a partial temporal ordering is a much safer avenue for assessing the relative occurrences of events. However, actual time can be incorporated into GEM by associating each event with a time parameter and requiring that the temporal ordering conform to these event time stamps: $(\forall\, e1(t1),\, e2(t2))\, [\, t1 < t2 \;\supset\; \Longrightarrow (e1(t1), e2(t2))\,]$.

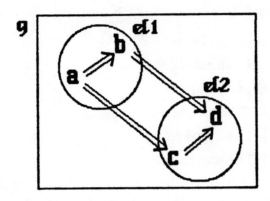

$$\Longrightarrow (a,b) \quad \Longrightarrow (a,c) \quad \Longrightarrow (b,d) \quad \Longrightarrow (c,d)$$
$$\varepsilon(a,el1) \quad \varepsilon(b,el1) \quad \varepsilon(c,el2) \quad \varepsilon(d,el2)$$
$$\varepsilon(el1,g) \quad \varepsilon(el2,g)$$

Figure 3: A World Plan

the simultaneity relation $\rightleftharpoons$ is reflexive, symmetric, and transitive, and models a *necessary* simultaneous occurrence of events.

In addition to being ordered, events are also clustered into *elements*. These elements (as well as other groups) are further clustered into *groups*. The events considered part of a group are precisely those belonging to the group's constituent elements and groups. The structure of a domain is conveyed by the set membership relation ε.

Particular domains are represented in GEM by domain specifications. Each specification will allow a set of world plans and the world executions conforming to those world plans. A specification is built by delineating locations of activity (elements and groups), stating the types of events that may occur at these locations, and, finally, imposing constraints on the possible relationships among those events. Some of these constraints are domain-specific (for example, the constraints that describe the seating rules of the restaurant domain); others apply to all domains (e.g., the total ordering constraint on events belonging to the same element). The basic form of a constraint is a first-order temporal-logic formula that is applied to the possible executions of a given world plan. The next section describes a semantics for such constraints.

World Executions: Histories and History Sequences

A world plan, as we have described it, is actually a structure that captures or represents many potential executions in the domain being modeled. For example, consider the world plan in Figure 3. It can actually be executed in three ways:

Execution 1:	1st a	2nd b	3rd c	4th d
Execution 2:	1st a	2nd c	3rd b	4th d
Execution 3:	1st a	2nd b,c	3rd d	

Note that, in the third execution, b and c occur simultaneously. Although we know that *one* of these world executions may occur, we cannot assume any one of them actually does.

The possible executions of a world plan may be viewed as linear sequences of " states," where each state is a record of past activity. We call such a state a *history* or *past*.[7] Each *history* α of a world plan W is simply a set of partially ordered events that is a *prefix* of that world plan; it therefore may be described in the same way as a world plan, i.e., for history α, we could use $< E_\alpha, EL_\alpha, G_\alpha, \Longrightarrow_\alpha, \rightsquigarrow_\alpha, \rightleftharpoons_\alpha, \varepsilon_\alpha >$, where $E_\alpha \subset E$, $EL_\alpha \subset EL$, $G_\alpha \subset G$, $\Longrightarrow_\alpha$ is a subrelation of $\Longrightarrow$, etc. Each history represents a possible point in an execution of the world plan, plus everything that has happened until then. Essentially, it is a record of past activity up to some moment in time.

For the world plan in Figure 3, there are six possible histories or pasts, consisting of the following sets of events (as well as their interrelationships):

α_0 :{} α_i :{a} α_j :{a,b} α_k :{a,c} α_m :{a,b,c} α_n :{a,b,c,d}

For instance, state α_j describes the state in which events a and b have occurred, and in which, moreover, the relations $\Longrightarrow_{\alpha_j}(a,b)$, $\varepsilon_{\alpha_j}(a, el1)$, $\varepsilon_{\alpha_j}(b, el1)$, and $\varepsilon_{\alpha_j}(el1, g)$ all hold.

Given this notion of history ("state"), the possible world executions permitted by a world plan may be described as sequences of histories – which we shall call *valid history sequences* (VHS). For each VHS, every history in the sequence (except the first) must be a superset of its predecessor. Moreover, two events may enter a given VHS in the same history only if it is possible for them to have occurred simultaneously, i.e., if there is no explicit temporal ordering relationship between them. For example, if $\Longrightarrow$(e1,e2), then e1 and e2 would have to enter a VHS in distinct histories. By the same token, if two events *must* take place simultaneously (e.g., $\rightleftharpoons$ (e1,e2)), they must always enter a given VHS in the same history. A history sequence is said to be *complete* if it starts with the empty history.

For the world plan in Figure 3, there are three possible complete VHSs — S1, S2, and S3 — corresponding to the three possible executions of the world plan given earlier:

S1:	α_0	α_i	α_j	α_m	α_n	$\equiv$	1st a	2nd b	3rd c	4th d
S2:	α_0	α_i	α_k	α_m	α_n	$\equiv$	1st a	2nd c	3rd b	4th d
S3:	α_0	α_i	α_m	α_n		$\equiv$	1st a	2nd b,c	3rd d	

Note that one way of representing the possible history sequences of a world plan might be as a branching tree. For example, we would have

$$
\begin{array}{ccccccccc}
& & & \nearrow & \alpha_j & \rightarrow & \alpha_m & \rightarrow & \alpha_n \\
\alpha_0 & \rightarrow & \alpha_i & \rightarrow & \alpha_k & \rightarrow & \alpha_m & \rightarrow & \alpha_n \\
& & & \searrow & \alpha_m & \rightarrow & \alpha_n & &
\end{array}
$$

----

[7]The reader should be warned that the term *history* has been used by others in different ways – for example, for a particular sequence of states. Here the term refers to a snapshot of the past – i.e. a record of the events that have occurred and their interrelationships.

This corresponds to the branching tree of states used by McDermott; a chronicle corresponds to a VHS [23]. However, by representing this tree as a *world plan* (i.e., the form depicted in Figure 3), information about possible world executions and observable relationships between events is conveyed in a more compact form.

Constraint Semantics

Now that we have valid history sequences, we have a framework for defining the semantics of formulas in first-order linear temporal logic. First, we consider simple nontemporal first-order formulas Q. Each such formula is composed in the standard fashion, with the usual quantifiers and connectives $(\wedge, \vee, \neg, \supset, \Longleftrightarrow, \forall, \exists, \exists!)$.[8] Event, element, and group instances, as well as event-parameter values, are used as constants, over which range event, element, group, and event-parameter variables. The predicates that may be used in these formulas are *occurred*, the infix predicates $\rightsquigarrow, \Longrightarrow, \rightleftharpoons, \varepsilon$, and equality, as well as arithmetic comparison of parameter values. The interpretation of formulas is standard. Given a history α described by $< E_\alpha, EL_\alpha, G_\alpha, \Longrightarrow_\alpha, \rightsquigarrow_\alpha, \rightleftharpoons_\alpha, \varepsilon_\alpha >$, we have

$$
\begin{aligned}
\alpha &\models occurred(e) &&\equiv\quad e \varepsilon E_\alpha \\
\alpha &\models e1 \Longrightarrow e2 &&\equiv\quad \Longrightarrow_\alpha (e1, e2) \\
\alpha &\models e1 \rightsquigarrow e2 &&\equiv\quad \rightsquigarrow_\alpha (e1, e2) \\
\alpha &\models e1 \rightleftharpoons e2 &&\equiv\quad \rightleftharpoons_\alpha (e1, e2) \\
\alpha &\models x \,\varepsilon\, y &&\equiv\quad \varepsilon_\alpha(x, y)
\end{aligned}
$$

A typical nontemporal first-order formula is the following: $(\forall\ e{:}E)[occurred(e) \supset (\exists\ f{:}F)[f \rightsquigarrow e]]$. This might be read as follows: "Every event of type E that has occurred must have been caused by an event of type F." Free variables in a formula are considered, by default, to be universally quantified.

Linear temporal operators are modal operators that apply formulas to sequences.[9] The most common temporal operators used are $\square$ (*henceforth*), $\diamondsuit$ (*eventually*), $\bigcirc$ (*next*), and $\cup$ (*weak until*). In most temporal logics they apply formulas to sequences of states [25]. GEM follows traditional formulations of linear temporal logic, but applies the modal operators to sequences of histories (i.e., to VHSs). Given a valid history sequence of the form $S = \alpha_0, \alpha_1, ...$, we use the notation $S[i]$ to denote the ith tail sequence of S – i.e., $\alpha_i, \alpha_{i+1}, ...$ Note that $S = S[0]$. Also notice that every tail sequence of a VHS is also a VHS.

---

[8] The quantifier $\exists!$ denotes existence of a unique object.

[9] This is in contrast to branching-time temporal logics, which regard time as a branching tree. In these logics, the modalities can vary according to how they are applied to the various paths through that tree. We have found linear temporal logic to be adequate and simpler to use.

We then define the semantics of temporal formulas as follows:

$$
\begin{aligned}
Henceforth\ P: \quad & S[i] \models \Box P & \equiv \quad & (\forall j \geq i)\ S[j] \models P \\
Eventually\ P: \quad & S[i] \models \Diamond P & \equiv \quad & (\exists j \geq i)\ S[j] \models P \\
Next\ P: \quad & S[i] \models \bigcirc P & \equiv \quad & S[i+1] \models P \\
P\ Until\ Q: \quad & S[i] \models P \cup Q & \equiv \quad & (\forall j \geq i)\ S[j] \models P\ \vee \\
& & & (\exists j \geq i)[\ S[j] \models Q \wedge (\forall k, i \leq k < j)\ S[k] \models P\ ]
\end{aligned}
$$

A nontemporal formula Q is true of $S[i]$ if it is true of α_i: $S[i] \models Q \equiv \alpha_i \models Q$.

To enhance the specification of properties dealing with past activity, we also introduce the backwards temporal operators $\triangle$ (*before*), $\overset{\leftarrow}{\Box}$ (*until now*), $P \overset{Q}{\underleftarrow{\quad}}$ (*Q back to P*), and $INIT$ (*initially*). Although somewhat nonstandard, they have been used elsewhere [3].

$$
\begin{aligned}
S[i] \models \triangle P & \equiv \quad S[i-1] \models P \\
S[i] \models \overset{\leftarrow}{\Box} P & \equiv \quad (\forall k, 0 \leq k \leq i)\ S[k] \models P \\
S[i] \models P \overset{Q}{\underleftarrow{\quad}} & \equiv \quad S[i] \models \overset{\leftarrow}{\Box} Q\ \vee \\
& \qquad (\exists j, 0 \leq j \leq i)[\ S[j] \models P \wedge (\forall k, j < k \leq i)\ S[k] \models Q\ ]
\end{aligned}
$$

We define $INIT\ P$ to be $\overset{\leftarrow}{\Box}\ [(\neg(\exists e)occurred(e)) \supset P]$. In other words, P is true of the empty history. At the beginning of a VHS, $S[0] \models \triangle P$ is *false* for all P.

Because we shall be creating structured specifications in which constraints are imposed on limited contexts, it is also useful to define *relativized* or scoped versions of the temporal operators. For example, what happens *next* in a particular context may be different from what happens next in the domain as a whole.

Suppose we have a VHS of form $\alpha_0....\alpha_n$. Let us assume that *context* is a set of events. We then define $\alpha_0....\alpha_n|_{context}$ to be the history sequence remaining after histories that satisfy the following formula have been removed:

$$occurred(e) \wedge \triangle \neg occurred(e) \supset \neg e\ \epsilon\ context.$$

In other words, we eliminate from $\alpha_0....\alpha_n$ all histories that are formed solely through the addition of events outside *context*. Given any valid history sequence S, we then define the scoped temporal operators as follows:

$$
\begin{aligned}
S \models \Box_{context}\ P & \equiv S|_{context} \models \Box\ P \\
S \models \Diamond_{context}\ P & \equiv S|_{context} \models \Diamond\ P \\
S \models \bigcirc_{context}\ P & \equiv S|_{context} \models \bigcirc\ P
\end{aligned}
$$

and similarly for other temporal operators.[10]

---

[10]The use of contexts may also be convenient for describing scoped or relativized forms of state. For example,

Finally, first-order temporal logic formulas may be applied to a GEM *world plan* by viewing a world plan W as the set of all its complete valid history sequences. A world plan satisfies a constraint if and only if all tail sequences of its complete valid history sequences satisfy that constraint: $W \models P \equiv (\forall \text{ complete VHS } S \text{ of } W)(\forall i \geq 0)S[i] \models P$.

For example, the world plan in Figure 3 satisfies $\square\,(occurred(d) \supset b \Longrightarrow d \wedge c \Longrightarrow d)$, but not $\square\,(occurred(c) \supset occurred(b))$ (VHS S2 and S3 do not satisfy it).[11]

Domain Specifications

In the next three sections, we demonstrate how GEM domain specifications are built by actually constructing a description of the restaurant scenario presented earlier. We begin with an overview of the general structure of the GEM specification language and describe how typical kinds of constraints are formed. In the ensuing sections, we address such issues as the specification of nonatomic actions, state description, and the frame problem. A complete specification of the restaurant scenario is given in a report based on this paper [14].

Specification Structure

The GEM specification language is a set of notational conventions for writing constraints on world plans. Viewed semantically, a specification σ is equivalent to (can be expanded into) a set of first-order temporal-logic formulas over valid history sequences. Each specification defines a class of world plans by stating explicitly

- What types of events may occur.

- How those events must be clustered into elements and how elements and groups are clustered into groups.

- What constraints exist on the relationships between events, what their parameter values are, etc.

Just as elements and groups model the structural aspects of a domain, they also serve as the structural components of our specification language. Each specification σ consists of a set of element and group declarations, along with a set of explicit constraints on the events that belong to those elements and groups. Each element is associated with a set of event types, and each group is composed of a set of elements and other subgroups. The events belonging

---

a state of the world α relative to a particular context would be a state α', where all noncontextual events have been removed. If a particular context corresponds to the events that are part of, or visible to, a particular agent, then the scoped state with respect to that agent would correspond to the agent's perspective upon, or beliefs about, the past.

[11]The temporal operator $\square$ can actually be removed from both of these constraints, because they apply to *all* tails of complete VHSs of a world plan.

to an element may be only of the designated types associated with it. The events belonging to a group are taken to be those belonging to the group's elements and subgroups. Constraints are "scoped" within the context in which they are declared; i.e., they are imposed only on those events that belong to the element or group with which they are associated. However, the temporal operators are scoped with respect to a context only if scoped temporal operators are used. Thus, if we write $\bigcirc P$, then P must be true of the next state in the *entire world execution*, not just the next state in which an event in the particular element or group occurs.

GEM also includes a mechanism for describing element and group *types*. These may be parameterized and are definable as refinements of other previously defined types. Each instance of a defined type is a unique element or group with a structure identical to that of its type description. From a semantic standpoint, the use of types and instances may be viewed as a simple text substitution facility; each type instance is shorthand for a separate but identical element or group declaration.

For example, we might describe the class of restaurant tables as follows:[12]

```
RestaurantTable (size:INTEGER) = ELEMENT TYPE
EVENTS
   Occupy(p:Party)
   Vacate(p:Party)
CONSTRAINTS

END RestaurantTable
```

A declaration of the form

```
table[1..5] = RestaurantTable(10) ELEMENT
```

would declare table[1]...table[5] to be tables of size 10. The notation table[1].size yields table[1]'s size value (in this case, 10). table[1].Occupy and table[1].Vacate refer to the class of Occupy and Vacate events belonging to table[1], respectively. The notation table[1].occupy(p) denotes a particular Occupy event instance.[13]

---

[12]This description models only two types of events that can take place at a table. Of course, if we wish a table to be associated with broader forms of activity, it could be modeled as an element with more event types or, alternatively, as a group consisting of many elements. For example, to represent the simultaneous lifting of both sides of a table, each side of a table could be modeled as an element associated with "lifting" events. We could also model these events as being performed by the agents that do the lifting. We could even do both (have lifting events at the table *and* the lifting agents) and identify the two. This form of event identification is illustrated later.

[13]A more typical event notation might be occupy(table[1].p). However, we have found dot notation to be very useful for denoting events that occur at particular elements or groups.

The structure laid out by a set of group and element declarations creates a framework associated with implicit (default) constraints. Domain-specific constraints are then added on top of this framework. Default constraints include the following (we give only an informal description of these constraints here; for a more formal description, see [18]):

- The only events, elements, and groups allowed within a valid world plan will be those delineated by the specification. We are essentially minimizing the potential structure of world plans with respect to the domain specification. Events must be clustered into elements and element/group structures must be formed as described in the specification.

- All events belonging to the same element must be totally ordered temporally:
  $(\forall$ e1.e2.elem$)$ [e1εelem $\wedge$ e2εelem $\wedge$ e1$\neq$e2 $\supset$ e1 $\Longrightarrow$ e2 $\vee$ e2 $\Longrightarrow$ e1].
  For instance, we might represent the restaurant lobby as follows:

      lobby = ELEMENT
      EVENTS
        Enter(f:Friend)
      END lobby

While lobby is not associated with any explicit constraint, its events must still be totally ordered – i.e., people may enter the lobby only one at a time.

- As stated earlier, we use groups as a way of representing limitations of causal effect. Essentially, the "walls" of a group form a boundary through which causal effect may probe outward, but not inward.[14] The one exception to this rule is the use of *ports*: "holes" in the group boundary. If an event is a port for a group g, that event can be affected by other events outside g. Let us assume that the atomic formula $port(e,g)$ is true for every event e that is a port of group g. The formal constraints on the causal relation imposed by group structure may be described as follows.

  Suppose that e1εel1 and e2εel2. Then e1 may cause e2 (e1 $\rightsquigarrow$ e2) only if:

$$access(el1, el2) \vee [port(e2, g) \wedge access(el1, g)].$$

We define $access(x, y)$ to be true if either (1) x and y belong to the same group or (2) there is some surrounding group g' such that y belongs to g' and x is contained within g' – i.e., y is "global" to x. We say that an element el or group g *belongs* to a group g' if it is explicitly declared as one of the components of group g'. We say that el (or g) is *contained* within g' if there is some hierarchical scoping of groups $g1...gn$ such that el belongs to $g1$, $g1$ belongs to $g2$, ... and gn belongs to g'. (By convention, we assume that all elements and groups modeling the world are contained within a single surrounding group.)

For example, the specification structure for the restaurant domain is shown in Figure 4 (only one party with one friend, one taxi, and one restaurant table are depicted). Notice

---

[14]This is much like the notion of scope in programming languages, except that groups may overlap as well as form hierarchies.

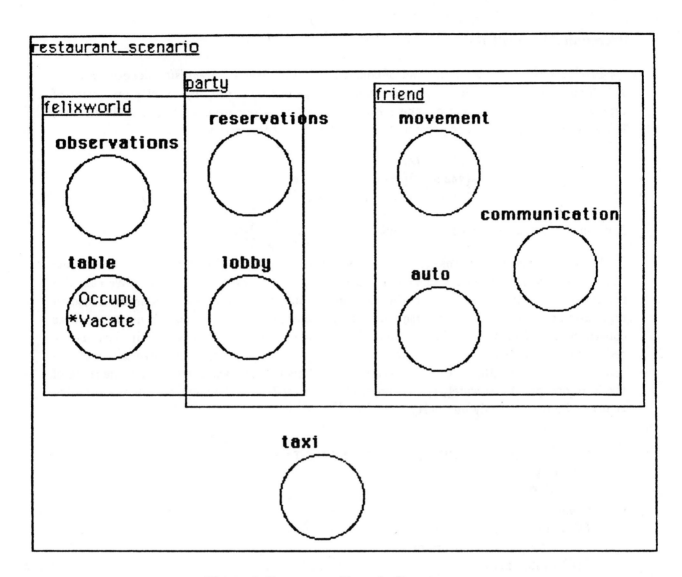

Figure 4: Restaurant Domain Structure

how the friend has access to the taxi, the reservation desk, the restaurant lobby, and also to the Vacate actions at the table (an asterisk marks port event types). However, a friend cannot affect Felix's personal observations, nor can she directly occupy a table (guests must be seated by Felix).

We now define some of the domain-specific constraints for the restaurant domain. Because many constraint forms arise repeatedly, it is useful to have abbreviations for them. We shall take some liberties in devising these abbreviations, appealing to the reader's intuition. However, all of these constraints are more rigorously defined elsewhere [18].

Prerequisite Constraints

Probably the most common kind of constraint is the *strong prerequisite*, denoted $E1 \longrightarrow E2$. This constraint requires that each event of type $E2$ be caused by exactly one event of type $E1$, and that each event of type $E1$ can cause at most one event of type $E2$. In essence, this is a one-to-one causal requirement. The definition of this constraint is as follows:

$$E1 \longrightarrow E2 \equiv$$
$$(\forall e2 : E2)(\exists! \, e1 : E1)[e1 \leadsto e2]] \wedge$$
$$(\forall e1 : E1)(\exists \text{ at most one } e2 : E2)[e1 \leadsto e2]$$

Note that many other forms of prerequisite could easily be described as well.[15]

In the next section we use a strong-prerequisite constraint to describe the one-to-one causal relationship between reservation and seating events: Reserve $\longrightarrow$ Seat. We can also use it to define the constraints of the RestaurantTable element type. Constraint 1 uses a regular-expression notation as shorthand for a more complicated pattern of strong-prerequisite constraints.[16] Each Vacate(p) event must have a one-to-one causal relationship with a preceding Occupy(p) event, and each Occupy event (except the first) must have a one-to-one causal relationship with a preceding Vacate event. This restricts the events at a table to be of the form occupy(p1)$\leadsto$vacate(p1)$\leadsto$occupy(p2)$\leadsto$vacate(p2)$\leadsto$.... Namely, a table is a resource that can be used by only one party at a time.[17]

```
RestaurantTable (size:INTEGER) = ELEMENT TYPE
EVENTS
    Occupy(p:Party)
    Vacate(p:Party)
CONSTRAINTS
1) ( Occupy(p) ⟶ Vacate(p) )*⟶
END RestaurantTable
```

Taxis and cars are other resources that are described in a similar fashion. In the following we use the element type hierarchy to first describe a Vehicle element type, and then further define taxis and personal automobiles as Vehicles.

---

[15]In two earlier reports, [16,18] I described nondeterministic forms of prerequisites in which causal requirements are imposed between an event and an undetermined member of a set of events. Combinations of prerequisites are also used to form causal forks and joins into an event.

[16]$(x)* \longrightarrow$ denotes zero or more repetitions of x separated by $\longrightarrow$. A formal semantics for prerequisite expressions is given my dissertation [18].

[17]Note that, although a party may "occupy" a table only once before it vacates, this does not preclude members of a party from leaving the table in the interim. As we shall see later, while some of the seating actions of party members are identified with "occupying" the table, not all are. Likewise not all departures from the table are identified with the party's actually vacating the table.

```
Vehicle = ELEMENT TYPE
EVENTS
   Occupy
   Drive(loc1,loc2:Location)
   Vacate
CONSTRAINTS
1) ( Occupy ⟶ Drive(loc1,loc2) ⟶ Vacate )*⟶
END Vehicle
```

```
Taxi = Vehicle ELEMENT TYPE
Auto = Vehicle ELEMENT TYPE
```

Priority, Mutual Exclusion, Eventuality

To specify Felix's seating rules, we need a way of describing synchronization properties among events. This is easily accomplished with temporal formulas. First we define the abbreviation e1 cbefore E2 (e1 is causally before the class of events E2) as follows:

$$e1 \ cbefore \ E2 \ \equiv \ occurred(e1) \wedge \neg(\exists e2 : E2)[e1 \rightsquigarrow e2]$$

This may be read, "e1 has occurred but has not yet caused an event of type $E2$."

We can now express priority and mutual-exclusion properties by using the following kinds of constraints:

- *Priority of causal transitions from e1 to events of type $E2$ over those from e3 to events of type $E4$:*

$$(e1 \ cbefore \ E2 \ \wedge \ e3 \ cbefore \ E4) \ \supset \ \Box \ [(\exists e4 : E4)e3 \rightsquigarrow e4 \supset (\exists e2 : E2)e1 \rightsquigarrow e2]$$

   In other words, if e1 is pending at $E2$ *and* e3 is pending at $E4$ at the same time, then, from that moment on, if e3 actually does cause an event e4, e1 must have already caused an event e2 (e1 must cause its corresponding event before e3 does).

- *Mutual exclusion between intervals in which e1 and e3 are causally pending:*

$$\neg(e1 \ cbefore \ E2 \wedge e3 \ cbefore \ E4)$$

If we define *tbefore* as follows:

$$e1 \ tbefore \ E2 \ \equiv \ occurred(e1) \wedge \neg(\exists e2 : E2)[e1 \Longrightarrow e2]$$

then temporal forms of mutual exclusion and priority can be expressed as well – e.g., constraints of the form $\neg(e1 \ tbefore \ E2 \wedge e3 \ tbefore \ E4)$.

Going back to the restaurant scenario, we have the following description of Felix's reservation desk:

reservations = ELEMENT
EVENTS
   Reserve(p:Party, b:Bribe)
   Seat(p:Party, t:RestaurantTable)
CONSTRAINTS
1) To be seated, a party must have a reservation. Moreover, each reservation is
   good for only one seating.
   Reserve(p,b) $\longrightarrow$ Seat(p,t)

2) Parties can be seated only at tables of the right size.
   occur(seat) $\supset$ seat.p.size = seat.t.size

3) A bigger bribe will get you seated faster.
   reserve1 cbefore Seat $\wedge$ reserve2 cbefore Seat $\wedge$ reserve1.b > reserve2.b $\supset$
   $\square$ [($\exists$ seat2:Seat) reserve2$\rightsquigarrow$seat2 $\supset$ ($\exists$ seat1:Seat) reserve1$\rightsquigarrow$seat1]

4) All other things being equal, seating is first-come-first-served.
   reserve1(p1,b1)$\Longrightarrow$reserve2(p2,b2) $\wedge$ b1=b2 $\wedge$
   present(p1) $\wedge$ present(p2) $\supset$
   $\square$ [($\exists$ seat2:Seat) reserve2$\rightsquigarrow$seat2 $\supset$ ($\exists$ seat1:Seat) reserve1$\rightsquigarrow$seat1]

5) A \$50 bribe will definitely get you seated.
   reserve.b $\geq$ \$50 $\supset$ $\diamondsuit$ ($\exists$ seat:Seat) reserve$\rightsquigarrow$seat
END reservations

Note how the temporal operator $\diamondsuit$ (eventually) is used to describe the rule for eventual seating, given a \$50 bribe. The state description **present(p)** represents states in which all members of party **p** are present in the lobby. It is defined to be true precisely at the time all the friends in party **p** have arrived in the restaurant lobby but have not yet been seated (later we introduce a prerequisite constraint that requires all the friends to enter before they can be seated).

present(p) $\equiv$ ($\forall$ f:Friend, fεp) ($\exists$ enter(f):Lobby.Enter)
         enter(f) cbefore Reservations.Seat

Simultaneity

One way of establishing relationships between the private events of restaurant guests and those of the restaurant's logical components is to form identifications between them. For example, we can identify a reservation event performed by one of the friends in a party with the reservation event at the restaurant desk. Similarly, we require that Felix's seating of a party coincides with a sitting action by each member of the party. These identifications will force all restaurant guests to comply with Felix's seating rules. Event identification (as well as other forms of required simultaneity) is accomplished by using the simultaneity relation $\rightleftharpoons$. In particular, we use the following kinds of constraints:

$$E1 \sim E2 \;\equiv\; (\forall e1 : E1)(\exists e2 : E2)[e1 \rightleftharpoons e2]$$
$$E1 \approx E2 \;\equiv\; (\forall e1 : E1)(\exists e2 : E2)[e1 \rightleftharpoons e2] \wedge (\forall e2 : E2)(\exists e1 : E1)[e1 \rightleftharpoons e2]$$

Note that $E1 \approx E2$ is equivalent to $E1 \sim E2 \wedge E2 \sim E1$. The constraint $E1 \sim E2$ identifies all events of type $E1$ with events of type $E2$, but not vice versa. For example, all of Felix's Seat events must be identified with Sit actions by members of a party, but not all Sit actions by a particular person need be identified with seating by Felix.

We begin with a preliminary description of a friend. Each friend is made up of movement events, communication events, and use of a personal automobile. Note that events at each of the elements composing a friend must be sequential, but events occurring at different elements may be simultaneous (as long as they conform to the domain constraints).[18] Thus, people can potentially talk and move at the same time.

```
Friend = GROUP TYPE (m:Movement, c:Communication, a:Auto)

Movement = ELEMENT TYPE
EVENTS
   Ride(loc1,loc2:Location)
   Walk(loc1,loc2:Location)
   Sit(tableloc:Location)
   Eat
END Movement

Communication = ELEMENT TYPE
EVENTS
   Reserve(p:Party, b:Bribe)
   OrderFood(food:Food)
END Communication
```

A party consists of a set of friends, the reservation desk, and the lobby: [19]

---

[18]Expanded versions of these specifications appear in a recent technical note [14].

[19]The notation f.c.Reserve denotes events of type Reserve occurring at the Communication element c of Friend f. SELF is used to denote the group constant associated with each particular group instance. Thus, when the Party type definition is instantiated, SELF will be replaced by each Party instance's group constant. The function setsize yields the cardinality of a set.

Party(size:INTEGER) = GROUP TYPE ({f}:SET OF Friend,reservations,lobby)
CONSTRAINTS

1) size must be the size of the set of friends.
   size = setsize({f})

2) A reservation by a friend is identified with a reservation at the desk.
   f.c.Reserve(p,b) $\approx$ reservations.Reserve(p,b)

3) All members of a party must be seated simultaneously.
   ($\forall$ f' ϵ {f}) reservations.Seat(SELF,t) $\sim$ f'.m.Sit(t)

4) In order to be seated, all members of the party must be present.
   ($\forall$ f' ϵ {f}) lobby.Enter(f') $\longrightarrow$ reservations.Seat(SELF,Table)

5) The first friend to enter the lobby must make a reservation.
   ($\forall$ f1,f2 ϵ {f}) occurred(lobby.enter1(f1)) $\wedge$
      $\neg$($\exists$ lobby.enter2(f2)) [lobby.enter2(f2)$\Longrightarrow$lobby.enter1(f1)] $\supset$
   $\Diamond$ ($\exists$ reserve1:f1.c.Reserve(SELF,b)) occurred(reserve1)
END Party

We can also now specify Felix's world, consisting of the reservation desk, the lobby, a set of tables table[1]...table[10] (these are assumed to have been instantiated), as well as Felix's personal observations or thoughts. One sort of observation that Felix may make is whether a table is empty. Later on we shall add an extra constraint that allows Felix to make such observations only if the table is indeed empty. For now, however, we assume that Felix always makes accurate observations. He will not seat a party unless *he* thinks a table is unoccupied. Note that this is different from saying that a seating may take place when the table is free.[20]

observations = ELEMENT
EVENTS
   EmptyTable(t)
END observations

felixworld = GROUP (reservations, table[1..10], lobby, observations)
            PORTS(table[i].Vacate)
CONSTRAINTS

1) Felix must observe that a table is empty before he can seat a party there.
   observations.EmptyTable(table[i]) $\longrightarrow$ reservations.Seat(Party,table[i])

2) Seating a party at a table is the same as occupying the table.
   reservations.Seat(p,table[i]) $\approx$ table[i].Occupy(p)
END felixworld

---

[20] We could have chosen to do this as well; we just wanted to illustrate the use of "observation" events.

Nonatomic Events and Hierarchical Description

We now digress from our development of the restaurant domain specification to discuss the use of nonatomic events within the GEM framework. The inclusion of such events is relatively straightforward once it is realized that a nonatomic event can be described by using two or more atomic events. In particular, we associate each nonatomic event type E with two atomic event types E' and E'', representing the initiation and termination of E. We also add an additional constraint: $E' \longrightarrow E''$ (there must be a one-to-one causal relationship between the initial event and terminal event for each nonatomic event). A nonatomic event e is *in progress* if the formula e' cbefore E" is true. Using this notation, we can describe the various possible ordering relationships between two nonatomic events a and b as follows (these are the same interval relationships used by Allen [1]):[21]

$$
\begin{array}{lll}
\text{a before b} & \equiv & \text{a}'' \Longrightarrow \text{b}' \\
\text{a equal b} & \equiv & \text{a}' \rightleftharpoons \text{b}' \wedge \text{a}'' \rightleftharpoons \text{b}'' \\
\text{a meets b} & \equiv & \text{occursnext(a}'') \supset \bigcirc \text{occursnext(b}') \\
\text{a overlaps b} & \equiv & \text{a}' \Longrightarrow \text{b}' \wedge \text{a}'' \Longrightarrow \text{b}'' \\
\text{a during b} & \equiv & \text{b}' \Longrightarrow \text{a}' \wedge \text{a}'' \Longrightarrow \text{b}'' \\
\text{a starts b} & \equiv & \text{a}' \rightleftharpoons \text{b}' \wedge \text{a}'' \Longrightarrow \text{b}'' \\
\text{a finishes b} & \equiv & \text{b}' \Longrightarrow \text{a}' \wedge \text{b}'' \rightleftharpoons \text{a}''
\end{array}
$$

The use of initial and terminal events will be the basis for our addition of nonatomic events to the GEM domain model. We extend world plans to include nonatomic events, and also add a relation κ, which models the composition of a nonatomic event – i.e., if $\kappa(e, f)$, then e is a part of nonatomic event f. Thus, we now have world plans of the form

$$
W = <E, EL, G, \Longrightarrow, \leadsto, \rightleftharpoons, \varepsilon, F, \kappa> .
$$

where F is a set of nonatomic events, and $\kappa : ((E \cup F) \times F)$ is the part-of relation between atomic (or nonatomic) events and nonatomic events. We require that, in all world plans, there should exist for each nonatomic event f two atomic events f' and f'' (its initial and terminal events) such that $\kappa(f', f)$ and $\kappa(f'', f)$. We also have the following additional constraints:

$$
\begin{array}{l}
occurred(f) \supset f' \leadsto f'' \\
e \leadsto f \supset e \leadsto f' \\
e \Longrightarrow f \supset e \Longrightarrow f' \\
f \leadsto e \supset f'' \leadsto e \\
f \Longrightarrow e \supset f'' \Longrightarrow e \\
e \rightleftharpoons f \supset e \varepsilon F \wedge f' \rightleftharpoons e' \wedge f'' \rightleftharpoons e''
\end{array}
$$

---

[21]The abbreviation occursnext(e) is defined by $\neg$ occurred(e) $\wedge \bigcirc$ occurred(e).

$$f \varepsilon el \supset f' \varepsilon el \wedge f'' \varepsilon el$$
$$f \varepsilon g \supset f' \varepsilon g \wedge f'' \varepsilon g$$

Note that a nonatomic event can be simultaneous only with another nonatomic event. We consider them to be simultaneous if their endpoints are simultaneous. This is equivalent to Allen's relation equal (see [1]).

To model a nonatomic domain action, we can now simply use two atomic events – its initial and terminal events. Usually, however, it is preferable to associate nonatomic actions with a particular form of behavior. For example, we might want to associate a nonatomic event type with particular intervals over which some formula holds.

Suppose we have a formula P that is true of particular histories.[22] By using the following constraint, we can identify a nonatomic event type E with every convex interval in which P is true:

P $\wedge$ $\triangle \neg$P $\supset$
($\exists$ e':E') justoccurred(e') $\wedge$ P $\cup$ ($\neg$ P $\wedge$ ($\exists$ e":E") [lastoccurred(e") $\wedge$ e'$\rightsquigarrow$e"])

where
justoccurred(e) $\equiv$ occurred(e) $\wedge$ $\triangle \neg$ occurred(e)
lastoccurred(e) $\equiv$ $\triangle$ justoccurred(e)

Namely, in any history in which P becomes true, there occurs some event e' and, when P is about to become false again, e'' occurs.

Alternatively, we can choose to model nonatomic actions as particular patterns of behavior. This is actually much more appealing in an event-based framework. To describe how a nonatomic event is achieved, we use an abbreviation of the following form:

F $\doteq$ E1 $\longrightarrow$... event pattern ... $\longrightarrow$En

This states that the nonatomic event type F is composed of a pattern of other event types, beginning with an atomic *initial*-event type (here E1) and ending with an atomic *terminal*-event type (En). These initial and terminal event types are then identified (by using $\sim$) with F' and F" respectively. If more than one way of achieving F is supplied, events f' and f" for each nonatomic event f may be identified with any of the possible initial-event/terminal-event pairs of event patterns that could compose f. Finally, we require that for all events ei of type E1 ... En that compose an event f, $\kappa(ei, f)$ must hold. Any arbitrary event pattern or set of constraints may be used to describe the set of events composing a nonatomic event. Such

---

[22]In other words, P is a *state description*.

nonatomic events are therefore very similar to the notion of process used by Georgeff and me [10].

We now return to the restaurant scenario. We can use a nonatomic-event description to define the different methods the friends have for traveling to the restaurant. Earlier we associated each friend with a Movement element containing an event type Ride(loc1,loc2). We can now view Ride as a nonatomic event that can be expanded in two ways:

$$\text{Ride(loc1,loc2)} \doteq \text{auto.Occupy} \longrightarrow \text{auto.Drive(loc1,loc2)} \longrightarrow \text{auto.Vacate}$$

$$\text{Ride(loc1,loc2)} \doteq \text{taxi.Occupy} \longrightarrow \text{taxi.Drive(loc1,loc2)} \longrightarrow \text{taxi.Vacate}$$

The element variables auto and taxi must be bound to the friend's personal automobile or to any taxi, respectively.

Note that, once Ride events have been expanded, they may cause interference with other events in the domain that were not observable beforehand. For example, if there is only one taxi in town and no friend wishes to use his or her personal auto, the Ride events for all friends will, after expansion, be forced into a total ordering.

Unfortunately, it seems inevitable that the expansion of *arbitrarily* defined nonatomic events will result in added complications (or even a violation of domain constraints) at the resulting lower level of description. It is precisely for these reasons that hierarchical planners such as NOAH must *recheck* domain constraints after each event expansion. This is clearly an undesirable state of affairs. It can lead to a combinatorial explosion in the cost of reasoning about and planning in such domains.

One way of getting around this problem is to limit the forms of behavior that can constitute a nonatomic event. This limited form of behavior must lack interaction with other events in the domain; it must somehow be encapsulated. Group structure, with its associated causal limitations, is a candidate for achieving this needed encapsulation.

Consider a nonatomic event type F occurring at element *elem*. Rather than assume that initial- and terminal-event types F' and F'' also belong to *elem* (as is normally done), we create a group g with port event types F' and F'' (see Figure 5). Port events of the form f' and f'' serve as an interface between the rest of the domain and the protected forms of activity within group g (which compose events of type F). We use the abbreviation

$$F \doteq g \quad E1 \longrightarrow \ldots \longrightarrow En$$

for this kind of protected or limited event expansion. All events composing an event of type F must belong to group g.

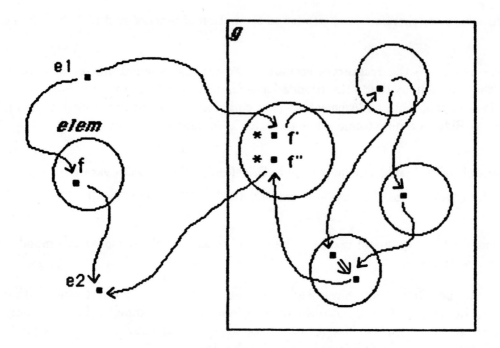

Figure 5: Protected Nonatomic-Event Expansion

We can use protected event expansion to describe the nonatomic event type OrderFood(food) in the Friend specification. To each Friend group we add a new subgroup of type FoodOrdering.

FoodOrdering = GROUP TYPE (r:Sight, t:Thought, s:Speech)

Each Sight element is assumed to have an event type Read(menu), Thought has an event type Choose(food), while Speech has an event type Utter(food). We then add to the Friend specification the following constraint (fo denotes the FoodOrdering group belonging to the particular Friend):

OrderFood(food) $\doteq fo$
fo.Sight.Read(menu) $\longrightarrow$ fo.Thought.Choose(food) $\longrightarrow$ fo.Speech.Utter(food)

Each FoodOrdering group has no ports other than those of type OrderFood' and OrderFood". Thus, if no constraints refer to events in the FoodOrdering group other than those constraints explicitly associated with FoodOrdering, and if these constraints are also localized (i.e. they utilize scoped modal operators), then interactions between a friend's food ordering activity and other domain events cannot take place.

State Description

As we have been trying to illustrate throughout this paper, many domain properties can easily be described without the use of state predicates and, in some cases, more naturally. However, such predicates are often useful for encoding or abbreviating aspects of past behavior. Thus, we might want to write a constraint of the form "P is a precondition of event e," without also stating in that constraint how P was achieved. For example, given some sort of definition for P, we could use the Precondition constraint defined below:[23]

Precondition(e,P) $\equiv$ occursnext(e) $\supset$ P ,

where
occursnext(e) $\equiv \neg$ occurred(e) $\land \bigcirc$ occurred(e)

The approach we will take to atomic state formulas once again emphasizes the duality between state-based and event-based representations; just as many state-based descriptions represent events as relations between states, so shall we represent state predicates dually as formulas pertaining to events. The truth or falsity of an atomic state formula will thus depend on the definition of its predicate.

In some cases, these defining formulas will form a complete description of the state predicate. For example, we might define a predicate TableEmpty as follows:

TableEmpty(table) $\equiv$
$\neg$ ($\exists$ occupy:table.Occupy) occurred(occupy) $\lor$
($\exists$ vacate:table.Vacate) vacate cbefore table.Occupy

If, for some history and table, there has never been a table.Occupy event *or* there is a table.Vacate event that has not yet been followed by a corresponding Occupy event (i.e, the table has been vacated but not yet reoccupied), then TableEmpty(table) is true in that history. If this formula evaluates to false, TableEmpty(table) is also false.

We shall call such formulas *complete predicate definitions*. Given the TableEmpty definition, we have the following constraint on Felix's observations:

($\forall$ empty(t):observations.EmptyTable) Precondition(empty(t),TableEmpty(t)).

Notice that no frame problem arises when complete predicate definitions are used; the atomic formula TableEmpty(table) is defined to be true for a particular table if and only if its corresponding formula is true. Consequently, there can be no question about the effects of

---

[23]To say that P is a precondition of *all* events of type E, we would write: ($\forall$ e:E) Precondition(e,P).

unrelated events on its truth value; once true (or false), TableEmpty(table) remains true (or false) for a particular value of table until its defining formula becomes false (or true).

Sometimes, however, we shall want to use weaker, *incomplete* predicate definitions – e.g., assertions of the form formula1 ⊃ P and formula2 ⊃ ¬ P. In this case, we know that, if formula1 is true, so is P. However, if formula1 is false, we *cannot* conclude ¬ P. This would be the case, however, if formula2 were true.[24] Other types of incomplete predicate definitions might include use of the temporal operators. These describe ways of attaining P for particular histories. For example, we might have formula1 ⊃ ◯ P or INIT P.

We may also want to build predicate definitions not only with behavioral (i.e., event-based) formulas, but also with formulas that utilize other state predicates. For example, we might have

¬ P ∨ Q ∨ formula1 ⊃ R

formula2 ≡ P

R ∨ formula3 ⊃ Q ,

where formula1, formula2, and formula3 are purely event-based. To find valuations for P, Q, and R in a particular history, we could use an iterative-evaluation mechanism. Behavioral portions of formulas would be evaluated first and then the formulas would be iteratively simplified wherever possible. Of course, sometimes this will not yield a truth value for all atomic formulas. For example, if formula2 and formula3 are true and formula1 is false, then we have R ∧ P ∧ Q. However, if formula1 and formula3 are false and formula2 is true, we can conclude P but nothing more about R and Q (except that $R \Longleftrightarrow Q$).

In order to apply incompletely-defined predicates to *all* histories in an execution, it is necessary to have some sort of frame rule to assert the persistence of P (or $\neg P$) despite the occurrence of other events. Such a rule is defined later, which essentially minimizes the effect of events on state formulas. In the future we hope to explore the use of circumscription in the GEM framework [21].

Note that, unlike formalisms based on STRIPS-like action descriptions, the use of predicate definitions (both complete and incomplete) suffers from none of the problems created by the possibility of simultaneous action. Since effects upon a world state are not prescribed in the context of individual event descriptions (as is normally done in many state-based frameworks), there is no confusion regarding the effect of simultaneous activity or any other form of behavior. If the formula defining the truth-value of an atomic formula P is true of a history, P itself is true of the history.

---

[24]Of course, for these definitions of P and $\neg P$ to be consistent, $\neg(formula1 \land formula2)$ must hold.

For example, suppose we have a domain with two events $e1$ and $e2$, plus the requirement that, if $e1$ and $e1$ occur simultaneously, Q will be true. Otherwise P will be true. In GEM we would simply state that $e1 \rightleftharpoons e2 \supset Q$ and $\neg\, e1 \rightleftharpoons e2 \supset P$. These effects on P and Q cannot be expressed in the classical STRIPS framework nor in in any framework that does not accommodate event simultaneity and explicit relationships between events.

Add/Delete Axioms

The add/delete lists used in STRIPS-like frameworks to define the effects of events on state can easily be cast in terms of predicate definitions. Let $\tilde{v}$, $\tilde{w}$, $\tilde{x}$, $\tilde{y}$, and $\tilde{z}$ denote tuples of free variables and/or constants. Event type $E(\tilde{x})$ denotes the class of events of type E whose parameters match $\tilde{x}$; and $P(\tilde{z})$ matches those atomic formulas formed from predicate symbol P and a tuple of variables or constants matching $\tilde{z}$.

Given this notation, for every event type $E(\tilde{x})$ that adds $R(\tilde{y})$ under precondition $P(\tilde{z})$, we use a declaration of the form $AdderE(\tilde{x}), P(\tilde{z}), R(\tilde{y}))$ and, for every event type $F(\tilde{w})$ that deletes $R(\tilde{y})$ under precondition $Q(\tilde{v})$, we have $Deleter(F(\tilde{w}), Q(\tilde{v}), R(\tilde{y}))$. If these $Adder$ and $Deleter$ declarations characterize the effects on $R(\tilde{y})$ completely, we can use the following predicate definition for $R(\tilde{y})$:[25]

$$R(\tilde{y}) \equiv$$
$$(\exists\, e{:}E(\tilde{x}))\, [\, Adder(E(\tilde{x}), P(\tilde{z}), R(\tilde{y})) \wedge occurred(e) \wedge \overset{\leftarrow}{\square}\ precondition(e, P(\tilde{z})) \wedge$$
$$\neg\, (\exists\, f{:}F(\tilde{w}))\, [\, Deleter(F(\tilde{w}), Q(\tilde{v}), R(\tilde{y})) \wedge \overset{\leftarrow}{\square}\ precondition(f, Q(\tilde{v})) \wedge e{\Longrightarrow}f\,]\,]$$

This states that $R(\tilde{y})$ is true if and only if it has been made true and has not been subsequently deleted. Of course, we might want to create other rules using $Adder$ and $Deleter$ (for example, stating that something is true *unless* deleted), or use $Adder$ and $Deleter$ to build incomplete rather than complete definitions. For example, if we stated that the above formula only *implies* $R(\tilde{y})$, it would be equivalent to the STRIPS rule (i.e. the value of $R(\tilde{y})$ would become *undefined* after a $Deleter$ event occurs). Notice that we have also assumed that all relevant $Deleter$ and $Adder$ events have been explicitly stated. Thus, we have invoked a form of closed-world assumption. Another alternative might have been to use some form of circumscription over $Adder$ and $Deleter$ specifications. While we tend to assume some form of minimization of the effects of events in this paper, we do not wish to take a particular stand on how it is done. We intend to explore this further in future work.

---

[25]Note that this formula can be expanded into a first-order formula by taking a disjunction over all possible combinations of *Adders* and *Deleters*.

The Frame Problem

In many ways, several of the difficulties often associated with the frame problem find relief in our structured event-based model. GEM's ability to structure events into elements and groups automatically imposes constraints that limit their effects upon each other. For example, events occurring within nonintersecting groups cannot causally affect one another except through explicitly-defined ports. Likewise, events occurring within the same element cannot occur simultaneously, thereby limiting the amount of reasoning necessary to determine the effects of simultaneity. Another important aspect of group/element structure is that it provides a well-defined *framework* in which nonmonotonic reasoning can take place. For example, while we may discover new qualifications on previously known preconditions for starting a car (e.g. no potato in tailpipe), groups provide a structure in which to add and use these qualifications. If we model the car as a group, we could simply add new ports to that group which allow for the newly discovered kinds of effects.

While we may effectively use group/element structure to alleviate aspects of the frame problem, there is still a need for frame rules in GEM. In particular, we still need a way to complete incompletely-defined predicates. As we have so far described, the truth or falsity of a state-based formula with respect to a particular history must be derived from predicate definitions. Given that we want to build a computational system based on our model, it will be inefficient to reevaluate these definitions for every history. This problem is somewhat alleviated by the fact that event-based domain descriptions do not often employ state predicates. Still, some sort of frame rule for carrying over atomic-formula valuations from one history to the next seems to be necessary. The same rule can also be used for extending incomplete predicate definitions to form complete predicate definitions.

We now describe a semantic frame rule of the form used by Georgeff [9]. Such semantic rules avoid the difficulties usually associated with syntactic approaches to the frame problem. For each n-ary predicate symbol P and event e in a world plan, we add a formula $\delta_P(e, \widetilde{x})$ to the world plan, where $\widetilde{x}$ is an n-tuple of free variables. This states that, for every $\widetilde{x}$, if $\delta_P(e, \widetilde{x})$ holds, then $P(\widetilde{x})$ may be affected by e. (Note the similarity between δ and the *Adder/Deleter* classifications used in the previous section.[26]) We then have the following frame rule:

$$\triangle P(\widetilde{x}) \wedge \neg(\exists e)[justoccurred(e) \wedge \delta_P(e, \widetilde{x})] \supset P(\widetilde{x}).$$

In other words, if $P(\widetilde{x})$ is true in a given history and no event occurs that can affect $P(\widetilde{x})$, then $P(\widetilde{x})$ remains true.

While the formula $\delta_P(e, \widetilde{x})$ may certainly be different for every P, e, and $\widetilde{x}$, a useful way of defining δ formulas in general is to assume that the predicate definitions in a particular

---

[26] And, as stated in the previous section, while we may wish to minimize δ, we take no stand in this paper on exactly how this is to be done.

specification are complete. In other words, we could assume that only events of types explicitly designated as affecting $P(\widetilde{x})$ can affect $P(\widetilde{x})$. Suppose we define $eventset(P(\widetilde{x}))$ to be precisely the set of events so designated. We then assert: $\delta_P(e, \widetilde{x}) \iff e \in eventset(P(\widetilde{x}))$. The frame rule then reduces to: $\triangle P(\widetilde{x}) \wedge \neg(\exists e \in eventset(P(\widetilde{x})))justoccurred(e) \supset P(\widetilde{x})$.

Conclusion

This paper has presented a structured, event-based framework for representing the properties of domains with parallel activity. We have attempted to demonstrate its utility in describing the complex properties of such domains in a coherent and semantically sound fashion. Our model, designed explicitly for describing parallel domains, has a well understood semantics (the semantics of first-order temporal logic) that has been used elsewhere in concurrency theory. By the use of first-order temporal-logic constraints on *history sequences*, complex synchronization properties based on causality, temporal ordering, and simultaneity can be expressed easily and naturally.

An important aspect of our model is its explicit representation of event location. This is used to embody the structural aspects of a domain, to scope domain constraints, and to impose constraints on the temporal ordering as well as on causal access. The model also includes the notion of nonatomic events. State-based specifications can be incorporated by describing state in terms of past behavior. We have presented a semantic frame rule for such uses of state. However, we have also stressed the fact that many properties can be expressed without resorting to state-based description.

We are currently constructing a planning system (GEMPLAN) based on the formalism described in this paper. It is being written in Prolog on a Sun 3/50. The present system is capable of generating multiagent solutions to blocks world problems [15]. Given an event-based specification for a domain, the planner builds an initial world plan that reflects a particular problem's initial and goal states. This event network is then filled in through a process of incremental constraint satisfaction.

The planning search space in GEMPLAN may be viewed as a tree with a partial plan at each node. When a node is reached, a constraint is checked and the search space branches for each of the possible plan "fixes" to satisfy that constraint. Since the kinds of constraints that must be satisfied are much broader than the simple pre- and post-conditions used by other planners, the derivation of constraint fixes is a nontrivial problem.

Highlights of the current system include a table-driven search mechanism that can be adapted to specific domains, an efficient representation of world plans, facilities for plan explanation, and nonatomic-event expansion. Initial work has also begun on delayed binding of event parameters, on accumulating constraints on unbound variables, and on dependency-directed search and backtracking.

Especially promising is current work on structuring and guiding the search in a way that makes use of the domain structure itself. The planning space is partitioned to reflect the element/group structure of the domain and search through this partitioned space is guided by the aforementioned table-driven mechanism, which is tailorable to the domain. The result is a planning architecture that can generate plans in a manner that can vary according to the specific application, ranging from loosely coordinated, distributed forms of planning (for less tightly synchronized applications) to more tightly coordinated, centralized planning (for those applications in which synchronization constraints are strong and complex).

Another useful result is an algorithm that transforms an n-robot solution into an m-robot solution where $n > m$. By using this algorithm, maximally parallel solutions are generated and then made less parallel as resource constraints warrant. We expect this development to be applicable to many other resource planning problems besides the blocks world and we shall be reporting on it at a later date.

To satisfy violated constraints, we are currently using predefined fixes for common constraint forms. The identification of a useful set of constraint forms that can be used to construct domain specifications is similar to utilizing Chapman's notion of *cognitive cliches* [4]. However, we are also working on techniqes for deriving some fixes automatically from the logical form of a constraint, at least for a subset of the logic. Synchronization techniques such as those conceived by Manna and Wolper [20] (and implemented by Stuart [30]) may eventually be applied.

Acknowledgments

I would like to thank Michael Georgeff for his critical reading of several drafts of this paper as well as many enlightening discussions on multiagent-domain representation and planning. Thanks also to David Fogelsong for his help in constructing GEMPLAN and for his constructive comments in reviewing this paper.

References

[1] Allen, J.F. "Towards a General Theory of Action and Time," *Artificial Intelligence*, Vol. 23, No. 2, pp. 123-154 (1984).

[2] Allen, J.F. and J.A.Koomen, "Planning Using a Temporal World Model," *IJCAI-83, Proceedings of the Eighth International Joint Conference on Artificial Intelligence*, Karlsruhe, West Germany, pp. 741-747 (August 1983).

[3] Barringer, H. and R. Kuiper, "Hierarchical Development of Concurrent Systems in a Temporal Logic Framework," *Proceedings of the NSF/SERC Seminar on Concurrency*, Carnegie Mellon University, Pittsburgh, Pennsylvania (July 1984).

[4] Chapman,D. "Cognitive Cliches," AI Working Paper 286, MIT Laboratory for Artificial Intelligence, Cambridge, Massachusetts (April 1986).

[5] Chapman, D. "Planning for Conjunctive Goals," Masters Thesis, Technical Report MIT-AI-TR-802, MIT Laboratory for Artificial Intelligence, Cambridge, Massachusetts (1985).

[6] Davidson, D. Essays on Actions and Events, Clarendon Press, Oxford, England (1980).

[7] Cheeseman, P. "A Representation of Time for Automatic Planning," *Proceedings of the IEEE International Conference on Robotics*, Atlanta, Georgia (March 1984).

[8] Fikes, R.E, P.E.Hart, and N.J.Nilsson, "Learning and Executing Generalized Robot Plans," *Artificial Intelligence*, 3 (4), pp. 251-288 (1972).

[9] Georgeff, M. "The Representation of Events in Multiagent Domains," *AAAI-86, Proceedings of the Fifth National Conference on Artificial Intelligence*, Philadelphia, Pennsylvania (August 1986).

[10] Georgeff, M. and A. Lansky, "Procedural Knowledge," *Proceedings of the IEEE, Special Issue on Knowledge Representation*, pp.1383-1398 (October 1986).

[11] Hewitt, C. and H.Baker Jr. "Laws for Communicating Parallel Processes," *IFIP 77*, B.Gilchrist,ed., pp. 987-992, North-Holland, Amsterdam, Holland (1977).

[12] Ladkin, P. "Comments on the Representation of Time," *in Proceedings of 1985 Workshop on Distributed Artificial Intelligence*, Sea Ranch, California, pp. 137-158 (1985).

[13] Lamport, L. "Times, Clocks, and the Ordering of Events in a Distributed System," *Communications of the ACM* Vol. 21, No. 7, pp. 558-565 (July 1978).

[14] Lansky, A.L. "A Representation of Parallel Activity Based on Events, Structure, and Causality," Technical Note 401, Artificial Intelligence Center, SRI International, Menlo Park, California (1986).

[15] Lansky, A.L. "GEMPLAN: Event-based Planning Through Temporal Logic Constraint Satisfaction," Forthcoming Working Paper, Artificial Intelligence Center, SRI International, Menlo Park, California (1987).

[16] Lansky, A.L. "Behavioral Specification and Planning for Multiagent Domains," Technical Note 360, Artificial Intelligence Center, SRI International, Menlo Park, California (1985).

[17] Lansky, A.L. "A 'Behavioral' Approach to Multiagent Domains," *in Proceedings of 1985 Workshop on Distributed Artificial Intelligence*, Sea Ranch, California, pp. 159-183 (1985).

[18] Lansky, A.L. "Specification and Analysis of Concurrency," Ph.D. Thesis, Technical Report STAN-CS-83-993, Department of Computer Science, Stanford University, Stanford, California (December 1983).

[19] Lansky, A.L. and S.S.Owicki, "GEM: A Tool for Concurrency Specification and Verification," *Proceedings of the Second Annual ACM Symposium on Principles of Distributed Computing*, pp.198-212 (August 1983).

[20] Manna, Z. and P.Wolper, "Synthesis of Communicating Processes from Temporal Logic Specifications," *ACM Transactions on Programming Languages and Systems*, 6 (1), pp.68-93 (January 1984).

[21] McCarthy, J. "Circumscription – A Form of Non-Monotonic Reasoning," *Artificial Intelligence*, Vol. 13, No. 1-2, pp.27-39 (1980).

[22] McCarthy, J. and P.Hayes, "Some Philosophical Problems from the Standpoint of Artificial Intelligence," *Machine Intelligence*, Vol.4, B.Meltzer and D.Michie, eds., pp. 463-502, American Elsevier, New York, New York (1969).

[23] McDermott, D. "A Temporal Logic for Reasoning About Processes and Plans," *Cognitive Science* 6, pp.101-155 (1982).

[24] Nilsson, N. Principles of Artificial Intelligence, Tioga Publishing Company, Palo Alto, California (1980).

[25] Owicki, S. and L.Lamport, "Proving Liveness Properties of Concurrent Programs," *ACM TOPLAS 4*, 3, pp.455-492 (July 1982).

[26] Pednault, E.P.D. "Toward a Mathematical Theory of Plan Synthesis," Ph.D. thesis, Department of Electrical Engineering, Stanford University, Stanford, California (forthcoming).

[27] Sacerdoti, E.D. A Structure for Plans and Behavior, Elsevier North-Holland, Inc., New York, New York (1977).

[28] Shoham, Y. "A Logic of Events," Working Paper, Department of Computer Science, Yale University, New Haven, Connecticut (1985).

[29] Shoham, Y. and T.Dean, "Temporal Notation and Causal Terminology," Working Paper, Department of Computer Science, Yale University, New Haven, Connecticut (1985).

[30] Stuart, C. "An Implementation of a Multi-Agent Plan Synchronizer Using a Temporal Logic Theorem Prover," *IJCAI-85, Proceedings of the Eighth International Joint Conference on Artificial Intelligence*, Los Angeles, California (August 1985).

[31] Tate, A. "Generating Project Networks," *IJCAI-77, Proceedings of the Fifth International Joint Conference on Artificial Intelligence*, Cambridge, Massachusetts, pp. 888-893 (August 1977).

[32] Vere, S.A. "Planning in Time: Windows and Durations for Activities and Goals," *IEEE Transactions on Pattern Analysis and Machine Intelligence*, Vol. PAMI-5, No.3, pp. 246-267 (May 1983).

[33] Wilkins, D. "Domain-independent Planning: Representation and Plan Generation," *Artificial Intelligence*, Vol. 22, No. 3, pp. 269-301 (April 1984).

BRANCHING REGULAR EXPRESSIONS AND MULTI-AGENT PLANS

Christopher J. Stuart
Monash University
Clayton, Victoria
AUSTRALIA

ABSTRACT

A plan synchronizer resolves potential conflicts in plans for multiple agents by restricting the possible executions with synchronization primitives. A useful technique is to describe the possible and safe executions of a plan using a temporal logic, and to use a theorem prover to generate a structure corresponding to safe possible executions. This structure guides the plan modification.

The generality of this technique depends on the expressiveness of the logic. Previous work of this kind using linear time temporal logic has required extensions to the logic allowing *regular* properties to be represented. We review such an extension which incorporates regular expression connectives corresponding directly to plan constructs.

Linear time logics are inadequate in the case where a plan has alternative executions for differing external circumstances. This case can be handled by branching time logic, but as for standard linear logic, regular properties cannot be expressed. An extension is presented analogous to the given extension of linear logic, in which plans may be considered to induce strategies for a game with the environment, rather than action sequences to be imposed upon it. The extended logic incorporates *branching regular expressions*.

SYNCHRONIZING PLANS

A plan is a specification of the activity of an agent. The execution of a plan directs activity in some purposeful manner; possibly towards the achievement of a desired goal, or the maintenance of some state of affairs, or the avoidance of catastrophic situations. In the case where several agents are acting together, plans must take into account the interactions between agents. An important part of the planning process is *conflict resolution*, in which plans are refined to prevent undesirable interaction between component parts. For multiple concurrent agents, this often corresponds to synchronizing the plans.

This paper is not concerned with issues of communication or antagonism with other independent intelligent entities. It may be assumed that agents have some common control (or can agree to constraints on their activity) as is the case in planning for robots on an automated assembly line, or choreography for a dance company. A discrete model of time is assumed throughout. The passage of time is a sequence of distinct moments, and at each moment the world is in one of some class of static situations.

As an introduction to the synchronization of plans, a quick overview is given of the multi-agent plan synchronizer produced by the author, which is in turn based on the program synchronizer of Manna and Wolper[8]. In both cases, actions take place over time and may overlap, so plans (or programs) induce sequences of moments at which actions start or end. These are called *execution* sequences. For parallel plans, the possible execution sequences are interleavings of sequences for the component sub-plans. Some of these interleavings may allow undesirable interactions. The synchronizer is given a characterization of the unsafe execution sequences – those for which conflicts may occur. It inserts synchronization primitives into the original plan which restrict the possible execution sequences to those which are safe.

Manna and Wolper assume that the synchronizer is given the safety constraints, and that the plan to be synchronized has been simplified down to a skeleton exposing the critical components for timing. Actions in this case correspond to critical regions. The multi-agent plan synchronizer is given action definitions, and automatically generates the safety constraints and simplifies the given plan. This paper is concerned only with the nature of activity for agents executing plans: this would be the basis for any subsequent work on simplifying plans and generating constraints.

Propositional temporal logic (PTL) is interpreted by sequences, and so may be used to express properties of execution sequences. If the properties of being a possible execution sequence of a given plan and of being a safe execution sequence are expressed in PTL, then a theorem prover may be used to build a structure accepting all the safe executions of the plan. Unfortunately, PTL is not sufficiently expressive to describe the possible execution sequences for plans in general. The class of PTL-definable sets is exactly the class of star-free ω-languages[12], which means that plans or programs involving loops are not generally representable.

To address this problem, Wolper has augmented PTL with automata connectives[17], which are temporal connectives corresponding to finite automata. Thus a countable set of connectives is introduced, with which any regular property of a sequence may be expressed. Equivalent expressive power may be obtained with three distinct types of automata connectives, or by allowing quantification over propositions[18].

These logics do allow those properties to be expressed which are necessary to capture general program or plan executions, and which are not expressible in PTL. Another approach was taken in the multi-agent plan synchronizer, which was to use regular expressions directly. This latter approach avoids a plethora of automata connectives, and provides a more natural way of expressing the execution sequences of a particular program, since programs are usually represented as syntactic objects resembling regular expressions, rather than as objects resembling finite automata (grammars). Using ω-regular expressions (regular expressions with infinite iteration) gives the same expressiveness as the other approaches, but since planning is usually concerned with terminating plans, we assumed that plans always terminate, and defined a temporal logic on finite sequences. The use of ω-regular expressions introduces some difficult but not insurmountable problems cf. [3]. The expressiveness of the resulting logic RPTL is not comparable with PTL, but is well suited to the types of reasoning used in synchronizing plans.

In the following summary of the notation used, X is a set, σ and υ are sequences, and A and B are sets of sequences. The same symbol will sometimes be used as a logical connective, and also to denote an operation which is used to define the semantics of that connective.

TABLE 1. Notation

ε	The empty sequence.
X^*	The set of finite sequences of elements from X.
X^ω	The set of infinite sequences of elements from X.
$|\sigma|$	The length of the sequence σ, or if σ is a set, the cardinality of the set.
σ_i	The ith element of the sequence σ. (σ_i is only defined for $1 \le i \le |\sigma|$.)
$\sigma\upsilon$	The sequence formed by concatenating σ and υ.
$O\sigma$	The sequence formed by stripping one element from the front of σ. By definition, $O\varepsilon = \varepsilon$.
AB	If A and B are sets of sequences, then AB is $\{\sigma\upsilon : \sigma \in A, \upsilon \in B\}$.
A^*	The set of sequences which may be formed by concatenating a finite number of sequences from A. This includes ε, the concatenation of no sequences.
$\sigma \parallel \upsilon$	The *interleaving* of two sequences $\sigma \parallel \upsilon$ is the *set* of sequences consisting of the elements of both sequences in order, but interspersed arbitrarily.

RPTL: A LOGIC FOR PLANS

> There's no limit to how complicated things can get, on account of one thing always leading to another.
> E.B. White (1939)

A RPTL formula is composed of elementary *propositions*, and *connectives*. The truth value of a RPTL formula is defined with respect to a *model*, which is a (possibly empty) finite sequence of *states*, together with a relation between states and propositions which are true in the given state.

States correspond to moments, following one another in time, for which propositions are given truth values. Let a non-empty set of states Z, and a non-empty set of propositions P be given, and let $R \subseteq Z \times P$ be the relation between states and propositions true in that state.

The following table provides a recursive definition of well-formed RPTL formulae, and of their truth for an arbitrary sequence $\sigma \in Z^*$. For a formula α and a sequence $\sigma \in Z^*$, we write $\sigma \models \alpha$ if α is true for that sequence. The *interpretations* of a formula are the models (sequences) for which it is true. $p \in P$ is a proposition, and α and β are formulae.

TABLE 2. RPTL semantics

formula	condition for truth for σ	intuitive meaning
p	$|\sigma| = 1$ AND $(\sigma_1, p) \in R$	There is one moment and p is true.
λ	$\sigma = \varepsilon$	empty sequence
μ	$|\sigma| = 1$	singleton sequences
$\sim\alpha$	NOT $\sigma \models \alpha$	not α
$\alpha \vee \beta$	$\sigma \models \alpha$ OR $\sigma \models \beta$	α or β
$O\alpha$	$O\sigma \models \alpha$	α next
$\alpha U \beta$	$\exists i \geq 1: \sigma_i \models \beta$ AND $\forall 1 \leq j < i: \sigma_j \models \alpha$	α until β, and β eventually occurs
$\alpha ; \beta$	$\exists \sigma_\alpha \exists \sigma_\beta : \sigma_\alpha \models \alpha$ AND $\sigma_\beta \models \beta$ AND $\sigma = \sigma_\alpha \sigma_\beta$	α then β in sequence
α^*	$\sigma \in \{\sigma' : \sigma' \models \alpha\}^*$	α repeated a finite number of times
$\alpha \| \beta$	$\exists \sigma_\alpha \exists \sigma_\beta : \sigma_\alpha \models \alpha$ AND $\sigma_\beta \models \beta$ AND $\sigma \in (\sigma_\alpha \| \sigma_\beta)$	α in parallel with β

Other connectives may be introduced in the usual way as shorthand for more complex formulae:

formula	condition	intuitive meaning
τ	$p \vee \sim p$	always true
$\alpha \Rightarrow \beta$	$\sim\alpha \vee \beta$	α implies β
$\alpha \Leftrightarrow \beta$	$(\alpha \Rightarrow \beta) \wedge (\beta \Rightarrow \alpha)$	α is equivalent to β
$\alpha \wedge \beta$	$\sim(\sim\alpha \vee \sim\beta)$	α and β
$\Diamond\alpha$	$\tau U \alpha$	eventually α
$\Box\alpha$	$\sim\Diamond\sim\alpha$	always α
$!\alpha$	$\mu \wedge \alpha$	There is one moment and α is true
$@\alpha$	$(!\alpha)\mu^* \vee (\alpha \wedge \lambda)$	α is true for the initial singleton

As usual, parentheses may be used to enforce a particular parsing, and in their absence precedence rules are used. The binding order for connectives is: $\{! @ * ; \| \sim O \Box \Diamond U \wedge \vee \Rightarrow \Leftrightarrow\}$. PTL is similar to RPTL, but without the connectives $\{\lambda \mu ! @ * ; \|\}$. Another distinction is that PTL models are infinite sequences. The connectives ! and @ correspond to two ways of regarding propositional formulae appropriate to the regular connectives $\{* ; \|\}$ and the PTL connectives {O [] ◊ U}, respectively. There is a complete and consistent axiom system for RPTL, a decision procedure, and a precise relationship with PTL[16].

PLANS AND THE LINEAR WORLD VIEW.

Since models for RPTL formulae are finite sequences, they are well suited to characterizing the terminating execution sequences of plans or programs. Sequence, selection, parallelism and iteration are common concepts often used in plans, and may be represented directly. The empty plan, which terminates immediately, corresponds to the formula λ. A singleton plan, having a single instantaneous action, corresponds to a single proposition for that action; the only execution sequence is that containing the one moment when the action is executed.

If a is a primitive action which takes a finite amount of time, then let a_B and a_E be propositions true at the moments when the action begins and ends, respectively. The RPTL formula $a_B ; a_E$ is true for execution sequences of the plan consisting only of the action a. The plan which executes actions a and b in sequence is characterized by $a_B ; a_E ; b_B ; b_E$.

Non-deterministic choice is represented by disjunction. The possible executions of a conditional selection are captured by asserting tests with sub-plans. For example, the following formula is true for the possible executions of a conditional plan: either it is raining in the initial moment, and the plan gets a raincoat; or it is not raining, and the plan gets a sun dress.

$$(@\,raining \wedge (get\_raincoat_B ; get\_raincoat_E)) \vee (@\,\sim raining \wedge (get\_sundress_B ; get\_sundress_E))$$

Similar methods apply to loops. The following formula is true for sequences of nail hammering actions which end in a state where the nail is driven home.

$$(hammer\_nail_B ; hammer\_nail_E)^* \wedge \mu^* ; nail\_flush$$

A parallel plan for multiple agents may be represented using the parallel connective. If α and β are RPTL formulae for the execution sequences of two plans, then $\alpha \| \beta$ is true for execution sequences of those plans interleaved in any order. Two propositions are introduced for each action so that actions may overlap. While parallelism does not increase the expressiveness of RPTL, it does permit parallel plans for multiple agents to be represented directly.

The PTL connectives may used to express correctness constraints. If (a, b, c) are actions which respectively (assert, retract, require) some condition, then such a constraint might be

$$[](@b_B \Rightarrow @\sim c_B \; U \; (@b_E \wedge @\sim c_B \; U \; (@a_B \wedge @\sim c_B U@a_E)))$$

This states that once the *retract* action has begun, the *require* action will not begin until the *retract* has ended, and the *assert* has begun and ended. This gives an idea of the constraints on plans which may be considered; the multi-agent plan synchronizer generates a variety of constraints for different cases. Other such constraints may define the effect of actions. For example

$$[]@\,(get\_hammer_E \Rightarrow have\_hammer)$$

states that at any moment when the action get_hammer ends, you have the hammer.

To test if a program might execute safely is to test for the satisfiability of the conjunction of RPTL formulae characterizing possible executions and safe executions. Presented with this conjunction, a theorem prover demonstrates satisfiability by finding the interpretations for the formula which are safe possible executions. In the multi-agent synchronizer, the theorem prover produces a finite automaton which accepts *all* such interpretations. This is then used to synchronize the plan by inserting synchronization primitives which restrict executions to those of the automaton. These primitives may cause parts of a plan to pause until it is safe to proceed. They may also be used as guards on selection between alternative subplans, allowing one branch or another to proceed depending on what has gone before, or ruling out one alternative entirely. We are not concerned here with the nature of these primitives, or with the insertion algorithm. The issue addressed is that of finding structures to represent constrained plans.

AN ALTERNATIVE VIEW OF PLANS.

It is a bad plan that admits of no modification.

Publilius Syrus (1st c. BC)

Now comes the moment for springing a trap which has been left for the unwary in the previous discussion. A problem arises from an overly simplistic characterization of plans. It is implicit in the RPTL and PTL synchronizers that the operation of an agent executing a plan may be characterized by a set of possible execution sequences, which may be arbitrarily reduced when the plan is synchronized. However, in general this is not so. For example, in the plan given previously for getting dressed prior to taking a walk, the synchronizer should not restrict executions to the sunny case. It is not sufficient to represent a plan as a set of possible execution sequences which may be arbitrarily restricted, since it may be crucial for the plan to have alternative executions for varying circumstances.

It would be possible to build a synchronizer which is given additional information about the permissible restrictions of a plan, but in this case a linear temporal logic theorem prover alone is not sufficient to build a structure corresponding to the synchronized plan. One of the reasons logic is used in describing and solving problems is that it allows us to be precise in our understandings, and may permit the use of general tools and techniques. Consideration of the nature of plans will lead to an alternative logic which captures the necessary concepts.

A distinction can be made between *angelic* and *demonic* non-determinism[7]. Angelic non-determinism corresponds to choices of the agent. In a plan, this means there are alternative ways to proceed towards a final goal. For example, a plan to go to the city may involve taking a bus or a train, but the choice is not critical. It is permissible, but not necessary, for a synchronizer to restrict such choices. Demonic non-determinism corresponds to choices under the control of the external environment, and which must remain in a synchronized plan. Conditional action usually corresponds to this case.

Parallel plans may exhibit both types of non-determinism. Mutual exclusion and other safety constraints may require some agent (or process) to pause under certain circumstances. This implies angelic choice of an agent to proceed, which may be constrained when a plan is synchronized. Liveness or priority constraints may require that some agents always be permitted to proceed from a given point. This implies demonic choice of the proceeding agent at execution time.

A plan operates in an incompletely specified world, and execution must cater for the unexpected or unknown. Executing a plan can be like playing a game with an environment. The plan corresponds not to a set of execution sequences, but rather to a *set of strategies* for dealing with circumstances determined by the environment, such as rain or train strikes.

Definition 1.

An *arena* is a pair (Z, A) such that Z is an arbitrary set, $A \subseteq Z^*$ is a set of finite sequences, and:

- $\varepsilon \in A$. The empty sequence is in A.

- $\forall \sigma \in A \exists z \in Z : \sigma z \in A$. Every sequence in A can be extended by some element to give another sequence in A.

◇

Consider the plan concepts introduced so far. From RPTL we have sequence, iteration, selection, parallelism, the empty plan and the singleton plan. These have been understood in terms of possible execution sequences. There is now the notion of demonic nondeterminism. All these concepts can be understood in terms of games in arenas. The players are the environment, and the agent executing the plan. They take turns to pick elements from Z, such that at every stage, the sequence of elements chosen so far is in A. The execution sequence depends on both players, and each moment involves a choice of *both* players. Thus the execution sequence is a sequence of *pairs* of moves, one from each player. Possible execution sequences are sequences of even length in the arena, divided into pairs. Propositions are given truth values for each pair.

Since the games we have defined are infinite, a special mechanism is needed to deal with terminating plans. This can be done by using a special termination state, and restricting A to contain sequences in which any occurrence of this state is followed only by more occurrences of the termination state. The empty plan corresponds to an arena where the only state used is the termination state. A plan corresponding to a single instantaneous action corresponds to an arena in which every sequence of length 2 is a pair where the proposition is true, and every longer sequence is formed by adding termination states.

Given two arenas corresponding to two plans, consider the plans which are demonic and angelic selection respectively of one of the two given plans. The arena corresponding to such a selection will be a combined arena such that the first pair of moves chosen will determine in which of the two sub-arenas play proceeds. Suppose that the environment has the first move. In this case, demonic selection is simply the case where the environment may chose the first move from either sub-arena, and the agent must chose the next move in that same arena. Angelic selection is defined by having the initial move of the environment correspond to a pair of initial moves, one from each sub-arena. The following move by the agent may be a successor to either of these initial moves, and thus defines the arena in which play continues. Both these cases have the same set of possible execution sequences, but only in the angelic case is there a strategy for the agent which limits the execution sequences to those of a particular sub-plan.

There are temporal logics appropriate to this branching view of time. These are *branching time* logics[1]. Whereas truth for linear time logical formulae is defined with respect to sequences, truth for branching time logical formulae is defined with respect to *trees*. Trees will correspond to strategies for the agent to apply in an arena; the *set* of strategies corresponding to a plan may be arbitrarily reduced in synchronization. Execution sequences correspond to branches of the tree; for a given tree (agent strategy), the final execution sequence depends on the environment.

The following notation will be used: (X, Y are sets; $R \subseteq X \times Y$, $S \subseteq X \times X$ are relations.)

TABLE 3. Notation

$X \backslash Y$	Set difference.
2^X	The set of subsets of X (the power set) .
R^{-1}	The inverse relation to R: $\{(y, x): (x, y) \in R\}$.
$R(x)$	For $x \in X$, $R(x)$ is the set $\{y: (x, y) \in R\}$. R is *total* if $\forall x \in X$ $\exists y \in Y: (x, y) \in R$. R is a *function* if $\forall x \in X: |R(x)| = 1$, and is a *partial function* if $\forall x \in X: |R(x)| \leq 1$. As usual, if R is known to be a function, $R(x)$ is the unique y such that $(x, y) \in R$.
$R(W)$	For $W \subseteq X$, the set $\{y: \exists x \in W: (x, y) \in R\}$.
$R^\bullet$	Elements not mapped by R: $\{x \in X: R(x) = \varnothing\}$
S^c	The reflexive transitive closure of S.
$S^\rightarrow$	The set of S-branches is $S^\rightarrow = \{\sigma \in X^\omega \cup (X^* S^\bullet): \forall 1 \leq i < |\sigma| : (\sigma_i, \sigma_{i+1}) \in S\}$. These are paths in the graph defined by S which are infinite, or cannot be extended.
$S^\rightarrow(x)$	For $x \in X$, $S^\rightarrow(x) = \{\sigma \in S^\rightarrow: \sigma_1 = x\}$.
$Inf(\sigma)$	If $\sigma \in X^\omega$, then $Inf(\sigma) \subseteq X$ is the set $\{x: x = \sigma_i$ for infinitely many $i\}$.

SYNCHRONIZING BRANCHING TIME PLANS.

We review here a simplification of the "Computation Tree Logic" (CTL), which is used in a program synchronizer written by Emerson and Clarke[4]. This simplification is a straight forward extension of the logic of "Unified Branching Time" (UB)[1] with *until* connectives, and uses connectives resembling those of PTL but which also contain an implicit quantifier.

The full CTL used by Emerson and Clarke is a little more complex: it has distinct next-time connectives for each agent, which makes it possible to express parallel plans. The structure for interpreting plans is also more complex. However, all the benefit of these extra connectives can also be obtained by adding an extra proposition for each agent, and using these propositions to identify actions taken by particular agents. Thus the added complexity will be overlooked, and throughout this paper, CTL will be taken to mean the simplified case described here. In all that follows, P is assumed to be a fixed non-empty set of propositions.

Definition 2.

A *forest* is a triple (Z, S, R), where

- Z is a set of states, which may also be called *moments*.

- $S \subseteq Z \times Z$ is the possible next state, or *successor*, relation. S must be total and acyclic, and S^{-1} must define a partial function. i.e. S defines an infinite tree on the *descendants* of any moment, which are given by S^c, the reflexive transitive closure of S.

- $R \subseteq Z \times P$ is relation between moments and propositions true at that moment.

A *tree* is a 4-tuple (Z, S, R, z_r), such that (Z, S, R) is a forest, and $z_r \in Z$ is a distinguished state called the *root* of the tree.

<>

Truth values for CTL formulae are defined for trees; or equivalently for moments in a forest. The references above use related equivalent models, with no change to the theory of CTL. The following table gives a recursive definition of truth for CTL formulae in the forest (Z, S, R). p is a proposition, and α and β are CTL formula. For a formula α, we write $z \models \alpha$ if α is true for the tree (Z, S, R, z).

TABLE 4. CTL semantics

formula	truth at moment z_r		intuition
p	true if $(z_r, p) \in R$		p is true at the moment
$\sim\alpha$	NOT $z_r \models \alpha$		not α
$\alpha \vee \beta$	$z_r \models \alpha$ OR $z_r \models \beta$		α or β
$\exists O \alpha$	$\exists z \in S(z_r): z \models \alpha$		possibly α next
$\forall O \alpha$	$\forall z \in S(z_r): z \models \alpha$		necessarily α next
$\alpha \exists U \beta$	$\exists \rho \in S^{\rightarrow}(z_r): \exists i \geq 1: \rho_i \models \beta$ AND $\forall 1 \leq j < i: \rho_j \models \alpha$		possibly α until β
$\alpha \forall U \beta$	$\forall \rho \in S^{\rightarrow}(z_r): \exists i \geq 1: \rho_i \models \beta$ AND $\forall 1 \leq j < i: \rho_j \models \alpha$		necessarily α until β
$\forall \Diamond \alpha$	$\tau \forall U \alpha$	(by substitution)	necessarily eventually α
$\exists \Diamond \alpha$	$\tau \exists U \alpha$	"	possibly eventually α
$\forall \Box \alpha$	$\sim \exists \Diamond \sim \alpha$	"	necessarily always α
$\exists \Box \alpha$	$\sim \forall \Diamond \sim \alpha$	"	possibly always α

Propositional connectives $\{\tau \wedge \Rightarrow \Leftrightarrow\}$ are defined by substitution as for RPTL.

Emerson and Clarke have written a program synchronizer based on CTL[4]. The operation of this synchronizer is similar to that of the multi-agent plan synchronizer mentioned earlier: a theorem prover demonstrates satisfiability by generating a structure accepting interpretations of a given formula.

The CTL theorem prover constructs an AND/OR graph from which interpretations of a given formula may be found. OR-nodes are labeled with arbitrary CTL-formulae: the initial OR-node is labeled with the given formula. For each OR-node, successors are found by converting the corresponding formula into a disjunctive normal form of *elementary* formulae. Elementary formulae are either atomic, or have one of the next-time connectives as the main connective. The successors of an OR-node are AND-nodes labeled with the conjunctions so obtained. Successors of AND-nodes are conjunctions of "next" cases. For every elementary formula of the form $\exists O\alpha$ (or for $\exists O\tau$ if no such α exists), take the conjunction of α with all the formulae β for which there is an elementary formula $\forall O\beta$, and make the OR-node corresponding to that conjunction a successor.

Trees satisfying the original formula are obtained from this graph, but some special attention must be paid to *eventuality* restrictions. Every tree node corresponds to an OR-node/AND-node pair. The algorithm associates with each OR-node a *set* of formulae which are consequences of the formula labeling the node. For any tree node, the sub-tree rooted at that node must satisfy the label of the corresponding OR-node, and hence all the formulae of the OR-node. Trees must be constructed so that nodes satisfying $\alpha \forall U \beta$ have a descendant satisfying β on every branch from that node; and nodes satisfying $\alpha \exists U \beta$ have a descendant satisfying β on some branch from that node. The details are given in[4].

If there is a tree satisfying the original formula, then such a tree can be obtained from the graph: however the algorithm used does not produce a graph from which every such tree is obtained, and hence the graph does not fully characterize the formula. It would be possible to extend this theorem prover to define a graph accepting all and only the trees satisfying the formula: but this is not necessary to demonstrate satisfiability.

This graph defines an arena: arena states are the AND/OR nodes, and the arena sequences are finite paths though the graph. At an OR (AND) node, the next state is chosen by the agent (environment). This arena limits the environment's initial choice to a particular root OR-node of the graph. A *strategy* for an agent in this arena is a function which specifies which AND-node is chosen for a given finite path through the graph ending at an OR-node. The strategies correspond to the trees obtained from the graph.

Note that synchronization does not correspond to choosing a strategy. Synchronization *restricts* the allowed strategies so that correctness constraints are satisfied. It is often useful to separate the functional component of a plan or program from the timing component. Temporal logic provides a natural way of specifying the timing component, and the synchronizer enables new scheduling algorithms to be implemented very easily.

Unfortunately, CTL as presented, and as used in Emerson and Clarke's synchronizer, suffers from a limitation analogous to that of standard linear time logics: regular plans – the functional component – are not generally representable. Emerson and Sistla[5] have shown that CTL may be augmented with existential quantification over propositions to obtain the logic EQCTL. As in the linear case, this is sufficiently expressive, but does not relate to the structure of plans as directly as regular expressions.

Just as linear time logics may be extended with regular expressions to represent naturally the execution sequences induced by plans, it is possible to extend branching time logic in a similar way.

BRANCHING REGULAR EXPRESSIONS

There is a generalized notion of regular expression which extends CTL in the same way that standard regular expressions extend PTL. We present formulae and interpretations for "Regular Branching Logic" (RBL), which incorporates branching regular expressions, and we relate these to plans and their execution.

Normal regular expressions have a very close relationship with finite automata, which are the structures produced by the linear time theorem prover. Automata accepting infinite trees rather than sequences were introduced by Rabin[13], and the relationship of these to branching time logics has been explored[5]. The relationship is not direct, since the usual definition of tree automata is for trees with a fixed number of successors for all nodes in the tree, and with an order defined on the successors of any given node.

The following section provides an automaton definition based on the notion of an AND/OR graph, which is directly suited to representing formulae of CTL, EQCTL, and RBL. These *branching automata* accept trees corresponding to the interpretations of a particular plan. In order to represent terminating plans, we require a notion of plan termination: thus trees will have special termination states with no successors.

Definition 3.

The definitions of *forest* and *tree* given above are superseded. A triple (Z, S, R) is a *forest* if it satisfies the previous definition in every respect except that S need not be total. The states with no successors (written $S^{\bullet}$) are called *termination* states. Only non-terminal states will be referred to as *moments*. R need not be defined on $S^{\bullet}$.

A 4-tuple (Z, S, R, z_r) is a *tree* if (Z, S, R) is a forest, and $S(z_r) \neq \emptyset$. That is, the root cannot be a termination state.

<>

RBL formulae will be given truth values with respect to trees. The termination states do *not* correspond to moments at which termination occurs, or indeed to any moment at all. If $z \in S^{\bullet}$, then z cannot be the root of a tree, and $z \models \alpha$ is undefined. Termination states mark their *parent* as a moment at which the environment may choose to define no further moments. Termination is not an event, but is the condition of having no more events.

RBL uses the CTL connectives, but the definitions take account of the existence of termination states. The following table gives truth values for RBL formulae. Note that in the definition of the until connectives, if a terminating branch is used, β is satisfied at a node strictly before the termination state. Also, the universal next time connective $\forall\bigcirc$ does not imply that a "next" moment actually exists. The CTL connectives defined by substitution are unchanged.

TABLE 5. RBL semantics

formulae	condition for truth in (Z, S, R, z_r)		intuition
p	true if $(z_r, p) \in R$		p true initially
$\sim\alpha$	NOT $z_r \models \alpha$		not α
$\alpha \vee \beta$	$z_r \models \alpha$ OR $z_r \models \beta$		α or β
$\exists\bigcirc\alpha$	$\exists z \in S(z_r)\backslash S^\bullet: z \models \alpha$		possibly α next
$\forall\bigcirc\alpha$	$\forall z \in S(z_r)\backslash S^\bullet: z \models \alpha$		necessarily α next
$\alpha\exists U\beta$	$\exists\rho \in S^\rightarrow(z_r): \exists 1 \le i < |\rho|: \rho_i \models \beta$ AND $\forall 1 \le j < i: \rho_j \models \alpha$		possibly α until β
$\alpha\forall U\beta$	$\forall\rho \in S^\rightarrow(z_r): \exists 1 \le i < |\rho|: \rho_i \models \beta$ AND $\forall 1 \le j < i: \rho_j \models \alpha$		necessarily α until β
λ	$S(z_r) \subseteq S^\bullet$		must terminate
μ	$\forall z \in S(z_r): z \notin S^\bullet$ AND $z \models \lambda$		tree is of depth 1
$\alpha\otimes\beta$	$\exists Z_\alpha \subseteq S(z_r)\ \exists Z_\beta \subseteq S(z_r):$	$S(z_r) = Z_\alpha \cup Z_\beta$	demonic selection
	AND	$(Z, \{(z, z') \in S : z \ne z_r \text{ OR } z' \subseteq Z_\alpha\}, R, z_r) \models \alpha$	
	AND	$(Z, \{(z, z') \in S : z \ne z_r \text{ OR } z' \subseteq Z_\beta\}, R, z_r) \models \beta$	

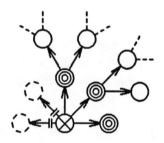

The intuition for the definition of $\otimes$ is that Z_α defines a *cut* of the tree; if all parts of the tree not descending from Z_α are pruned, then what remains satisfies α. Note that for what remains to satisfy anything, $Z_\alpha \ne \emptyset$. The same is true for Z_β. The two subtrees together make up the whole of the original, and may overlap. The environment can chose a path in either sub-tree.

$\otimes$ root, satisfies α with indicated cuts

$\circledcirc$ in Z_α

FIGURE 1. Demonic selection

Truth values for the remaining RBL connectives in a given tree depend on the existence of an *equivalent* tree satisfying some condition which might not be preserved under the mapping which defines equivalence. The intuition for equivalence is that equivalent trees have the same *behaviour*: RBL is intended to describe the observable behaviour of agents, rather than the internal workings which give rise to behaviour. For example, since branching within a tree represents alternatives which are taken depending on choices of the environment, it follows that duplication of subtrees provides an additional choice for the environment which makes no difference to the agent. Thus duplicating subtrees within a given tree gives rise to an equivalent tree. The notions of behaviour and observational equivalence are explored in detail by Milner[11] for a structure related to, but distinct from, trees as defined here.

Definition 4.

The trees (Z, S, R, z_r) and (Z', S', R', z'_r) are *equivalent* if there is a relation $E \subseteq S^c(z_r) \times S'^c(z'_r)$ between the descendants of the respective roots such that

- $(z_r, z'_r) \in E$

- $\forall (z, z') \in E: \quad R(z) = R'(z') \text{ AND } S'(E(z)) = E(S(z)) \text{ AND } S(E^{-1}(z')) = E^{-1}(S'(z'))$

The first tree *reduces* to the second if this relation is a function.

◇

The following table gives semantics for RBL connectives which depend on the existence of *frontiers*. This concept will not be formally defined: intuitively it represents the moment when execution of one subplan ends, and another begins. Frontiers are not preserved under the equivalence mapping, and so we introduce the notion of *direct acceptance*. A formula is *true* for a given tree if that tree is *equivalent* to some other tree which is *directly accepted* by the formula.

TABLE 6. Further RBL semantics

formula	condition for direct acceptance of (Z, S, R, z_r)		intuition
$\alpha; \beta$	$\exists Z_\alpha \subseteq Z \setminus \{z_r\}:$	$S^\bullet \subseteq S^c(Z_\alpha)$	α then β in sequence
	AND	$\forall z \in Z_\alpha: S^c(z) \cap Z_\alpha = \{z\}$	
	AND	$(Z, \{(z, z') \in S : z \notin Z_\alpha\}, R, z_r) \models \alpha$	
	AND	$\forall z \in S^{-1}(Z_\alpha): (Z, \{(z', z'') \in S : z' \neq z \text{ OR } z'' \in Z_\alpha\}, R, z) \models \beta$	
α^ω	$\exists \{Z_i\}_{i=1}^\infty:$	$Z_1 = S(z_r)$	α repeated
	AND	$\forall i \geq 1: Z_{i+1} \subseteq S^c(Z_i)$	
	AND	$\forall i \geq 1 \, \forall z \in Z_i : S^c(z) \cap Z_i = \{z\}$	
	AND	$S^\bullet = \bigcap_{i=1}^\infty Z_i$	
	AND	$\forall i \geq 1 \, \forall z \in S^{-1}(Z_i):$ $(Z, \{(z', z'') \in S : z' \notin Z_{i+1} \text{ AND } z'' \in S^c(Z_i)\}, R, z) \models \alpha$	

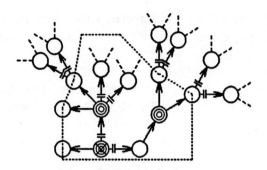

Z_α defines a *frontier*. No path terminates before reaching the frontier, or meets the frontier twice. An infinite path might not reach the frontier. If all arcs going beyond the frontier are cut, the remaining sub-tree satisfies α. For any node just inside the frontier, prune arcs not reaching the frontier to get a subtree rooted at that node satisfying β.

⊗ root, satisfies α if nodes outside the frontier are pruned

◎ in $S^{-1}(Z_\alpha)$, satisfies β if nodes inside the frontier are pruned

⊘ in Z_α, the frontier

FIGURE 2. Sequence

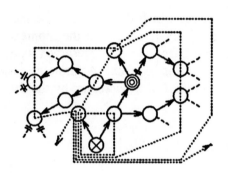

Z_i is a sequence of concentric frontiers. Every path cuts the first frontier in its first step, and other frontiers in turn. A terminating path cuts all frontiers. For any node just inside a frontier, prune all arcs not reaching the frontier, and all nodes beyond the next frontier. The resulting subtree satisfies α, and (except for the root) is *between* frontiers.

◎ satisfies α with indicated cuts

FIGURE 3. Iteration

The only remaining connective is for parallelism. Consider what parallelism means in the context of branching time. The execution of plans in parallel corresponds to the concurrent activity of distinct agents. Thus the environment of a particular agent includes the activity of all the other agents. We use the interleaving model of concurrency, and so every moment is reached by a step of exactly one sub-plan.

A given strategy for parallel plan execution may include restrictions on the execution order of the sub-plans. Thus at any moment, a strategy specifies some non-empty set of sub-plans which may proceed. These sub-plans are said to be *enabled*. The final choice of the particular sub-plan to proceed at a given moment is demonic. This sub-plan is said to be *selected*. Thus there is angelic choice, corresponding to choosing a strategy for a parallel plan, amongst all possible degrees of demonic choice of execution order of the component plans.

The behaviour of a *synchronized* parallel plan may be described with the conjunction of a parallel RBL formula and some other RBL formula expressing the additional constraints imposed by the synchronization primitives. The possible strategies satisfy *both* formulae.

Angelic choice *within* a sub-plan is also resolved by a parallel strategy. That choice may depend on the execution *sequences* of other agents, since execution sequences correspond to branches through the tree representing the parallel strategy, and different nodes in the tree define different sub-trees, which correspond to different resolutions of angelic choice. The concepts of strategy and choice are formalized in the next section. A tree satisfying a particular sub-plan may be extracted from a parallel tree by specifying the execution sequences of the other sub-plans.

The interested reader may compare this mapping from states to sub-plans with the parallel models used by Emerson and Clarke in the CTL program synchronizer[4], where parallelism is built into the underlying model by giving an explicit partitioning the successor relation on a tree as part of the CTL model.

The situation here is complicated by the possibility of termination: if a *selected* sub-plan terminates, then the subsequent moment must be due to another sub-plan, since termination states do not correspond to moments. In general, a moment in the parallel tree will correspond to termination states for any number of sub-plans, and an execution step of exactly one sub-plan.

The following diagram shows a *decomposition* of a tree corresponding to a parallel plan with two sub-plans. Each node may correspond to states for either sub-plan, and if a node corresponds to both, then it must be a termination state for at least one of them. Given a decomposition, many different trees can be *extracted* for a given sub-plan, depending on execution sequences of the other sub-plan. Four such extractions are shown for sub-plan 1. These concepts will be defined formally, and then informally justified with reference to the diagram.

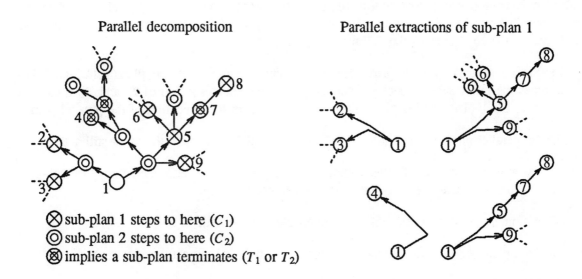

Parallel decomposition   Parallel extractions of sub-plan 1

$\otimes$ sub-plan 1 steps to here (C_1)
$\odot$ sub-plan 2 steps to here (C_2)
$\otimes$ implies a sub-plan terminates (T_1 or T_2)

FIGURE 4. Parallelism

Definition 5.

A *parallel decomposition* of a tree (Z, S, R, z_r) is a pair of sets of states $(Z_1, Z_2) \in 2^Z \times 2^Z$ such that $Z_1 \cup Z_2 = S^c(z_r) \setminus \{z_r\}$, and the following conditions hold:

Let $\quad C_1 = Z_1 \backslash Z_2 \qquad\qquad\qquad\qquad C_2 = Z_2 \backslash Z_1$

$\qquad T_1 = Z_1 \cap Z_2 \cap \{z : S^c(z) \subseteq \{z\} \cup C_2\} \quad T_2 = Z_1 \cap Z_2 \cap \{z : S^c(z) \subseteq \{z\} \cup C_1\}$

1) $T_1 \cup T_2 = Z_1 \cap Z_2$

2) $S^\bullet \subseteq S^c(T_1 \cup T_2)$

3) $\forall z \in Z : (S^c(z) \subseteq C_1 \Rightarrow z \in S^c(T_2))$ AND $(S^c(z) \subseteq C_2 \Rightarrow z \in S^c(T_1))$

4) $\forall z \in \{z : S(z) \cap (Z_1 \backslash T_2) \neq \emptyset$ AND $S(z) \cap (Z_2 \backslash T_1) \neq \emptyset\}:$

4.1) $\qquad\qquad S^\bullet \cap S(z) \neq \emptyset$ IFF $(T_1 \cap S(z) \neq \emptyset$ AND $T_2 \cap S(z) \neq \emptyset)$

4.2)   AND   IF $T_2 \cap S(z) \neq \emptyset$ THEN $C_1 \cap S(z) \neq \emptyset$ IFF $(T_2 \backslash T_1) \cap S(z) \neq \emptyset$

4.3)   AND   IF $T_1 \cap S(z) \neq \emptyset$ THEN $C_2 \cap S(z) \neq \emptyset$ IFF $(T_1 \backslash T_2) \cap S(z) \neq \emptyset$

◇

The tree Z is an interpretation of a parallel plan containing two sub-plans. Z_1 (Z_2) is the set of states corresponding to sub-plan 1 (sub-plan 2). The states in C_1 correspond to non-terminating steps of sub-plan 1, made when it was selected to proceed by the environment. The states in T_1 correspond to moments when sub-plan 1 was selected to proceed and it terminated, so that sub-plan 2 advanced a step. States in $T_1 \cap T_2$ correspond to the case where both plans terminate together.

In the diagram of parallel decomposition, the *parent* of node 4 is a point at which sub-plan 1 is *enabled*, but the angelic choice for sub-plan 1 at that point is such that it will only terminate. The angelic choice for sub-plan 2 at that point is such that it will either terminate (node 4) or make a step (sibling of node 4), depending on the environment. However, sub-plan 2 is not actually enabled. If it had been enabled, then there would be a successor corresponding to the selection of sub-plan 2, without sub-plan 1 terminating. On the other hand, at node 5, both sub-plans are enabled, both may make a non-terminating step, and only sub-plan 2 may terminate. The intuition behind each of the conditions in the definition is given.

1)   Simultaneous steps in both plans can only occur when one of the plans terminate. This enforces the interleaving model of concurrency. From the definition of T_1 and T_2, it follows that after a sub-plan terminates, it takes no further part in the execution of the parallel plan.

2)   For the parallel plan to terminate, one sub-plan must terminate with the other still active.

3)   At any moment when all further moments correspond to one sub-plan, the other sub-plan must have terminated. i.e. A strategy may not force starvation.

4) z is a moment at which both sub-plans are enabled to proceed.

4.1)   Both sub-plans may terminate when selected if and only if they can terminate together.

4.2)   If sub-plan 2 can terminate, then sub-plan 1 can be selected to make a non-terminating step if and only if it can make a non-terminating step as a result of sub-plan 2 terminating.

4.3) This is a dual to (4.2) for sub-plan 2. These three conditions effectively prevent an enabled agent from waiting to see whether another agent terminates before making an angelic choice. If an agent is enabled, it must make an angelic choice which may or may not permit either termination or continuation; and it is up to the environment to determine which occurs.

Definition 6.

A *parallel extraction* of a tree (Z, S, R, z_r) is a tree (Z', S', R', z'_r) and a triple (Z_1, Z_2, f) such that (Z_1, Z_2) is a parallel decomposition of the tree Z, and $f : Z' \to Z$ is a mapping between the nodes of the trees such that:

Let C_1, C_2, T_1, T_2 be as given in the previous definition.
              $S_2 = S \cap (Z \times C_2)$ (the non-terminating steps for 2 without 1 terminating)

1) $f(z'_r) = z_r$
2) $\forall z' \in Z' : R'(z') = R(f(z'))$
3) $\forall z' \in Z' : \quad z' \in S'^\bullet \text{ IFF } f(z') \in T_1 \cup S^\bullet$
4) $\forall z' \in Z' \ \exists z \in S_2^\natural(f(z')):$
4.1) $f(S'(z')) \subseteq S(z) \cap Z_1$
4.2)   AND   (EITHER $(S(z) \cap T_2 \neq \varnothing$ AND $S(z) \cap T_2 \subseteq f(S'(z'))$)
                    OR $(S(z) \cap (C_1 \cup T_1) \neq \varnothing$ AND $S(z) \cap (C_1 \cup T_1) \subseteq f(S'(z'))$))

$\diamond$

The intuition for this definition is that Z' is a tree extracted from a parallel tree, for a component sub-plan. States in the extracted tree map to states in the parallel tree corresponding to that sub-plan. In the diagram above, four extraction mappings are given by the numbers in the nodes. Note that several nodes may map to a single node in the parallel tree. In the upper right hand mapping, two nodes map to node 6 of the parallel tree.

1)   The root of the extracted tree maps to the root of the parallel tree.

2)   Propositional interpretations are preserved in the mapping.

3)   A node in the extracted tree is terminal if and only if it maps to a state in which sub-plan 1 terminates when selected, or to a terminal state in the parallel tree.

4)   For every state in the extracted tree, there is a path in the parallel tree of non-terminating steps from sub-plan 2, to a moment at which steps for sub-plan 1 are extracted. If the path contains only one node, then $z = f(z')$.

4.1) The successors of a state in the extracted tree correspond to steps of sub-plan 1 in the parallel tree from the moment given in (4).

4.2) The successors of a state in the extracted tree correspond to a set of states in the parallel tree which includes either all the steps taken as a result of sub-plan 1 being selected (given that this is possible), or all the steps taken as a result of sub-plan 2 terminating when selected (given that this is possible). Steps for both cases may be permitted, as is the case at node 5 in the upper right hand extraction of the diagram.

Semantics for the parallelism connective follow directly from the concepts of parallel decomposition and parallel extraction. As for sequence and iteration, a structure is imposed on a parallel tree which is not preserved under the tree equivalence mapping. A formula is true for a given tree if and only if there is an equivalent tree which is directly accepted.

This definition incorporates quantification over all trees. This is not formally a set. It is possible to give an alternative definition using a standard quantifier over a restricted class of trees which can be treated as a set, but the definition given here is more directly related to intuitive understanding.

TABLE 7. Condition for direct acceptance of (Z, S, R, z_r) by $\alpha \parallel \beta$

$\exists (Z_\alpha, Z_\beta)$, a parallel decomposition, such that for any tree (Z', S', R', z'_r)

$\forall f : Z' \to Z :$ IF (Z_α, Z_β, f) is a parallel extraction THEN $Z' \models \alpha$

       AND   IF (Z_β, Z_α, f) is a parallel extraction THEN $Z' \models \beta$

Lemma 1.

Two finitely generated trees satisfy all the same RBL (CTL) formulae if and only if they are equivalent.

Proof.

All proofs are shortened outlines only. For the IF case, the finitely generated assumption is not necessary, and follows from simple induction on the length of formulae.

For the ONLY IF case, assume that two given trees accept the same sets of RBL formulae. Prove that every successor of the root of one tree must satisfy the same set of formulae as some successor of the root of the other tree. For each node, there is a set of formulae which are true at that node. Associate with each node the sequence of sets of formulae corresponding to the path from the root to that node. The equivalence mapping relates nodes which give the same sequence. For this purpose, note that termination nodes accept no formulae.

                                            ∎

BRANCHING AUTOMATA AND PLAN EXECUTION.

A difficulty with the use of trees to interpret plans is that there is no possibility of representing demonic choice in the initial moment. Any tree gives a precise specification of the initial moment. Initial demonic choice could be given by using sets of disjoint trees (a *grove*?) to define the truth of formulae, or equivalently by associating propositions with all moments except the initial root moment, since a grove is a tree with the root removed. The interpretations of plans will be trees with an initial *dummy* moment having an unrestricted propositional interpretation, and execution sequences will correspond to branches with this initial moment removed.

A plan having a single action and a dummy root node corresponds to the formula $\mu;(\alpha \wedge \lambda)$. For convenience, this is defined by substitution to be $!\alpha$. This connective will normally only be applied to propositional expressions, and is used to represent primitive actions in plans. *Branching regular expressions* are RBL formulae made up of sub-formulae of the form $!p$ for some purely proposition propositional formula p, combined with the connectives $\{\lambda \vee \otimes \omega ; \| \}$. These connectives "maintain" the dummy root node, and so branching regular expressions can be used to represent plans with potential initial demonic choice, and still permit the CTL connectives to be defined in terms of trees, which is more useful for representing safety constraints. For example, the plan for getting dressed prior to taking a walk in any weather now becomes

$$!get\_raincoat_B ; !get\_raincoat_E \otimes !get\_sundress_B ; !get\_sundress_E$$

An extra proposition about raining could be added, but there is no need; the semantics for RBL ensures that any interpretation of this plan contains the two choices. Consider iterative plans for giving away money. If you are doing it altruistically, then termination is by angelic choice. If you are the victim of a hold-up, then termination is by demonic choice. The corresponding plans, with sample interpretations (there are others), are shown in the following figure.

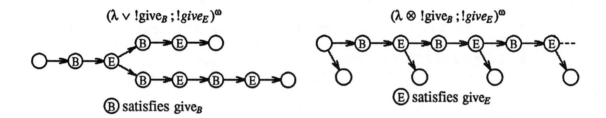

FIGURE 5. Angelic and demonic loop termination

As a final example, consider a plan for a reader and writer to run in parallel, in which the writer terminates demonically, and the reader terminates angelically.

$$(\lambda \vee !read_B ; !read_E)^\omega \| (\lambda \otimes !write_B ; !write_E)^\omega$$

With this plan, additional correctness constraints could be required, which might, for example, prevent simultaneous reading and writing. If it is intended to model a finite buffer, then correctness constraints may limit interpretations to those in which the writer will pause when the buffer is overfull. The interpretation given on the left of the following diagram is one which satisfies such constraints for a buffer of size 2: it is the function of a plan synchronizer to insert synchronization primitives so that only such interpretations will arise from the execution of the plan. The interpretation on the right has a reader completing a read action on the upper branch, before the writer completes its first write action. If the horizontal branch is extended indefinitely, then this interpretation is one in which the reader is enabled in the initial moment, and if selected to proceed by the environment, it will terminate. This choice is revoked if the writer proceeds first (upper branch), because the reader is enabled in all nodes shown on that branch. Of course, the definition of acceptable behaviour is dependent on the application.

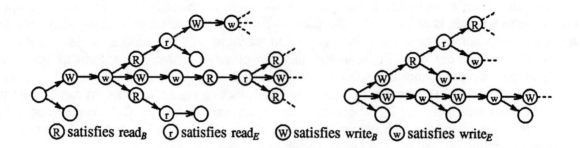

$\circledR$ satisfies read$_B$ $\circledr$ satisfies read$_E$ $\circledW$ satisfies write$_B$ $\circledw$ satisfies write$_E$

FIGURE 6. Parallel reader/write interpretations

A tree which is an interpretation of a given plan will correspond to a *strategy* for playing a game defined by a *branching automaton*.

Definition 7.

A *branching automaton* is a 7-tuple $(X, Y, S_X, S_Y, R, A, x_r)$, such that:

- X and Y are finite sets of nodes, called OR-nodes and AND-nodes respectively.

- $S_X \subseteq X \times Y$ and $S_Y \subseteq Y \times X$ are successor relations from X-nodes to Y-nodes and from Y-nodes to X-nodes. S_Y must be total; $S_X^{\bullet}$ is the set of X-nodes with no successors.

- $R \subseteq Y \times 2^P$ defines a family of *sets* of true propositions for any Y-node.

- $A \subseteq 2^Y$ is a family of sets of Y-nodes, called the *acceptance* sets.

- $x_r \in X \backslash S_X^{\bullet}$ is a distinguished non-terminal X-node called the *initial* node.

For a branching automaton $(X, Y, S_X, S_Y, R, A, x_r)$, a *run* on that automaton is a tree (Z, S_Z, R_Z, z_r) and mappings $f_X : Z \to X$, $f_Y : Z \backslash S_Z^{\bullet} \to Y$ such that:

- $f_X(z_r) = x_r$

- $\forall z \in Z : z \in S_Z^{\bullet}$ IFF $f_X(z) \in S_X^{\bullet}$

- $\forall z \in Z \backslash S_Z^{\bullet} : R_Z(z) \in R(f_Y(z))$

- $\forall z \in Z \backslash S_Z^{\bullet} : f_Y(z) \in S_X(f_X(z))$

- $\forall z \in Z \backslash S_Z^{\bullet} : S_Y(f_Y(z)) = \{f_X(z') : z' \in S_Z(z)\}$

The run *wins* if for every branch $\rho \in S_Z^{\to}(z_r)$, the set of corresponding Y-nodes which occur infinitely often is in A. i.e. $Inf(\{f_Y(\rho_i)\}_{i=1}^{\infty}) \in A$. The automaton *accepts* a tree if there is a winning run which reduces to that tree. If ρ is a finite branch, then $Inf(\{f_Y(\rho_i)\}_{i=1}^{\infty}) = \emptyset$.

<>

Branching automata are similar to the infinite-tree automata defined by Rabin[13], which have a set of nodes X corresponding to relations $x \subseteq \Sigma \times X^n$, where n is the arity of the trees accepted by the automaton, and Σ is an alphabet with which trees nodes are labeled. We have taken tree nodes to be labeled with set of propositions, so $\Sigma = 2^P$. In branching automata, the two successor mappings and the labeling of Y-nodes give for each X-node a relation $x \subseteq 2^P \times 2^X$. The distinction is that branching automata impose no order on the successors of a node, and allow an arbitrary number of successors. Tree automata do not have these two properties, and so do not relate directly to branching time logics cf. [5]

An alternative definition of acceptance may be given in terms of games.

Definition 8.

Given an automaton $(X, Y, S_X, S_Y, R, A, x_r)$ and a tree (Z, S_Z, R_Z, z_r), define the following game between the tree and the automaton. The arena for the game is a set of sequences from $(X \cup Y \cup Z)^*$, called *partial plays*. Moves by the automaton add two elements to a sequence. Play defines paths concurrently in the tree and the automaton. At every stage, let x, y, and z be the most recent nodes chosen from X, Y and Z respectively. Initially, the tree choses one of x_r or z_r, and the automaton choses the other. Play continues as follows:

(1)   The automaton then choses a new $y \in S_X(x)$. If $R_Z(z) \notin R(y)$ then the automaton loses.

(2)   The tree choses any node from $S_Y(y) \cup S_Z(z)$.

(3)   If the last node chosen by the tree was in X, then the automaton choses a node from $S_Z(z)$, otherwise it choses a node from $S_Y(y)$.

(4)   If $x \in S_X^\bullet$ AND $z \in S_Z^\bullet$, then the game ends, and the automaton wins if and only if $\varnothing \in A$.

(5)   Otherwise, if $x \in S_X^\bullet$ OR $z \in S_Z^\bullet$, then the game ends, and the automaton loses.

(6)   Go back to step one.

If play continues forever, then the automaton wins if and only if the set of nodes from Y which are chosen infinitely often is in A.

Choices for the tree are taken from $X \cup Z$, and for the automaton are taken from $(X \cup Z) \times Y$ (the automaton choses two nodes in each move). The tree is accepted by the automaton if and only if there is a strategy (a function which maps partial plays onto choices) for the automaton which ensures it will win the above game.

<>

Lemma 2.

The definition of acceptance given above is equivalent to the earlier definition.

Proof.

A strategy in the second definition corresponds to a winning run and a reduction in the first.

∎

Lemma 3.

If one automaton accepts all the finitely generated trees accepted by a second automaton, then it accepts all the trees accepted by the second automaton.

Proof.

By a general result on the determinacy of games proven by Martin[9], either the tree or the automaton has a winning strategy in the acceptance game. Let a tree be given which is rejected by the first automaton and accepted by the second. Define a critical set of tree nodes to be those nodes which may be chosen by the tree in its winning strategy against the first automaton, or by the second automaton in its winning strategy. Since there are only a finite number of partial plays leading up to any given tree node, any given tree node will have only a finite number of critical successors.

Prune the successor relation of this tree to delete all pairs leading to a non-critical node, except that if all successors of a node are non-critical, leave one arbitrarily. The resulting tree is finitely generated (though there may not be an upper bound on the number of successors for an arbitrary node). The given strategies will still win on this tree, which contradicts the assumption.

∎

DECIDING RBL

The main result we present is that every RBL formula corresponds to a branching automaton. This involves showing that branching automata are closed under negation. The proof of this result is based on a similar result for infinite binary tree automata proven by Gurevich and Harrington[6]. Their proof is slightly easier, in that it is restricted to infinite binary trees.

Definition 9.

If V is a set, $\sigma \in V^*$ is a sequence, and $B \subseteq V^*$ is a set of sequences, define $\sigma^{-1}B = \{\sigma' : \sigma\sigma' \in B\}$.

For any set Y, define $Y^{disp} \subseteq Y^*$ to be those sequences in which no element is repeated.

Define $LAR(\sigma, Y) \in Y^{disp}$ to be the sequence formed from σ by deleting every element not in Y, and then deleting all elements which are followed in σ by another copy of themselves. If Y is omitted, simply apply the second deletion rule. LAR is called the *last appearance record*.

◇

Lemma 4.

For a finitely generated tree and an automaton given as in the game definition above, let B be the set of partial plays. Then either the tree has a winning strategy $f : B \to (X \cup Z)$ or the automaton has a winning strategy $f : B \to (X \cup Z) \times Y$ such that

$$\forall \sigma \in B \ \forall \upsilon \in B : \quad \text{IF } \sigma^{-1}B = \upsilon^{-1}B \text{ AND } LAR(\sigma, Y) = LAR(\upsilon, Y) \text{ THEN } f(\sigma) = f(\upsilon)$$

A strategy having this property is called *forgetfully deterministic*.

Proof.

This is a corollary of a game theoretic result proven by Gurevich and Harrington[6], restated here:

If a game is defined as follows:

Let $(Move, B)$ be an arena such that $Move$ is finite. Let Y be a finite subset of $Move$. Let $A \subseteq 2^Y$ be some family of subsets of Y. Let two players play an infinite game by chosing elements from $Move$ alternately so that the sequence of moves remains in B. Let the first player win a play $\rho \subseteq Move^\omega$ if $Inf(\rho) \cap Y \in A$

then one of the players has a winning strategy $f : B \to Move$ such that

$$\forall \sigma, \upsilon \in B : \quad \text{IF } |\sigma| = |\upsilon| \text{ AND } LAR(\sigma, Y) = LAR(\upsilon, Y) \text{ AND } \sigma^{-1}B = \upsilon^{-1}B \text{ THEN } f(\sigma) = f(\upsilon)$$

The hypothesis is stronger than necessary. Their proof is still valid with the finiteness assumption for $Move$ replaced by the weaker assumption that $\{ m \in Move : \sigma m \in B \}$ is finite for any sequence $\sigma \in B$, which allows their result to be applied to this lemma when the tree is finitely generated.

∎

Theorem 5.

Branching automata are closed under complementation.

Proof.

Let an automaton $(X, Y, S_X, S_Y, R, A, x_r)$ be given. Let $X' = X \cup \{\tau\}$ be X augmented with a single special element. Each move by a tree in the acceptance game is either in X or in the tree itself. This latter case will be represented by τ. Let Σ be the set of mappings $f : Y^{disp} \to X'$, and let Σ' be the powerset of Y^{disp}. Let a tree (Z, S_Z, R_Z, z_r) be given, and mappings $f' : Z \to \Sigma$ and $g' : Z \to \Sigma'$, such that

$$\forall z \in Z \ \forall \sigma \in Y^{disp} : \quad \text{IF } f'(z, \sigma) = \tau \text{ THEN } \exists z' \in S_Z(z) : \sigma \in g'(z') \tag{1}$$

The mappings define the following strategy for the tree in the acceptance game:

For any partial play ρ in which the tree has the next move, let $d = LAR(\rho, Y)$, and let z be the most recent Z-node chosen. If $f'(z, d) \in X$, then the tree choses this X-node as its next move. Otherwise, it choses some tree node $z' \in S(z)$ such that $d \in g'(z')$.

Every forgetfully deterministic strategy corresponds to some such mapping, and any such mapping corresponds to a forgetfully deterministic strategy. Thus by the previous lemma, the tree is rejected if and only if maps f' and g' can be found so that the tree wins by the above strategy. The complementation problem thus reduces to the problem of finding a branching automaton which accepts trees labeled so as to give such a winning strategy. In such an automaton, the relation R, which gives possible propositional interpretations for a node, is extended to give possible values for f' and g' at a node (values are taken from Σ and Σ', which are finite). The complement of the original automaton is then obtained by discarding the Σ and Σ' values in the extended R, to give only the possible propositional interpretations.

There are two conditions to be satisfied for a labeling to correspond to a winning strategy. First, it must be a legitimate labeling, as defined by condition (1) above. This is easily tested by a branching automaton.

Second, the strategy must be a winning strategy. This may be expressed as a property of branches in the tree. Informally, for every branch in the tree, every sequence of plays by the automaton which could cause that branch to be traversed will also cause the automaton to lose. Paths in the automaton will be sequences $\{(x_i, y_i)\}_{i=1}^{\infty}$ of elements from $X \times Y$. For each such sequence, the sequence $\{d_i = LAR(y_1 \cdots y_i)\}_{i=1}^{\infty}$ can be defined. Let $\{(a_i, f_i, g_i)\}_{i=1}^{\infty}$ be the sequence of elements from $2^P \times \Sigma \times \Sigma'$ obtained from an infinite path in the tree. (Consideration of finite paths requires the addition of an additional special element, and is omitted here for simplicity.) For every such sequence, the following condition must hold:

$$\forall \{x_i\}_{i=1}^{\infty} \in X^* \ \forall \{y_i\}_{i=1}^{\infty} \in Y^* \ \forall \{d_i\}_{i=1}^{\infty} \in (Y^{disp})^* : \qquad \text{For all automaton paths}$$

$$\begin{aligned}
&\text{IF} & &x_1 = x_r \text{ AND } d_1 = (y_1) \\
&\text{AND} & &\forall i \geq 1 : d_{i+1} = LAR(d_i y_{i+1}) & &\{d_i\} \text{ defined by } \{y_i\} \\
&\text{AND} & &\forall i \geq 1 : (y_i \in S_X(x_i) \text{ AND } x_{i+1} \in S_Y(y_i)) \\
&\text{AND} & &\forall i \geq 1 : a_i \in R(y_i) & &\text{if the play is legal} \\
&\text{AND} & &\forall i \geq 1 : f_i(d_i) = x_{i+1} \text{ OR } (f_i(d_i) = \tau \text{ AND } d_i \in g_{i+1}) \\
&\text{THEN} & &Inf(\{y_i\}_{i=1}^{\infty}) \notin A & &\text{then the automaton loses}
\end{aligned}$$

This property can be expressed in S1S, the second order theory of natural numbers (N) with the successor relation. S1S allows quantification over sets of natural numbers, and the use of the subset and successor relations. The successor relation between two sets of numbers holds if both sets contain a single element, and the standard successor relation on natural numbers holds on those elements. Formally, $Succ(X, Y)$ is true if and only if $\exists n \in N : X = \{n\}$ AND $Y = \{n+1\}$. A sequence over a finite alphabet corresponds to a set of sets of numbers, one for each letter in the alphabet. The set for a given letter is the set of indices of those elements of the sequence equal to that letter.

For a given automaton, the condition on infinite branches presented above can be represented in S1S. By the theory of Büchi and McNaughton[2][10] there is a linear finite automaton accepting such sequences if the states appearing infinitely often on the corresponding path through the automaton are in some distinguished family of sets. This linear automaton is easily converted to a branching automaton accepting trees where every path though the tree satisfies this property. The OR-nodes of the branching automaton correspond to nodes in the linear automaton; the AND-nodes have only one successor each, and correspond to arcs in the linear automaton.

By taking the conjunction of the branching automaton accepting all possible labelings, with the branching automaton accepting the winning labelings, the complement of the original is obtained. Conjunction of branching automata is a straightforward process, and the result follows.

Theorem 6.

For any RBL formula, there exists a branching automaton accepting all and only the trees for which that formula is true.

Proof.

The proof is by induction on the length of formulae, and requires a case by case analysis for each RBL connective. The most difficult case, negation, follows from the previous theorem.

As an example showing some of the techniques, we present an informal construction for the sequence connective. Constructions for other connectives are omitted. Take two automata corresponding to RBL formulae α and β, respectively: $(X_\alpha, Y_\alpha, S_{X\alpha}, S_{Y\alpha}, R_\alpha, A_\alpha, x_\alpha)$ and $(X_\beta, Y_\beta, S_{X\beta}, S_{Y\beta}, R_\beta, A_\beta, x_\beta)$. Every node in Y_α which has a successor in $S_{X\alpha}^\bullet$ corresponds to a point at which the tree may chose to terminate the α-game. This must be changed so that the tree may chose to begin the β-game.

Replace any such node $y \in Y_\alpha : \exists x \in S_{Y\alpha}(y) \cap S_{X\alpha}^\bullet$ with a set of nodes corresponding to pairs of Y-nodes from the α and β automata $\{(y, y') : y' \in S_{X\beta}(x_\beta)\}$, one for every successor of the root of β. Any OR-node which had the original node as a successor now has all these new nodes as successors. This allows the automaton to chose how the β-game should start, should the tree terminate the α-game. For any such new node (y, y'), the successors are successors of either y or y'. Thus the tree may chose to continue the α-game, or to play in the β-game. For these new nodes, the set of acceptable propositional interpretations (given by the relation R) is defined by the intersection of the sets of interpretations of the two associated nodes. $R((y, y')) = R_\alpha(y) \cap R_\beta(y')$.

The sets of AND-nodes which may be repeated infinitely often are the sets from A_β, or the non-empty sets from A_α. Thus a terminating play must correspond to a terminating play of the second game, but there may be infinitely long plays in α which never reaches β.

This gives a branching automaton accepting $\alpha;\beta$. There are two steps to proving that this is so.

- First, let a tree be given which is accepted by the constructed automaton. Find a run of the automaton which reduces to this accepted tree. Define a frontier on the run tree to be all tree nodes which map to an AND-node which was inserted in the above process. This frontier is used in the definition of ";" given above to show that $\alpha;\beta$ is true on that tree.

- Second, let a tree be given for which $\alpha;\beta$ is true. Thus, by the definition of ";", there is a frontier on this tree, for which α is true on the sub-tree inside the frontier, and β is true on all sub-trees outside the frontier. Take runs for these sub-trees on the appropriate automata. These runs can be combined to form a run for the complete tree on the constructed automaton.

∎

WHERE DO WE GO FROM HERE?

Considering the distinction between demonic and angelic non-determinism leads to a generalization of branching time logic incorporating constructs used in plans. Among the problems of interest currently being considered, but not covered in detail in this paper, are the following:

- Is there an axiomization for RBL?

- Is RBL expressively complete with respect to branching automata? It is probably necessary to allow path quantifiers to be associated with arbitrary linear time expressions rather than a single connective. Emerson describes such an extension to CTL called CTL*.[5]

- The emptiness problem for branching automata can be solved by application of the theorem on the existence of forgetfully deterministic strategies.

- What is the relationship between branching automata and the second order monadic theory of infinite trees? This intersting question is prompted by the use of the second order monadic theory of two successors by Emerson and Sistla to show a relationship between EQCTL and infinite binary tree automata.[5].

- Consideration is being given to the implementation of a plan synchronizer based on an RBL theorem prover. Time and space requirements of the algorithm are to be explored.

Branching regular expressions extend the expressive power of standard branching time logic, and give a natural way of describing the behaviour of plans. There is potential application for the resulting logic to planning, synchronization, and proving properties of plans.

Acknowledgements

This investigation is being conducted at Monash University; thanks are also due to SRI International and the SRI AI Center for support during the initial stages, to Michael Georgeff for guidance, ideas and practical assistance, and to John Crossley for comments on drafts and for help with the mathematics where it is not in my comfort zone. Also, since artificial intelligence research is used in technological and military solutions to problems which require deeper human solutions, I offer my thanks to those who work for effective peace and justice; my pledge to resist the application of my own work to projects which threaten the same; and my request to us all to consider if our efforts are used for sophisticated military applications at the expense of hopes for genuine peace and security.

References

1. M. Ben-Ari, Z. Manna and A. Pnueli, The Temporal Logic of Branching Time, *8th Annual ACM symposium on Principles of Programming Languages*, 1981.

2. J. R. Büchi, On a Decision Method in the Restricted Second Order Arithmetic, *Proc. 1960 international congress on Logic, Methodology, and Philosophy of Science*, 1962, 1-11.

3. P. Darondeau and L. Kott, A formal proof system for Infinitary Rational Expressions, in *Automata on Infinite Words* , Lecture Notes in Comp. Sci., vol. 192, M. Nivat and D. Perrin, (eds.), Springer-Verlag, 1984, 68-80.

4. E. A. Emerson and E. M. Clarke, Using Branching Time Temporal Logic to Synthesize Synchronization Skeletons, *Science of Computer Programming 2* , 3, (1982), 241-266.

5. E. A. Emerson and A. P. Sistla, Deciding Branching Time Logic, *16th Annual ACM symposium on Theory of Computing*, 1984, 14-24.

6. Y. Gurevich and L. Harrington, Trees, Automata, and Games, *Proc. ACM symposium on Theory of Computing*, San Francisco, May, 1982, 60-65.

7. C. A. R. Hoare, *Communicating Sequential Processes*, International series in Computer Science, Prentice-Hall, 1985.

8. Z. Manna and P. Wolper, Synthesis of Communicating Processes from Temporal Logic Specifications, STAN-Comp. Science-81-872, Stanford Uni., 1981.

9. D. A. Martin, Borel Determinacy, *Annals of Mathematics 102* , (1975), 363-371.

10. R. McNaughton, Testing and Generating Infinite Sequences by a Finite Automaton, *Information and Control 9* , (1966), 521-530.

11. R. Milner, *A Calculus of Communicating Systems*, Lecture Notes in Comp. Sci., vol. 92, Springer-Verlag, 1980.

12. J. Pin, Star-free ω-languages and First Order Logic., in *Automata on Infinite Words* , Lecture Notes in Comp. Sci., vol. 192, M. Nivat and D. Perrin, (eds.), Springer-Verlag, 1984, 56-67.

13. M. O. Rabin, Decidability of Second-order Theories and Automata on Infinite Trees., *Transactions of the A.M.S. 141* , (1969), 1-35.

14. C. J. Stuart, An Implementation of a Multi-agent Plan Synchronizer, TN 350, SRI International, Menlo Park, California, Dec., 1985.

15. C. J. Stuart, An Implementation of a Multi-agent Plan Synchronizer, *Internat. Joint Conf. on Artificial Intelligence*, Aug., 1985, 1031-1033.

16. C. J. Stuart, Regular Expressions as Temporal Logic, Tech. Rep. 64, Monash University, Clayton, Victoria, Jan., 1986.

17. P. Wolper, Temporal Logic can be more expressive, *22nd Annual symposium on Foundations of Computer Science*, Nashville, Tennessee, 1981, 340-348.

18. P. Wolper, M. Y. Vardi and A. P. Sistla, Reasoning about Infinite Computation Paths, *Proc. 24th IEEE symposium on Foundations of Computer Science*, Tuscon, 1983, 185-194.

A representation of action and belief for automatic planning systems

Mark E. Drummond

AI Applications Institute,
University of Edinburgh, 80 South Bridge,
Edinburgh, Scotland, U.K. EH1 1HN

Net Address: M.Drummond%Uk.Ac.Edinburgh@ucl-cs.arpa
Telephone: (031) 225-4464

ABSTRACT

A plan representation is presented which can describe sensory, iterative, and conditional behaviors. The representation builds on previous research in parallel plans, action teleology, reason maintenance, iterative plans, action disjunction and action-ordering plan structures. The new representation is motivated by demonstrating that current methods of operator description are unable to describe the sensory effects of actions, and by arguing that existing action-ordering plan representations cannot easily describe iterative behavior. A new representation is defined which overcomes these difficulties, and sample plans are given. Comments are made about the relationship between this new representation and what has come before.

Financial support for this work has been provided by the University of Edinburgh through a Postgraduate Studentship, by the British Government through the ORS award scheme, and by the British Council, in the form of a Foreign and Commonwealth Office Scholarship.

If there were a verb meaning "to believe falsely," it would not have any significant first person, present indicative.
-- Wittgenstein

There can never be any reason for rejecting one instinctive belief except that it clashes with others. It is of course *possible* that all or any of our beliefs may be mistaken, and therefore all ought to be held with at least some element of doubt. But we cannot have *reason* to reject a belief except on the ground of some other belief.
– Russell

1. Introduction.

Over the past few years, a great deal of research has gone into representation and reasoning relating to *automatic planning*. There are many ideas in the literature regarding parallel (or non-linear) plans [31, 32, 13, 14], action-on-node plans [31, 32, 36, 37, 44, 45], iterative constructs [13, 14, 9], reason maintenance systems [4, 5, 6, 7, 8], teleology of action [11, 35, 39, 45], formal plan construction reasoning [2, 27], disjunction of action [13, 14, 43], and multiple-agent theories of knowledge and action [20, 21, 22, 16]. The time seems ripe to attempt a synthesis of some of the underlying ideas into a coherent framework. This paper presents such a synthesis in the form of a new representation for plans. The representation is essentially an action-on-node network, and it explicitly addresses the issues of parallel action, iterative constructs, reason maintenance, action teleology, and action disjunction. Two restrictions are in force. First, although part of the representation includes a mechanism for *analyzing* possible plan behaviors, this paper does not explicitly address the complex issue of automated plan construction. Second, the structures we present are intended to form the basis of a *single* agent's representation for plans. We do not consider the multi-agent case, or the problems involved with reasoning about what *other* agents can *know* or *believe*.

The first two sections of this paper present basic arguments against certain features of current plan representations. We argue that the classic STRIPS [11] method of action characterization does not permit description of an action's *sensory* results. We also show that the now classic method of stringing together action descriptions as *procedural nets* does not allow for natural description of iterative behavior. Apart from these two brief explanatory sections, we assume basic familiarity with relevant previous work. A new plan representation is developed which can represent the results of sensory actions and which can describe iterative behavior. This representation builds on much of the work referenced above. Sensory and iterative example plans are presented. The basic relationship between this representation and previous work is also discussed. We conclude with some points which require further thought.

2. A problem: planning to sense.

The issues we address in this section are all intimately connected to the so-called *frame problem* [15]; that is, the problem of finding adequate "laws of motion". A law of motion is a law, or rule, used to infer the properties of new "states", given old. The goal of this section is to show that the classic STRIPS [11] method of characterizing actions through operators containing precondition-lists, delete-lists, and add-lists is limited. Such operators cannot be naturally used to characterize the *sensory* results of an action. To deal with this, we present the essentials of a novel method for dealing with the frame problem. We assume familiarity with the advantages offered by the STRIPS method of operator description; in particular, we assume that the reader is aware how the "STRIPS assumption" [42] solves much of the frame problem incurred by the simpler situation calculus [18, 19] formulation of time and change. However, it actually doesn't matter a great deal which representation is discussed. As far as our argument is concerned, the situation calculus makes the same basic commitments as STRIPS, so the criticisms still apply. We simply choose STRIPS as the more visible of two available targets.

Understand that comments made here regarding STRIPS operators apply to the plan representations employed in more recent systems, such as NOAH [31, 32], Nonlin [37], Deviser [40, 41], SIPE [44, 45], and O-Plan [3]. These newer systems *do* extend the current planning paradigm in various ways. New features include the ability to represent and reason about metric time and resources. Sophisticated plan execution monitoring abilities are also evidenced [38, 46]. However, the plan representations used by *all* these systems still follow the STRIPS convention of using precondition-lists, add-lists, and delete-lists to characterize actions. Thus, our argument against STRIPS operators still applies.

The overall framework we assume is as follows. A planning system is part of an intelligent (one hopes) computer agent. Classically, the planning system is required to have access to a *world model*. This world model is an internal data structure which describes the environment for the agent. Essentially, this world model is a database of formulas in some *mental* language. It is extremely important for us to be clear about the basic status of these formulas. In this paper, we take the view that each formula occurring in an agent's world model is best considered to be either a *belief* or an *assumption* of that agent.

This position is not entirely new. Doyle [5, p.234] has argued that "... we should study justified belief or reasoned argument, and ignore questions of truth. Truth enters into the study of extra-psychological rationality and into what common sense truisms we decide to supply to our programs, but truth does not enter into the narrowly psychological rationality by which our programs operate.". Hayes [15, p.223], suggests that "by *belief* is meant any piece of information which is explicitly stored in the robot's memory.". It is quite certainly the case that this semi-technical notion of belief is inadequate for discussing the rich variety of human belief; it does, however, accord with our basic intuition of what a belief might be. Similar thoughts are expressed by Moore and Hendrix [23]. Levesque [17, p.198] says "because what is represented in a knowledge base in typically not required to be *true*, to be consistent with most philosophers and computer scientists, we are calling the attitude involved here 'belief' rather than 'knowledge'." It is also possible to argue that these world model formulas are *necessarily* beliefs; see Fodor [12] for a convincing essay. Later on, we will define the conditions under which a given world model assertion is a *belief* or an *assumption* for the agent. For now, we will use "belief" as a slightly imprecise blanket term to cover both notions.

It seems quite clear that STRIPS operators do not adequately characterize the changes to an agent's beliefs under action occurrence. However, we briefly explore STRIPS operators in a "belief context", in order to see exactly what the problems are, and to motivate the solution we present.

Consider the *action* in which an agent moves some block *A* from an object *B* to another object *C*. During the course of the action, suppose that a weight sensor in the agent's arm supplies information regarding the weight of block A. The notional effect of the action is to make block A be on top of block C. How might this action with all its results be represented to the agent via the STRIPS operator formalism? This question can be answered in two parts, one answer for each of the add-list and delete-list.

What would the add-list be? Should this list contain a formula of the form *weight(a,X)*, and a formula of the form *on(a,c)*? In different situations, the agent will want to achieve different results -- packing these two formulas into a single add-list ensures that the agent will not be able to reference the action for *required* results. Some of the action's results are realized in the environment; in this case, these are results which involve blocks actually being on top of each other. Other of the action's results are internal to the agent; that is, they are *mental* results, and only involve the agent in coming to *believe* something about its environment. These two sorts of results are quite different, and an operator representation language must distinguish between them if the agent is to be expected to invoke actions as appropriate, depending on its goals. STRIPS operators do not provide for making this distinction, and thus cannot be used by the agent to plan to sense the world *and* to effect changes in it.

And what should the delete-list for the *move* action be? First, what is the delete-list intended to describe? The operator of which it is a part is intended to describe an action. Following operator application, the formulas in the delete-list will be removed to derive a successor "model" to the one in which the operator is applied. Thus, the delete-list appears to determine the beliefs that the action described by the operator would remove from the world model, were it to actually occur. This seems rather suspect. It appears strange to say that performance of the block movement action forces out old beliefs. Instead, we might want to say that the actual additions to the beliefs of the agent under the modelled occurrence of the action is what would cause old beliefs to be rejected. However, this suggests that what is rejected depends on what is actually added, and perhaps, what is already believed. Such a suggestion is antithetical to the idea embodied in STRIPS delete-lists.

Consider the following delete-list scenario. An operator somehow calls for the addition of a formula *on(a,b)*. What should be deleted? Clearly, this depends *only* on the agent's current beliefs regarding a and b. What if b is believed to be a table? Then it would be fine for the agent to believe as well that b is clear. However, what if b is believed to be a block? (Say that being a block implies unit-support capability.) Then it would seem impossible for the agent to believe as well that b is clear, since a is on it. In addition, consider the object denoted by a. What beliefs regarding it should be deleted? If it is a block, then b must be the only object it is on; if not, then it may well be on b *and* some other object(s) simultaneously. The situation can be summarized as follows. The beliefs that must be deleted under operator application are only a function of what is currently believed by the agent, and what is being "added" by the operator. Such a view on belief deletion permits the use of a *single* block movement operator in most blocks world domains. The only operator required is one for moving a block from an initial support to a final support. Standard STRIPS-like formulations require four operators. (See, for instance, [25, p.281].)

3. Another problem: no iteration with procedural nets.

Most modern planners use some form of Sacerdoti's [31, 32] *procedural net*. (See, for instance, [37, 40, 45, 3].) We next suggest that this sort of representation has problems describing iterative behavior. Note that by the term "procedural net", we mean the entire class of action-ordering plan representations which derive from it.

The order in a procedural net is a strict partial order: irreflexive and transitive, thus asymmetric. This is intuitively sound, since the ordering is intended to reflect the "flow" of time. If one action α is *before* another action β, then β cannot be before α. No loops can ever exist in time, so no loops can exist in a procedural net. This poses a problem when attempting to model iterative behavior; for instance, agents can hammer nails, can walk until they come to a bar, and can dial a number on a telephone until someone answers. If agents can take part in such activities, it seems natural to suggest that their representation for plans be able to capture the required notions. We would not want to attempt a solution to the problem by introducing "special" nodes into a net which describe *iterative* actions. (See [32], for instance.) Such a ploy would hide the notion of process inside an inaccessible black box: if iteration is to be represented, it must be done in such a way that permits reasoning about it. This is not to say that we would not want the ability to abstract away from iterative constructs, and view them as single-step actions. It is important however, to be *able* to include iterative constructs in the basic net representation of a plan. In this paper, we adopt the philosophy that in order to describe iterative behavior, a richer action-ordering plan structure is required.

4. A new representation.

We now define plan nets, consistency maintenance, plan net projection, assumptions, problems, and potential solutions. The block movement action presented above is developed as an example.

We assume that Π denotes powerset, that "$-$" denotes set difference, and that ρ^* denotes the transitive closure of the relation ρ. Given a relation σ, we often abbreviate $(x,y)\in \sigma$ as $x\sigma y$.

Some of the formalism we use comes from Net Theory [1]. While a few Net Theory constructions are borrowed directly, most are unique to this work. Readable introductions to Petri Nets and Net Theory in general can be found in [24, 30, 28, 29].

4.1. Structure.

We begin by defining the *terms* of a base language, L. These terms are used below in the definition of the basic formulae from which plan nets are built.

Definition 1. The *terms* of L are of two categories:

(1)   A denumerably infinite set of *constants* $Co = \{a_1,a_2,a_3, \cdots \}$. We will sometimes use a to stand for a_1, b to stand for a_2, and c to stand for a_3. We extend this set of constants as required for each domain. There is nothing fundamental in this extension. Each new constant introduced can be considered to stand for some $a_i \in Co$.

(2)   A denumerably infinite set of *individual variables* $Va = \{v_1, v_2, v_3, \cdots\}$. We will sometimes use w to stand for v_1, x to stand for v_2, y to stand for v_3, and z to stand for v_4.

Formulae of the language L_B (for Belief Language) are defined using terms from the base language L, and arbitrary *n-place* predicates. Formulae are formed in the obvious way using the predicates and terms. A formula from L_B will be interpreted here as a *possible* belief. A set of formulae of L_B is to be interpreted as a possible state of belief. If any given formula of L_B is in the agent's *world model*, then the agent might *currently* believe that formula. Other sets of formulae of L_B are only *possible* states of belief. We are only concerned here with states of belief that are possible for the agent in the future. We make this precise later, by defining the projection of a plan into the future, and by defining when any given L_B formula is a justified belief and when it is only an assumption.

Definition 2. The *basic expressions* of L_B are of two categories:

(1)   The terms of L.

(2)   A set of *1-place predicates*, a set of *2-place predicates*, ..., a set of *n-place predicates*.

Definition 3. The *formation rules* of L_B consist of the following:

(1)   If σ is an n-place predicate of L_B and $\alpha_1, \alpha_2, \alpha_3, \cdots, \alpha_n$ are terms of L, then $\sigma(\alpha_1, \alpha_2, \alpha_3, \cdots, \alpha_n)$ is a *formula* of L_B.

(2)   Nothing else is a formula of L_B.

For example, let $\{clear, block, table\}$ be the one-place predicates of L_B, and let $\{weight, on\}$ be the two place predicates. Let $\{a, b, c, 1, 2, 3\}$ be constants, and let $\{w, x, y, z\}$ be variables. The constants $\{a, b, c\}$ denote objects, and $\{1, 2, 3\}$ denote (respectively) light objects, objects of moderate weight, and extremely heavy objects. The predicates *on* and *clear* have the obvious interpretation. *block* is true if its argument denotes a block; and *table* is true if its argument denotes a table. A formula $weight(b,2)$ is true if the object denoted by b weighs the amount denoted by 2. Valid first arguments for *weight* are objects; valid second arguments must be drawn from the set $\{1, 2, 3\}$.

Similarly, we now construct the language L_E (Event Language). L_E formulae use terms from the base language L, and predicates of arbitrary arity. Formulae of L_E are built analogously to those of L_B. Each formulae of L_E is intended to denote an action.

Definition 4. The *basic expressions* of L_E are of two categories:

(1)   The terms of L.

(2)   A set of *1-place predicates*, a set of *2-place predicates*, ..., a set of *n-place predicates*.

Definition 5. The *formation rules* of L_E consist of the following:

(1)   If σ is an n-place predicate of L_E and $\alpha_1, \alpha_2, \alpha_3, \cdots, \alpha_n$ are terms of L, then $\sigma(\alpha_1, \alpha_2, \alpha_3, \cdots, \alpha_n)$ is a *formula* of L_E.

(2)   Nothing else is a formula of L_E.

For our simple example, we require a single three place predicate: *move*. This predicate must only be applied to objects, and denotes the action of moving a block from an initial support to a final support. For this example, we suppose that the agent has a weight sensor in its robot arm, such that following the movement of any given block, the agent will hold a belief regarding the block's weight. The weight will be measured in our trinary 1, 2, 3 scheme. For instance, *move(a,b,c)* denotes the action of moving the block denoted by *a* from the object denoted by *b* (table or block) to the object denoted by *c* (table or block). Following execution of this action, the agent will hold a belief about the weight of the block denoted by *a*.

Using formulae of L_B and L_E, we can now define the basic net structure used to build plans. A net is a 3-tuple consisting of a set of formulae of L_B, a set of formulae of L_E, and a flow relation.

Definition 6. A 3-tuple $N = (B,E;F)$ is called a *net* iff

(1) $B \subseteq L_B$ (B is a set of formulae of L_B);

$E \subseteq L_E$ (E is a set of formulae of L_E);

$B \cap E = \emptyset$ (B and E have no intersection);

B and E are finite. (We call $b \in B$ a *b-element*, and $e \in E$ an *e-element*.)

(2) $F = (In0,In1,Out0,Out1)$ is a four-tuple where $In0 \subseteq (B \times E)$, the *enable-out* relation; $In1 \subseteq (B \times E)$, the *enable-in* relation; $Out0 \subseteq (E \times B)$, the *external-results* relation; $Out1 \subseteq (E \times B)$, the *internal-results* relation.

Graphical convention. We represent a b-element by a circle labelled with the b-element, and an e-element as a box labelled with the e-element. The four relations in F are drawn as shown in figure 1.

A blocks-world net constructed according to definition 6 appears in figure 2. The corresponding graphical presentation is given in figure 3. The intended interpretation of a net's flow relation is discussed below.

Notational convention. Let $N = (B,E;F)$ be a net. We sometimes denote the three components B, E, and F

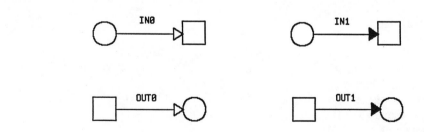

Figure 1: Graphical convention for plan net relations.

by B_N, E_N, and F_N, respectively. If confusion can be excluded, we also write N for $B \cup E$, and F for $In0 \cup In1 \cup Out0 \cup Out1$. We sometimes denote the four components of F by $In0_N$, $In1_N$, $Out0_N$, and $Out1_N$, respectively.

We often want to make reference to net elements that are connected to each other. Given some particular element of a net, it is useful to be able to refer abstractly to those elements which are directly associated with this element in one of the relations in F. To do this, we introduce the following notation.

Definition 7. Let $N = (B,E;F)$ be a net.

(1)   For $x \in N$

$^{\pm}x = \{y \mid y \, F_N \, x\}$ is called the *basic preset* of x;

$x^{\pm} = \{y \mid x \, F_N \, y\}$ is called the *basic postset* of x.

For $X \subseteq N$, let $^{\pm}X = \bigcup_{x \in X} {^{\pm}x}$ and let $X^{\pm} = \bigcup_{x \in X} x^{\pm}$

(2)   For $x \in E$

$^{-}x = \{y \mid y \, In0_N \, x\}$ is called the *enable-out preset* of x;

$^{+}x = \{y \mid y \, In1_N \, x\}$ is called the *enable-in preset* of x;

$x^{-} = \{y \mid x \, Out0_N \, y\}$ is called the *external-results postset* of x;

$x^{+} = \{y \mid x \, Out1_N \, y\}$ is called the *internal-results postset* of x.

As in definition 7.1 (above), we extend this notation to cover sets $X \subseteq E$.

(3)   A pair $(b,e) \in B_N {\times} E_N$ is called a *self-loop* iff $(b \, F_N \, e)$ & $(e \, F_N \, b)$. N is called *pure* iff F_N does not contain any self-loops.

N = (B,E;F)

B = {block(x), on(x,y), clear(y), clear(x), on(x,z), weight(x,w)}
E = {move(x,z,y)}

F = (In0,In1,Out0,Out1)

In0 = ∅
In1 = {(block(x), move(x,z,y)),
        (clear(y), move(x,z,y)),
        (clear(x), move(x,z,y)),
        (on(x,z),   move(x,z,y))}
Out0 = {(move(x,z,y), on(x,y))}
Out1 = {(move(x,z,y), weight(x,w))}

Figure 2: A sample blocks-world net.

(4) $x \in N$ is called *isolated* iff $^{\pm}x \cup x^{\pm} = \emptyset$.

(5) N is called *simple* iff distinct elements do not have the same basic preset and basic postset, i.e.

$$\forall \ x,y \in N: (^{\pm}x = {}^{\pm}y \ \& \ x^{\pm} = y^{\pm}) \rightarrow x = y.$$

The net given in figure 2 is pure, contains no isolated elements, and is simple.

The four ordering relations on e-elements and b-elements describe the relationship between any given action and that action's enabling conditions and results. The intention is that the enable-in preset of a given e-element describes those formulas that must be *in* the agent's world model for the event denoted by the e-element to occur. The e-element's enable-out preset describes those formulas that must not be in the world model if the denoted event is to be enabled. The e-element's external-results postset describes the external, or physical, results of the denoted action; and the internal-results postset describes the internal, or mental, results of the denoted action.

Consider again the net of figures 2 and 3. This net contains only one e-element: *move(x,z,y)*. The e-element denotes the action of moving the block denoted by *x* from an initial support denoted by *z* to a final support denoted by *y*. The basic preset of the e-element describes what must and must not be in the agent's world model if the denoted action is to be enabled. More specifically, the e-element's enable-in preset says that the action denoted can only occur if the formulas *block(x)*, *clear(y)*, *clear(x)*, and *on(x,z)* are all *in* the agent's world model. No formulas are required to be out of the world model.

The net also determines that the *move* action has two results, specified by the e-element's basic postset. In particular, the move action has the external result that the block denoted by *x* is on the object denoted by *y*. This action also has the internal result that the block denoted by *x* has a weight denoted by *w*. Thus, this action is "sensory", in that it imparts to the agent a measure of the moved block's weight. It is certainly true that the block would have a weight before the action occurs; however, the agent may or may not have had any beliefs regarding

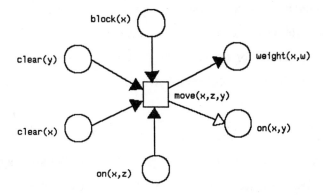

Figure 3: The net of figure 2, graphically presented.

this weight. After the action occurs, the agent *will* have some sort of belief about the weight of *x*.

We can now define plans (and operators) as nets which have certain properties. We include the definition of a *before* relation, used to constrain the way in which a plan can execute. Here, the before relation is simply introduced as a part of a plan. How this is used is made clear in the definition of problems and their solution, below. Intuitively, the before order is a specification of which events must occur before which other events, if a plan is to run to its intended completion.

Definition 8. A 2-tuple $O = (N,A)$ is called a *plan net* iff

(1) N is a pure and simple net.

(2) $A \subseteq \Pi(E_N) \times \Pi(E_N)$ is called the *before relation*. This relation must be a strict partial order: irreflexive and transitive, thus asymmetric. We use the terms *before relation* and *execution advice* interchangeably. (In graphical presentations, if $A = \emptyset$, nothing will be shown for the execution advice; otherwise, the pairs in A will be listed with the plan net.)

(3)   If $|E_N| = 1$ then we also say that O is an *operator*.

What is the difference between an operator and a plan? As used here, the terms reflect two perspectives. We will call a net plus advice an *operator* when it is given (perhaps with other operators) to a planner to be used in solving a specified problem. To be useful, such an operator will usually contain individual variables, but this is not always so. An operator might be of some use in solving a problem even if it contains only constants. A net/advice two-tuple will be called a *plan* when it is produced by a planner as a potential solution to a problem. Of course, this plan may later be used as an operator, if the problem solver has the ability to store and re-use previous solutions. Thus there is no fundamental distinction between operators and plans in this formalism, and the terms will be used as appropriate, depending on context. This is similar to what is done by NonLin [37], SIPE [45], and O-Plan [3].

According to definition 8, we can construct an operator from the net N which appears in figure 2 as $O = (N,\emptyset)$; thus O is an operator with execution advice that is the empty set. This seems reasonable, since it's hard to imagine requiring ordering advice for the execution of a single action! For a larger example, see [9]. The formalism we use in that paper is slightly different, but is similar enough to see what a larger plan net structure might look like.

4.2. Consistency.

It is not enough to have a simple *structural* account of a plan of action. We also require some means for describing the behaviors it specifies. We use a state-space account, which we call a *projection*. In order to define a plan's projection, we must first address the definition of the belief consistency maintenance function, μ. This function will be used in defining a basic state transition, the atomic "step" from which plan projections will be constructed.

The basic idea of the μ function is as follows. Given a set of current beliefs, and a set of new observations (potential beliefs), we must arrive at a peaceful union of the two sets. It is this union that is to become the new set of current beliefs. Clearly, the new observations and the old beliefs may be incompatible. What is required then, is a deletion of old beliefs, such that the set obtained through belief deletion is compatible with the new observations. In saying this, we have made a simplifying assumption: none of the new beliefs may be among those deleted. This can be thought of as saying that our agent will never disbelieve what it senses. The role of the function μ then, is this: given a set of current beliefs, and a set of new observations, return the set of possible deletion sets from the current beliefs, such that any one of the possible deletion sets, when removed from the current beliefs, makes the union of the current beliefs and new observations consistent. Consistency is defined with respect to a set of domain constraints. A reasonable place to begin then, is by defining consistency for a set of beliefs. To do this we start with the notion of a *valuation*.

Definition 9. A function $\beta: Va \rightarrow Co \cup Va$ is called a *valuation*. We will often find it convenient to apply a valuation to arbitrary terms of L, and not just individual variables. To facilitate this, given any particular valuation β, we define $\hat{\beta}: Va \cup Co \rightarrow Va \cup Co$ as follows.

$$\hat{\beta}(v) = v' \text{ iff } v \in Va \ \& \ \beta(v) = v'$$
$$\hat{\beta}(v) = v \text{ iff } v \in Va \ \& \ \beta(v) \text{ is undefined}$$
$$\hat{\beta}(c) = c \text{ iff } c \in Co$$

This usage induces, canonically, a mapping $\hat{\beta}: L_E \cup L_B \rightarrow L_E \cup L_B$
by $\hat{\beta}(\sigma(\alpha_1,\alpha_2, \cdots ,\alpha_n)) = \sigma(\hat{\beta}(\alpha_1),\hat{\beta}(\alpha_2), \cdots ,\hat{\beta}(\alpha_n))$.
We also expand $\hat{\beta}$ for sets of formulae $T \subseteq L_E \cup L_B$ by $\hat{\beta}(T) = \{\hat{\beta}(t) \mid t \in T\}$.

Definition 10. Let $c,c' \subseteq L_B$, and let $X \subseteq \Pi(L_B)$. c and c' are called *cases*, and X is called a set of *domain constraints*.

(1)   We say that c' *can be bound in* c, iff there exists an injective valuation $\beta: \hat{\beta}(c') \subseteq c$. An injective valuation is one which, for all $x,y \in domain(\beta)$, if $x \neq y$, then $\beta(x) \neq \beta(y)$. Requiring the valuation to be injective ensures that different variables in a domain constraint will be bound to different constants when attempting to detect constraint violations.

(2)   We say that c *is consistent with respect to* $X \subseteq \Pi(L_B)$ iff $\forall \ x \in X: x$ cannot be bound in c.

Definition 11. Let $c,c' \subseteq L_B$ be cases, and let $X \subseteq \Pi(L_B)$ be a set of domain constraints.

(1)   A set $q \subseteq L_B$ is said to *reconcile* c *with* c' *(with respect to X)* iff
a) $(c \cup c') - q$ is consistent with respect to X;
b) $c' \subseteq (c \cup c') - q$ (or, equivalently, $q \cap c' = \varnothing$);
c) $\neg \exists \ q' \subseteq L_B$ such that $q' \subset q \ \& \ (c \cup c') - q'$ is consistent with respect to X.

(2)   We define the *consistency maintenance function*, $\mu: (\Pi(L_B) \times \Pi(L_B)) \rightarrow \Pi(\Pi(L_B))$, with respect to X, as
$$\mu_X(c,c') = \{q \subseteq L_B \mid q \text{ reconciles } c \text{ with } c' \text{ (with respect to X)}\}.$$

For example, imagine that the agent's domain constraints, $X \subseteq \Pi(L_B)$ are the following.

$$\{\{ on(x_1,y_1), clear(y_1), block(y_1) \},$$
$$\{ on(x_2,y_2), on(x_2,z_2), block(x_2) \},$$
$$\{ on(x_3,y_3), on(z_3,y_3), block(y_3) \},$$
$$\{ block(x_4), table(x_4) \},$$
$$\{ weight(x_5,x_6), weight(x_5,x_7) \}\}$$

The first of these says that it is impossible for the agent to believe there is any block y_1 which is both clear and under some other object. The second says that it is impossible for the agent to believe that there is any block x_2 which is on top of two different objects simultaneously. The third domain constraint specifies that it is impossible to believe that there is any block y_3 which is under two different blocks. The fourth says that it is impossible for the agent to believe that any given object x_4 is both a block and a table. The final constraint specifies that it is impossible to believe that one object has more than one weight.

Notice that this sort of belief *consistency* maintenance is *not explicitly* addressed by classical reason maintenance systems. Doyle [7, p.349] states that his RMS "... does not maintain consistency of beliefs in any important sense.". Once the *reasoner* using Doyle's RMS has decided which beliefs conflict, RMS calculates the follow-on consequences of the decision. μ formalizes the calling program's *reasons* for detecting inconsistencies. However, as noted below, we could benefit from the addition of RMS's dependency directed backtracking ideas when removing beliefs to reconcile inconsistencies. The mechanism which we define below that uses μ is unnecessarily "direct" in its operation.

There will often be many ways of reconciling any given inconsistency. In the formalisation which follows, we insist that one of the possible reconciliations be chosen, and the rest ignored. To this end, we require a reconciliation set selection function, $\psi: \Pi(\Pi(L_B)) \rightarrow \Pi(L_B)$. In the definitions below we assume that such a function exists, but do not explicitly define it. ψ incorporates a heuristic about which reconciliation set looks "best", and is thus extremely domain dependent. It must be specified as required for each application domain.

4.3. Projection.

We now use the consistency maintenance function in the definition of the simulated execution of an action. We must first define when a given e-element has *concession;* that is, when the event it denotes is believed by the agent to be enabled. In addition, we must define how a case (interpreted as a possible state of belief) changes under the *occurrence* of the action denoted. This definition of e-element occurrence gives us an accessibility relation on belief states for the agent. E-element occurrence will be used as a "state generator", permitting the definition of state-space structures which describe the behaviors sanctioned by a plan.

We have here a rather interesting decision to make, regarding the sort of story we would like to tell about plan projection. There are two obvious projection stories, and they differ as to what they say about how to use an e-element's external-results and internal-results postsets. Recall the motivation behind the introduction of these sets:

one set describes the external-results of an action (like STRIPS), and the other set describes the internal-results of the action.

How should these sets be used in deriving "successor" belief states? One answer is to use only an e-element's internal-results postset as a source of formulae to add to a generated state. This would seem to accurately model the occurrence of the action denoted by the e-element: the action's internal effects (e^+) are added to generate the successor state, and the action's external effects (e^-) have no effect on the belief state of the agent. Given a case c, and an e-element e which has concession in c, we refer to the state transition specified by a next-state generator which uses only e^+ as a *realistic transition*. Plan projections built from realistic transitions will be called realistic projections.

Using only realistic projections to explain net behavior would be tedious at best. If actions have been included in a plan on the basis of their declared external results postsets, it might prove efficacious for the agent to simply *assume* that the actions will actually function as the e-elements specify. To do this, the agent could use the external-results postset of an e-element to generate successor belief states. In this way, the e-element would be giving the agent sufficient cause to *assume* given formulas. Given a case c, and an e-element e which can occur in c, we refer to the state transition specified by a next-state generator which uses $e^{\pm}$ as an *assumptive transition*. Plan projections built from assumptive transitions will be called assumptive projections.

So which is the more appropriate execution story to tell? In general, it will depend on the nature of the agent's environment and plan execution system. If the external results of actions are likely to be sensed without intentional action towards that end, then an assumptive projection is adequate. If a domain is "extended" in such a way that the external effects of an action often occur beyond the agent's immediate sensory range, then it would be more appropriate to employ a realistic projection. However in general, it seems unnecessary to require that each relevant external action effect be monitored by the inclusion of explicit sensory actions in a plan.

It is important to realize that the particular execution story told does not affect the agent's ability to construct sensory plans. The internal and external results of an action are distinguished for the agent by e^+ and e^-, and it is this distinction that allows the agent to index the appropriate "sensory" and "motor" actions, as required. This indexing is performed in terms of the agent's goals, so actions are retrievable for the appropriate result.

We now define both a realistic and assumptive transition. However, in what follows, we will focus primarily on the assumptive transition, and the plan projection structures which are constructed from it.

Definition 12. Let $P = (B,E;F,A)$ be a plan, let $c \subseteq L_B$ be a case, let $X \subseteq \Pi(L_B)$ be a set of domain constraints, and let $\psi: \Pi(\Pi(L_B)) \rightarrow \Pi(L_B)$ be a reconciliation set selection function.

(1) Let $e \in E$. We say that e *has concession in c* (is *c-enabled*) iff $^+e \subseteq c$ & $\forall$ *valuations* β: $\beta(^-e) \cap c = \emptyset$.

(2) Let $e \in E$, and e be c-enabled. The *realistic follower case to c under e (respecting X)* is c', given by

$$c' = (c \cup e^+) - \psi(\mu_X(c,e^+)).$$

This is written as $c \xrightarrow[e]{X} c'$, with a particular ψ to be understood from context.

(3)   Let $e \in E$, and e be c-enabled. The *assumptive follower case to c under e (respecting X)* is c', given by

$$c' = (c \cup e^{\pm}) - \psi(\mu_X(c,e^{\pm})).$$

This is written as $c \overset{X}{\underset{e}{\Rightarrow}} c'$, with a particular ψ to be understood from context.

Graphical convention. When drawing a case $c \subseteq L_B$, in terms of a plan $P = (B,E;F,A)$, we place a dot (a *token*) inside each and only those circles labelled with formulae in B which are also in c.

Definition 12.1 expresses the conditions under which any given e-element is allowed to occur (has concession, or is enabled). We interpret the enable-out preset of any e-element as containing those b-elements (formulae from L_B) that must not be in the world model if the action referenced by the e-element is to be enabled. This is captured in definition 12.1 by insisting that a condition on e-element concession is: $^-e \cap c = \varnothing$; that is, by insisting that the element's enable-out preset has no intersection with the given case. Similarly, the enable-in preset is understood to contain those formulae that must be in the world model if the action is to be enabled. This appears as the requirement: $^+e \subseteq c$. This condition on concession ensures that the e-element's enable-in preset *is* contained within the given case.

Notice that neither definition of e-element occurrence allows e-elements to directly remove b-elements from the case in which they occur. This is interpreted as saying that no action *directly* causes the agent to stop believing anything. B-elements are only removed through the consistency maintenance function μ, in conjunction with the domain specific reconciliation set selector ψ. What is suggested for removal is a function of the enabling case, and the appropriate postset of the e-element that occurs. The only way a belief is ever removed from the enabling case is if the consistency maintenance function requires it. This means that old beliefs are only removed when they can be shown to be inconsistent with new ones. This is more general than having each e-element commit itself to specifying a "delete-list". What is deleted is quite literally a function of what is currently the case and what is being added to the current case.

We now define what it means to apply a *set* of e-elements to a case, since it may be possible for some number of actions to occur at the same time. By defining the occurrence of a set of e-elements, we achieve the ability to perform least-commitment action-ordering plan construction: if some actions are causally independent, the e-elements which model them can be applied as a set and reasoning can continue from the resulting case. To define this more carefully, we begin by specifying when a set of e-elements is *detached*; that is, when the actions they denote are causally independent.

Definition 13. Let $P = (B,E;F,A)$ be a plan, let $X \subseteq \Pi(L_B)$ be a set of domain constraints, and let $c, c', c'' \subseteq L_B$ be cases.

(1)   Let $e_1, e_2 \in E$ be c-enabled. We say that e_1 and e_2 are *causally independent in c* iff
$c \overset{X}{\underset{e_1}{\Rightarrow}} c'$ with e_2 being c'-enabled, and $c \overset{X}{\underset{e_2}{\Rightarrow}} c''$ with e_1 being c''-enabled.

(2)   A set of events $G \subseteq E$ is called *detached in c* iff $\forall e \in G$: e is c-enabled & $\forall e_1, e_2 \in G$, $e_1 \neq e_2$: e_1 and e_2 are causally independent in c.

(3)   Let G be detached in c. G is called an *assumptive step from c to c' (respecting X)*, written $c \overset{X}{\underset{G}{\Rightarrow}} c'$, where c' is given by $c' = (c \cup G^{\pm}) - \psi(\mu_X(c, G^{\pm}))$. (With a particular ψ understood from context.)

Notice that if G contains only one element, i.e., if $G = \{e\}$, then $c \overset{X}{\underset{G}{\Rightarrow}} c'$ is equivalent to $c \overset{X}{\underset{e}{\Rightarrow}} c'$.

It is possible to define an exactly analogous *realistic step*, simply by replacing the assumptive transition specification with a realistic one. However, we define only the assumptive step, since it is generally more useful.

To enable simple state-space reasoning over a plan net, we must define the projection of a plan as a directed graph structure. The nodes of any projection graph are *cases*, that is, sets of L_B formulae, and the arcs are labelled with sets of e-elements from the plan net being projected. Thus, if an initial node of the projection of a plan is a subset of the current world model, the nodes reachable from that node in the projection describe possible future belief states for the agent. A state-space structure is easily represented as a graph. Unfortunately, we do not have room here to present all required graph definitions. Basic familiarity with graph theory concepts is therefore assumed.

Definition 14. Let $G = (H, P)$ be a graph, let $c \subseteq L_B$ be a case, and let $h \in H$ be a node in G.

(1)   We define the *subgraph of G rooted at h as* $G' = (H', P')$, where $H' \subseteq H$ is given by
$$H' = \{h' \in H \mid \exists \ a \ path \ in \ G \ h_i l_i h_j l_j \cdots h' \ \& \ h_i = h\},$$
and $P' \subseteq P$ is given by $P' = \{(h, l, h') \in P \mid h, h' \in H'\}$.

(2)   We say that $h \in H$ *satisfies c* iff $\exists$ *a finite path* $h_1 l_1 h_2 l_2 \cdots h'$, such that $c \subseteq h' \ \& \ h = h_1$.

(3)   We say that a graph G *satisfies c* iff $\forall$ initial nodes h, h satisfies c.

(4) $h \in H$ is called a *choice point* iff $\mid \{(h_1, l, h_2) \in P \mid h_1 = h\} \mid > 1$.

(5)   We denote the set of *choices available at h* by $\bar{h} = \{h_j \mid (h_i, l, h_j) \in P \ \& \ h_i = h\}$.

Definition 15. Let $P = (B, E; F, A)$ be a plan, let $c \subseteq L_B$ be a case, and let $X \subseteq \Pi(L_B)$ be a set of domain constraints. We define the *assumptive projection of P from c (respecting X)* as the graph $S_{PX} = (H, R)$, where the set of nodes, H, is given by $H = \{c' \subseteq L_B \mid c \ r_P^* \ c'\}$,

and $r_P \subseteq \Pi(L_B) \times \Pi(L_B)$ is given by $c_1 \ r_P \ c_2 \iff \exists \ G \subseteq E: c_1 \overset{X}{\underset{G}{\Rightarrow}} c_2$,

and the set of arcs, R, is given by $R = \{(c_1, G, c_2) \in (H \times \Pi(E) \times H) \mid \exists \ G \subseteq E: c_1 \overset{X}{\underset{G}{\Rightarrow}} c_2\}$.

Definition 15 uses the definition of a step to construct a reachability relation r_P on cases. Under transitive closure, this relation can be used to find all the cases reachable from an initial case, c. This is how the set of nodes, H, is derived. The set of arcs, R, is built up by finding nodes in H that are reachable from each other in a single step. An exactly analogous definition for the *realistic projection of P from c (respecting X)* can be given, simply by replacing the assumptive step specification $\overset{X}{\underset{G}{\Rightarrow}}$, with the realistic step $\overset{X}{\underset{G}{\rightarrow}}$.

We now suggest a definition of *sound* execution advice. The idea is that a plan's advice must contain the information required to remove harmful residual non-determinism within the plan. The advice should not restrict legitimately causally independent actions from occurring concurrently, but it should prevent planned actions from occurring in an order permitted by the causal structure of the plan but unintended by the agent. A classic example of this occurs in blocks-world tower construction problems: given the problem of creating a tower with block C on the bottom, block B in the middle, and block A on top, the plan construction reasoning must order the two required stack actions to reflect the agent's overall goals. To see this, assume that all blocks are initially clear and on the table. If a plan calls for stacking A on B, and B on C, then *either* stack action can actually proceed from the initial state. It is not an ordering enforced by *teleology* that requires the stacking of B on C before A on B. Rather, it is the agent's *intention* regarding overall plan outcome that directs the action sequencing.

Definition 16. Let $P = (B,E;F,A)$ be a plan, let $c,c' \subseteq L_B$ be cases, let $X \subseteq \Pi(L_B)$ be a set of domain constraints, and let $S_{PX} = (H,R)$ be the assumptive projection of P from c (respecting X).

(1)   We say that the execution advice A is *sound with respect to* c' iff $\forall h \in H$, if h is a choice point and $\exists\, h' \in \bar{h}$, such that h' satisfies c', then either

      a) $\forall h' \in \bar{h}$, h' satisfies c' or

      b) $\forall h' \in \bar{h}$, if h' does not satisfy c' then $\exists\, (G',G) \in A$ such that

            i) $(h,G,h') \in R$ and

            ii) $(h,G',h'') \in R$ & h'' *satisfies* c'

This says that for all choice points in a plan's assumptive projection, if there is *any* hope for success at the choice point, then either all choices lead to success, or for each choice point that could lead to failure, there is advice about another possible alternative, such that the suggested alternative *can* lead to success. In essence, when there is still hope for success, the advice prevents the wrong choice from being made.

4.4. Assumptions and reasons.

We now define various modes of existence for formulae of L_B. The basic idea is that, given a case c and an L_B formula p, we can classify p as *in c*, or *not in c*, and in addition say whether or not there is a *reason* for this formula being in or not in c. Notice that this is a more symmetrical relationship than commonly occurs in reason maintenance formalisms. Here, we are interested in giving a reason for a formula's *out*-ness, as well as its *in*-ness. In our framework, to give a reason for an *in* formula is to justify *belief* in it; we consider all other *in* formulae to be *assumptions*. To give a reason for p being out is to give reason to *disbelieve* it; if no such reason can be given, the formula is simply *not believed*. The difference between lack of belief and disbelief is missing from standard reason maintenance accounts of belief and reason.

Definition 17. Let $c \subseteq L_B$ be a case, let $P = (B,E;F,A)$ be a plan, let $X \subseteq \Pi(L_B)$ be a set of domain constraints, and let $p \in L_B$ be a formula of L_B.

(1) *p is in c* iff $p \in c$.

(2) *p is out of c* (or *p is not in c*) iff $\{p\} \cap c = \varnothing$.

(3) Let *p* be in *c*. If $\exists\, e \in E_P \,\exists\, c' \subseteq L_B: c' \xrightarrow[e]{X} c$ & $\{p\} \cap c' = \varnothing$ then we say that *p is believed in c with reason e* (or *p is a belief with respect to c and P*), otherwise we say that *p is assumed in c* (or *p is an assumption with respect to c and P*).

(4) Let *p* be out of *c*. If $\exists\, r \in R: \mu_X(c, \{p\}) = R$ & $r \neq \varnothing$ then we say that *p is disbelieved in c with reason r* (or *p is a disbelief with respect to c and X*), otherwise we say that *p is not believed in c* (or *p is a non-belief with respect to c and X*).

Thus, a given formula is *in* with respect to a set of formulae if it is a member of the set; it is *not in* if it is not a member of the set. Definitions 17.3 and 17.4 capture the idea of providing *reasons* for a formula being *in* or *out*. A reason for being *in* is formalised as an e-element which under realistic application can produce the desired formula. Informally, we sometimes say that the b-element can be *discharged* by an e-element that is a reason for it. A reason for being *out* is a reconciliation set which would have to be removed from the set of formulae if the individual formula were to be added. This is formalized using μ: if the case which the formula is not in would become inconsistent by adding the formula, then there is a reason not to add it. The reason is one of the reconciliation sets that it would be necessary to remove, were the single formula to be added. The empty set, $\varnothing$, is not considered to be an adequate reason for disbelief.

4.5. Defining problems.

Using the definitions of a plan and a projection, we can now formalize *problems* and *potential solutions*.

Definition 18. A 4-tuple $R = (O, X, i, g)$ is called a *planning problem* iff

(1) *O* is a set of operators;

(2) $X \subseteq \Pi(L_B)$ is a set of domain constraints;

(3) $i \subseteq L_B$ is called the *initial case;*

(4) $g \subseteq L_B$ is called the *goal case.*

Definition 19. Let $P = (B, E; F, A)$ be a plan, let $R = (O, X, i, g)$ be a planning problem, let $S_{PX} = (H, R)$ be the assumptive projection of *P* from *i*, respecting *X*, and let $E_O = \bigcup\limits_{(B', E'; F', A') \in O} E'$ be the set of all e-elements in the operators in *O*. *P* is called a *potential solution* to *R* iff

(1) S_{PX} satisfies *g*.

(2) The execution advice *A* is sound with respect to *g*.

(3) $\forall e \in E_P \,\exists\, e' \in E_O \,\exists$ a valuation $\beta: e = \hat{\beta}(e')$. We say that the plan *P* is *composed* from the e-elements contained in the operators in *O*.

5. Two examples.

We now present two sample plan nets. We use the letters *v*, *w*, *x*, *y*, and *z* to denote variables, all other symbols are predicates or constants. The first plan net is shown graphically in figure 4, and describes the following behavior. The agent is initially at some location, *l1*. The goal is for the agent to be at some other location, *l2*. There are two preconditions for the agent moving from *l1* to *l2*: the formulas *at(me,l1)* and *signal(green)* must both be *in*. The scenario might be one in which the agent is on one side of a street, and wishes to cross to the other side. Being law-abiding, the agent will cross only when the pedestrian control light is green. The plan net calls for the possible occurrence of only three events: the agent moving from *l1* to *l2*, the signal changing from *red* to *green*, and the signal changing from *green* to *red*. According to the plan's structure, for the light to change from *green* to *red*, it must first be *green*. After changing, the light will be *red*. Similarly for the color change in the opposite direction.

The initial case (shown in figure 4) has the agent assuming itself to be at *l1*, and assuming that the signal light is *red*. The domain constraints for this example are {{*at(x,y)*, *at(x,z)*}, {*signal(v)*, *signal(w)*}}; these indicate

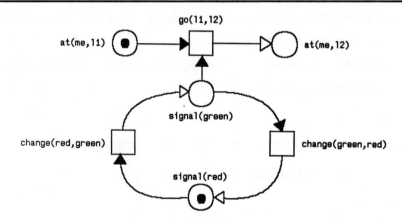

Figure 4: Crossing the road.

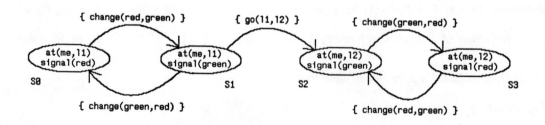

Figure 5: What the net of figure 4 can do.

that any object is only ever *at* one location, and that the traffic signal light is only ever one color. An assumptive projection is given in figure 5 which uses this initial case and these domain constraints. The projection has the initial case labelled as S_0. Three other cases are reachable from S_0. The projection indicates that the light can change state an infinite number of times before any movements by the agent occur. The preconditions for moving from *l1* to *l2* are only met in S_1. Once the agent does move, an assumption about its new location forces a change in belief state, and now an infinite number of signal light changes can occur, with the agent assuming that it will be safely at location *l2*. All the formulas in all the cases in the projection are assumptions, since none can be *discharged* by unapplying any of the e-elements contained in the given plan net.

Our second example calls for an agent to open a combination safe. The safe's combination is written on a scrap of paper which the agent has in its possession. The plan appears in figure 6; we cannot give a projection due to space restrictions. We formulate a plan using two e-elements: one to model the action of reading the value of the combination from the paper, and one to model the action of dialing the combination on the safe. The preconditions for reading the combination from the paper are the formulas *looking-at(paper)*, *light(on)*, and *written-on(combination,paper)*; all must be *in*. In the initial case given graphically in figure 6, these preconditions are met. The *read* e-element models the action of reading the combination as having an internal result of the combination having a certain value, *y*. The variable *y* is used to indicate that the value of the combination cannot be determined yet. So the action of reading the combination causes a belief for the agent about the value of the safe's combination. This belief, plus the *assumption* that this combination in fact opens the specified safe, enables the e-element which models dialing the combination on the safe. Dialing the combination on the safe is described as having the result of the safe being open.

The *dial* e-element is an example of an action specification that is not fully complete when plan execution begins. In order to constitute an *executable description* of the action of dialing a combination on a safe, it must have all of its variable parameters bound to constants. If an appropriate action as modelled by the *read* e-element

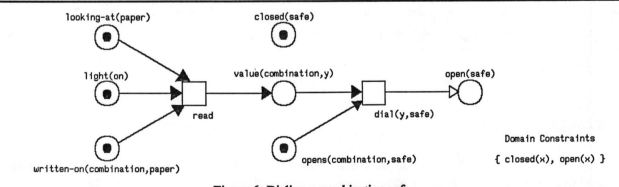

Figure 6: Dialing a combination safe.

does not actually occur, then no belief about the value of the safe's combination will be held by the agent when the time comes to open the safe. This is best considered to be a plan execution failure, since an action has not occurred as intended. If the *read* e-element is not realized as an action, then the *dial* e-element will not constitute an executable action description.

6. A brief discussion and conclusion.

It is possible to show that with appropriate restrictions, the existence of a path between two cases in a net's projection is equivalent to what Doyle [6, 7, 8] calls the *strict groundedness* of one set of beliefs in another; see [10] for a proof. The most obvious problem with what we have defined is the way that both the assumptive and realistic follower case generators *directly* remove one of the inconsistencies returned by μ. What is actually required is a *reasoned* retraction of inconsistencies, much as done by Doyle's RMS while performing dependency directed backtracking. Serious thought must also be given to the issue of plan net construction.

While plan nets do not yet provide a general reason maintenance facility, they do begin to tie together some of the required notions for use in a general purpose planning system. In particular, we now have an explicit representation for a plan's teleology [33, 34, 35, 36, 38, 39, 44, 45, 46, 26], have a clear definition of when actions are causally independent [31, 32], and now have the fundamentals of a plan representation which includes essential reason maintenance abilities as a fundamental component. The novel offerings of this representation are its ability to describe the sensory results of actions, and the way it allows for the specification of iterative behavior through its basic net structure.

ACKNOWLEDGEMENTS.

I'd like to thank Austin Tate, Peter Ross, and Alan Black for their careful reading of this paper and thoughtful comments. Alan pointed out a fault in the paper which I have not corrected: jay-walking is actually *not* illegal in Scotland. Graeme Ritchie has helped this work in many ways, especially in the formalization of μ_X. This work has been made possible only through the enthusiastic supervision of Austin Tate, to whom I extend my thanks.

REFERENCES.

[1] Brauer, W. (ed.). 1979. Springer-Verlag LNCS series. *Net theory and applications*. Proceedings of the Advanced Course on General Net Theory of Processes and Systems, Hamburg.

[2] Chapman, D. 1985. Nonlinear planning: a rigorous reconstruction. In proc. of *IJCAI-9*. pp. 1022-1024.

[3] Currie, K., & Tate, A. 1985. O-Plan: Control in the open planning architecture. *Proc. of the BCS Expert Systems '85 Conference.* Warwick (December), Cambridge University Press.

[4] de Kleer, J. 1984. Choices without backtracking. In proc. of *AAAI-84.* pp. 79-85.

[5] Doyle, J. 1979. A truth maintenance system. *AI Journal.* Vol. 12, pp. 231-272.

[6] Doyle, J. 1982. Some theories of reasoned assumptions: an essay in rational psychology. Department of Computer Science, Carnegie-Mellon University. (CMU-CS-83-125).

[7] Doyle, J. 1983. The ins and outs of reason maintenance. In proc. of *IJCAI-8.* pp. 349-351.

[8] Doyle, J. 1985. Reasoned assumptions and pareto optimality. In proc. of *IJCAI-9.* pp. 87-90.

[9] Drummond, M.E. 1985. Refining and extending the procedural net. In proc. of *IJCAI-9.* pp. 1010-1012.

[10] Drummond, M.E. 1986. Plan nets: a formal representation of action and belief for automatic planning systems. Ph.D. dissertation, Department of Artificial Intelligence, University of Edinburgh, Edinburgh, Scotland.

[11] Fikes, R.E., Nilsson, N.J. 1971. STRIPS: a new approach to the application of theorem proving to problem solving. *Artificial Intelligence 2.* pp. 189-208.

[12] Fodor, J. 1981. Methodological solipsism considered as a research strategy in cognitive psychology. In John Haugeland (ed.). *Mind Design.* Montgomery, Vt. Bradford Books.

[13] Georgeff, M. 1984. A theory of action for multiagent planning. In proc. of *AAAI-84.* Austin, TX. pp. 121-125.

[14] Georgeff, M., Lansky, A., Bessiere, P. 1985. A procedural logic. In proc. of *IJCAI-9.* pp. 516-523.

[15] Hayes, P. 1981. The frame problem and related problems in artificial intelligence. In *Readings in artificial intelligence.* B.L. Webber & N.J. Nilsson (eds.), Tioga publishing co., Palo Alto, CA. pp. 223-230. Originally appeared in *Artificial and human thinking.* A. Elithorn & D. Jones (eds.), Jossey-Bass. pp. 45-59.

[16] Konolidge, K. 1980. A first order formalization of knowledge and action for a multiagent planning system. *Artificial Intelligence Center Technical Note 232,* SRI International, Menlo Park, California. (Also in *Machine intelligence 10,* 1981).

[17] Levesque, H.J. 1984. A logic of implicit and explicit belief. In the proc. of *AAAI-84.* pp. 198-202.

[18] McCarthy, J. 1958. Programs with common sense. *Semantic information processing.* M. Minsky, ed., pp. 403-418. Cambridge: MIT Press.

[19] McCarthy, J., and Hayes, P.J. 1969. Some philosophical problems from the standpoint of artificial intelligence.

Machine Intelligence 4. B. Meltzer & D. Michie, eds. pp. 463-502. Edinburgh: Edinburgh University Press.

[20] Moore, R.C. 1977. Reasoning about knowledge and action. In proc. of *IJCAI-5.* pp. 223-227.

[21] Moore, R.C. 1980. Reasoning about knowledge and action. *Artificial Intelligence Center Technical Note 191,* SRI International, Menlo Park, CA.

[22] Moore, R.C. 1985. A formal theory of knowledge and action. In J.R. Hobbs & R.C. Moore (eds.) *Formal theories of the commonsense world.* Ablex series in artificial intelligence.

[23] Moore, R. C. and Hendrix, G. 1982. Computational models of belief and the semantics of belief sentences. In S. Peters & E. Saarinen (eds.). *Processes, beliefs, and questions.* D. Reidel Publishing Co. pp. 107-127.

[24] Nielsen, M., and Thiagarajan, P.S. 1984. Degrees of non-determinism and concurrency: a petri net view. *In proc. of the 4th conference on foundations of software technology and theoretical computer science.* (December).

[25] Nilsson, N. 1980. *Principles of Artificial Intelligence.* Tioga Publishing Co. Palo Alto, CA.

[26] Nilsson, N. 1985. Triangle tables: a proposal for a robot programming language. *Artificial Intelligence center Technical Note 347,* SRI International, Menlo Park, CA.

[27] Pednault, E.P.D. 1985. Preliminary report on a theory of plan synthesis. *Artificial Intelligence Center Technical Note 358,* SRI International, Menlo Park, CA.

[28] Peterson, J.L. 1977. Petri nets. *Computing surveys.* Vol. 9, No. 3, September.

[29] Peterson, J.L. 1980. *Petri net theory and the modeling of systems.* Prentice-Hall.

[30] Reisig, W. 1985. *Petri nets: an introduction.* Springer-Verlag, EATCS Monographs on theoretical computer science, vol. 4.

[31] Sacerdoti, E.D. 1975. The non-linear nature of plans. In the *advance papers of the 4th IJCAI,* Tbilisi, U.S.S.R.

[32] Sacerdoti, E.D. 1977. *A structure for plans and behavior.* American Elsevier, New York. Also SRI AI Tech. Note 109, August, 1975.

[33] Tate, A. 1974. Interplan: a plan generation system which can deal with interactions between goals. University of Edinburgh, Machine Intelligence Research Unit Memorandum MIP-R-109.

[34] Tate, A. 1975. Interacting goals and their use. In the *advance papers of the 4th IJCAI,* Tbilisi, U.S.S.R.

[35] Tate, A. 1975. *Using goal structure to direct search in a problem solver.* Ph.D. thesis, University of Edinburgh, Edinburgh, Scotland.

[36] Tate, A. 1976. Project planning using a hierarchic non-linear planner. University of Edinburgh, Department of Artificial Intelligence Research Report #25.

[37] Tate, A. 1977. Generating project networks. In proc. of *Proceedings of the 5th IJCAI*.

[38] Tate, A. 1984. Planning and condition monitoring in an FMS. International conference on Flexible Automation Systems. Institute of Electrical Engineers, London, UK (July).

[39] Tate, A. 1984. Goal structure -- capturing the intent of plans. *Proceedings of ECAI-84*. (September).

[40] Vere, S.A. 1983. Planning in time: windows and durations for activities and goals. *IEEE Transactions on Pattern Analysis and Machine Intelligence*. Vol. PAMI-5, No. 3, pp. 246-267.

[41] Vere, S.A. 1985. Splicing plans to achieve misordered goals. In proc. of *IJCAI-9*. pp. 1016-1021.

[42] Waldinger, R. 1977. Achieving several goals simultaneously. *Machine Intelligence 8*. In E.W. Elcock and D. Michie (Eds.), New York, Halstead/Wiley.

[43] Warren, D.H.D. 1974. Warplan: a system for generating plans. Memo 76, Computational Logic Dept., School of Artificial Intelligence, University of Edinburgh.

[44] Wilkins, D.E. 1983. Representation in a domain independent planner. In proc. of *IJCAI-8*. pp. 733-740.

[45] Wilkins, D.E. 1984. Domain independent planning: representation and plan generation. *Artificial Intelligence*, No. 22.

[46] Wilkins, D. 1985. Recovering from execution errors in SIPE. *Computational Intelligence 1*. pp. 33-45.

Possible Worlds Planning

Matthew L. Ginsberg
THE LOGIC GROUP
KNOWLEDGE SYSTEMS LABORATORY
Department of Computer Science
Stanford University
Stanford, California 94305

Abstract

General-purpose planning appears to be one of the most difficult theoretical problems in AI. I argue that this difficulty is due, at least in part, to the unavailability of an adequate formal framework for planning problems. STRIPS-like formalisms appear [8] to impose severe restrictions on the description of the planning domain, while approaches such as Green's [6] which are based on situation calculus [11] appear to have difficulty dealing with the frame and qualification problems [10].

I argue here that possible worlds [5] provide an alternative formalization of planning problems which can help address these issues. The formal description I present also will allow us to understand some existing techniques for controlling the search involved in planning, such as means-ends analysis [12] and consistency checking [2]. This understanding leads to a natural generalization of both of these methods, and we conclude by describing an implementation of these ideas.

1 Introduction

Existing formalizations of planning appear to be based, in one way or another, upon McCarthy's situation calculus [11]. My intention in this paper is to present another formalization based on the notion of possible worlds, and to argue that this formalization is better equipped than the conventional one to deal with some of the problems general-purpose planners must face.

These problems are of two sorts. Firstly, there are formalization issues which must be addressed. Coming to grips with the frame problem [10] is a necessity for any planning system; the ability to exploit the natural persistence of domain facts is crucial to the synthesis of complex plans. A second formalization problem is what McCarthy calls the *qualification problem* [10]: in general, the preconditions to any specific action include many "default" entries. McCarthy's example has to do with starting one's car in the morning. It is not sufficient to simply insert the key in the ignition and turn it; one must also guarantee (for example) that there is no potato in the tailpipe. Planners working in commonsense domains will need to handle qualified actions of this sort.

The second problem planners must address is a consequence of the enormous size of the search space generated during planning itself. A variety of methods have been proposed for this, such as consistency checking [2], which prunes portions of the search space which can be shown not to contain a valid plan for some goal, and hierarchical planning [16], which proceeds by first building a "skeletal" plan and then refining its details. Wilkins [22] has considered the possibility of planning subgoals separately and then combining the partial plans in ways which ensure that they do not conflict with one another.

Another possibility which has been principally ignored is to select planning subgoals after performing a limited amount of inference involving the interaction between the specified goal and the state of the planner's domain. Consistency checking is only a first step in this direction; an approach based on possible worlds can generalize this idea considerably.

A simple blocks world problem which will motivate some of the following work is presented in the next section. Section 3 describes the basic possible worlds construction; these ideas are also discussed in considerably greater detail in [5]. Section 4 proceeds to apply these ideas to planning matters, discussing applications both to formalization issues and to those involved in control of search.

A theoretical comparison with existing formulations is the subject of section 5. Again, formal and search issues are considered separately. We discuss the relation of a possible worlds formalization to that used by STRIPS, and to that derived

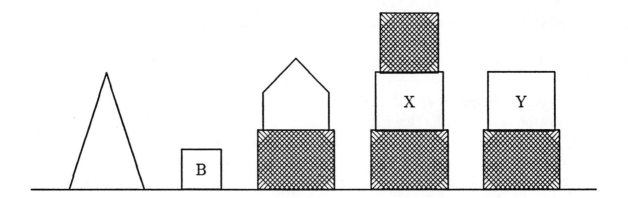

Figure 1: Put B on an unshaded object on the table

from situation calculus. The comparison between control based on possible worlds and search control based on previous ideas also allows us to draw some conclusions about the potential effectiveness of the protocol used to mediate between control and planning activity.

An implementation of these ideas is discussed in section 6. The prototype planner operates in a simple kitchen domain, attempting valiantly to boil some water. An experimental comparison with other methods is also drawn.

2   A blocks world example

Consider the scenario in figure 1. The goal is to put the small unshaded block B on any other unshaded object after moving the second object to the table.

Both formalization and search issues arise in solving this problem. The qualification problem appears because of the fact that if we attempt to move B onto either of the pyramid-like objects, it will fall off.

One solution, of course, would be to include in our rule describing allowable block movements a condition requiring that the target block not be pointed. The difficulty is that there are potentially an infinite number of such preconditions. It would be more effective and parsimonious to describe these apparent preconditions in terms of domain constraints indicating, for example, that pointed blocks can never have anything above them, and to have the planner check the consistency of the result of an action in terms of these domain constraints before including the action in a partial or potential plan. A car known to have a potato in its tailpipe cannot be started; a block known to be pointed cannot have another block placed above it.

Even after restricting our attention to the two rectangular unshaded blocks in the figure, we must decide on which we will attempt to place B. It is clear that the block Y, which is already clear, is a more sensible choice to pass to our planner than X is.

The reason, however, is *not* that the plan for getting B onto Y will work out to be shorter than the plan for getting B onto X. It would be useful to be able to decide to plan using Y before we have actually generated any plans at all. This is a consequence of the fact that each of the planning steps involved (e.g., move Y to the table, clear off X, etc.) may be extremely complex.

Intuitively, the reason is clear: the presence of the additional block on top of X is an obstruction to our achievement of the goal. In terms of possible worlds, the world in which B is on X and X is on the table requires that we:

1. Get X on the table,

2. Clear the top of X, and

3. Put B on X,

while the possible world in which B is on Y and Y is on the table requires only that we:

1. Get Y on the table, and

2. Put B on Y.

The reason we focus our planning activities around Y is because the second world above is nearer to the current situation than the first is.

Of course, in the presence of additional information (such as that Y is very heavy and will be difficult to move to the table), this may not be the case. One attractive feature of the possible worlds approach is that it allows us to formalize this intuition in terms of a distance measure among the possible worlds involved.

3   Possible worlds

3.1   Formal description

I discuss in [5] the formal construction of a *possible world* corresponding to the addition of some new fact to a logical database. Informally, if we have some collection S of facts which describe the current situation, we wish to add to S some new fact

p (which may well be inconsistent with S) and to construct the "nearest" possible world in which p holds.

The formal construction proceeds by identifying subsets of S with these possible worlds, and noting that the nearness of a particular subset to the original situation described by S is reflected by how large the subset is; if $T_1 \subseteq T_2 \subseteq S$, T_2 is at least as close to S as T_1 is. We also allow for the possibility of there being some "protected" subset P of S (containing domain constraints, for example); the facts in P are assumed to be true in all possible worlds.

Formally, we have the following: Let S be a set of logical formulae, P the protected sentences in S, and suppose that p is some additional formula. Now define a *possible world for p in S* to be any subset $T \subseteq S$ such that $P \subseteq T$, $T \cup \{p\}$ is consistent and such that T is maximal under set inclusion subject to these constraints. We will denote the collection of all possible worlds for p in S by $W(p, S)$.

Returning to our blocks world example, suppose that we label the unlabeled blocks in the diagram by C, D, E, F, G and H (from left to right on the page, and top to bottom). We then might have the following description of the situation presented in figure 1:

	on(C,table)	unshaded(B)
*	on(B,table)	unshaded(C)
	on(D,E)	unshaded(D)
	on(E,table)	unshaded(X)
*	on(F,X)	unshaded(Y)
*	on(X,G)	
	on(G,table)	shaded(E)
	on(Y,H)	shaded(F)
	on(H,table)	shaded(G)
		shaded(H)
	pointed(C)	
	pointed(D)	

There are also the associated domain constraints:

$$on(x,y) \wedge y \neq z \;\rightarrow\; \neg on(x,z)$$
$$pointed(x) \;\rightarrow\; \neg on(z,x)$$
$$on(x,y) \wedge y \neq \texttt{table} \wedge x \neq z \;\rightarrow\; \neg on(z,y)$$

Assuming that we are not prepared to drop the domain constraints appearing at the end of the above description, there is a unique possible world corresponding to the goal $\text{on}(B, X) \wedge \text{on}(X, \texttt{table})$. This possible world corresponds to the removal of the three facts marked with an asterisk in the domain description.

There are two possible worlds corresponding to the satisfaction of the more general goal $\exists x.\text{unshaded}(x) \wedge \text{on}(B, x) \wedge \text{on}(x, \texttt{table})$. One of these binds x to X and matches the world described above. The other binds x to Y and removes only $\text{on}(B, \texttt{table})$ and $\text{on}(Y, H)$ from the initial description. Note, however, that since neither of the two subsets corresponding to these two worlds is included in the other, *both* of these are possible worlds associated with the general goal.

Selecting between these possible worlds requires adding domain-dependent information to this construction. This is also discussed in [5]; the essential idea is to consider the subsets of S as ordered not by set inclusion, but by some other partial order $\leq$ which generalizes it (so that $T_1 \subseteq T_2 \Rightarrow T_1 \leq T_2$). We now repeat the definition exactly, defining possible worlds to correspond to subsets which are not merely maximal in a set-theoretic sense, but which are maximal with respect to $\leq$ as well.

In our blocks world example, we might take $T_1 \leq T_2$ just in case $|T_1| \leq |T_2|$, so that we attempt to remove from S a subset of minimal cardinality. In this case, the unique possible world corresponding to the generalized goal would bind x to Y and remove the two sentences mentioned earlier.

Alternatively, it might be the case that Y is known to be very heavy and difficult to move. We could capture this by taking $\leq$ to be set inclusion, augmented by:

$$\texttt{on(Y,H)} \in T_1 - T_2 \Rightarrow T_1 > T_2.$$

In this case, the unique possible world for the generalized goal will bind x to X; we have accurately captured the information that moving Y involves a "substantial" change to the database.

3.2   Possible worlds and default logic

In the absence of domain-dependent information, this construction can also be described using either Reiter's default logic [13] or circumscription [10,9]. We present only the first description here; the second can be found in [5].

Let S be some collection of sentences, and P the protected subset of S. Now consider a default theory in which the default rules are given by

$$\frac{Mq}{q}$$

for each $q \in S - P$, so that q holds in the absence of information proving it false. The facts in the default theory consist of p, together with sentences in P. We now have the following:

Theorem 3.1 *The possible worlds for p in S are in natural correspondence with the extensions of the above default theory.*

Proof. See [5].   □

This correspondence is also discussed in [14]; Reiter goes on to show how it is possible to capture some sorts of domain-dependent information in this framework, although it does not yet appear that possible worlds generated using arbitrary partial orders will always correspond naturally to results obtained using some default theory.

3.3   Automatic generation of possible worlds

The existing implementation of the ideas presented in section 3.1 proceeds by examining proofs of the negation of the supplied premise p. Just enough (where "just" is interpreted using the partial order on subsets of S) must be removed from the original world description to invalidate each of these proofs; having done so, the result will necessarily be consistent with p.

Details on this process can be found in [5]; the point of interest as far as planning goes is that there is a fundamental difference in outlook between this approach and one which uses, for example, the implementation discussed by Reiter for default logic [13].

Reiter proceeds by developing extensions from the "base" set of those facts which are known to hold even in the absence of default information, gradually adding to these facts the consequences of the default rules of inference. The fact that there may be more than one extension of a given default theory corresponds to the fact that the order in which the default rules are applied may govern the subsequent applicability of other default rules.

The possible worlds approach is the reverse of this. Here, the ideas is to start with a "maximal" extension in which *all* of the default rules have been fired, and to then retract just as many of these conclusions as necessary to maintain consistency.

Clearly, there are problems for which either of the two approaches is more suitable than the other. But in dealing with (for example) the frame problem, which is described by a very *large* number of default rules (one for each database fact, essentially), and where almost all of these default rules will fire successfully (hence the applicability of the cartoonist's metaphor), it seems likely that the possible worlds approach, which modifies only that part of the picture which is changing while retaining the rest automatically, will be the more effective of the two. Of course, even within the space of planning problems, it will be possible to come up with domains which are changing so rapidly that Reiter's approach is the more useful one. But it seems unlikely that this will be the norm. In addition, it appears that the possible worlds approach is slightly the more powerful of the two epistemically, because of its general ability to deal with domain-dependent information. We compare these two approaches at greater length in section 5.1.2.

4   Possible worlds and planning

4.1   Formalization

Suppose that we are given some initial world description S, together with some collection A of actions. To each action $a \in A$ is associated a precondition $p(a)$ and a consequence $c(a)$. Informally, the precondition must hold if the action is to be possible, and the result of the action is to add the consequence $c(a)$ to the world description.

Now if we are given some world description S and some premise p such that $W(p, S)$ is nonempty, we will define the *result* of p in S, to be denoted $r(p, S)$, to be any collection of sentences such that

$$r(p, S) \models q \Leftrightarrow [W \in W(p, S) \rightarrow (W \cup \{p\} \models q)].$$

In other words, some fact is entailed by the result of p in S if and only if it is true in *every* possible world for p in S.

Now let $a_1, \ldots, a_n$ be a sequence of actions. We define a corresponding sequence of situations recursively by:

$$s_i = \begin{cases} S, & \text{if } i = 0, \\ r(c(a_i), s_{i-1}), & \text{if } 0 < i \le n. \end{cases} \tag{1}$$

We will say that a sequence of actions is *viable* if $s_{i-1} \models p(a_i)$ and $W(c(a_i), s_{i-1}) \ne \emptyset$ for all $i \in 1, \ldots, n$, and will say that the sequence *achieves* a goal g if $s_n \models g$.

The formalization difficulties arising from the frame problem are captured naturally by the possible worlds construction used to generate the result of an action. This is also discussed in [5].

For the qualification problem, consider again the car with a potato in its tailpipe. Now the action of turning the key in the ignition will supposedly have the consequence of the car's being running. Provided that there is a domain constraint in our database indicating that cars with potatoes in their tailpipes cannot be running, however, the (apparent) result of turning the key in the ignition will indeed be for the car to be running, *and also for the potato to be removed from the tailpipe*. It is straightforward to use this information by having the possible worlds generator inform the planner of this "hidden" precondition.

Formalizing this requires the addition of new information into our domain description. What we need to do is to make the set P of protected axioms in our domain description a function of the action being taken. (Alternatively, we might make the partial order dependent on the action being taken. This is a more powerful approach but will involve specifying much more additional domain information.) If block A is on block B and we move block A, it will necessarily no longer be on block B, so that $on(x, y)$ is unprotected for the action $move(x, z)$. Other domain facts are protected.

Returning to our potato and tailpipe example, removing the potato from the tailpipe is protected relative to turning the key in the ignition. This leads us to conclude that turning the key is not a viable plan for getting the car running. Of course, the plan would be viable were it not for the potato's being there in the first place.

This idea has wider application than merely the qualification problem. Suppose that we have domain constraints in a blocks world problem indicating that any block can be in only one place at a given time, and that a block can support as most one other. Suppose also that the single consequence of moving a block b to a location l is that the block is now on top of l. What should the preconditions of this action be?

The addition of the new fact $on(b,l)$ will require our removing from the database the fact giving b's original location and, if l is a block that initially had something else on it, say x, the fact $on(x,l)$ will also need to be removed. We have already seen that the first of these facts (essentially that the original supporting block was occupied) should be unprotected relative to the motion, while the second (that l can no longer support anything else, since b is on it) should not be. This will result in the planning formalism automatically generating the precondition of clearing the top of l before moving some other block onto it. Thus the only precondition which must be supplied by the user is that the block being moved be clear before the action can proceed. But note that this requirement does *not* follow from the existing constraints on the blocks world domain, and it is easy to imagine scenarios where entire stacks can be moved *en masse*, instead of only single blocks. It is fairly clear that the formalism we are proposing handles this exactly as it should, moving the entire stack from its original location to l.

4.2   Control

Formalization issues notwithstanding, controlling the size of the search space is one of the most difficult problems faced by a general-purpose planner. It appears that the possible worlds construction can be used to help control the size of this search space, and a discussion of this point is the aim of this section.

In order to provide a uniform framework for the discussion of both the possible worlds and other approaches to controlling planning search, I will present each of these approaches in terms of the A^* algorithm. Essentially, we will simplify the architecture of the planner by assuming that its aim is to find, via forward search, the shortest plan which achieves a fixed goal. This simplification will enable us to understand a variety of planning approaches in a uniform fashion, but the conclusions we will draw will remain valid as the architecture of the planner becomes more complex, involving backward search, means-ends analysis, hierarchical methods, or some other approach. Backward planning search is especially important in any domain of realistic complexity; the reason we have chosen to assume that our planner works forwards is to avoid the difficult formal issues involved in searching backwards through a domain which is fundamentally non-monotonic. Were these issues to be accurately addressed, the points we are making would carry through unchanged.

Repeating, the aim of the planner is to generate the shortest possible plan for achieving the given goal. Inputs to the planner are some initial state s_0, some goal condition g, and information about the set A of actions available. We also assume that the planner has some way to judge how far a general state S is from the goal g, and will denote this "distance" by $d^*(S, g)$. Then a natural way for the planner to proceed in its search is by using the A^* algorithm: if we label each node n in the portion of the search space explored thus far by $p(n)$, the number of planning steps required to reach n, the node to be expanded next is that for which the value $p(n) + d^*(n, g)$ is minimal. The algorithm terminates whenever a state is reached in which the goal holds.

Of course, the distance-judging function d^* is only an approximation to the *actual* distance from S to g, which we will denote by $d(S, g)$. If $d^*(S, g) \le d(S, g)$, so that we regularly underestimate the distance remaining to the goal, the approximating function d^* is called *admissible*. The usefulness of the A^* algorithm rests on following three observations:

1. If d^* is admissible, then the algorithm will succeed in finding an optimal path to the goal.

2. If d_1^* and d_2^* are both admissible, but $d_1^* \ge d_2^*$ for all S and g, the space explored

using the approximating function given by d_1^* will be a subset of that explored using that given by d_2^*.

3. If $d = d^*$, the algorithm is optimal, in that only nodes directly on the optimal path will be expanded.

One clearly admissible d^* is simply $d^*(S, g) = 0$; this corresponds to breadth-first search through the planning space. What is needed is some way to increase the approximating function while continuing to ensure its admissibility.

One possible way to address this depends on the descriptions of the planning domain and of the initial state S. Consider a blocks world application, where our database may well consist of a list of facts giving the location of each object in the domain. Individual actions can now change at most a single fact in the description of the world state.

Formally, given two lists of facts S_1 and S_2, we can define $|S_1 - S_2|$ to be the number of facts in S_1 whose negations are in S_2. Then the remarks of the previous paragraph amount to the observation that if S' is an immediate successor to S, then $|S' - S| \le 1$. We will refer to a planning domain with this property as *unitary*. For a single conjunctive goal $g = g_1 \wedge \cdots \wedge g_k$, we will abbreviate $|\{g_1, \ldots, g_k\} - S|$ to $|g - S|$.

Theorem 4.1 *In a unitary domain, the distance function $d_{me}^*(S, g) = |g - S|$ is admissible.*

Proof. Any plan which achieves g will necessarily reverse $|g - S|$ facts in the initial state. Since each action can reverse at most one such fact, the plan must be at least $|g - S|$ steps long. Thus

$$d(S, g) \ge |g - S| = d_{me}^*(S, g). \quad \square$$

The effect of using the above distance function is simply to ensure that we consider as early as possible actions that reduce the apparent distance to the goal. A similar result would hold in a backward planning system, ensuring that we act so as to minimize the apparent distance to the initial state.

A larger estimating function, but one which remains admissible, can be obtained using possible worlds. Specifically, suppose that we order the subsets of S not merely by set inclusion, but by cardinality, so that for $T, U \subseteq S$, $T < U$ if and only if $|T| < |U|$. We now have the following:

Theorem 4.2 *Consider the distance function given by:*

$$d_{pw}^*(S, g) = \begin{cases} |S| - |W|, & \text{where } W \text{ is a possible world for } g \text{ in } S; \\ \infty, & \text{if no such world exists.} \end{cases}$$

Then in a unitary domain, d^*_{pw} is admissible. In addition, $d^*_{pw} \geq d^*_{me}$.

Proof. There are two cases.

If there is no possible world for g in S, then there can be no plan which achieves g from S. Thus taking $d^*_{pw}(S, g) = \infty$ is admissible; clearly $\infty \geq d^*_{me}(S, g)$.

If there is a possible world for g in S, let W be such a world. Clearly any fact in S whose negation is in g must be missing from W, so that $d^*_{pw}(S, g) = |S| - |W| \geq |g - S| = d^*_{me}(S, g)$. To see that d^*_{pw} is admissible, let P be the shortest plan which achieves g from S, arriving at some final state s_n in which g holds. Now let S_n be that subset of S which holds in s_n. The length of P will be at least $|S| - |S_n|$, since the domain is unitary, but $|S_n| \leq |W|$ since $|W|$, as a possible world for g in S, is of maximal size. Thus

$$d(S, g) = |P| \geq |S| - |S_n| \geq |S| - |W| = d^*_{pw}(S, g). \qquad \square$$

Note that the possible worlds construction also addresses, to some extent, the issue of whether or not the goal g can be reached from the state S. If achieving the goal would involve the violation of some of the domain constraints, for example, there will be no possible world for g in S, and we will have $d^*_{pw}(S, g) = \infty$.

More importantly, this construction gives us a uniform way to consider our goal not as an independent unit (consistent or otherwise), but in terms of our current situation. Returning to the blocks world example in figure 1, we see that there can be no possible advantage to moving the shaded block above X because the state that would result is just as distant from the goal as is the initial state shown in the figure. Similar remarks hold for attempting to place B on either of the pointed blocks shown; our planning efforts are therefore directed in profitable directions.

At this point, we can relax our assumption that the planning domain being investigated be unitary. Specifically, we need only assume that the collection of all possible worlds (obtainable from *any* initial state) forms a *metric space*. We can use the metric ρ to define our partial order on possible worlds, saying that M_1 is closer to S than M_2 is if and only if

$$\rho(M_1, S) \leq \rho(M_2, S).$$

We now have:

Theorem 4.3 *Suppose that ρ is a metric on the possible worlds in some planning domain. For any goal g and initial state S, denote by $\rho(S, g)$ the distance between S and a possible world for g in S, taking $\rho(S, g) = \infty$ if no such world exists. Assume also that our actions are constrained in that, given any state S and any action a*

which can be applied to S, if S' is the result of the application, the $\rho(S, S') \leq \alpha$ for some fixed constant α. Now define

$$d^*(S, g) = \rho(S, g)/\alpha.$$

Then d^* is admissible.

Proof. Use the triangle inequality. If the shortest plan which achieves g from S consists of n actions $a_1, \ldots, a_n$, with intermediate states $S = s_0, s_1, \ldots, s_n$, where g holds in s_n, then

$$\rho(S, g) \leq \rho(S, s_n) \leq \rho(s_0, s_1) + \cdots + \rho(s_{n-1}, s_n) \leq n\alpha.$$

Therefore

$$d(S, g) = n \geq \rho(S, g)/\alpha. \qquad \square$$

Unitary domains are a special case of this result, having $\rho(S, g) = |S| - |W|$ and $\alpha = 1$.

If additional information is available regarding the structure of the space of possible worlds, it may be possible to incorporate this into our approach. Often, for example, the metric referred to in the above theorem will be a sum of distinct contributions (perhaps five blocks have to be moved and three need to be painted). Assuming that we have no move-and-paint actions, we might now replace $\rho(S, g)/\alpha$ in the theorem with

$$\sum_i \rho_i(S, g)/\alpha_i,$$

where i runs over the various "dimensions" in the combined metric. If actions exist which have advantageous effects in more than one of the dimensions being considered, we could replace the above sum with a maximization.

Finally, we should remark that there are many instances where the possible worlds approach will be of little or no help, since the metric used in theorem 4.3 may severely underestimate the actual planning distance to the goal.

Sussman's anomaly [21], pictured in figure 2, is typical. The goal is to get C on B on A; the situation is "anomalous" because the natural action of moving C onto B in fact takes us further from the goal. The possible worlds approach offers no help with this problem.

5   Comparison with existing work

5.1   Formalization

There are two existing formal characterizations of planning problems. One is that used by STRIPS [1], and the other is that of situation calculus. We discuss STRIPS

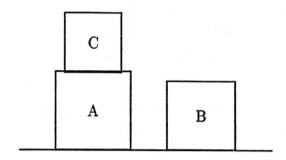

Figure 2: Sussman's anomaly

first.

5.1.1 STRIPS

STRIPS formalized actions in terms of preconditions, add lists and delete lists. The intention was that a given action could be executed if all of its preconditions were satisfied; the result of the execution was to add the facts in the add list to the world description while removing the facts in the delete list.

This approach is clearly extremely similar to ours. In both cases, a single model of the world is maintained, which is updated to reflect the result of any particular action (this is in contrast to the situation calculus approach). The difference is that in STRIPS, consistency is maintained after the execution of an action via the delete lists; in our approach, it is maintained inferentially using the constraints describing the domain in question.

In some sense, the STRIPS descriptions of the actions "compile" the interactions between these actions and the domain constraints; the delete lists contain the results of this compilation. As a consequence of this, effecting any particular action will generally be faster in a STRIPS-type system than in one based on possible worlds; unfortunately, the system designer is responsible for obtaining a satisfactory description of the actions.

As the domain becomes more complex, this will become an increasingly difficult task. Suppose, for example, that a block is capable of resting on several other blocks simultaneously, provided that those other blocks are close together. How are we to describe the fact that moving A to B should delete information regarding A's being on C only if B and C are fairly far apart? There seems to be no convenient way to do this within the STRIPS formalism.

This is a reflection of a more general problem. I point out in [5] that the problem of maintaining consistency of a database in the presence of new information is at best semi-decidable; it is therefore not theoretically possible for STRIPS to achieve this consistency maintenance via the simple mechanism of delete lists.

The STRIPS designers were aware of this. They get around the problem by requiring that the knowledge base contain only facts of a very specific nature, essentially guaranteeing through this that their description retains consistency. It is not clear how to maintain the validity of the restrictions on the knowledge base (essentially that it contain only atomic propositions) in more complex domains. Lifschitz [8] has also discussed this issue.

5.1.2 Situation calculus

Our argument against the formalism used by STRIPS was that although it was more efficient than the possible worlds approach, it was epistemologically inadequate. With regard to situation calculus, we make the other claim: that the approach we are presenting is computationally more efficient than the existing one.

The situational approach can be described using a predicate $\text{holds}(s, p)$, indicating that some proposition p holds in some state s. We are given an initial state s_0, together with information about it in the form of a variety of axioms $\text{holds}(s_0, p_i)$. We will generally abbreviate $\text{holds}(s, p)$ to p_s.

The situational approach can capture the frame axiom in one of two ways. The first, which we have already described, involves the use of the default rule

$$\frac{p_s \wedge \text{succ}(s, s') : M p_{s'}}{p_{s'}}. \tag{2}$$

In other words, if p holds in some situation s and s' is an (immediate) successor to s, then p holds in s' in the absence of information to the contrary.

The monotonic approach involves working through the example sufficiently to remove the defaults from the above description. Suppose, for example, that we denote by $\text{do}(s, \text{move}(x, y))$ the state obtained by moving x to y in state s. We now can replace (2) with:

$$\text{on}(x, y)_s \wedge x \neq z \rightarrow \text{on}(x, y)_{\text{do}(s, \text{move}(z, a))}. \tag{3}$$

In other words, if x is on y in some situation, x will remain on y after we move some other block z. Here is another example, stating that moving blocks does not change their color:

$$\text{color}(x, c)_s \rightarrow \text{color}(x, c)_{\text{do}(s, \text{move}(z, a))}.$$

In general, for each relation symbol in our domain and each possible action, we will need such a rule.

The efficiency question involves determining the computational cost of either describing the result of the action or determining whether or not some specific condition is satisfied after the action is complete.

In order to discuss this, suppose that we have some monotonic description of the planning domain, as in (3). Let r be a relation which appears in our domain description, and suppose that we have some "persistence rule" $k(r, a)$ such as (3) which describes the persistence of facts about r as action a takes place.

Now suppose that we are given some query q in which we are interested after completing some action. Suppose in addition that most of the facts in our domain do not change as a result of the action, so that the time needed to determine whether or not q holds will be approximately t, the (average) time it takes to check the antecedent of the relevant persistence rule.

Alternatively, we might be interested in the investigation of q after a sequence of n actions occurs. If investigating any single persistence rule involves looking up l facts in the database, in order to determine q at time n, we will need to investigate l facts at time $n - 1$, hence l^2 facts at time $n - 2$, and so on.

It will clearly be effective to cache the many facts which are investigated at early times. If we suppose that we are working in a domain containing d facts in the state description, a random collection of x of these facts (possibly with repetition) will involve, on average,

$$d \left[1 - \left(1 - \frac{1}{d} \right)^x \right]$$

distinct domain facts. The time spent investigating q will be spent investigating each of these domain facts at various times, and we need to evaluate:

$$\sum_{i=0}^{n-1} t \left\{ d \left[1 - \left(1 - \frac{1}{d} \right)^{\left(l^i \right)} \right] \right\}.$$

After some algebraic manipulation, this leads us to:

Theorem 5.1 *The time taken to investigate the query q in the monotonic approach is approximately given by:*

$$t(q) = \begin{cases} td(n - 1), & \text{if } l^{n-1} \gg d, \\ \frac{t(l^n - 1)}{l - 1}, & \text{if } l^{n-1} \ll d. \end{cases} \tag{4}$$

The possible worlds approach is somewhat simpler to analyze. Suppose that for each relation r, there are $c(r)$ domain constraints on r. If the result of an action is to add x new facts $p_1, \ldots, p_x$ to the database, the possible worlds construction now requires that we investigate each of these domain constraints to determine whether or not they lead to proofs of $\neg p_i$ for some i. If it takes time t' to examine each, the total time spent will therefore be approximately $\sum_1^x t'c(r_i)$, where r_i is the relation symbol appearing in p_i. Assuming that the constraints are distributed uniformly among the relation symbols, the time spent constructing the state corresponding to the consequences of the action will be $xt'c/r$, where c is the number of constraints on the domain in its entirety.

Theorem 5.2 *The time spent analyzing a sequence of n actions using the possible worlds approach is given by*

$$t(q) = \frac{nxt'c}{r}. \qquad \square \tag{5}$$

Both of these results are general; in order to compare the times required by the two approaches, we need to compare t' and c, which appear in the second theorem, with t and l, which appear in the first. Our basic plan for doing so will be to take a collection of persistence rules and derive domain constraints from them. The form of the derived domain constraints will enable us to estimate c and t'.

Suppose, then, that we have some domain constraint to the effect that if some condition α_+ holds, then q will persist through an action a. In other words, if q holds in s and the preconditions to a hold in s, then $\alpha_+ \to q_{do(s,a)}$:

$$q_s \wedge p(a)_s \to [\alpha_+ \to q_{do(s,a)}]. \tag{6}$$

We assume in addition that α_+ is a minimal persistence requirement, so that q persists *only* if α_+ holds. This allows us to strengthen the above expression to:

$$q_s \wedge p(a)_s \to [\alpha_+ \leftrightarrow q_{do(s,a)}]. \tag{7}$$

Related to the persistence of q is the persistence of $\neg q$, and we assume that α_- is a persistence condition for it:

$$\neg q_s \wedge p(a)_s \wedge \alpha_- \to \neg q_{do(s,a)}. \tag{8}$$

Note that we do not need to require α_- to be minimal.

We also have that

$$p(a)_s \to c(a)_{do(s,a)}.$$

Combining this with (7) gives us

$$q_s \wedge p(a)_s \wedge \neg\alpha_+ \to [c(a) \to \neg q]_{do(s,a)}. \tag{9}$$

Now suppose we can find some state-independent λ such that:

1. $q_s \wedge p(a)_s \wedge \neg\alpha_+ \to \lambda$, and

2. $\lambda \to \neg\alpha_+ \wedge \alpha_-$.

Then we maintain that (9) implies

$$p(a)_s \wedge \lambda \to [c(a) \to \neg q]_{\mathrm{do}(s,a)}. \tag{10}$$

To see this, suppose that (9) holds but (10) does not. Then from the falsity of (10), we have that λ and $p(a)_s$ hold but $[c(a) \to \neg q]_{\mathrm{do}(s,a)}$ does not, so that $c(a)_{\mathrm{do}(s,a)}$ holds and $q_{\mathrm{do}(s,a)}$ does as well.

The continuing validity of (9) implies that $q_s \wedge p(a)_s \wedge \neg\alpha_+$ is false. But we know that $p(a)_s$ is true, and since λ holds and $\lambda \to \neg\alpha_+$, $\neg\alpha_+$ must be true as well. This leads us to conclude $\neg q_s$. Again since λ holds, we know that α_-. Thus

$$\neg q_s \wedge p(a)_s \wedge \alpha_- \wedge q_{\mathrm{do}(s,a)},$$

in conflict with (8).

For some domain fact q and action a, if we can find an α_+ and α_- such that (7) and (8) are satisfied, we will call α_+ a *positive persistence condition* for q and a; α_- will be called a *negative persistence condition* for q and a. We have shown the following:

Theorem 5.3 *Let α_+ and α_- be positive and negative persistence conditions for q and a. Suppose also that λ is a state-independent condition such that:*

1. $q_s \wedge p(a)_s \wedge \neg\alpha_+ \to \lambda$, and

2. $\lambda \to \neg\alpha_+ \wedge \alpha_-$.

Then

$$p(a)_s \to [\lambda \wedge c(a) \to \neg q]_{\mathrm{do}(s,a)}. \qquad \square \tag{11}$$

Given this result, it seems appropriate to treat

$$\lambda \wedge c(a) \to \neg q$$

as a domain constraint for the domain in question, since this constraint holds in any state which can be reached by performing the action a.

As an example, let us return to the blocks world. We take $q = \mathrm{on}(x,y)$ as our domain fact, and $a = \mathtt{move}(u,v)$ as our action. The persistence rule is given by:

$$\mathrm{on}(x,y)_s \wedge u \neq x \to \mathrm{on}(x,y)_{\mathrm{do}(s,\mathtt{move}(u,v))},$$

so the persistence condition α_+ is $u \neq x$.

The preconditions of the action are $p(a) = \text{clear}(u) \wedge \text{clear}(v)$, and consequences are $c(a) = \text{on}(u, v)$. A negative persistence condition is given by $\alpha_- = v \neq y$, and it is not hard to see that $\lambda = (v \neq y \wedge u = x)$ satisfies the conditions of the theorem, so that the calculated domain constraint is:

$$v \neq y \wedge u = x \wedge \text{on}(u, v) \to \neg \text{on}(x, y),$$

which we can easily rewrite as:

$$v \neq y \wedge \text{on}(x, v) \to \neg \text{on}(x, y).$$

This is precisely the usual constraint indicating that a block can be in only one place at a time.

We will call a planning domain *persistence-constrained* if all of the domain constraints can be obtained in this fashion from the persistence rules. If there are r relation symbols and a action types in the domain, there will be ar persistence rules, and these will lead to $c = ar$ domain constraints. We can expect that the time t' needed to investigate each will be comparable to the sum of the time t needed to examine a persistence condition such as α_+ and the time t_c needed to examine the consequences $c(a)$ of the (now hypothetical) action a.

Theorem 5.4 *In a persistence-constrained domain with a action types and a large number d of domain facts, the times needed to investigate the validity of a single query after a sequence of n actions are*

$$\frac{t(l^n - 1)}{l - 1} \qquad \text{and} \qquad nx(t + t_c)a$$

for the monotonic and possible worlds approaches respectively.

The times needed by the two approaches to construct the entire state resulting from the actions are

$$ntd \qquad \text{and} \qquad nx(t + t_c)a$$

respectively.

Proof. This is essentially a compilation of earlier results. All intermediate facts should clearly be cached if we need to construct the final state in its entirety. □

One can expect x, t, t_c, l and a to all be approximately independent of the size of the domain being investigated. Given this assumption, we can expect the possible worlds approach to show substantial computation savings over the monotonic situational approach if either:

1. $l > 1$ and n is large, or

2. The entire final state needs to be constructed.

The first condition corresponds to a situation where a great many facts need to be investigated at early times in order to determine the validity of even a single one at a later time.

The comparison to the standard default approach represented by (2) is much simpler. Invoking a rule such as

$$\frac{p_s \wedge \text{succ}(s, s') : Mp_{s'}}{p_{s'}}$$

will generally take approximately as long as it does to check $Mp_{s'}$; in other words, as long is it takes to examine each of the c/r domain constraints relating to p:

Theorem 5.5 *The time taken to investigate the query q after a single action in the default approach is given by:*

$$t(q) = \frac{t'c}{r}. \qquad \square$$

Using this, we can repeat the analysis used to calculate the time needed to investigate the consequences of a series of actions using the monotonic approach. The results can be summarized as follows:

Theorem 5.6 *In a persistence-constrained domain with a action types and a large number d of domain facts, the times required by the various approaches are:*

	possible worlds	monotonic	default
single query	$nx(t + t_c)a$	$\frac{t(l^n - 1)}{l - 1}$	$\frac{(t + t_c)a(l^n - 1)}{l - 1}$
entire state	$nx(t + t_c)a$	ntd	$n(t + t_c)ad$

The performance of the default approach is worse than that of the monotonic approach. There is, however, an important mitigating factor in that the domain constraints constructed from the persistence conditions may be inefficiently represented. If, for example, some relation type *always* persists through an action type (such as `color` and `move` earlier), the persistence condition α_+ will be $\alpha_+ = t$ (truth). This leads to $\lambda = f$, and the resulting domain constraint will be trivial. This will decrease the time and space requirements of both the default and possible worlds approaches.

5.1.3   Qualification

There is little existing formal work on the qualification problem. Hanks and McDermott [7] have noted that the need to distinguish between defeasible preconditions
(such as the existence of a potato in the tailpipe) and defeasible consequences (such
as the car's being running) makes it impossible for any of the standard approaches
to non-monotonic reasoning to address this issue without the availability of additional information separating the qualification from the effect. They also note that
most existing formalisms are incapable of putting this sort of information to use.

Shoham [17] provides such a mechanism in his theory of *chronological ignorance*.
This is an idea he presents in order to discuss what he refers to as the *initiation*
problem; the problems he is addressing seem to be identical to those we have discussed.

Shoham's solution is to include temporal information in the description of any
action; he requires that the qualifications be simultaneous with the action, while
the consequences follow it in time. Thus he distinguishes between qualifications and
consequences essentially via a temporal order. By adding the assumption that default conditions are maintained for *as long a time as possible* (his notion of "chronological" ignorance), he ensures that the consequences of any particular action will
be defeated in preference to the removal of the qualifications.

Shoham's construction is extremely similar to ours. The difficulty with it is
that, once again, domain constraints are not being represented as such, but instead
are being temporally split. This may not always be possible.

Suppose I am attempting to take a photograph inside a cave. At great expense,
I bring in a power supply and a battery of lights. I also bring a camera.

Now, it turns out (this example is intended to take place in the near future)
that my camera has twelve on-board computers and must also be connected to the
power supply. Unfortunately, my power supply cannot both operate the camera
and run the lights. Thus, when I press the shutter release, two things will happen:
the shutter will open, and the lights will dim.

I need the lights on to take the photograph. And furthermore, I need them on
at the precise instant that the shutter opens. It is imperative that the qualification
to taking the photograph (that the lights are on) be simultaneous with the *effect* of
the action (that the shutter drop) in this example.

5.2   Control of search

The admissible distance function d_{me}^* discussed in section 4.2 corresponds to the
distance function used in means-ends analysis. If any clause in the goal is known

not to hold in the current state, then an action must be taken to correct it. Other than this, the planner searches blindly.

Consistency checking is an extension of this idea. In addition to counting the number of clauses remaining to be achieved, the goal is checked for consistency before any planning is attempted. We take:

$$d_{cc}^*(S, g) = \begin{cases} \infty, & \text{if } g \text{ is unsatisfiable,} \\ |g - S|, & \text{otherwise.} \end{cases}$$

Theorem 5.7 *In a unitary domain, the three distance approximation functions d_{me}^*, d_{cc}^* and d_{pw}^* are all admissible. In addition,*

$$d_{pw}^* \geq d_{cc}^* \geq d_{me}^*. \tag{12}$$

Proof. In light of the results in section 4.2, we must only show that d_{cc}^* is admissible and verify the inequality (12).

The admissibility of d_{cc}^* and the fact that $d_{cc}^* \geq d_{me}^*$ are both clear, since the distance functions agree except for unsatisfiable goals. Since $d_{pw}^* = d_{cc}^*$ except at points where $d_{cc}^* = d_{me}^*$, the second half of the inequality follows from theorem 4.2.
□

In spite of this result, there is a very general problem which will arise if we try to solve a planning problem using either the possible worlds approach or a consistency checking method. The reason for this is that both approaches require us to prove (or fail to prove) the negation of the goal, and performing this calculation may be arbitrarily expensive. This is a general problem in control [19,18]: some effort must be expended in pruning the search space, and a compromise must be struck between the need to prune this space and the need to examine it in order to find a solution to the problem. Genesereth [4] and Smith [19,18] have both discussed this problem in general terms; one solution they present involves interleaving base-level and meta-level deduction effort. This guarantees the discovery of a solution in a time no greater than twice that required by the better of the two methods.

Although improvements may exist on Genesereth's and Smith's suggestion that base-level and meta-level steps be interleaved one-for-one (as they themselves remark), it seems likely that a general protocol will involve some mixture of base- and meta-level activity. One attractive feature of the possible worlds approach is that it is able to make use of the meta-level proving activity to *incrementally* reduce the size of the space which the base-level planner must examine. This is in sharp contrast with consistency checking, which must wait until the proving activity is complete in order to obtain any benefit at all, since the distance function d_{cc}^* agrees with d_{me}^* except for goals which have been proven unsatisfiable.

The reason for this is that, as discussed in section 3.3, a possible world W is not constructed directly. Instead, it is constructed by an examination of the proofs of $\neg p$; each such proof provides additional information about the complement of W in S.

Consider the blocks world example, and suppose that we have domain constraints to the effect that any block can be on at most one other object, and that each block can support at most one other. We now generate a possible world in which B is on X and X is on the table by considering proofs of the negation of this goal. In other words, we try to prove

$$\neg\mathrm{on}(B, X) \vee \neg\mathrm{on}(X, \texttt{table}).$$

There are three proofs of the above proposition. We can prove $\neg\mathrm{on}(B, X)$ either by noting that B cannot be on X because it is on the table at the moment or by noting that X already has something else on it. We can prove $\neg\mathrm{on}(X, \texttt{table})$ by noting that X is currently on something else. Any possible world with X on B on the table must therefore remove from the database the three facts underlying these proofs. In the example as presented thus far, the removal of these three facts does indeed give us a possible world. Let us denote this possible world by S'.

Suppose now that the domain were much more complex, so that there were many other potential proofs that either B is not on X or X is not on the table. We might need to determine the structure of X and composition of B in order to know whether or not X can support the weight, or to check that there is room on the table, and so on.

Even in this case, the distance between the current state and that in which B is on X and X is on the table is *at least* as great as the distance to the state S' where B is not on the table and the blocks above and below X have been dealt with in some fashion. In the notation of theorem 4.3, it follows that $d(S, g) \geq \rho(S, S')/\alpha$, so that if we take $d^*(S, g) = \rho(S, S')/\alpha$, *this distance approximation function will still be admissible.*

This observation underlies our earlier remark. Suppose that we decide to implement a planner with consistency checking, but fix some limit as to just how much effort can be spent checking the consistency of a goal. If the goal is not proved inconsistent within this time, there will be absolutely no benefit from the meta-level analysis which has been done. But in the possible worlds approach, we may well have obtained useful lower bounds on the distance to the nearest possible world in which the goal holds; although not as sharp as the approximating function appearing in theorem 4.3, we will still have obtained an improvement over what was available previously. Additional incremental effort spent in generating possible worlds will lead to incremental increases in the distance-judging function, and thus to incremental pruning of the search space. This will enhance substantially the efficiency of a protocol that interleaves meta-level and base-level analysis, since the base-level effort is able to benefit from meta-level results even if they are not complete.

6   Implementation

Many of the ideas presented here have been implemented in a general purpose planner at Stanford. The planner proceeds in a backwards fashion, selecting from a list of subgoals and regressing the subgoal selected through possible actions until it has apparently been achieved. The actions generated are then executed; each action is assumed to cause a state transition from the current state to the nearest one in which the consequences of the action hold.

The planner operates in a simple kitchen domain. There are a variety of containers (pots, pans, etc.) which are in a cupboard, except for a bowl which has been left in the sink. There is a stove which may or may not be broken; in the closet are a variety of components which can be assembled into a nuclear reactor. The planner's goal is to boil some water; the constraints under which it must work are given in figure 3. The LISP description of the domain is given in figure 4.

All of the planning problems we have discussed are present in this domain. The frame problem is, of course, ubiquitous. It actually appears in a moderately nasty form in this domain because of the fact that the only indication that an object placed under a running tap will fill with water is an implication in the domain description. The qualification problem appears because the stove may or may not be broken, and also appears in the actual encoding of the move operator; the fact that the destination must be empty if it is small is essentially treated as a qualification on the action. This description in terms of a domain constraint seems much more natural than a modification of the precondition of the move operator.

Consistency checking is needed to determine that the bowl (which is temptingly in the sink when the planner is invoked) should not be used to boil the water. Finally, even if the stove is working, the planner must decide whether to construct the nuclear reactor or simply turn on the stove.

The metric used to estimate the distance between possible worlds involves simply counting the number of propositions which must be modified, as in theorem 4.2. Additionally, however, a possible world in which a default rule has been broken for no apparent reason is assumed to be quite distant. The effect of this is to have the planner avoid possible plans where, for example, it heats the pot before taking it to the sink and filling it with water.

1. If x is fillable and under the tap, and the tap is running, x will contain water. The bowl, cup, pot and pan are all fillable.

2. Anything in the sink is under the tap.

3. Anything on the stove will be hot if the stove is turned on.

4. Anything on the nuclear reactor will be hot if the nuclear reactor has been assembled.

5. If the nuclear reactor cannot be proven to be assembled, it is not assembled.

6. Any particular object which cannot be proven to be hot is not hot.

7. The sink can only hold one object at a time.

8. Anything flimsy will melt (and therefore hold nothing) if it gets hot. The bowl and the cup are flimsy.

9. The stove cannot be turned on if it is broken.

Figure 3: A kitchen

```
(if (and (fillable $x) (under $x tap) (running tap))
    (contains $x water))
(if (loc $x sink) (under $x tap))
(if (and (loc $x stove) (on stove)) (hot $x))
(if (and (loc $x n1) (assembled-nuke)) (hot $x))
(if (and (loc n1 n2) (loc n2 n3)) (assembled-nuke))
(if (underivable (assembled-nuke)) (not (assembled-nuke)))
(if (and (loc $x $1) (small $1) (unknown (= $x $y)))
    (not (loc $y $1)))
(if (and (loc $x $1) (unknown (= $k $1))) (not (loc $x $k)))
(if (and (fillable $c) (flimsy $c) (hot $c)) (not (contains $c $x)))
(if (broken $x) (not (on $x)))
(if (loc $x $y) (not (clear $y)))
(if (unprovable (loc $x $y)) (clear $y))
(if (stationary $x) (not (moved $x)))
(if (underivable (hot $x)) (not (hot $x)))
(if (on $x) (not (off $x)))  (if (off $x) (not (on $x)))


(small sink) (small n1) (small n2) (small n3)


(flimsy cup) (flimsy bowl)


(stationary cupboard) (stationary closet)


(fillable pot) (fillable pan) (fillable bowl) (fillable cup)


(surface sink) (surface stove)


(object pot) (object pan) (object bowl) (object cup) (object n1)
(object n2) (object n3)


(electrical stove)


(loc n1 closet) (loc n2 closet) (loc n3 closet)
(loc cup cupboard) (loc bowl sink) (loc pot cupboard)
(loc pan cupboard)
```

Figure 4: LISP description of the kitchen

search type	nodes expanded	time (minutes)	optimal solution?
depth first, possible worlds	30	1	yes
A^*, possible worlds	50	5	yes
depth first, blind	293	9	no
iterative deepening	> 7500	> 960	?

Figure 5: Experimental results

The planner immediately realizes that only the pot and pan are sturdy enough to boil water. In addition, it expands the goal of heating the water container first, since that goal involves defeating a default rule. (Since the planner is proceeding backwards through the search tree, this results in the actions taken to heat the water container being executed *last*.) The two possible expansions involve putting x (where x contains water) on the stove, and assembling the nuclear reactor and putting x on that. The second of these appears substantially more distant than the first, so the planner attempts to proceed by simply using the stove to boil the water. It has no difficulty removing the bowl from the sink, putting the pan from the cupboard into the sink, turning on the tap, bringing the pan to the stove, and turning on the stove.

A variety of search strategies were employed. The first simply proceeded through the search space in a depth-first fashion; when a particular search node was expanded, which of its children was examined next was determined using the possible worlds metric.

A second approach used the A^* algorithm as we have presented it. A third simply used depth-first search *without* choosing among the children of any particular node; since this approach generated a non-optimal plan (involving the construction of the nuclear reactor), a fourth approach which used iterative deepening [20] was also tried.

The results of these approaches are summarized in figure 5. For each approach, we give the number of planning nodes expanded, the time spent on the problem (running MRS [3,15] on a Symbolics 3600), and whether or not an optimal plan was found.

The performance of the two approaches based on possible-worlds is superior to the other methods. (It must be remarked, however, that the search for the blind methods truly is blind; although consistency checking *was* used for these methods, other improvements are surely possible.)

Also of interest is a comparison between the possible worlds methods themselves. The A^* approach took approximately five times as long as the depth-first approach; half of this difference was time spent deciding at each point which node to expand next. (The entire fringe of the search tree needed to be examined at each step.) The remainder is a result of the fact that the A^* algorithm expanded more nodes than the depth-first approach. This is basically a consequence of the horizon effect: since assembling the nuclear reactor is only slightly more difficult than turning on the stove (the nuclear reactor only has three components), the system investigated this possibility before it thoroughly explored the difficulties involved in filling the pan with water. The observation that the bowl would have to be removed from the sink before the pan could be placed in it was therefore avoided until some preliminary investigation of the nuclear reactor approach had been completed. In this particular example, the depth-first approach is extremely effective: the possible worlds metric focusses the search sufficiently that the planner did not need to backtrack at all.

Finally, we should note that the implementation currently carries to completion all of the meta-level calculations involved in the generation of the possible worlds. Work is under way to remove this constraint and to explore the effectiveness of a variety of protocols governing the distribution of base- and meta-level planning activities.

7   Conclusion

My aim in this paper has been to describe an approach to planning based on possible worlds and to explore the usefulness of this approach in dealing with three distinct theoretical difficulties a planner must face. These three difficulties are the frame problem, the qualification problem, and the size of the search space involved in planning problems.

A variety of formalisms capable of dealing with the frame problem have already been discussed in the literature. The approach used in STRIPS [1] is the most efficient of these (and is more efficient than a possible worlds solution as well), but appears [8] to be epistemologically inadequate. The other existing approaches, based on McCarthy's situation calculus, appear in general (theorem 5.6) to be less efficient than the one we have presented.

The qualification problem was introduced by McCarthy in 1980 [10] to describe situations in which some of the preconditions of an action are true by default. Hanks and McDermott [7] have noted that the need to distinguish between these defeasible preconditions and the defeasible consequences of the action involved is not within the scope of most non-monotonic reasoning systems. We have shown that the possible worlds approach is capable of handling this problem; Shoham's notion of chronological ignorance [17] also addresses this question.

Finally, we have argued that there are substantial advantages to be gained by examining a planning problem not merely in terms of the goal being achieved, but in terms of an entire possible world in which the goal holds. By constructing such a world (an inferential instead of a planning task), the search space involved in many planning problems can be reduced substantially. In addition, the effort involved in the generation of the possible world has the attractive property that it leads to incremental reductions in the search space even before the possible world construction is complete. This has substantial impact for practical planning systems, which need to allocate their time between control and search activities.

The theoretical ideas we have presented have been implemented in a prototype planning system using MRS [3,15] at Stanford. The planner operates in a moderately complex kitchen domain, and the practical benefits of the approach we have suggested have been verified experimentally.

Acknowledgement

I would like to thank the Logic Group for providing, as ever, a cooperative and stimulating — and demanding — environment in which to work. Dave Smith has been especially helpful in working with me on the material in section 5.1.2.

References

[1] R. Fikes and N. J. Nilsson. STRIPS: a new approach to the application of theorem proving to problem solving. *Artificial Intelligence*, 2:189–208, 1971.

[2] H. Gelernter. Realization of a geometry-theorem proving machine. In E. Feigenbaum and J. Feldman, editors, *Computers and Thought*, pages 134–152, McGraw-Hill, New York, 1963.

[3] M. R. Genesereth. An overview of meta-level architecture. In *Proceedings of the Third National Conference on Artificial Intelligence*, pages 119–124, 1983.

[4] M. R. Genesereth. *Partial Programs*. Knowledge Systems Laboratory Report KSL-84-1, Stanford University, Nov. 1984.

[5] M. L. Ginsberg. Counterfactuals. *Artificial Intelligence*, 1986.

[6] C. C. Green. Theorem proving by resolution as a basis for question-answering systems. In B. Meltzer and D. Mitchie, editors, *Machine Intelligence 4*, pages 183–205, American Elsevier, New York, 1969.

[7] S. Hanks and D. McDermott. Default reasoning, nonmonotonic logics and the frame problem. In *Proceedings of the Fifth National Conference on Artificial Intelligence*, pages 328–333, 1986.

[8] V. Lifschitz. On the semantics of STRIPS. In *Proceedings of the 1986 Workshop on Planning and Reasoning about Action*, Timberline, Oregon, 1986.

[9] J. McCarthy. Applications of circumscription to formalizing common sense knowledge. *Artificial Intelligence*, 28:89–116, 1986.

[10] J. McCarthy. Circumscription – a form of non-monotonic reasoning. *Artificial Intelligence*, 13:27–39, 1980.

[11] J. McCarthy and P. J. Hayes. Some philosophical problems from the standpoint of artificial intelligence. In B. Meltzer and D. Mitchie, editors, *Machine Intelligence 4*, pages 463–502, American Elsevier, New York, 1969.

[12] A. Newell and H. A. Simon. GPS, a program that simulates human thought. In E. A. Feigenbaum and J. Feldman, editors, *Computers and Thought*, pages 279–293, McGraw-Hill, New York, 1963.

[13] R. Reiter. A logic for default reasoning. *Artificial Intelligence*, 13:81–132, 1980.

[14] R. Reiter. *A Theory of Diagnosis from First Principles*. Technical Report 187/86, Computer Science Department, University of Toronto, 1985.

[15] S. Russell. *The Compleat Guide to* MRS. Technical Report STAN-CS-85-1080, Stanford University, June 1985.

[16] E. D. Sacerdoti. *A Structure for Plans and Behavior*. American Elsevier, New York, 1977.

[17] Y. Shoham. Chronological ignorance. In *Proceedings of the Fifth National Conference on Artificial Intelligence*, pages 389–393, 1986.

[18] D. E. Smith. *Controlling Inference*. PhD thesis, Stanford University, Aug. 1985.

[19] D. E. Smith and M. R. Genesereth. Ordering conjunctive queries. *Artificial Intelligence*, 26(2):171–215, 1985.

[20] M. E. Stickel and W. M. Tyson. An analysis of consecutively bounded depth-first search with applications in automated deduction. In *Proceedings of the Ninth International Joint Conference on Artificial Intelligence*, 1985.

[21] G. J. Sussman. *A Computational Model of Skill Acquisition*. Technical Report 297, Massachusetts Institute of Technology, 1973.

[22] D. E. Wilkins. Domain-independent planning: representation and plan generation. *Artificial Intelligence*, 22:269–301, 1984.

INTRACTABILITY AND TIME-DEPENDENT PLANNING

Thomas L. Dean
Department of Computer Science
Brown University
Box 1910
Providence, RI 02912

ABSTRACT

Many of the problems that a robot planner is likely to encounter in nontrivial domains are believed to be intractable (i.e., they belong to the class of *NP-complete* problems). Such problems occur frequently enough in practice that a planner simply cannot ignore issues concerning the difficulty of the problems it endeavors to solve. A practical planner for robotics applications must possess criteria for deciding what a good solution to a given problem should look like, and be able to quickly estimate the cost of computing such a solution. The criterion chosen in a particular set of circumstances will depend upon the algorithms available for computing a solution satisfying that criterion and the time available for producing a solution.

While it is true that all of a planner's tasks ultimately compete for the same limited resources (most notably time), the demands of common situations seldom dictate considering all tasks at once. To reduce the complexity of the problems it is presented with, a planner should routinely partition time into intervals containing tasks which taken together constitute problems that can be solved independently. If done properly, composite solutions formed by combining several independently computed solutions will often compare favorably with considerably more expensive solution methods that don't attempt a decomposition. This paper presents a framework for handling the sort of global decision making necessary for dealing with complex problems in situations in which time is an important factor.

1   Introduction

This paper challenges the assumption, often implicit in the operation of traditional planners [19] [20] [22], that planning consists primarily of making *local* decisions concerning the sequence of actions to be taken in carrying out a set of tasks. By *local*, it is meant that the decision making process does not have to consider the current set of tasks as a whole. For instance, having determined that two tasks conflict with one another, most planning systems attempt to resolve the conflict by considering only the two tasks in conflict. Unfortunately, such local decisions frequently turn out to be ill-advised, forcing the planner to engage in expensive backtracking. Suppose that a robot managing an industrial machine shop has several tasks, each of which requires operations performed on a particular piece of equipment. Assuming that these tasks have deadlines, the question of what order to perform two of them cannot be resolved from a consideration of the two alone. Any ordering decision is likely to have consequences that will affect all of the tasks.

It might be argued that producing optimal solutions to intractable problems is more than one can legitimately expect from a general purpose planning system. Unfortunately, in almost any interesting domain, (provably) hard problems occur with alarming frequency. It seems reasonable to expect that a planner distinguish between hard and easy problems and shift its problem solving strategy to suit. A planner that lacks such discrimination and is unaware of the consequences of adopting a particular solution criterion is quite likely to expend exponentially large amounts of resources in dealing with routine planning problems. In this paper, we will explore methods whereby a robot planning system might recognize the difficulty of the problems it is endeavoring to solve, and, depending on the time it has to consider the matter and what it stands to gain or loose, produce solutions that, if not optimal, are at least reasonable given the circumstances.

2   Global Decisions and Robot Problem Solving

The notion of solution used by most planning systems is stated in terms of "reducing" a set of given tasks to primitive (irreducible) tasks, ordered so as to eliminate any undesirable interactions (situations in which one task undoes the work performed by a second task before that work has had a chance to serve its intended purpose). The resulting solution criterion provides no means for comparing solutions or realizing when a partially constructed solution is exorbitantly expensive and probably worth abandoning. In addition to lacking flexible criteria for judging the cost of achieving a task or set of tasks, most planners have no conception of how much time it will take to formulate a solution that meets some criterion of goodness or optimality. If planning time is to be factored into the cost of a plan (as, one might argue, it must in real-time robotics applications), then having the planner take into account the time necessary to produce an acceptable solution is critical.

Many problems that require a more global analysis can be described as scheduling problems [2] [10] [17]. There are other planning operations besides the scheduling of tasks, however, that can benefit from considering several tasks together. The process of stepwise refinement (i.e., providing increasingly more detailed descriptions of how to carry out a task—also referred to as plan expansion in NOAH [19] and task reduction in NASL [14]) can be extended to range over sets of tasks. There are many situations in which only by considering sets of tasks does it become clear how refinement should proceed. Consider the predicament of a department store clerk confronted with several customers and trying to minimize the amount of time that they are kept waiting. A reasonable strategy might be to decompose each task into those operations that require the customer's presence (e.g., demonstrating products and filling out sales slips) and those that can be delayed until after the customer has left (e.g., reshelving items and completing the paperwork for items to be delivered). It can often easily be determined whether or not such a strategy is appropriate. If the expected number of customers is either small (≤ 2) or large (> 6), it is probably best not to follow this strategy (if small, the short time a customer is kept waiting is less important than having the store appear in good order which requires that stock be immediately replaced on the display shelves; if large, eventually all the accumulated clutter from the postponed tasks will serve to discourage that majority of customers that would normally fend for themselves upon noticing an overworked clerk). The above example illustrates how decomposition and postponement strategies might be invoked on the basis of a fairly simple deduction concerning the number of tasks of a given type expected over an interval of time. In order to recognize when such strategies apply, we will have to consider methods for breaking up time into appropriate intervals and making predictions about the likelihood of tasks that might fall within such intervals. These issues will be addressed in Sections 5 and 8 respectively.

Instead of using libraries of plans to provide progressively more detailed descriptions of single tasks [16], a planner capable of reasoning about sets of interdependent tasks would have a library of strategies that would apply to sets of tasks confined to restricted intervals of time. Other examples of strategies might involve preemption and coroutining (e.g., if there are several clients, a clerk may consider jumping back and forth between them) or various clustering techniques (e.g., segregating clients interested in the same merchandise).

In any given situation, there will be a number of strategies that might apply. Hence, there must be some method of combining strategies where possible and criteria for choosing between strategies that are not compatible. To this end, strategies must be able to provide some estimate of the utility of applying them in a particular set of circumstances.

In order to direct the planning process, it must also be clear when and to what the system should try to apply a given strategy. In the approach described in this paper, intervals corresponding to convenient chunks of the planner's time (e.g., the morning work hours from 9:00 AM until noon) are annotated with the type and number of tasks scheduled to be carried out within them. This annotation plus the interval's offset in time from the current moment direct the planner as to what strategies to consider.

Keeping track of when a given task is likely to be carried out and how long it is likely to take often require that the system have some complete schedule for at least all those tasks preceding the task in question. On the other hand, given that the planner does not always have good reasons for ordering tasks one way or the other, it is often convenient to keep tasks partially ordered [19]. This presents somewhat of a conflict. In an attempt to keep fairly accurate estimates on the duration and time of occurrence of tasks and at the same time reap some of the benefits of maintaining a partial order, we introduce the notion of an *activity stream*, used to capture information about the length of time sets of tasks are likely to take. A set of tasks is represented in an activity stream as an interval whose duration provides some estimate of the amount of time that the planner is occupied in carrying out those tasks. If it turns out that there are significant differences in the time taken by a set of tasks depending upon what order they are performed, then the system attempts to partition the set of tasks into smaller sets of tasks. Since the sets of tasks in an activity stream are often distinguished by their common dependence upon a given resource or location, one often has to take into account *transition tasks* allowing for the time necessary for the planner to turn its attention from one set of tasks to another. Transition tasks are the glue that binds actions into continuous streams of activity.

Examples of transition tasks include: repositioning a spacecraft's camera between taking pictures of different objects in space [22], moving between naval vessels in carrying out refueling tasks [21], and moving between work stations in a factory domain [16]. In every case, the detailed description of the transitions depends upon the order in which the tasks are performed. In the factory domain, a robot performs tasks with deadlines using machines located throughout a large work area. Operations on different machines require that the robot travel between those machines. In order to determine how much time it will take to move from one task to another, the robot has to know where it will be following the earlier task and where it has to be before beginning the later task. Only by considering total orderings on tasks can the planner be sure of avoiding deadline failures. In order to make use of procrastination techniques like Sacerdoti's *least commitment* principle [19], strategies are used to partition tasks into components (sets) so that transitions between tasks in a component are negligible. Activity streams reflect these partitions, noting only transition tasks between components (e.g., travel time necessary to move between tasks to be performed in area14 and those to be performed in area17).

By partitioning its time into reasonable chunks and maintaining accurate activity streams, it is possible for a planner to keep account of the time required to specify its tasks in sufficient detail so that they can actually be executed. The process of partitioning and assigning tasks to particular intervals bounds the size of the problems that are being considered and serves to identify the types of computations that will be required. Partitioning strategies are not difficult to come by and they can often dramatically reduce the cost of planning with little appreciable reduction in performance. If a planner has n tasks divided evenly between k intervals, then the general scheduling problem might require $O(f(n))$ where f depends upon the particular optimality criteria chosen. The partitioned scheduling problem, on the other hand, might be solved in $O(\sum_{i=1}^{k} f(k/n))$. If $f(n)$ is n^2, $n = 12$, and $k = 4$, we're looking at the difference between 144 and 36. If $f(n)$ is exponential in n, then the difference is even more significant.

While the above observation is fairly obvious and uninteresting from the standpoint of classical complexity theory, in practical planning systems realizing such savings is a necessity. A robot cannot look at its entire future as one big scheduling problem. In any realistic robotics application, it will be necessary to interleave planning and execution. It is better to delay detailed consideration of tasks in the future until a sufficient amount is known about what the future holds. If time is a consideration (as it ultimately must be), then a planner will have to account for the time required to carry out the deductions necessary to formulate a plan. An effective planner must possess some understanding of

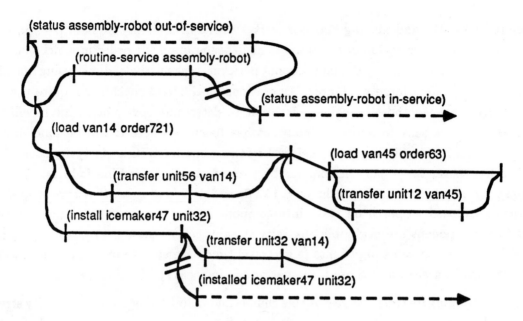

Figure 1: Fragment of a time map for planning in the warehouse domain

how hard a (planning) problem is, how much time it has available (for both planning and execution), and what is to be gained or lost by exerting more (planning) effort on a given problem.

In the following sections, we will explore the ideas sketched above and attempt to convince the reader that in many cases a robot should be able to deal efficiently with problems that require a more expansive reasoning strategy than that handled by traditional planning systems.

3   Reasoning about Time

In the following, we will make use of a representation of events and their effects over time called a *time map* [15] [4]. Time maps are meant to capture a planner's beliefs concerning the past, present, and expected future(s). In time maps, the classical data base assertion is replaced by the notion of *time token* corresponding to a particular interval of time during which a general *type* of occurrence (a fact or event) is said to be true. The *type* of a time token is denoted by a formula such as (location obj42 area17) or (move obj42 area17 area34). A time map is a graph whose vertices refer to *points* (or *instants*) of time corresponding to the beginning and ending of time tokens. Points are related to one another using *constraints*: directed edges linking two points, labeled with an upper and lower bound on the distance (in time) separating the two points. These bounds allow us to represent incomplete information concerning the duration and time of occurrence of events.

In the FORBIN planner, planning consists of constructing a time map that describes a picture of the world changing over time, in which the robot carries out a detailed set of actions to achieve its purposes. This time map represents a commitment on the part of the planner to behave in a particular manner and a set of predictions concerning how other processes active in the world might react to that behavior. The underlying data base routines used to manage time maps [5] see to it that the robot's predictions satisfy some notion of causal coherence as expressed in rules that determine the physics of a particular domain. The resulting *temporal reason maintenance system* allows a planner to specify the temporal and causal reasons for making certain commitments so that unsupported commitments are quickly noticed and the time map at all times accurately reflects the planner's beliefs.

Figure 1 shows a time map describing a situation in the warehouse domain (Section 4). Time tokens corresponding to events are depicted as two vertical bars connected by a horizontal bar (e.g., |—|), whereas time tokens corresponding to facts are depicted as two vertical bars or a vertical bar and a right arrow (indicating that the associated interval persists indefinitely into the future) connected by a dashed line (e.g., |----→). Constraints (depicted as curved lines) indicate simple precedence or coincidence in the case where a curved line is intersected by double hash marks.

4   A Domain for Exploring Planning Issues

The application domain chosen for the examples in the rest of this paper involves an automated materials handler (e.g., a computer controlled forklift) given the task of filling orders and shelving stock in an industrial warehouse setting. The physical layout used in the warehouse domain is shown in Figure 2. Shipments of supplies (appliances in the examples provided in this paper) arrive in tractor/trailer trucks at the unloading dock and their contents have to be catalogued and stored in the appropriate (predesignated) storage areas. Vans arrive at the loading dock with stock orders. To fill an order the robot must load the van with the items specified on the order. Shipments and orders can arrive at any time. The numbers of orders and shipments over an interval of time can be predicted

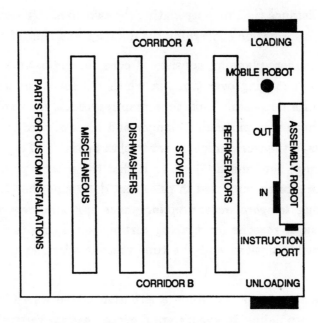

Figure 2: Physical layout of the appliance warehouse domain

with a certain probability as a function of the current time and the current (known) set of orders and shipments. The sequence in which tasks are handled is up to the discretion of the planner controlling the robot. Orders have deadlines. If an order is not filled by its deadline, then there is a penalty that accrues as a function of the time that the van picking up the order remains waiting in the loading dock. In addition, the warehouse is charged by the hour for any time over a set limit that a tractor/trailer truck sits waiting to be unloaded. To complicate matters somewhat, orders may require certain assembly operations. In the warehouse domain, assembly involves installing options in stock items (e.g., adding an ice maker or decorative panel to a refrigerator). Installation consists of taking the stock item and the parts for the installation to a stationary robot that actually carries out the neccessary modifications. These complications are not meant to focus on the problems of assembly, rather they allow us to address certain issues involving the coordination of tasks with steps that can be carried out by independent processses operating in parallel. The assembly robot provides two additional sources of uncertainty: the time required for a given assembly task is described by a random variable and there is a probability, depending upon the machine's last service date, that the assembly robot will halt requiring replenishment of its reserves of hydraulic and lubrication fluids.

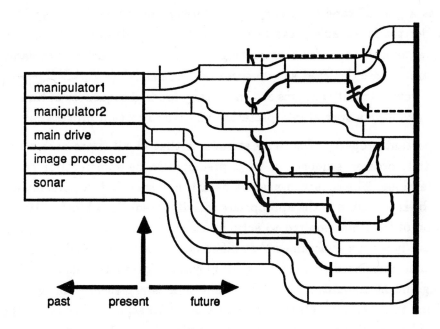

manipulator1

manipulator2

main drive

image processor

sonar

past   present   future

Figure 3: Scheduling activity streams for a multi-processor robot

5   Activity Streams

From the perspective of this paper, the objective of a planning system is to construct what are called *activity streams*: sequences of time tokens corresponding to operations requiring the services of some portion of the robot's computational and/or mechanical equipment. We will assume that a robot has some number of processors each dedicated to a specific function (e.g., manipulator movement or image processing). The system constructs a continuous activity stream for each processor. The time tokens in an activity stream represent computations to be carried out by a processor. The duration of a time token's associated interval describes just how long the computation will take; the constraints on its time of occurrence determine when the computation will be carried out. It is the job of the planner to ensure that when it is time to carry out a given portion of an activity stream, the tokens in that portion of the stream are of a type readily interpreted by the associated processor.

Each processor constitutes a special purpose planner capable of carrying out a restricted class of tasks. The planner can be viewed as weaving together threads of prediction and commitment into a fabric that becomes increasingly more detailed as the commitments draw nearer. A time map so constructed is like a multi-track tape in which each track corresponds to an activity stream destined for a particular processor. The processors are synchronized to behave as a ganged tape head that moves forward over the time map interpreting its contents under the inexorable pressure of time. Figure 3 attempts to capture this image of the planner as a machine for constructing and interpreting activity streams. In Figure 3, activity streams are depicted as sequences of "tape cells" (e.g., ⬚⬚). In the time map, however, activity streams are just totally ordered sequences of time tokens whose types happen to have a special interpretation relative to certain processors[1].

One important property of activity streams is that at all times each stream accounts for some totally ordered sequence of tasks predicted to be sufficient for carrying out the planners intentions. The sequence needn't be actually specified; a partially ordered set of tasks might be represented in the appropriate activity stream as a block of time constituting an estimation of the time required to actually execute some total ordering of those tasks. In such a case, it is usually assumed that differences between schedules are negligible with respect to some associated cost estimate. If moving between two sets of tasks is likely to require a significant amount of time, then that time is represented in an activity stream as a transition task. Activity streams provide the information necessary for the planner to keep track of how much time it has available for planning and acting.

6   Task Accommodation Strategies

To direct the process of constructing and refining activity streams, the planner employs what are called *task accommodation strategies*: a generalization of the notion of plan used in NOAH [19] and NONLIN [20]. Task accommodation strategies are employed to direct planning and restrict search in a manner similar to the way that SIPE [23] uses the notion of constraints to achieve the same purpose. Task accommodation strategies are used to prescribe both reduction and scheduling methods. The strategies are applied to sets of tasks occurring within specific intervals of time offset from the current moment.

The planner tries to maintain a picture of the future in which imminently executable tasks are well specified (the corresponding portions of activity streams can be interpreted

---

[1]It is quite possible to have tasks described at a sufficiently abstract level that the planner doesn't know what processor (or processors) will be used in actually carrying out the task. The earlier a planner can commit to a set of processors for a given task, the more accurate a picture it will have of its activities and available resources. On the other hand, the longer the planner can procrastinate the more information it will have to make a well informed choice. Establishing a reasonable tradeoff is nontrivial.

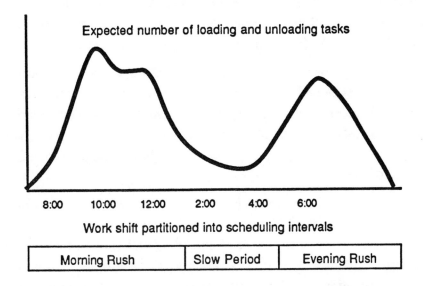

Figure 4: Partitioning a work shift into periods of light and heavy loads

by an appropriate processor), and the more distant in time a task is, the vaguer its representation in the time map. Plan detail is essentially a function of the time remaining until execution. Future tasks are often not individuated but rather treated in groups (e.g., the loading tasks for this afternoon) and represented as an interval of time likely to occupy the robot in carrying out a particular group of tasks. If we are willing to consider entities such as "the set of loading tasks to be performed between 2:00 and 5:00 tomorrow afternoon" as a single (albeit high level) task, then what we are suggesting here shouldn't seem all that foreign to traditional hierarchical planning approaches [18]. Having predicted such high level tasks, the planner should be able to make planning decisions that take them into account (e.g., if the later portion of the morning is likely to be particularly busy it might be prudent to finish clearing the loading dock now and delay maintenance tasks until later in the day).

To handle this process of formulation, the planner routinely applies certain strategies whose purpose it is to partition the future into component intervals of time during which sets of tasks are expected to occur that should be considered together. In the warehouse domain, the planner can estimate the number of loading and unloading tasks it is likely to encounter over any given interval. Using this information the planner partitions its eight hour work shift into three periods as shown in Figure 4. These periods are annotated in the time map to reflect their expected use: the first and third periods correspond to anticipated high numbers of loading and unloading tasks, whereas the middle period is likely to be relatively free of such tasks. The planner makes use of such annotations to schedule newly derived tasks (e.g., perform routine maintenance on the assembly robot).

Each time token representing a task or set of tasks has a set of strategies that apply to it depending on its type and time until execution. The planner continually updates the time map as execution proceeds and applies new strategies as they become appropriate. By restricting the number of tasks of a given type in a specified interval the planner can also carefully manage the computational cost of scheduling those tasks using a particular accommodation strategy.

In the warehouse domain, the robot has to deal with a steady stream of deliveries that need to be unloaded and shelved and orders that require fetching items and loading them on trucks. We'll assume that the number of unloading and loading tasks varies predictably during the course of the day. Suppose that according to the robot's "rough" predictions, it will be impossible to carry out all of the anticipated tasks by their associated deadlines. At the highest level of abstraction, an unloading task consists of a block or interval of time required for the robot to make the necessary trips from the truck on the unloading dock to the area of the warehouse where the newly arrived items are to be stored. This description is potentially misleading in at least two important respects: (1) the interval of time is only an estimate of the amount of time that the robot will be engaged in carrying out the task and (2) the actual time spent by the robot may be broken up into several intervals spread out over time. In making a rough prediction, the robot tries to find some schedule (sequence of tasks) such that all the tasks are completed at or before their respective deadlines. The prediction is "rough" in that it does not consider the possibility of decomposing the high level task descriptions into subtasks for which it might have tighter time bounds or more sophisticated scheduling techniques. Such rough estimates are extremely useful in that they can be used to alert the robot to potential problems, and thus serve to direct decision making so as to avoid expensive backtracking during planning. In response to a warning that no penalty-free schedule appears possible, the robot might apply certain (higher cost) strategies for decomposing high-level tasks. One strategy might involve removing the items from the waiting tractor/trailer trucks, placing them temporarily on the unloading dock, and postponing the task of actually shelving the newly arrived items until a convenient time. By delaying the (sub)tasks of shelving new deliveries, the robot can formulate penalty-free task schedules in situations where otherwise it would be impossible. It should be fairly simple to convince yourself that there is no single strategy that will work in all such situations. The robot actually has to anticipate the future behavior of other processes (suppliers and consumers in this case) in order to instigate actions *now* that will allow it to deal with those processes *later* in an effective manner. This is a critical issue in what is referred to as *strategic* planning [5].

Having decided to delay the shelving tasks until afternoon, the planner has to make sure that there is enough time available in the afternoon to fit in these tasks. But, given that the afternoon tasks are represented in an activity stream, it is fairly simple and inexpensive to determine if enough time is available in the afternoon and, if so, to modify the existing activity stream to accomodate the shelving tasks.

Each task accommodation strategy has associated with it an application criterion. This criterion restricts what sorts of tasks the strategy can be applied to. For strategies involving classic job-shop scheduling, we use the classification criteria of [10]. Strategies are classified by optimality criteria (how schedules are to be rated), factors such as whether or not the cost of preempting a task can be considered as negligible, and computational efficiency (how much time will it take to compute a schedule that satisfies the given optimality criterion). In the warehouse domain, loading and unloading tasks are assumed to have the tardiness optimality criterion (schedules are rated by the sum over all tasks of the time past a task's deadline it takes to complete the task). The cost of delaying a maintenance task past its deadline is assumed to be a constant. There are certain situations in which it is reasonable to assume that the cost of preempting a loading/unloading task is actually negligible. Factors such as preemptibility and choice of optimality criterion can significantly influence complexity and hence computational efficiency. The cost of scheduling n tasks can range from $O(n \log n)$ in the case where the cost of preemption is negligible and optimality is in terms of tardiness, to $O(n^2)$ where optimality is in terms of minimizing the maximum lateness of a single task, to $O(2^n)$ for almost any problem involving minimizing total cost and not allowing preemption. In some situations, the planner simply doesn't have the time to apply an expensive strategy. By maintaining activity streams the planner is able to take note of this and apply the best strategy it can given the time available.

There are strategies for dealing with travel time minimization, path planning, and resource management. Some of these strategies correspond to heuristics used in approximating solutions to vehicle routing problems (e.g., spatial segregation techniques for the traveling salesman problem [12] and methods for dealing with uncertainty [11]). There are also strategies that make use of more complicated heuristic path planning algorithms [17]. A special class of strategies for handling resource management problems deal with restricted cases of the transaction scheduling problem [8] that are known to be tractable. These resource management strategies are akin to what Chapman calls *cognitive cliches* [3].

The actual manipulations performed by a given strategy are relatively unimportant in our discussion. What is important is that for any given problem the planner encounters there are several appropriate strategies and these strategies have varying computational costs and likelihoods of producing good solutions by various criteria.

The reason we have shifted to a planning paradigm that makes use of large number of strategies is that we were dissatisfied with the generality and extensibility of the techniques used in the FORBIN planner [16] [7]. FORBIN employs a single scheduling program that handles all ordering decisions. Plan choice is managed by a second program and the two programs communicate with one another through a rather narrow-bandwidth communication channel. Each program appeared as a black box to the other, and it was always a battle to see to it that one box didn't swallow the other in an effort to better direct the decision making process. The methods presented here are an attempt to banish inscrutable monolithic decision making programs of the sort that FORBIN relied upon.

If you were to open up FORBIN's plan choice and scheduling black boxes you would be faced with an assortment of heuristics embedded in a complicated LISP program. These heuristics embody special purpose knowledge of the sort captured by the task accommodation strategies that we have been discussing in this section. Having banished the black boxes, we will have to supply some means of determining when and how to apply strategies, and, more importantly, some means of choosing between strategies where more than one apply and their recommendations are at odds.

7   Choosing Between Strategies

Each strategy has an associated utility function that returns some measure of the result of applying a given strategy to a particular set of tasks occuring in a specified interval. In addition, there are standard methods for determining whether or not the results of two strategies are compatible. For instance, certain strategies suggest restrictions on partially ordered sets of tasks; two such strategies are said to be compatible if their combined restrictions are consistent. Two strategies are comparable if they apply to the same interval and set of tasks, and their respective utility functions return values in the same units. This mechanism for comparing strategies involves a rather limited application of classical decision theory [1]. Rather than explore large decision trees, however, the planner must content itself with fairly shallow deductions. Most strategies take into account some form of probabilistic information (see Section 8). In addition, each strategy employs an optimality criteria that enables it to compute an estimate of the cost of the situation resulting from applying that strategy. The cost estimates and probablities are combined in a single number using standard decision theoretic methods.

In classical decision theory, you decide how to act one step at a time. Each action and the information that results from carrying it out change the probabilities and require reevaluation of plans that were instigated earlier but not completely carried out. In point of fact, plans really have no place in the classical approach; there are just actions to be carried out in service to a goal. Having performed certain steps in what might be identified as a plan, it is more likely that a decision theoretic robot "sequencer" would choose to complete the remaining steps in the plan. But this is simply because already completed steps often make it easier (more cost effective) to complete the remaining steps. Note that in this approach handling tests and conditionals is built in; every action that introduces new information is a test and each new action is chosen conditional on the information gathered in the preceding actions. While the sort of continual reevaluation employed in the decision theoretic framework might be reasonable for a planner with virtually unlimited computational resources, it is impractical in realistic situations.

A partially executed plan represents not only an investment in physical effort, but also an investment in planning effort: laying out the problem, gathering the necessary information to ensure its success, and attending to the critical aspects of its execution. A planner has to make commitments and then stick with them as long as the initial reasons for making the commitment remain valid. If the planner has some indication that a plan might go awry then it must explicitly plan to monitor the execution of that plan, and be prepared to switch to an alternative plan if circumstances dictate. There must also be mechanisms built into the planner that keep track of the reasons for certain decisions and detect when those reasons are undermined and the decisions no longer warranted [6] [5]. Given that the reasons in this context depend on probability estimates, there appears to be a need for more sophisticated reason maintenance systems, perhaps along the lines of [9], that would allow a planner to express confidence in a given commitment conditional upon its associated utility staying above some threshold.

It is not fundamental to this approach that the final arbiter in decisions concerning the application of strategies involve the use of decision theory. What is required, however, is some means of comparing and combining information from various and disparate knowledge sources. Since statistical inference techniques in general and decision theory in particular are concerned with just these problems we hope to benefit from these approaches as much as possible.

8   Expectation Based Planning

The techniques described in this paper rely upon the implicit assumption that the planner pretty much knows what to expect in all situations. The only hint of backtracking was introduced in the previous section concerning the need for sophisticated reason maintenance to determine when it might be reasonable to reconsider a given strategy. By maintaining activity streams and using strategies that range over sets of tasks we hope to eliminate much of the backtracking that previous planners are prone to. While some means of recovering from poor choices is ultimately necessary, we will not be considering such issues in this paper. If a planner can't anticipate a problem that requires complex preparation to deal with, then it simply will perform poorly with regard to such problems. We can't, of course, expect a planner to anticipate everything, but it should be capable of making guesses about what might happen. Such guesses or expectations will have to be periodically reassessed. Sometimes new information will serve to confirm or disconfirm an expectation. At other times a planner will find itself performing useless maneuvers in order to anticipate nonexistent events or stumbling into situations that it is unprepared to deal with. The possibility of failure notwithstanding, a planner will have to make guesses concerning the likelihood of certain events and plan accordingly. This sort of probabilistic prediction and noticing should constitute a significant part of planning. Our current effort is aimed at dealing with situations that the planner is relatively familiar with. On the basis of past experience and current observations we assume that the planner should be able to predict the immediate future rather accurately and the more distant future (e.g., this afternoon's loading tasks) with only a moderate decrease in precision. Factors such as incoming loading and unloading tasks are represented as stochastic processes [13]. Strategies consult these probabilistic representations in order to construct activity streams that take into account not only fixed tasks (e.g., lubricate the assembly unit by 3:00 so as not to void its warranty) but also tasks predicted by currently observed trends.

For instance, if the robot predicts that the afternoon will be particularly busy, it might choose to perform certain routine maintenance tasks during the relatively idle period around noon. Maintenance tasks are instigated by the planner and not initially assigned a time slot. The utility of a maintenance task for a given machine is computed as a function of the time since the last maintenance task. After a fixed time determined by the machine manufacturer's warranty this utility rises sharply. In general, there will be many tasks not associated with a particular chunk of time in an existing activity stream. These tasks (e.g., (routine-maintenance lathe14) or (clear-passage aisle7)) are created by special tasks called *policies* [14]. Examples of policies in the warehouse domain include general tasks to maintain machines according to their warranty conditions, and to keep heavily traveled passages free of obstructions. Policies serve to generate other tasks and establish criteria (deadlines and utility functions) to guide in scheduling such tasks. As an interval of time defined by a partitioning strategy draws near to execution time, the planner applies certain strategies whose purpose it is to assess and possibly reduce the amount of idle time currently available in the interval. These strategies attempt to splice in those homeless tasks generated by policies.

As another example of probabilistic reasoning in the warehouse domain, suppose that the robot is moving an item in the vicinity of the assembly unit at the same time that an assembly process is supposed to be underway. By making a short detour the robot could splice in a task to check on the progress of the assembly process. If the assembly unit is stalled awaiting service, then the planner might wish to interrupt its current transfer task to perform the necessary service. If the assembly process is complete, then that information might prove useful in enabling the robot to meet a particular deadline. The actual decision as to whether or not the detour is cost effective will depend on several factors, including the past performance of the assembly unit and the importance of the task that gave rise to the assembly process. The task accomodation strategy responsible for suggesting the detour would be applied to the entire set of loading and unloading tasks occuring within the partition component to which the transfer task under consideration was assigned. This allows the system to compare the utility of doing nothing with the utility of actually interrupting the transfer task.

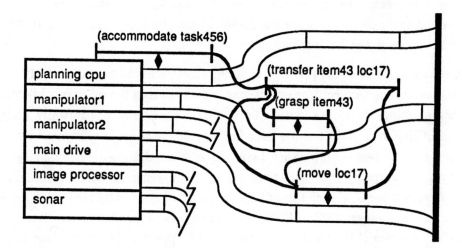

Figure 5: Activity streams that take into account planning time

9   Interleaved Planning and Execution

In any realistic robotics application, some method of interleaving planning and execution will have to be devised. In time dependent situations, a planner will have to carefully manage the time available for planning. In the approach described here, it is quite simple to represent operations on the time map such as scheduling and expansion as tasks to be performed on a special processor dedicated to that purpose. Some sort of primitive scheduler (i.e., a scheduler whose cost per task is essentially constant and thus can be trivially factored into the total cost of accommodating additional tasks) would have to generate an activity stream for this planning processor that would ensure that a task to expand or schedule a set of tasks would be executed before the activity stream associated with those tasks is due for execution. Figure 5 depicts a planning system with a dedicated planning processor.

Of course, operations on the time map are just tasks and hence, it might be argued, that they should be handled by task accommodation strategies just like any other activity of the robot. While this is perhaps true, there is good reason for calling a halt at some point to this sort of meta-circular digression. The scheme we are currently investigating relies upon a primitive scheduling mechanism that takes each newly generated task (or set of tasks) and splices chunks of time for both accommodating and carrying out that task into appropriate activity streams. The initial estimates on the duration of these chunks and their distribution among the robot's available processors may be quite rough. Nevertheless, as was shown in experiments with the FORBIN planner [7], even these rough estimates can provide a planner with much needed information to guide its decision making. The information associated with strategies and the intervals and sets of tasks they can be applied to is used to compute quick estimates of the expected time to actually apply those strategies. These estimates are used at various times by the primitive scheduler to choose from among the applicable strategies those that can be applied in the time allotted. Given the wide range of strategies available and our assumptions concerning the relative benevolence of the factory domain, it is expected that the planner will always have some strategy that can be applied; the planner will just perform less well when it is pressed for time. There is a danger that the planner will expend an inordinate amount of time to produce an optimal solution when a slightly less than optimal solution could be had for a fraction of the cost. This might lead the planner to waste effort in getting a slight improvement in one interval only to suffer a more substantial loss in a later interval having squandered all but a small portion of the available planning time on the earlier occurring interval. A method of computing reliable and inexpensive measures of the *expected* utility of a strategy has proven rather elusive, but some such method will have to be devised in order deal with the above problem.

10   Conclusions

The world seldom presents us with neatly packaged problems to solve. We essentially have to determine for ourselves what problems are worth solving and what problems we are capable of solving. The complete specification of a problem includes a criterion for what a solution should look like. In the past, most planning systems have relied upon fairly simplistic criteria for choosing between proposed solutions to planning problems. Such systems exhibit extreme inflexibility, often failing to terminate or reporting that no solution exists in situations where a slightly less restrictive solution criterion would quickly yield an acceptable, if not optimal, solution. It would be unwise to tell such a planner to finish all tasks by their respective deadlines without telling it what to do if this turns out to be impossible or what to do if the factory is burning down and there are tasks yet to do. What we would like is to specify certain general policies and have the robot formulate for itself a set of problems that it is both capable of solving and that make the most of its abilities. The criterion for what constitutes a solution to a given planning problem should depend upon the time available to formulate a solution, the time and resources available for carrying out a solution, and just how important solving such a problem is.

This paper describes a framework in which a planning system might determine for itself what problems are worth attempting, and which solution criteria are appropriate given the time available for generating a solution. The framework is designed to deal with problems that cannot be handled using purely local decision methods. Since the general problems involving deadlines, travel time, and resource management are intractable it is important to (a) correctly categorize problems so as to avoid doing unnecessary work and (b) somehow restrict the size of the problem so as to maintain a reasonable level of performance. The solution proposed here involves the use of strategies that are applied to sets of tasks confined to carefully specified intervals of time. Two or more strategies applicable to the same set of tasks can be compared using decision theoretic techniques. Other strategies are employed to partition the future into intervals to which tasks are assigned so as to effectively decompose complex scheduling problems. These intervals serve to partition time on the basis of distance in the future and predictions as to how many and what sort of tasks are likely to materialize and what sort of deadlines they are liable to have. Each strategy is applicable only at specified times as an interval or set of tasks draws near to execution time. This constitutes a form of hierarchical planning in which the detail with which a task is specified becomes a function of the time until that task is actually scheduled to be carried out. The representations and techniques presented here suggest a method for taking seriously the constraints involved in real-time processing and continuous interleaved planning and execution. Using the notion of processor-specific activity streams, a planning system can take into account the time required for task expansion and scheduling. The techniques presented here provide an extensible framework for dealing with situations in which a planner can make reasonable but not infallible predictions.

References

1. Barnett, V., *Comparative Statistical Inference* (John Wiley and Sons, 1982).

2. Bodin, L. and Golden, B., Classification in Vehicle Routing and Scheduling, *Networks* **11** (1981) 97–108.

3. Chapman, David, *Planning for Conjunctive Goals,* Technical Report AI-TR-802, MIT AI Laboratory, 1985.

4. Dean, Thomas, *Time Map Maintenance,* Technical Report 289, Yale University Computer Science Department, 1983.

5. Dean, Thomas, *Temporal Imagery: An Approach to Reasoning about Time for Planning and Problem Solving,* Technical Report 433, Yale University Computer Science Department, 1985.

6. Doyle, Jon, A truth maintenance system, *Artificial Intelligence* **12** (1979) 231–272.

7. Firby, R. James, Dean, Thomas L., Miller, David P., Efficient Robot Planning with Deadlines and Travel Time, *Proceedings of the 6th International Symposium on Robotics and Automation, Santa Barbara, Ca.,* IASTED, 1985.

8. Garey, Michael R. and Johnson, David S., *Computing and Intractibility: A Guide to the Theory of NP-Completeness* (W. H. Freeman and Company, 1979).

9. Ginsberg, M.L., Does Probability Have a Place in Non-monotonic Reasoning?, *Proceedings IJCAI 9, Los Angeles, Ca.,* IJCAI, 1985.

10. Graham, R.L., Lawler, E.L., Lenstra, J.K. and Rinnooy Kan, A.H.G., Optimization and Approximation in Deterministic Sequencing and Scheduling: A Survey, *Proceedings Discrete Optimization,* Vancouver, 1977.

11. Jaillet, P., *Probabilistic Traveling Salesman Problems,* Technical Report TR-185, Operations Research Center, MIT, 1985.

12. Karp, R., Probabilistic Analysis of Partitioning Algorithms for the Traveling Salesman Problem in the Plane, *Math. Oper. Res.* **2** (1977) 209–224.

13. Lindley, D.V., *Introduction to Probability and Statistics,* (Cambridge University Press, 1980).

14. McDermott, Drew V., *Flexibility and Efficiency in a Computer Program for Designing Circuits,* Technical Report 402, MIT AI Laboratory, 1977.

15. McDermott, Drew V., A temporal logic for reasoning about processes and plans, *Cognitive Science* **6** (1982) 101–155.

16. Miller, David P., Firby, R. James, Dean, Thomas L., Deadlines, Travel Time, and Robot Problem Solving, *Proceedings IJCAI 9, Los Angeles, Ca.,* IJCAI, 1985.

17. Miller, David P., *Planning by Search Through Simulations,* Technical Report 423, Yale University Computer Science Department, 1985.

18. Sacerdoti, Earl, Planning in a Hierarchy of Abstraction Spaces, *Artificial Intelligence* **7** (1974) 231–272.

19. Sacerdoti, Earl, *A Structure for Plans and Behavior* (American Elsevier Publishing Company, Inc., 1977).

20. Tate, Austin, Generating Project Networks, *Proceedings IJCAI 5, Cambridge, Ma.,* IJCAI, 1977.

21. Tate, A. and Whiter, A.M., Planning with Multiple Resource Constraints and an Application to a Naval Planning Problem, *Proceedings of the First Conference on the Applications of Artificial Intelligence,* 1984.

22. Vere, Steven, Planning in Time: Windows and Durations for Activities and Goals, *IEEE Transactions on Pattern Analysis and Machine Intelligence* **5** (1983) 246–267.

23. Wilkins, David, Domain Independent Planning: Representation and Plan Generation, *Artificial Intelligence* **22** (1984) 269–302.

Goal Structure, Holding Periods and "Clouds"

Austin Tate†
Artificial Intelligence Applications Institute
University of Edinburgh
80 South Bridge
Edinburgh EH1 1HN
United Kingdom

Abstract

This paper briefly describes the representation of plans as used in the Edinburgh O-Plan knowledge-based planning system. The representation allows for the modelling of relative and metric time and metric resource constraints. The O-Plan system structure is mentioned.

The main body of the paper describes the representation of effects and conditions in a plan. It lists the Support Operations often required in an AI planner. The use of a "cloud" as an abstraction of a potentially large set of effects (and effects caused by events external to the plan) and how this structure is used within the planner to replace earlier "Goal Structure" maintenance packages in planners is described.

† Electronic mail to A.Tate@uk.ac.edinburgh

O-Plan Plan State

The plan representation used in O-Plan (Open Planning Architecture) generalises the representation used in the earlier NOAH (Sacerdoti, 1975) and NONLIN (Tate, 1977) planners and extensions of these planners such as in DEVISER (Vere, 1983), SIPE (Wilkins, 1983) and NONLIN+ (Tate and Whiter, 1984). The O-Plan Plan State thus represents activities and their orderings, effects, conditions, protections, goal interactions, time and resource constraints, uncertainty, etc. An overview of O-Plan can be found in Currie and Tate (1985).

The O-Plan Plan State consists of "fixed" and "pending" parts. The fixed side represents the results and consequences of all choices and deductions made during planning up to that stage. The fixed side includes:

The "network" of nodes

- the set of activity nodes included in the plan at various levels of abstraction
- ordering constraints on the nodes
- annotation of these nodes with time windows, resource usage, objects manipulated, etc.

Other Constraints

- restrictions on bindings for object variables included in the node annotations
- lower and upper numeric bounds for numeric variables included in the node annotations
- symbolic constraints and relationships between node annotations

Effects and Conditions

- TOME/GOST†: Effect and Condition recording and maintenance information

Interactive User Aids

- JOTTER: extra "effects" used for information deposited by user interface routines whilst exploring alternatives

Even though we say that the foregoing items are on the "fixed" side of the Plan State, the entries represent uncertainty through partial orderings on nodes, levels of abstraction and aggregation, representation of alternatives, object variable choice sets, numeric variable bounds, etc.

The "pending" side is represented as a (structured) agenda of tasks that still must be carried out to make the plan acceptable. These will represent planning steps which have been put off for later processing as

---

† Table Of Multiple Effects / GOal Structure Table

in MOLGEN (Stefik, 1981) for example. The system will report success when nothing remains on this side. It will fail if *any* pending task cannot be achieved. Of course, tasks often may be carried out in several ways, not all of which are compatible with particular choices made for other tasks.

The "pending" agenda entries may represent tasks such as:

- expand a particular node (if not primitive)

- choose a binding for a variable (if not bound)

- correct an outstanding interaction

- etc

O-Plan Task Scheduler

O-Plan has a scheduler to decide which "pending" task to choose from the agenda next. Dynamically computed measures of "opportunism" are used together with static information extracted when the possible activities' expansions are compiled (from a language called "Task Formalism" which extends NONLIN's simpler TF). This static information concerns time and resource usage as well as relevance to achieving certain conditions or expanding/refining certain (abstract) activities. In the present version of O-Plan, a procedural scheduler is used. A rule-based scheduler is currently being defined.

O-Plan Knowledge Sources

Relevant "Knowledge Sources" are called for a selected pending task on each problem solving cycle. The Knowledge Source will find the alternative ways that its task can be achieved and terminate after representing these in the Plan State. This can be done by any or all of the following:

1. making further "fixed" side entries

2. posting additional "pending" tasks via the agenda

3. recording dependencies and assumptions such that the alternatives will be reconsidered should the (single) chosen option fail

4. (notionally) spawning multiple alternative Plan States in which the choices will be considered (using a context mechanism).

5. if any Knowledge Source can find no way to carry out its task, the Plan State is such that it can never lead to a solution. Hence, it can be POISONED.

The O-Plan system supports (structure shared) context layered alternative Plan States for relatively "dumb" Knowledge Sources. Intelligent Knowledge Sources can record the dependencies or assumptions for one choice made in a form that will still allow the alternatives to be re-considered later. The design aim of the overall O-Plan planner is to reduce the number of "dumb" Knowledge Sources. Many

Knowledge Sources are sufficiently knowledgeable to be able to record the information and allow the planner to act non-monotonically. Any alternatives that are spawned by "dumb" Knowledge Sources can be rapidly selected, some work done on them and then put back into abeyance for later, without chronological backtracking.

Faults raised during planning that are not locally corrected are noted on the "pending" task agenda in the Plan State to await correction by Fault Correction Knowledge Sources (as in McDermott, 1978). Hence, a list of interactions found when a new effect is added to a plan which violates some essential protection would be added to the "pending" side of a Plan State as a "fault" to be corrected when appropriate.

The present O-Plan planning algorithm consists of a set of Knowledge Sources for planning that replicates many of the types of task carried out by a NONLIN-like planner such as:

- expand/refine an activity

- establish a condition

- correct an interaction

- choose a value for an object variable

- etc.

However, the architecture allows for a greater degree of experimentation. New Knowledge Sources and a more sophisticated scheduler are now being written to provide an opportunistic planner able to operate on realistic applications.

Support Operations on an O-Plan Plan State

Given a representation of a plan, a planner will be required to make the following queries or performs the following operations on that representation:

a) query the temporal relationship between points in the plan (before, after or uncertain) or establish such relationships.

b) make a query at some point in the plan (question answering):

   b1)   with some relatively restricted query to establish whether there is support for a condition at some point or perhaps to suggest variable bindings.

   b2)   with a relatively general query to get a "picture" of the state of the application world model that the plan would imply - this can be used for simulation tasks and for user presentation.

c) seek assistance to establish a condition at some point by the proposition of changes to the Plan State (e.g., by establishing further temporal relationships or restricting the bindings for variables).

d) record the effects of actions in the plan.

e) record and maintain the conditions at points in the plan.

f) record the assumptions or dependencies that underly entries in the plan. [This is not discussed in this paper but is needed in a full planning system.]

The implementations of a support system for a planner that provides these services must cope with:

i)   scale - by splitting the relevant information from the irrelevant.

ii)   uncertainty in temporal relationships (ordering and time windows), uncertainty in object selection (variable choice sets and numeric bounds), multiple possible alternatives, etc.

iii) aids to the planner to recover (or take appropriate action) when assumptions prove unjustified, temporal relationships change, new effects interact with conditions, variables are bound inconsistently, etc.

O-Plan Effect and Condition Maintenance

Underlying O-Plan are two support packages (TOME/GOST Maintainer and Network Manager) to help the planner perform the Support Operations described in the previous section. The two packages themselves sit on a context layered entity/relationship data base system (O-Base) of the sort often used in AI planners.

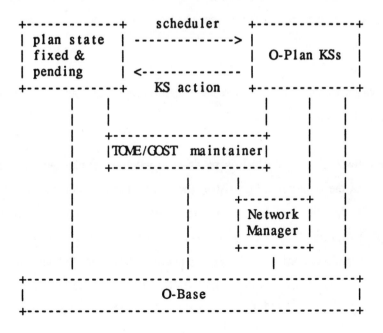

All effects are recorded as:

$$P = V \text{ at } \text{<point>} \quad \text{(e.g., on(a,b) = true at node-41)}.$$

The TOME/GOST Maintainer module interface is very simple. There is a "query" mode and a "do" mode. The "query" mode is always used prior to the "do" mode. These modes apply to adding an effect at a point or establishing a condition at a point. "do" will only work if the caller takes responsibility for dealing with all problems returned by the TOME/GOST Maintainer during a query. These "problems" are usually interactions or lack of commitment between alternatives that are still open. If required, the query mode proposes all the alternative ways to remove the problems or make the commitment (they are returned in a lazy-evaluated summary form for use by the Knowledge Source that will need them). A Knowledge Source can deal with such problems by posting relevant agenda entries.

The temporal relationships which the TOME/GOST Maintainer can use in carrying out its functions involve the normal links specifying ordering constraints on nodes. Also, metric temporal information is used in the form of pairs of numbers that bound time constraints of various types:

- start time window for each activity
- finish time window for each activity
- duration bounds for each activity
- delay bounds between any specified pair of activities

The numeric bounds will be computed from the symbolic constraints on these values using an interval arithmetic package (Bundy, 1984) and an equation simplification system based on PRESS (Bundy and Welham, 1981). A simplified module is included in the present O-Plan prototype to demonstrate feasibility.

It is the job of the Network Manager to store and maintain these relationships and constraints. It also answers queries about ordering relationships between nodes.

A propagation algorithm in the Network Manager which is sensitive to incremental changes is used to keep the ordering constraints and all the time bounds consistent (or to signal inconsistency). The temporal constraint graph propogation algorithm has been shown to be equivalent to a Linear Program (LP). The O-Plan algorithm (Bell & Tate, 1985) extends the simple Critical Path Method facility in NONLIN and the time window comparison routines in DEVISER (Vere, 1983). The O-Plan algorithm also deals with looping problems that would occur with the DEVISER algorithms. The O-Plan addition of a representation of the delay between any specified pair of activities extends the types of plans and problems that can be represented.

O-Plan "Clouds"

The representation of effect holding periods, associated conditions, time points and temporal relationships is unified in O-Plan. The representation allows for scale by aggregating information not needed at any particular stage of planning. We use a single skeletal representation for all effect holding periods with form:

P = V from {C} to {T}

This specifies what we call a "cloud". **P** is a proposition and **V** is a value. {C} is a set of "contributor" points and {T} is a set of "terminator" points. A cloud is an aggregation of effect holding periods for which all effects included match the **P = V** template over a particular time window. The template can contain "don't care" specifiers written as ??.

The effects are known to hold over a period constrained by the earliest time that (any of) the contributor points(s) and the latest time that (any of) the terminator point(s) can be scheduled. One contributor can be the start of the plan or a "zero time" point. One terminator may be the end of the plan or an "infinity" point.

A Cloud's P=V specifier might be:

- highly generalised, e.g., on(??,??) = ??

- quite specific, e.g., on(??,table) = true

- or fully bound, e.g., on(a,table) = true

The representation chosen for clouds allows for approximate reasoning. The aim is to allow for a vague representation of a whole set of effects and their holding periods. The aggregation representation of the clouds only requires two things of the TOME/GOST Maintainer:

i)   that the cloud's P=V specifier represents all effects associated with the cloud.
ii) that the cloud's time window bounds the earliest time of any of the "contributor" points and the latest time of any of the "terminator" points.

These can be maintained efficiently as effects are added to a cloud without considering all the temporal relationships involved between points *within* the cloud. It is not necessary to ensure that overlapping clouds have disjoint P=V specifiers. However, it is usually more efficient to perform queries if they are disjoint.

The TOME/GOST Maintainer need only get concerned about a particular cloud if it is asked to establish and/or maintain a condition (say P'=V') that matches the proposition side of the P=V specifier for the cloud at a point that overlaps with the cloud's time window. Then, clouds are made as explicit as necessary to establish support for the condition (or indicate why it is not at present possible to establish support for it). This involves a process we term "splitting" the cloud. In general, the result is two P=V clouds joined by a "holding period" for the (more) specific P'=V' that matches the conditions required.

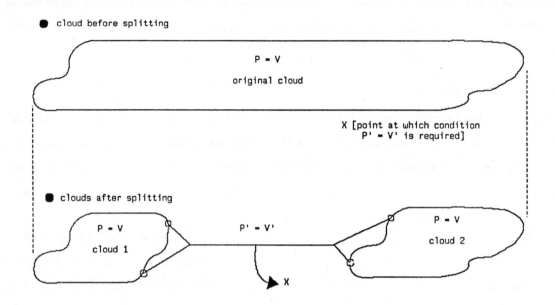

After splitting, the centre holding period for P'=V' is in exactly the same representation as a cloud - this simplifies operations and proofs. In practice, a third cloud may be produced by splitting whenever P'=V' is more restricted (instantiated) than the original P=V specifier.

Any holding period may have associated condition(s). Hence the P'=V' condition on X can be "supported by" the holding period. The set of contributors in the holding period represents a set of effects, any one of which could satisfy the condition. In addition in O-Plan, as in NONLIN, a type is associated with the condition to aid the TOME/GOST Maintainer and the O-Plan Knowledge Sources when they first establish a condition and when they deal with protection violations or other problems.

The TOME/GOST Maintenance package has to ensure, for holding periods supporting conditions, that at least one contributor continues to be available and that no terminator intrudes between that contributor and the point at which the condition is required.

Clouds or holding periods can be merged when no conditions rely on them, so long as the P=V specifier continues to represent the collection of effect holding periods. As mentioned realier, merging can improve query performance.

Comparison with earlier work

Early work on goal protection mechanisms in AI planners was based on HACKER (Sussman, 1973) and the STRIPS' MACROPS triangle table (Fikes, Hart and Nilsson, 1972). INTERPLAN (Tate, 1975) used a holding period or protection maintenance mechanism called "ticklists" summarised in the AI Handbook (Barr & Feigenbaum, 1981) that was the basis of much of our later work on "Goal Structure" maintenance in plans. The Table of Multiple Effects (TOME) in NOAH (Sacerdoti, 1975) and NON-LIN, and the Goal Structure Table (GOST) in NONLIN were data structures used alongside the temporal relationships represented in the network of activity nodes to record and maintain protections for those planners. NOAH used an active "criticise" phase to detect problems with plans. NONLIN used a Goal Structure Maintenance Package that signalled any faults when the establishment of new effects, conditions or temporal relationships was attempted. This same package could be used in a "question answering" mode and could propose new temporal relationships to resolve a protection violation or achieve a required condition.

The cloud/holding period concept is based on a mixture of earlier formalisms used in planning, especially:

- Hacker's Protection Interval (Sussman, 1973).

- the NOAH TOME (Sacerdoti, 1975) with its pattern directed lookup of relevant facts.

- the NONLIN Goal Structure (GOST) Range with its multiple alternative contributors format:
  P=V at \<point\> from {C}

- NONLIN's typing of conditions to restrict search in the planner (Tate, 1984).

- the DEVISER time windows (Vere, 1983).

- and DEVISER's alternative terminators to time ranges (Vere, 1984) - proposed independently.

Dean (1985) recently described the Time Map Manager (TMM) which performs some of the Support Operations described earlier and which are carried out by the O-Plan TOME/GOST Maintainer, cloud representation and Network Manager.

Summary

The O-Plan Cloud Scheme provides a partitioning mechanism that allows the natural incorporation of large bases of background plan information (such as external ongoing events) as well as keeping a planner's own side effects clear of the information that must be monitored during planning and execution. The representation can be used to carry out efficiently several Support Operations required in AI planners.

Acknowledgements

Ken Currie has been responsible for much of the implementation of O-Plan. Colin Bell of the University of Iowa helped set the direction for work on time window and resource management in O-Plan. Mark Drummond provided helpful comments on this paper. The U.K. Science and Engineering Research Council and the U.K. Alvey Programme provided financial support and computing facilities. Systems Designers provided support for the Knowledge Based Planning Group at AIAI.

References

Bell, C.E. and Tate, A. (1985) Using Temporal Constraints to Restrict Search in a Planner, Third Alvey IKBS SIG Workshop, Sunningdale, UK. Also in AIAI-TR-5, AIAI, University of Edinburgh.

Barr, A. & Feigenbaum, E.A. (1981) The Handbook of Artificial Intelligence, William Kaufmann, Los Angeles, CA, USA.

Bundy, A. (1984) A Generalized Interval Package and its Use for Semantic Checking, Dept. of A.I. Research Paper No. 217, University of Edinburgh.

Bundy, A. and Welham, B. (1981) Using Meta-level Inference for Selective Application of Multiple Re-write Rules in Algebraic Manipulation, Artificial Intelligence, 16(2), pp 189-212.

Currie, K.W. and Tate, A. (1985) O-Plan: Control in the Open Planning Architecture, Proceedings of the BCS Expert Systems 85 Conference, Warwick, UK, Cambridge University Press.

Dean, T. (1985) Temporal Reasoning Involving Counterfactuals and Disjunctions, IJCAI-85, Los Angeles, CA, USA.

Fikes, R.E., Hart, P.E. and Nilsson, N.J. (1972) Learning and Executing Generalised Robot Plans, Artificial Intelligence, 3.

McDermott, D.V. (1978) Planning and Acting, Cognitive Sciences 2.

Sacerdoti, E.D. (1975) The Non-linear Nature of Plans, IJCAI-75, Tbilisi, USSR.

Stefik, M.J. (1981) Planning with Constraints, Artificial Intelligence 16, pp 111-140.

Sussman, G.A. (1973) A Computation Model of Skill Acquisition, MIT AI Laboratory Memo AI-TR-297, Cambridge, MA, USA.

Tate (1975) Using Goal Structure to Restrict Search in a Planner, Ph.D Thesis, University of Edinburgh.

Tate, A. (1977) Generating Project Networks, IJCAI-77, pp 888-893, Cambridge, Mass., USA.

Tate, A. (1984) Goal Structure: Capturing the Intent of Plans. Proceedings of the Sixth European Conference on Artificial Intelligence (ECAI-84), Pisa, Italy, pp 273-276.

Tate, A. and Whiter, A.M. (1984) Planning with Multiple Resource Constraints and an Application to a Naval Planning Problem, First Conference on the Applications of Artificial Intelligence, Denver, Colorado, USA.

Vere, S. A. (1983) Planning in Time: Windows and Durations for Activities and Goals. IEEE Trans. on Pattern Analysis and Machine Intelligence, Vol. PAMI-5, No. 3, May 1983, pp 246-267.

Vere, S. A. (1984) Temporal Scope of Assertions and Window Cutoff, JPL AI Research Group Memo.

Wilkins, D.E. (1983) Representation in a Domain-Independent Planner, IJCAI-83, Karlsruhe, West Germany.

A MODEL OF PLAN INFERENCE THAT DISTINGUISHES BETWEEN THE BELIEFS OF ACTORS AND OBSERVERS

Martha E. Pollack
Artificial Intelligence Center, SRI International
and
Center for the Study of Language and Information

ABSTRACT

Existing models of plan inference (PI) in conversation have assumed that the agent whose plan is being inferred (the actor) and the agent drawing the inference (the observer) have identical beliefs about actions in the domain. I argue that this assumption often results in failure of both the PI process and the communicative process that PI is meant to support. In particular, it precludes the principled generation of appropriate responses to queries that arise from invalid plans. I describe a model of PI that abandons this assumption. It rests on an analysis of plans as mental phenomena. Judgements that a plan is invalid are associated with particular discrepancies between the beliefs that the observer ascribes to the actor when the former believes that the latter has some plan, and the beliefs that the observer herself holds. I show that the content of an appropriate response to a query is affected by the types of any such discrepancies of belief judged to be present in the plan inferred to underlie that query. The PI model described here has been implemented in SPIRIT, a small demonstration system that answers questions about the domain of computer mail.

This paper also appears in the Proceedings of the 24th Annual Meeting of the Association for Computational Linguistics, June 1986. Used by permission of the Association for Computational Linguistics; copies of the publication from which this paper is derived can be obtained from Dr. Donald E. Walker (ACL) – MRE 2A379, Morristown, N.J., 07960-1961, U.S.A.

Introduction

The importance of plan inference (PI) in models of conversation has been widely noted in the computational-linguistics literature. Incorporating PI capabilities into systems that answer users' questions has enabled such systems to handle indirect speech acts [13], supply more information than is actually requested in a query [2], provide helpful information in response to a yes/no query answered in the negative [2], disambiguate requests [17], resolve certain forms of intersentential ellipsis [6,11], and handle such discourse phenomena as clarification subdialogues [11], and correction or "debugging" subdialogues [16,11].

The PI process in each of these systems, however, has assumed that the agent whose plan is being inferred (to whom I shall refer as the *actor*), and the agent drawing the inference (to whom I shall refer as the *observer*), have identical beliefs about the actions in the domain. Thus, Allen's model, which was one of the earliest accounts of PI in conversation[1] and inspired a great deal of the work done subsequently, includes, as a typical PI rule, the following: "$SBAW(P) \rightarrow_i SBAW(ACT)$ if P is a precondition of ACT" [2, page 120]. This rule can be glossed as "if the system (observer) believes that an agent (actor) wants some proposition P to be true, then the system may draw the inference that the agent wants to perform some action ACT of which P is a precondition." Note that it is left unstated precisely who it is—the observer or the actor—that believes that P is a precondition of ACT. If we take this to be a belief of the observer, it is not clear that the latter will infer the actor's plan; on the other hand, if we consider it to be a belief of the actor, it is unclear how the observer comes to have direct access to it. In practice, there is only a single set of operators relating preconditions and actions in Allen's system; the belief in question is regarded as being both the actor's and the observer's.

In many situations, an assumption that the relevant beliefs of the actor are identical with those of the observer results in failure not only of the PI process, but also of the communicative process that PI is meant to support. In particular, it precludes the principled generation of appropriate responses to queries that arise from invalid plans. In this paper, I report on a model of PI in conversation that distinguishes between the beliefs of the actor and those of the observer. The model rests on an analysis of plans as mental phenomena: "having a plan" is analyzed as having a particular configuration of beliefs and intentions. Judgements that a plan is invalid are associated with particular discrepancies between the beliefs that the observer ascribes to the actor when the former believes that the latter has some plan, and the beliefs observer herself holds. I give an account of different types of plan invalidities, and show how this account provides an explanation for certain regularities that are observable in cooperative responses to questions. The PI model described here has been implemented in SPIRIT, a small demonstration system that answers questions about the domain of computer mail. More extensive discussion of both the PI model and SPIRIT can be found in my dissertation [14].

---

[1]Allen's article [2] summarizes his dissertation research [1].

Plans as Mental Phenomena

We can distinguish between two views of plans. As Bratman [5, page 271] has observed, there is an ambiguity in speaking of an agent's plan: "On the one hand, [this] could mean an appropriate abstract structure—some sort of partial function from circumstances to actions, perhaps. On the other hand, [it] could mean an appropriate state of mind, one naturally describable in terms of such structures." We might call the former sense the *data-structure view of plans*, and the latter the *mental phenomenon view of plans*. Work in plan synthesis (e.g., Fikes and Nilsson [8], Sacerdoti [15], Wilkins [18], and Pednault [12]), has taken the data-structure view, considering plans to be structures encoding aggregates of actions that, when performed in circumstances satisfying some specified preconditions, achieve some specified results. For the purposes of PI, however, it is much more useful to adopt a mental phenomenon view and consider plans to be particular configurations of beliefs and intentions that some agent has. After all, inferring another agent's plan means figuring out what actions he "has in mind," and he may well be wrong about the effects of those intended actions.

Consider, for example, the plan I have to find out how Kathy is feeling. Believing that Kathy is at the hospital, I plan to do this by finding out the phone number of the hospital, calling there, asking to be connected to Kathy's room, and finally saying "How are you doing?" If, unbeknownst to me, Kathy has already been discharged, then executing my plan will not lead to my goal of finding out how she is feeling. For me to have a plan to do β that consists of doing some collection of actions Π, it is not necessary that the performance of Π actually lead to the performance of β. What is necessary is that I believe that its performance will do so. This insight is at the core of a view of plans as mental phenomena; in this view a plan "exists"—i.e., gains its status as a plan—by virtue of the beliefs, as well as the intentions, of the person whose plan it is.

Further consideration of our common-sense conceptions of what it means to have a plan leads to the following analysis [14, Chap. 3][2]:

(**P0**) An agent G has a plan to do β, that consists in doing some set of acts Π, provided that

1. G believes that he can execute each act in Π.

2. G believes that executing the acts in Π will entail the performance of β.

3. G believes that each act in Π plays a role in his plan. (See discussion below.)

4. G intends to execute each act in Π.

5. G intends to execute Π as a way of doing β.

6. G intends each act in Π to play a role in his plan.

---

[2]Although this definition ignores some important issues of commitment over time, as discussed by Bratman [4] and Cohen and Levesque [7], it is sufficient to support the PI process needed for many question-answering situations. This is because, in such situations, unexpected changes in the world that would force a reconsideration of the actor's intentions can usually be safely ignored.

The notion of an act *playing a role in* a plan is defined in terms of two relationships over acts: *generation*, in the sense defined by Goldman [9], and *enablement*. Roughly, one act *generates* another if, by performing the first, the agent also does the second; thus, saying to Kathy "How are you doing?" may generate asking her how she is feeling. Or, to take an example from the computer-mail domain, typing **DEL** . at the prompt for a computer mail system may generate deleting the current message, which may in turn generate cleaning out one's mail file. In contrast, one act *enables* the generation of a second by a third if the first brings about circumstances that are necessary for the generation. Thus, typing **HEADER 15** may enable the generation of deleting the fifteenth message by typing **DEL .**, because it makes message 15 be the current message, to which '.' refers.[3] The difference between generation and enablement consists largely in the fact that, when an act α generates an act β, the agent need only do α, and β will automatically be done also. However, when α enables the generation of some γ by β, the agent needs to do something more than just α to have done either β or γ. In this paper, I consider only the inference of a restricted subset of plans, which I shall call *simple plans*. An agent has a simple plan if and only if he believes that all the acts in that plan play a role in it by generating another act; i.e., if it includes no acts that he believes are related to one another by enablement.

It is important to distinguish between types of actions (act-types), such as typing **DEL .**, and actions themselves, such as my typing **DEL** . right now. Actions or acts—I will use the two terms interchangeably—can be thought of as triples of act-type, agent, and time. Generation is a relation over actions, not over act-types. Not every case of an agent typing **DEL** . will result in the agent deleting the current message; for example, my typing it just now did not, because I was not typing it to a computer mail system. Similarly, executability—the relation expressed in Clause (1) of (P0) as "can execute"—applies to actions, and the objects of an agent's intentions are, in this model, also actions.

Using the representation language specified in my thesis [14], which builds upon Allen's interval-based temporal logic [3], the conditions on G's having a simple plan to do β can be encoded as follows:

(P1) SIMPLE-PLAN$(G,\alpha_n,[\alpha_1,\ldots,\alpha_{n-1}],t_2,t_1)\leftrightarrow$

    (i) BEL$(G,\text{EXEC}(\alpha_i,G,t_2),t_1)$, for i $= 1,\ldots$,n $\wedge$

    (ii) BEL$(G,\text{GEN}(\alpha_i, \alpha_{i+1},G,t_2),t_1)$, for i $= 1,\ldots$,n-1 $\wedge$

    (iii) INT(G,α_i, t_2,t_1), for i $= 1,\ldots$, n $\wedge$

    (iv) INT$(G,by(\alpha_i, \alpha_{i+1}), t_2,t_1)$, for i $= 1,\ldots$,n-1

The left-hand side of (P1) denotes that the agent G has, at time t_1, a simple plan to do α_n, consisting of doing the set of acts $\{\alpha_1,\ldots,\alpha_{n-1}\}$ at t_2. Note that all these are simultaneous

---

[3]Enablement here thus differs from the usual binary relation in which one action enables another. Since this paper does not further consider plans with enabling actions, the advantages of the alternative definition will not be discussed.

acts; this is a consequence of the restriction to simple plans. The right-hand side of (P1) corresponds directly to (P0), except that, in keeping with the restriction to simple plans, specific assertions about each act generating another replace the more general statement regarding the fact that each act plays a role in the plan. The relation BEL(G,P,t) should be taken to mean that agent G believes proposition P throughout time interval t; INT(G,α, t_2, t_1) means that at time t_1 G intends to do α at t_2. The relation EXEC(α,G,t) is true if and only if the act of G doing α at t is *executable*, and the relation GEN(α, β, G, t) is true if and only if the act of G doing α at t *generates* the act of G doing β at t. The function *by* maps two act-type terms into a third act-type term: if an agent G intends to do $by(\alpha, \beta)$, then G intends to do the complex act β-by-α, i.e., he intends to do α in order to do β. Further discussion of these relations and functions can be found in Pollack [14, Chap. 4].

Clause (i) of (P1) captures clause (1) of (P0).[4] Clause (ii) of (P1) captures both clauses (2) and (3) of (P0): when i takes the value n-1, clause (ii) of (P1) captures the requirement, stated in clause (2) of (P0), that G believes his acts will entail his goal; when i takes values between 1 and n-2, it captures the requirement of clause (3) of (P0), that G believes each of his acts plays a role in his plan. Similarly, clause (iii) of (P1) captures clause (4) of (P0), and clause (iv) of (P1) captures clauses (5) and (6) of (P0).

(P1) can be used to state what it means for an actor to have an invalid simple plan: G has an invalid simple plan if and only if he has the configuration of beliefs and intentions listed in (P1), where one or more of those beliefs is incorrect, and, consequently, one or more of the intentions is unrealizable. The correctness of the actor's beliefs thus determines the validity of his plan: if all the beliefs that are part of his plan are correct, then all the intentions in it are realizable, and the plan is valid. Validity in this absolute sense, however, is not of primary concern in modeling plan inference in conversation. What is important here is rather the observer's judgement of whether the actor's plan is valid. It is to the analysis of such invalidity judgements, and their effect on the question-answering process, that we now turn.

Plan Inference in Question-Answering

Models of the question-answering process often include a claim that the respondent (R) must infer the plans of the questioner (Q). So R is the observer, and Q the actor. Building on the analysis of plans as mental phenomena, we can say that, if R believes that she has inferred Q's plan, there is some set of beliefs and intentions satisfying (P1) that R believes Q has (or

---

[4]In fact, it captures more: to encode Clause (i) of (P0), the parameter i in Clause (i) of (P1) need only vary between 1 and n-1. However, given the relationship between EXEC and GEN specified in Pollack [14], namely

$$EXEC(\alpha, G, t) \land GEN(\alpha, \beta, G, t) \rightarrow EXEC(\beta, G, t)$$

the instance of Clause (i) of (P1) with i=n is a consequence of the instance of Clause (i) with i=n-1 and the instance of Clause (ii) with i=n-1. A similar argument can be made about Clause (iii).

is at least likely to have). Then there are particular discrepancies that may arise between the beliefs that R ascribes to Q when she believes he has some plan, and the beliefs that R herself holds. Specifically, R may not herself believe one or more of the beliefs, corresponding to Clauses (i) and (ii) of (P1), that she ascribes to Q. We can associate such discrepancies with R's judgement that the plan she has inferred is invalid.[5] The type of any invalidities, defined in terms of the clauses of (P1) that contain the discrepant beliefs, can be shown to influence the content of a cooperative response. However, they do not fully determine it: the plan inferred to underlie a query, along with any invalidities it is judged to have, are but two factors affecting the response-generation process, the most significant others being factors of relevance and salience.

I will illustrate the effect of invalidity judgements on response content with a query of the form "I want to perform an act of β, so I need to find out how to perform an act of α," in which the goal is explicit, as in example (1) below[6]:

(1) "I want to prevent Tom from reading my mail file. How can I set the permissions on it to faculty-read only?"

In questions in which no goal is mentioned explicitly, analysis depends upon inferring a plan leading to a goal that is reasonable in the domain situation. Let us assume that, given query (1), R has inferred that Q has the simple plan that consists only in setting the permissions to faculty-read only, and thereby directly preventing Tom from reading the file, i.e.:

(2) BEL(R,SIMPLE-PLAN(Q, prevent(mailfile,read,tom),

[set-permissions(mailfile,read,faculty)]$,t_2, t_1$),

t_1)

Later in this paper, I will describe the process by which R can come to have this belief. Bear in mind that, by (P1), (2) can be expanded into a set of beliefs that R has about Q's beliefs and intentions.

The first potential discrepancy is that R may believe to be false some belief, corresponding to Clause (i) of (P1), that, by virtue of (2), she ascribes to Q. In such a case, I will say that

---

[5]This assumes that R always believes that her own beliefs are complete and correct. Such an assumption is not an unreasonable one for question-answering systems to make. More general conversational systems must abandon this assumption, sometimes updating their own beliefs upon detecting a discrepancy.

[6]The analysis below is related to that provided by Joshi, Webber, and Weischedel [10]. There are significant differences in my approach, however, which involve (i) a different structural analysis, which applies *unexecutability* to actions rather than plans and introduces *incoherence* (this latter notion I define in the next section); (ii) a claim that the types of invalidities (e.g., formedness, executability of the queried action, and executability of a goal action) are independent of one another; and (iii) a claim that recognition of any invalidities, while necessary for determining what information to include in an appropriate response, is not in itself sufficient for this purpose. Also, Joshi et al. do not consider the question of how invalid plans can be inferred.

she believes that some action in the inferred plan is *unexecutable*. Examples of responses in which R conveys this information are (3) (in which R believes that at least one intended act is unexecutable) and (4) (in which R believes that at least two intended acts are unexecutable):

(3) "There is no way for you to set the permissions on a file to faculty-read only. What you can do is move it into a password-protected subdirectory; that will prevent Tom from reading it."

(4) "There is no way for you to set the permissions on a file to faculty-read only, nor is there any way for you to prevent Tom from reading it."

The discrepancy resulting in (3) is represented in (5); the discrepancy in (4) is represented in (5) plus (6):

(5) $BEL(R,BEL(Q,EXEC(\text{set-permissions}(\text{mailfile},\text{read},\text{faculty}),Q,t_2),t_1),t_1) \wedge$
    $BEL(R,\neg EXEC(\text{set-permissions}(\text{mailfile},\text{read},\text{faculty}),Q,t_2),t_1)$

(6) $BEL(R,BEL(Q,EXEC(\text{prevent}(\text{mailfile},\text{read},\text{tom}),Q,t_2),t_1),t_1) \wedge$
    $BEL(R,\neg EXEC(\text{prevent}(\text{mailfile},\text{read},\text{tom}),Q,t_2),t_1)$

The second potential discrepancy is that R may believe false some belief corresponding to Clause (ii) of (P1) that, by virtue of (2), she ascribes to Q. I will then say that she believes the plan to be *ill-formed*. In this case, her response may convey that the intended acts in the plan will not fit together as expected, as in (7), which might be uttered if R believes it to be mutually believed by R and Q that Tom is the system manager:

*(7) "Well, the command is **SET PROTECTION** = (Faculty:Read), but that won't keep Tom out: file permissions don't apply to the system manager."*

The discrepancy resulting in (7) is (8):

(8) $BEL(R,BEL(Q,GEN(\text{set-permissions}(\text{mailfile},\text{read},\text{faculty}),$
    $\text{prevent}(\text{mailfile},\text{read},\text{tom}),$
    $Q,t_2),t_1),t_1)$
    $\wedge$
    $BEL(R,\neg GEN(\text{set-permissions}(\text{mailfile},\text{read},\text{faculty}),$
    $\text{prevent}(\text{mailfile},\text{read},\text{tom}),$
    $Q,t_2), t_1)$

Alternatively, there may be some combination of these discrepancies between R's own beliefs and those that R attributes to Q, as reflected in a response such as (9):

(9) *"There is no way for you to set the permissions to faculty-read only; and even if you could, it wouldn't keep Tom out: file permissions don't apply to the system manager."*

The discrepancies encoded in (5) and (8) together might result in (9).

Of course, it is also possible that no discrepancy exists at all, in which case I will say that R believes that Q's plan is *valid*. A response such as (10) can be modeled as arising from an inferred plan that R believes valid:

(10) *"Type* **SET PROTECTION** $=$ (Faculty:Read)."

Of the eight possible combinations of formedness, executability of the queried act and executability of the goal act, seven are possible: the only logically incompatible combination is a well-formed plan with an executable queried act, but unexecutable goal act. This range of invalidities accounts for a great deal of the information conveyed in naturally occurring dialogues. But there is an important regularity that the PI model does not yet explain.

A Problem for Plan Inference

In all of the preceding cases, R has intuitively "made sense" of Q's query, by determining some underlying plan whose components she understands, though she may also believe that the plan is flawed. For instance in (7), R has determined that Q may mistakenly believe that, when one sets the permissions on a file to allow a particular access to a particular group, no one who is not a member of that group can gain access to the file. This (incorrect) belief explains why Q believes that setting the permissions will prevent Tom from reading the file.

There are also cases in which R may not even be able to "make sense" of Q's query. As a somewhat whimsical example, imagine Q saying:

(11) *"I want to talk to Kathy, so I need to find out how to stand on my head."*

In many contexts, a perfectly reasonable response to this query is "Huh?". Q's query is *incoherent*: R cannot understand why Q believes that finding out how to stand on his head (or standing on his head) will lead to talking with Kathy. One can, of course, construct scenarios in which Q's query makes perfect sense: Kathy might, for example, be currently hanging by her feet in gravity boots. The point here is not to imagine such circumstances in which Q's query would be coherent, but instead to realize that there are many circumstances in which it would not.

The judgement that a query is incoherent is not the same as a judgement that the plan inferred to underlie it is ill-formed. To see this, contrast example (11) with the following:

(12) "I want to talk to Kathy. Do you know the phone number at the hospital?"

Here, if R believes that Kathy has already been discharged from the hospital, she may judge the plan she infers to underlie Q's query to be ill-formed, and may inform him that calling the hospital will not lead to talking to Kathy. She can even inform him why the plan is ill-formed, namely, because Kathy is no longer at the hospital. This differs from (11), in which R cannot inform Q of the reason his plan is invalid, because she cannot, on an intuitive level, even determine what his plan is.

Unfortunately, the model as developed so far does not distinguish between incoherence and ill-formedness. The reason is that, given a reasonable account of semantic interpretation, it is transparent from the query in (11) that Q intends to talk to Kathy, intends to find out how to stand on his head, and intends his doing the latter to play a role in his plan to do the former and that he also believes that he can talk to Kathy, believes that he can find out how to stand on his head, and believes that his doing the latter will play a role in his plan to do the former.[7] But these beliefs and intentions are precisely what are required to have a plan according to (P0). Consequently, after hearing (11), R can, in fact, infer a plan underlying Q's query, namely the obvious one: to find out how to stand on his head (or to stand on his head) in order to talk to Kathy. Then, since R does not herself believe that the former act will lead to the latter, on the analysis so far given, we would regard R as judging Q's plan to be ill-formed. But this is not the desired analysis: the model should instead capture the fact that R cannot make sense of Q's query here—that it is incoherent.

Let us return to the set of examples about setting the permissions on a file, discussed in the previous section. In her semantic interpretation of the query in (1), R may come to have a number of beliefs about Q's beliefs and intentions. Specifically, all of the following may be true:

(13) BEL(R,BEL(Q,EXEC(set-permissions(mailfile,read,faculty),Q,t_2),t_1),t_1)
(14) BEL(R,BEL(Q,EXEC(prevent(mailfile,read,tom),Q,t_2),t_1),t_1)
(15) BEL(R,BEL(Q,GEN(set-permissions(mailfile,read,faculty),
$\qquad\qquad\qquad$ prevent(mailfile,read,tom),
$\qquad\qquad$ Q,t_2), t_1),t_1)
(16) BEL(R,INT(Q,set-permissions(mailfile,read,faculty),t_2,t_1),t_1)
(17) BEL(R,INT(Q,prevent(mailfile,read,tom),t_2,t_1),t_1)

---

[7]Actually, the requirement that Q have these beliefs may be slightly too strong; see Pollack [14, Chap. 3] for discussion.

(18) BEL(R,INT(Q,*by*(set-permissions(mailfile,read,faculty),prevent(mailfile,read,tom)),
t_2,t_1),t_1)

Together, (13)-(18) are sufficient for R's believing that Q has the simple plan as expressed in (2). This much is not surprising. In effect Q has stated in his query what his plan is—to prevent Tom from reading the file by setting the permission on it to faculty-read only—so, of course, R should be able to infer just that. And if R further believes that the system manager can override file permissions and that Tom is the system manager, but also that Q does not know the former fact, R will judge that Q's plan is ill-formed, and may provide a response such as that in (7). There is a discrepancy here between the belief R ascribes to Q in satisfaction of Clause (ii) of (P1)—namely, that expressed in (15)—and R's own beliefs about the domain.

But what if R, instead of believing that it is mutually believed by Q and R that Tom is the system manager, believes that they mutually believe that he is a faculty member? In this case, (13)-(18) may still be true. However we do not want to say that this case is indistinguishable from the previous one. In the previous case, R understood the source of Q's erroneous belief: she realized that Q did not know that the system manager could override file protections, and therefore thought that, by setting permissions to restrict access to a group that Tom is not a member of, he could prevent Tom from reading the file. In contrast, in the current case, R cannot really understand Q's plan: she cannot determine why Q believes that he will prevent Tom from reading the file by setting the permissions on it to faculty-read only, given that Q believes that Tom is a faculty member. This current case is like the case in (11): Q's query is incoherent to R.

To capture the difference between ill-formedness and incoherence, I will claim that, when an agent R is asked a question by an actor Q, R needs to attempt to ascribe to Q more than just a set of beliefs and intentions satisfying (P1). Specifically, for each belief satisfying Clause (ii) of (P1), R must also ascribe to Q another belief that explains the former in a certain specifiable way. The beliefs that satisfy Clause (ii) are beliefs about the relation between two particular actions: for instance, the plan underlying query (12) includes Q's belief that his action of calling the hospital at t_2 will generate his action of establishing a communication channel to Kathy at t_2. This belief can be explained by a belief Q has about the relation between the act-types "calling a location" and "establishing a communication channel to an agent." Q may believe that acts of the former type generate acts of the latter type provided that the agent to whom the communication channel is to be established is at the location to be called. Such a belief can be encoded using the predicate CGEN, which can be read "conditionally generates," as follows:

(19) BEL(Q, CGEN(call(X),establish-channel(Y),at(X,Y)), t_1)

The relation CGEN(α, β, C) is true if and only if acts of type α performed when condition

C holds will generate acts of type β. Thus, the sentence $\mathrm{CGEN}(\alpha, \beta, C)$ can be seen as one possible interpretation of a hierarchical planning operator with header β, preconditions C, and body α. Conditional generation is a relation between two act-types and a set of conditions; generation, which is a relation between two actions, can be defined in terms of conditional generation.

In reasoning about (12), R can attribute to Q the belief expressed in (19), combined with a belief that Kathy will be at the hospital at time t_2. Together, these beliefs explain Q's belief that, by calling the hospital at t_2, he will establish a communication channel to Kathy. Similarly, in reasoning about query (1) in the case in which R does not believe that Q knows that Tom is a faculty member, R can ascribe to Q the beliefs that, by setting the permissions on a file to restrict access to a particular group, one denies access to everyone who is neither a member of that group nor the system manager, as expressed in (20):

(20) $\mathrm{BEL}(\mathrm{R}, \mathrm{BEL}(\mathrm{Q}, \mathrm{CGEN}(\text{set-permissions}(\mathrm{X},\mathrm{P},\mathrm{Y}), \text{prevent}(\mathrm{X},\mathrm{P},\mathrm{Z}), \neg \text{member}(\mathrm{Z},\mathrm{Y})), t_1), t_1)$

She can also ascribe to Q the belief that Tom is not a member of the faculty, (or more precisely, that Tom will not be a member of the faculty at the intended performance time t_2), i.e.,

(21) $\mathrm{BEL}(\mathrm{R}, \mathrm{BEL}(\mathrm{Q}, \mathrm{HOLDS}(\neg \text{member}(\text{tom}, \text{faculty}), t_2), t_1), t_1)$

The conjunction of these two beliefs explains Q's further belief, expressed in (15), that, by setting the permissions to faculty-read only at t_2, he can prevent Tom from reading the file.

In contrast, in example (11), R has no basis for ascribing to Q beliefs that will explain why he thinks that standing on his head will lead to talking with Kathy. And, in the version of example (1) in which R believes that Q believes that Tom is a faculty member, R has no basis for ascribing to Q a belief that explains Q's belief that setting the permissions to faculty-read only will prevent Tom from reading the file.

Explanatory beliefs are incorporated in the PI model by the introduction of *explanatory plans*, or *eplans*:

(P2) $\mathrm{BEL}(\mathrm{R}, \mathrm{EPLAN}(\mathrm{Q}, \alpha_n, [\alpha_1, \ldots, \alpha_{n-1}], [\rho_1, \ldots, \rho_{n-1}], t_2, t_1), t_1) \leftrightarrow$

   (i) $\mathrm{BEL}(\mathrm{R}, \mathrm{BEL}(\mathrm{Q}, \mathrm{EXEC}(\alpha_i, \mathrm{Q}, t_2), t_1), t_1)$, for $i = 1, \ldots, \mathrm{n} \wedge$

   (ii) $\mathrm{BEL}(\mathrm{R}, \mathrm{BEL}(\mathrm{Q}, \mathrm{GEN}(\alpha_i, \alpha_{i+1}, \mathrm{Q}, t_2), t_1), t_1)$, for $i = 1, \ldots, \mathrm{n}\text{-}1 \wedge$

   (iii) $\mathrm{BEL}(\mathrm{R}, \mathrm{INT}(\mathrm{Q}, \alpha_i, t_2, t_1), t_1)$, for $i = 1, \ldots, \mathrm{n} \wedge$

   (iv) $\mathrm{BEL}(\mathrm{R}, \mathrm{INT}(\mathrm{Q}, by(\alpha_i, \alpha_{i+1}), t_2, t_1), t_1)$, for $i = 1, \ldots, \mathrm{n}\text{-}1$

   (v) $\mathrm{BEL}(\mathrm{R}, \mathrm{BEL}(\mathrm{Q}, \rho_i, t_1), t_1)$,
      where each ρ_i is $\mathrm{CGEN}(\alpha_i, \alpha_{i+1}, C_i) \wedge \mathrm{HOLDS}(C_i, t_2)$

Saying that an agent R believes that another agent Q has some eplan is shorthand for describing a set of beliefs possessed by R. I claim that the PI process underlying cooperative question-answering can be modeled as an attempt to infer an eplan, i.e., to form a set of beliefs about the questioner's beliefs and intentions that satisfies (P2). Thus the next question to ask is: how can R come to have such a set of beliefs?

The Inference Process

In the complete PI model, the inference of an eplan is a two-stage process. First, R infers beliefs and intentions that Q plausibly has. Then when she has found some set of these that is large enough to account for Q's query, their epistemic status can be upgraded, from beliefs and intentions that R believes Q plausibly has, to beliefs and intentions that R will, for the purposes of forming her response, consider Q actually to have. Within this paper, however, I will blur the distinction between attitudes that R believes Q plausibly has and attitudes that R believes Q indeed has; in consequence I will also omit discussion of the second stage of the PI process.

A set of plan inference rules encodes the principles by which an inferring agent R can reason from some set of beliefs and intentions—call this the antecedent eplan—that she thinks Q has, to some further set of beliefs and intentions—call this the consequent eplan—that she also thinks he has. The beliefs and intentions that the antecedent eplan comprises are a proper subset of those that the consequent eplan comprises. To reason from antecedent eplan to consequent eplan, R must attribute some explanatory belief to Q on the basis of something other than just Q's query. In more detail, if part of R's belief that Q has the antecedent eplan is a belief that Q intends to do some act α, and R has reason to believe that Q believes that act-type α conditionally generates act-type γ under condition C, then R can infer that Q intends to do α in order to do γ, believing as well that C will hold at performance time. R can also reason in the other direction: if part of her belief that Q has some plausible eplan is a belief that Q intends to do some act α and R has reason to believe that Q believes that act-type γ conditionally generates act-type α under condition C, then R can infer that Q intends to do γ in order to do α, believing that C will hold at performance time.

The plan inference rules encode the pattern of reasoning expressed in the last two sentences. Different plan inference rules encode the different bases upon which R may decide that Q may believe that a conditional generation relation holds between some α, an act of which is intended as part of the antecedent eplan, and some γ. This ascription of beliefs, as well as the ascription of intentions, is a nonmonotonic process. For arbitrary proposition P, R will only decide that Q may believe that P if R has no reason to believe Q believes that $\neg P$.

In the most straightforward case, R will ascribe to Q a belief about a conditional generation relation that she herself believes true. This reasoning can be encoded in the representation language in rule (PI1):

(PI1) $\text{BEL}(R,\text{EPLAN}(Q,\alpha_n,[\alpha_1,\ldots,\alpha_{n-1}],[\rho_1,\ldots,\rho_{n-1}],t_2,t_1),t_1) \wedge$
$\quad\quad \text{BEL}(R,\text{CGEN}(\alpha_n,\gamma,C),t_1)$
$\quad\quad \rightarrow$
$\quad\quad \text{BEL}(R,\text{EPLAN}(Q,\gamma,[\alpha_1,\ldots,\alpha_n],[\rho_1,\ldots,\rho_n],t_2,t_1),t_1)$
$\quad\quad \text{where } \rho_n = CGEN(\alpha_n,\gamma,C) \wedge HOLDS(C,t_2)$

This rule says that, if R's belief that Q has some eplan includes a belief that Q intends to do an act α_n, and R also believes that act-type α_n conditionally generates some γ under condition C, then R can (nonmonotonically) infer that Q has the additional intention of doing α_n in order to do γ—i.e., that he intends to do $by(\alpha_n,\gamma)$. Q's having this intention depends upon his also having the supporting belief that α_n conditionally generates γ under some condition C, and the further belief that this C will hold at performance time. A rule symmetric to (PI1) is also needed since R can not only reason about what acts might be generated by an act that she already believes Q intends, but also about what acts might generate such an act.

Consider R's use of (PI1) in attempting to infer the plan underlying query (1).[8] R herself has a particular belief about the relation between the act-types "setting the permissions on a file" and "preventing someone access to the file," a belief we can encode as follows:

(22) $\text{BEL}(R,\text{CGEN}(\text{set-permissions}(X,P,Y),\text{prevent}(X,P,Z),\neg\text{member}(Z,Y) \wedge \neg\text{system-mgr}(Z)), t_1)$

From query (1), R can directly attribute to Q two trivial eplans:

(23) $\text{BEL}(R,\text{EPLAN}(Q,\text{set-permissions}(\text{mailfile,read,faculty}),[],t_2,t_1),t_1)$
(24) $\text{BEL}(R,\text{EPLAN}(Q,\text{prevent}(\text{mailfile,read,tom}),[],t_2,t_1),t_1)$

The belief in (23) is justified by the fact that (13) satisfies Clause (i) of (P2), (16) satisfies Clause (iv) of (P2), and Clauses (ii), (iii), and (v) are vacuously satisfied. An analogous argument applies to (24).

Now, if R applies (PI1), she will attribute to Q exactly the same belief as she herself has, as expressed in (22), along with a belief that the condition C specified there will hold at t_2. That is, as part of her belief that a particular eplan underlies (1), R will have the following belief:

(25) $\text{BEL}(R,\text{BEL}(Q, \text{CGEN}(\text{set-permissions}(X,P,Y),$
$\quad\quad\quad\quad\quad\quad\quad\quad\quad \text{prevent}(X,P,Z),$
$\quad\quad\quad\quad\quad\quad\quad\quad\quad \neg\text{member}(Z,Y) \wedge \neg\text{system-mrg}(Z)) \wedge$

---

[8]I have simplified somewhat in the following account for presentational purposes. A step-by-step account of this inference process is given in Pollack [14, Chap. 6].

$$HOLDS(\neg member(tom, faculty) \wedge \neg system\text{-}mgr(tom), t_2), t_1), t_1)$$

The belief that R attributes to Q, as expressed in (25), is an explanatory belief supporting (15). Note that it is not the same explanatory belief that was expressed in (20) and (21). In (25), the discrepancy between R's beliefs and R's beliefs about Q's beliefs is about whether Tom is the system manager. This discrepancy may result in a response like (26), which conveys different information than does (7) about the source of the judged ill-formedness.

(26) *"Well, the command is* **SET PROTECTION = (Faculty:Read)**, *but that won't keep Tom out: he's the system manager."*

(PI1) (and its symmetric partner) are not sufficient to model the inference of the eplan that results in (7). This is because, in using (PI1), R is restricted to ascribing to Q the same beliefs about the relation between domain act-types as she herself has.[9] The eplan that results in (7) includes a belief that R attributes to Q involving a relation between act-types that R believes false, specifically, the CGEN relation in (20). What is needed to derive this is a rule such as (PI2):

(PI2) $BEL(R, EPLAN(Q, \alpha_n, [\alpha_1, \ldots, \alpha_{n-1}], [\rho_1, \ldots, \rho_{n-1}], t_2, t_1), t_1) \wedge$
$BEL(R, CGEN(\alpha_n, \gamma, C_1 \wedge \ldots \wedge C_m), t_1)$
$\rightarrow$
$BEL(R, EPLAN(Q, \gamma, [\alpha_1, \ldots, \alpha_n], [\rho_1, \ldots, \rho_n], t_2, t_1), t_1)$
where $\rho_n = CGEN(\alpha_n, \gamma, C_1 \wedge \ldots \wedge C_{i-1} \wedge C_{i+1} \wedge \ldots \wedge C_m) \wedge$
$HOLDS(C_1 \wedge \ldots \wedge C_{i-1} \wedge C_{i+1} \wedge \ldots \wedge C_m, t_2)$

What (PI2) expresses is that R may ascribe to Q a belief about a relation between act-types that is a slight variation of one she herself has. What (PI2) asserts is that, if there is some CGEN relation that R believes true, she may attribute to Q a belief in a similar CGEN relation that is stronger, in that it is missing one of the required conditions. If R uses (PI2) in attempting to infer the plan that underlies query (1), she may decide that Q's belief about the conditions under which setting the permissions on a file prevents someone from accessing the file do not include the person's not being the system manager. This can result in R attributing to Q the explanatory belief in (20) and (21), which, in turn, may result in a response such as that in (7).

Of course, both the kind of discrepancy that may be introduced by (PI1) and the kind

---

[9] Hence, existing PI systems that equate R's and Q's beliefs about actions could, in principle, have handled examples such as (26) which require only the use of (PI1), although they have not done so. Further, while they could have handled the particular type of invalidity that can be inferred using (PI1), without an analysis of the general problem of invalid plans and their effects on cooperative responses, these systems would need to treat this as a special case in which a variant response is required.

that is always introduced by (PI2) may be present simultaneously, resulting in a response like (27):

(27) "Well, the command is **SET PROTECTION** = (Faculty:Read), *but that won't keep Tom out: he's the system manager, and file permissions don't apply to the system manager."*

(PI2) represents just one kind of variation of her own beliefs that R may consider attributing to Q. Additional PI rules encode other variations and can also be used to encode any typical misconceptions that R may attribute to Q.

Implementation

The inference process described in this paper has been implemented in SPIRIT, a System for Plan Inference that Reasons about Invalidities Too. SPIRIT infers and evaluates the plans underlying questions asked by users about the domain of computer mail. It also uses the result of its inference and evaluation to generate simulated cooperative responses. SPIRIT is implemented in C-Prolog, and has run on several different machines, including a Sun Workstation, a Vax 11-750, and a DEC-20. SPIRIT is a demonstration system, implemented to demonstrate the PI model developed in this work; consequently only a few key examples, which are sufficient to demonstrate SPIRIT's capabilities, have been implemented. Of course, SPIRIT's knowledge base could be expanded in a straightforward manner. SPIRIT has no mechanisms for computing relevance or salience and, consequently, always produces as complete an answer as possible.

Conclusion

In this paper I demonstrated that modeling cooperative conversation, in particular cooperative question-answering, requires a model of plan inference that distinguishes between the beliefs of actors and those of observers. I reported on such a model, which rests on an analysis of plans as mental phenomena. Under this analysis there can be discrepancies between an agent's own beliefs and the beliefs that she ascribes to an actor when she thinks he has some plan. Such discrepancies were associated with the observer's judgement that the actor's plan is invalid. Then the types of any invalidities judged to be present in a plan inferred to underlie a query were shown to affect the content of a cooperative response. I further suggested that, to guarantee a cooperative response, the observer must attempt to ascribe to the questioner more than just a set of beliefs and intentions sufficient to believe that he has some plan: she must also attempt to ascribe to him beliefs that explain those beliefs and intentions. The *eplan* construct was introduced to capture this requirement. Finally, I described the process of inferring eplans—that is, of ascribing to another agent beliefs and intentions that explain his query and can influence a response to it.

Acknowledgements

The research reported in this paper has been made possible in part by an IBM Graduate Fellowship, in part by a gift from the Systems Development Foundation, and in part by support from the Defense Advanced Research Projects Agency under Contract N00039-84-K-0078 with the Space and Naval Warfare Command. The views and conclusions contained in this document are those of the author and should not be interpreted as representative of the official policies, either expressed or implied, of the Defense Advanced Research Projects Agency or the United States Government. I am grateful to Barbara Grosz, James Allen, Phil Cohen, Amy Lansky, Candy Sidner and Bonnie Webber for their comments on an earlier draft.

References

[1] James F. Allen. *A Plan Based Approach to Speech Act Recognition.* Technical Report TR 121/79, University of Toronto, 1979.

[2] James F. Allen. Recognizing intentions from natural language utterances. In Michael Brady and Robert C. Berwick, editors, *Computational Models of Discourse*, pages 107–166, MIT Press, Cambridge, Mass., 1983.

[3] James F. Allen. Towards a general theory of action and time. *Artificial Intelligence*, 23(2):123–154, 1984.

[4] Michael Bratman. *Intention, Plans and Practical Reason.* Harvard University Press, Cambridge, Ma., forthcoming.

[5] Michael Bratman. Taking plans seriously. *Social Theory and Practice*, 9:271–287, 1983.

[6] M. Sandra Carberry. *Pragmatic Modeling in Information System Interfaces.* PhD thesis, University of Delaware, 1985.

[7] Philip R. Cohen and Hector J. Levesque. Speech acts and rationality. In *Proceedings of the 23rd Conference of the Association for Computational Linguistics*, pages 49–59, Stanford, Ca., 1985.

[8] R. E. Fikes and Nils J. Nilsson. Strips: a new approach to the application of theorem proving to problem solving. *Artificial Intelligence*, 2:189–208, 1971.

[9] Alvin I. Goldman. *A Theory of Human Action.* Prentice-Hall, Englewood Cliffs, N.J., 1970.

[10] Aravind K. Joshi, Bonnie Webber, and Ralph Weischedel. Living up to expectations: computing expert responses. In *Proceedings of the Fourth National Conference on Artificial Intelligence*, pages 169–175, Austin, Tx., 1984.

[11] Diane Litman. *Plan Recognition and Discourse Analysis: An Integrated Approach for Understanding Dialogues*. PhD thesis, University of Rochester, 1985.

[12] Edwin P.D. Pednault. *Preliminary Report on a Theory of Plan Synthesis*. Technical Report 358, SRI International, 1985.

[13] C. Raymond Perrault and James F. Allen. A plan-based analysis of indirect speech acts. *American Journal of Computational Linguistics*, 6:167–182, 1980.

[14] Martha E. Pollack. *Inferring Domain Plans in Question-Answering*. PhD thesis, University of Pennsylvania, 1986.

[15] Earl D. Sacerdoti. *A Structure for Plans and Behavior*. American Elsevier, New York, 1977.

[16] Candace L. Sidner. Plan parsing for intended response recognition in discourse. *Computational Intelligence*, 1(1), 1985.

[17] Candace L. Sidner. What the speaker means: the recognition of speakers' plans in discourse. *International Journal of Computers and Mathematics*, 9:71–82, 1983.

[18] David E. Wilkins. Domain-independent planning: representation and plan generation. *Artificial Intelligence*, 22:269–301, 1984.

Persistence, Intention, and Commitment

Philip R. Cohen
Artificial Intelligence Center
and
Center for the Study of Language and Information
SRI International
and
Hector J. Levesque
Department of Computer Science
University of Toronto*

Abstract

This paper establishes basic principles governing the rational balance among an agent's beliefs, actions, and intentions. Such principles provide specifications for artificial agents, and approximate a theory of human action (as philosophers use the term). By making explicit the conditions under which an agent can drop his goals, i.e., by specifying how the agent is *committed* to his goals, the formalism captures a number of important properties of intention. Specifically, the formalism provides analyses for Bratman's three characteristic functional roles played by intentions [7,8], and shows how agents can avoid intending all the forseen side-effects of what they actually intend. Finally, the analysis shows how intentions can be adopted relative to a background of relevant beliefs and other intentions or goals. By relativizing one agent's intentions in terms of beliefs about another agent's intentions (or beliefs), we derive a preliminary account of interpersonal commitments.[1]

---

*Fellow of the Canadian Institute for Advanced Research.

[1]This research was made possible in part by a gift from the Systems Development Foundation, and in part by support from the Defense Advanced Research Projects Agency under Contract N00039-84-K-0078 with the Naval Electronic Systems Command. The views and conclusions contained in this document are those of the authors and should not be interpreted as representative of the official policies, either expressed or implied, of the Defense Advanced Research Projects Agency or the United States Government. This paper is reprinted with the permission of the MIT Press.

Introduction

Sometime in the not-so-distant future, you are having trouble with your new household robot. You say "Willie, bring me a beer." The robot replies "OK, boss." Twenty minutes later, you screech "Willie, why didn't you bring that beer?" It answers "Well, I intended to get you the beer, but I decided to do something else." Miffed, you send the wise guy back to the manufacturer, complaining about a lack of commitment. After retrofitting, Willie is returned, marked "Model C: The Committed Assistant". Again, you ask Willie to bring a beer. Again, it accedes, replying "Sure thing". Then you ask: "What kind did you buy?" It answers: "Genessee". You say "Never mind." One minute later, Willie trundles over with a Genessee in its gripper. This time, you angrily return Willie for overcommitment. After still more tinkering, the manufacturer sends Willie back, promising no more problems with its commitments. So, being a somewhat trusting consumer, you accept the rascal back into your household, but as a test, you ask it to bring you your last beer. Willie again accedes, saying "Yes, Sir." (Its attitude problem seems to have been fixed). The robot gets the beer and starts toward you. As it approaches, it lifts its arm, wheels around, deliberately smashes the bottle, and trundles off.

Back at the plant, when interrogated by customer service as to why it had abandoned its commitments, the robot replies that according to its specifications, it kept its commitments as long as required — commitments must be dropped when fulfilled or impossible to achieve. By smashing the last bottle, the commitment became unachievable.

Despite the impeccable logic, and the correct implementation, Model C is dismantled.

Rational Balance

This paper is concerned with specifying the "rational balance" [2] needed among the beliefs, goals, plans, intentions, commitments, and actions of autonomous agents. For example, it would be reasonable to specify that agents should act to achieve their intentions, and that agents should adopt only intentions that they believe to be achievable. Another constraint might be that once an agent has an intention, it believes it will do the intended act. Furthermore, we might wish that agents keep (or commit to) their intentions over time and not drop them precipitously. However, if an agent's beliefs change, it may well need to alter its intentions. Intention revision may also be called for when an agent tries and fails to fulfill an intention, or even when it succeeds. Thus, it is not enough to characterize what it means for an agent to have an intention; one also needs to describe how that intention affects the agent's beliefs, commitments to future actions, and ability to adopt still other intentions during plan formation.

Because autonomous agents will have to exist in *our* world, making commitments to us and obeying our orders, a good place to begin a normative study of rational balance is to examine

---

[2] I thank Nils Nilsson for this apt phrase.

various commonsense relationships among people's beliefs, intentions, and commitments that seem to justify our attribution of the term "rational". However, rather than just characterizing agents in isolation, we propose a logic suitable for describing and reasoning about these mental states in a world in which agents will have to interact with others. Not only will a theorist have to reason about the kinds of interactions agents can have, agents may themselves need to reason about the beliefs, intentions, and commitments of other agents. The need for agents to reason about others is particularly acute in circumstances requiring communication. In this vein, the formalism serves as a foundation for a theory of speech acts [13,12], and applies more generally to situations of rational interaction in which communication may take place in a formal language.

In its emphasis on formally specifying constraints on the design of autonomous agents, this paper is intended to contribute to Artificial Intelligence research. To the extent that our analysis captures the ordinary concept of intention, this paper may contribute to the philosophy of mind. We discuss both areas below.

Artificial Intelligence Research on Planning Systems

AI research has concentrated on algorithms for finding plans to achieve given goals, on monitoring plan execution [17], and on replanning. Recently, planning in dynamic, multiagent domains has become a topic of interest, especially the planning of communication acts needed for one agent to affect the mental state and behavior of another [1,3,4,15,14,13,19,20,27,39,38]. Typically, this research has ignored the issues of rational balance — of precisely how an agent's beliefs, goals, and intentions should be related to its actions.[3] In such systems, the theory of intentional action embodied by the agent is expressed only as code, with the relationships among the agent's beliefs, goals, plans, and actions left implicit in the agent's architecture. If asked, the designer of a planning system may say that the notion of intention is defined operationally: A planning system's intentions are no more than the contents of its plans. As such, intentions are representations of possible actions the system may take to achieve its goal(s). This much is reasonable; there surely *is* a strong relationship between plans and intentions.[4] However, what constitutes a plan for most planning systems is itself often a murky topic.[5] Thus, saying that the system's intentions are the contents of its plans lacks needed precision. Moreover, operational definitions are usually quite difficult to reason with and about. If the program changes, then so may the definitions, in which case there would not be a fixed set of specifications that the program implements. This paper can be seen as providing both a logic in which to write specifications for autonomous agents, and an initial theory cast in that logic.

---

[3]Exceptions include the work of Moore [34], analyzed the relationship of knowledge to action, Appelt [4], Konolige [26,25]. However, none of these works addressed the issue of goals and intention.

[4]See [36] for a definition of plans in terms of intentions.

[5]Rosenschein [40] discusses some of the difficulties of hierarchical planners, and presents a formal theory of plans in terms of dynamic logic.

Philosophical Theories of Intention

Philosophers have long been concerned with the concept of intention, often trying to reduce it to some combination of belief and desire. We shall explore their territory here, but cannot possibly do justice to the immense body of literature on the subject. Our strategy is to make connection with some of the more recent work, and hope our efforts are not yet another failed attempt, amply documented in philosophers' big book of classical mistakes.

Philosophers have drawn a distinction between future-directed intentions and present-directed ones [9,8,41]. The former guide agents' planning and constrain their adoption of other intentions [8], whereas the latter function *causally* in producing behavior [41]. For example, one's future-directed intentions may include cooking dinner tomorrow, and one's present-directed intentions may include moving an arm now. Most philosophical analysis has examined the relationship between an agent's doing something intentionally and the agent's having a present-directed intention. Recently, Bratman [9] has argued that intending to do something (or having an intention) and doing something intentionally are not the same phenomenon, and that the former is more concerned with the coordination of an agent's plans. We agree, and in this paper, we concentrate primarily on future-directed intentions. Hereafter, the term "intention" will be used in that sense only.

Intention has often been analyzed differently from other mental states such as belief and knowledge. First, whereas the content of beliefs and knowledge is usually considered to be in the form of propositions, the content of an intention is typically regarded as an action. For example, Casteñada [10] treats the content of an intention as a "practition", akin (in computer science terms) to an action description. It is claimed that by doing so, and by strictly separating the logic of propositions from the logic of practitions, one avoids undesirable properties in the logic of intention, such if one intends to do an action a one intends to do a or b. However, it has also been argued that needed connections between propositions and practitions may not be derivable [7].

Searle [41] claims that the content of an intention is a causally self-referential representation of its conditions of satisfaction.[6] That is, for an agent to intend to go to the store, the conditions of satisfaction would be that the intention should cause the agent to go to the store. Our analysis is incomplete in that it does not deal with this causal self-reference. Nevertheless, the present analysis will characterize many important properties of intention discussed in the philosophical literature.

A second difference among kinds of propositional attitudes is that some, such as belief, can be analyzed in isolation — one axiomatizes the properties of belief apart from those of other attitudes. However, intention is intimately connected with other attitudes, especially belief, as well as with time and action. Thus, any formal analysis of intention must explicate these relationships. In the next sections, we explore what theories of intention should handle.

---

[6]See also [24].

Desiderata for a Theory of Intention

Bratman [8] argues that rational behavior cannot just be analyzed in terms of beliefs and desires (as many philosophers have held). A third mental state, intention, which is related in many interesting ways to beliefs and desires but is not reducible to them, is necessary. There are two justifications for this claim. First, noting that agents are resource-bounded, Bratman suggests that no agent can continually weigh his competing desires, and concomitant beliefs, in deciding what to do next. At some point, the agent must just *settle on* one state-of-affairs for which to aim. Deciding what to do establishes a limited form of *commitment*. We shall explore the consequences of such commitments.

A second reason is the need to coordinate one's future actions. Once a future act is settled on, i.e., intended, one typically decides on other future actions to take with that action as given. This ability to plan to do some act A in the future, and to base decisions on what to do subsequent to A, requires that a rational agent *not* simultaneously believe he will *not* do A. If he did, the rational agent would not be able to plan past A since he believes it will not be done. Without some notion of commitment, deciding what else to do would be a hopeless task.

Bratman argues that unlike mere desires, intentions play the following three functional roles:

1. *Intentions normally pose problems for the agent; the agent needs to determine a way to achieve them.* For example, if an agent intends to fly to New York on a certain date, and takes no actions to enable him to do so, then the intention did not affect the agent in the right way.

2. *Intentions provide a "screen of admissibility" for adopting other intentions.* Whereas desires can be inconsistent, agents do not normally adopt intentions that they believe conflict with their present and future-directed intentions. For example, if an agent intends to hardboil an egg, and knows he has only one egg (and cannot get any more in time), he should not simultaneously intend to make an omelette.

3. *Agents "track" the success of their attempts to achieve their intentions.* Not only do agents care whether their attempts succeed, but they are disposed to replan to achieve the intended effects if earlier attempts fail.

In addition to the above functional roles, it has been argued that intending should satisfy the following properties. If an agent intends to achieve p, then:

4. *The agent believes p is possible.*

5. *The agent does not believe he will not bring about p.* The rationale for this property was discussed above.

6. *Under certain conditions, the agent believes he will bring about p.*

7. *Agents need not intend all the expected side-effects of their intentions.* [7]

For example, imagine a situation not too long ago in which an agent has a toothache. Although dreading the process, the agent decides that she needs desperately to get her tooth filled. Being uninformed about anaesthetics, the agent believes that the process of having her tooth filled will necessarily cause her much pain. Although the agent intends to ask the dentist to fill her tooth, and, believing what she does, she is willing to put up with pain, the agent could surely deny that she thereby *intends* to be in pain.

Bratman argues that what one intends is, loosely speaking, a subset of what one chooses. Consider an agent as choosing one desire to pursue from among his competing desires, and in so doing, choosing to achieve some state of affairs. If the agent believes his action(s) will have certain effects, the agent has chosen those effects as well. That is, one chooses a "scenario" or a possible world. However, one does not intend everything in that scenario, for example, one need not intend harmful expected side-effects of one's actions (though if one knowingly brings them about as a consequence of one's intended action, they have been brought about intention*ally*.) Bratman argues that side-effects do not play the same roles in the agent's planning as true intentions do. In particular, they are not goals whose achievement the agent will track; if the agent does not achieve them, he will not go back and try again.

We will develop a theory in which expected side-effects are *chosen*, but not intended.

These properties are our desiderata for a treatment of intention. However, motivated by AI research, we add one other, as described below:

The "Little Nell" Problem: Not giving up too soon.

McDermott [33] points out the following difficulty with a naively designed planning system:

> Say a problem solver is confronted with the classic situation of a heroine, called Nell, having been tied to the tracks while a train approaches. The problem solver, called Dudley, knows that "If Nell is going to be mashed, I must rescue her." (He probably knows a more general rule, but let that pass.) When Dudley deduces that he must do something, he looks for, and eventually executes, a plan for doing it. This will involve finding out where Nell is, and making a navigation plan to get to her location. Assume that he knows where she is, and she is not too far away; then the fact that the plan will be carried out will be added to Dudley's world model. Dudley must have some kind of data-base-consistency maintainer to make sure that the plan is deleted if it is no longer necessary. Unfortunately, as

---

[7]Many theories of intention are committed to the undesirable view that expected side-effects to ones intentions are intended as well.

soon as an apparently successful plan is added to the world model, the consistency maintainer will notice that "Nell is going to be mashed" is no longer true. But that removes any justification for the plan, so it goes too. But that means "Nell is going to be mashed" is no longer contradictory, so it comes back in. And so forth. (p. 102).

The agent continually plans to save Nell, and abandons its plan because it believes it will be successful. McDermott attributes the problem to the inability of various planning systems to express "Nell is going to be mashed *unless* I save her", and to reason about the concept of prevention. Haas [21] blames the problem on a failure to distinguish between actual and possible events. The planner should be trying to save Nell based on a belief that it is possible that she will be mashed, rather than on the belief that she in fact will be mashed. Although reasoning about prevention, expressing "unless", and distinguishing between possible and actual events are important aspects of the original formulation of the problem, the essence of the Little Nell puzzle is the more general problem of an agent's giving up an intention too soon. We shall show how to avoid it.

As should be clear from the previous discussion, much rides on an analysis of intention and commitment. In the next section, we indicate how these concepts can be approximated.

Intention as a Composite Concept

Intention will be modeled as a composite concept specifying what the agent has chosen and how the agent is committed to that choice. First, consider the desire that the agent has chosen to pursue as put into a new category. Call this chosen desire, loosely, a goal.[8] By construction chosen desires are consistent. We will give them a possible-world semantics, and hence the agent will have chosen a set of worlds in which the goal/desire holds.

Next, consider an agent to have a *persistent goal* if he has a goal (i.e., a chosen a set of possible worlds) that will be kept at least as long as certain facts hold. For example, a fanatic is persistent with respect to believing his goal has been achieved or is impossible. If either of those circumstances hold, the fanatical agent must drop his commitment to achieving the goal. Persistence involves an agent's *internal* commitment to a course of events over time.[9] Although persistent goal is a composite concept, it models a distinctive state of mind in which agents have both chosen and committed to a state of affairs.

We will model intention as a kind of persistent goal. This concept, and especially its variations allowing for subgoals, interpersonal subgoals, and commitments relative to certain other conditions, is interesting for its ability to model much of Bratman's analysis. For example, the analysis shows that agents need not intend the expected side-effects of their intentions because agents need not be committed to the expected consequences of those intentions. To

---

[8]Such desires are ones that speech act theorists claim to be conveyed by illocutionary acts such as requests.

[9]This is not a *social* commitment. It remains to be seen if the latter can be built out of the former.

preview the analysis, persistence need not hold for expected side-effects because the agent's *beliefs* about the linkage of the act and those effects could change.

Strictly speaking, the formalism predicts that agents only intend the logical equivalences of their intentions, and in some cases intend their logical consequences. Thus, even using a possible-worlds approach, one can get a fine-grained modal operator that satisfies many desirable properties of a model of intention.

Methodology

Strategy: A Tiered Formalism

The formalism will be developed in two layers: atomic and molecular. The foundational atomic layer provides the primitives for the theory of rational action. At this level can be found the analysis of beliefs, goals, and actions. Most of the work here is to sort out the relationships among the basic modal operators. Although the primitives chosen are motivated by the phenomena to be explained, few commitments are made at this level to details of theories of rational action. In fact, many theories could be developed with the same set of primitive concepts. Thus, at the foundational level, we provide a framework in which to express such theories.

The second layer provides new concepts defined out of the primitives. Upon these concepts, we develop a partial theory of rational action. Defined concepts provide economy of expression, and may themselves be of theoretical significance because the theorist has chosen to form some definitions and not others. The use of defined concepts elucidates the origin of their important properties. For example, in modeling intention with persistent goals, one can see how various properties depend on particular primitive concepts.

Finally, although we do not do so in this paper (but see [12]), one can erect theories of rational interaction and communication on this foundation. By doing so, properties of communicative acts can be derived from the embedding logic of rational interaction, whose properties are themselves grounded in rational action.

Successive Approximation

The approach to be followed in this paper is to approximate the needed concepts with sufficient precision to enable us to explore their interactions. We do not take as our goal the development of an exceptionless theory, but rather will be content to give plausible analyses that cover the important and frequent cases. Marginal cases (and arguments based on them) will be ignored when developing the first version of the theory.

Idealizations

The research presented here is founded on various idealizations of rational behavior. Just as initial progress in the study of mechanics was made by assuming frictionless planes, so too can progress be made in the study of rational action with the right idealizations. Such assumptions should approximate reality — e.g., beliefs can be wrong and revised, goals not achieved and dropped — but not so closely as to overwhelm. Ultimately, choosing the right initial idealizations is a matter of research strategy and taste.

A key idealization we make is that no agent will attempt to achieve something forever — everyone has limited persistence. Similarly, agents will be assumed not to procrastinate forever. Although agents may adopt commitments that can only be given up when certain conditions (C) hold, the assumption of limited persistence requires that the agent eventually drop each commitment. Hence, it can be concluded that eventually conditions C hold. Only because of this assumption are we able to draw conclusions from an agent's adopting a persistent goal. Our strategy will be first to explore the consequences of fanatical persistence — commitment to a goal until it is believed to be achieved or impossible. Then, we will weaken the persistence conditions to something more reasonable.

Map of the Paper

In the next sections of the paper we develop elements of a formal theory of rational action, leading up to a discussion of persistent goals and the consequences that can be drawn from them with the assumption of limited persistence. Then, we demonstrate the extent to which the analysis satisfies the above-mentioned desiderata for intention, and show how the analysis of intention solves various classical problems. Finally, we extend the underlying concept of a persistent goal to a more general one, and briefly illustrate the utility of that more general one for rational interaction and communication. In particular, we show how agents can have interlocking commitments.

Elements of A Formal Theory of Rational Action

The basis of our approach is a carefully worked out theory of rational action. The theory is expressed in a logic whose model theory is based on a possible-worlds semantics. We propose a logic with four primary modal operators — BELief, GOAL, HAPPENS (what event happens next), and DONE (which event has just occurred). With these operators, we shall characterize what agents need to know to perform actions that are intended to achieve their goals. The world will be modeled as a linear sequence of events (similar to linear time temporal models [28,29]). [10] By adding GOAL, we can model an agent's intentions.

---

[10]This is unlike the integration of similar operators by Moore [34], who analyzes how an agent's knowledge affects and is affected by his actions. That research meshed a possible-worlds model of knowledge with a situation-calculus-style, branching-time, model of action [32]. Our earlier work [13] used a similar branching time/ dynamic logic model. However, the model's inability to express beliefs about the future that were not

Intuitively, a model for these operators includes courses of events, which consist of sequences of primitive events, that characterize what has happened and will happen in each possible world. [11] Possible worlds can also be related to one another via accessiblity relations that partake in the semantics of BEL and GOAL. Although there are no simultaneous primitive events in this model, an agent is not guaranteed to execute a sequence of events without events performed by other agents intervening.

As a general strategy, the formalism will be too strong. First, we have the usual consequential closure problems that plague possible-worlds models for belief. These, however, will be accepted for the time being, and we welcome attempts to develop finer-grained semantics (e.g., [6,16]). Second, the formalism will describe agents as satisfying certain properties that might generally be true, but for which there might be exceptions. Perhaps a process of nonmonotonic reasoning could smooth over the exceptions, but we will not attempt to specify such reasoning here (but see [35]). Instead, we assemble a set of basic principles and examine their consequences for rational interaction. Finally, the formalism should be regarded as a description or specification *of* an agent, rather than one that any agent could or should use.

Most of the advantage of the formalism is stems from the assumption that agents have a limited tolerance for frustration; they will not work forever to achieve their goals. Yet, because agents are (often) persistent in achieving their goals, they will work hard to achieve them. Hence, although all goals will be dropped, they will not be dropped too soon.

Syntax

For simplicity, we adopt a logic with no singular terms, using instead predicates and existential quantifiers. However, for readability, we will often use constants. The interested reader can expand these out into the full predicative form if desired.

$\langle$**Action-var**$\rangle$ ::= $a, b, a_1, \ldots, a_n, b_1, \ldots, b_n, \ldots, e, e_1, e_2, \ldots, e_n$

$\langle$**Agent-var**$\rangle$ ::= $x, y, x_1, \ldots, x_n, y_1, \ldots, y_n, \ldots$

$\langle$**Regular-var**$\rangle$ ::= $i, j, i_1, \ldots, i_n, j_1, \ldots, j_n, \ldots$

$\langle$**Variable**$\rangle$ ::= $\langle$Agent-var$\rangle$ | $\langle$Action-var$\rangle$ | $\langle$Regular-var$\rangle$

$\langle$**Pred**$\rangle$ ::= $(\langle$Pred-symbol$\rangle$ $\langle$Variable$\rangle_1, \ldots, \langle$Variable$\rangle_n)$

$\langle$**Wff**$\rangle$ ::= $\langle$Pred$\rangle$ | $\sim \langle$Wff$\rangle$ | $\langle$Wff$\rangle \vee \langle$Wff$\rangle$ | one of the following:

---

beliefs about what might possibly occur led to many difficulties.

[11]For this paper, the only events that will be considered are those performed by an agent. These events may be thought of as event types, in that they do not specify the time of occurrence, but do include all the other arguments. Thus John's hitting Mary would be such an event type.

(HAPPENS ⟨ActionExpression⟩) —
   meaning that in the given course of events, one of the (sequence of) events
   described by ⟨ActionExpression⟩ happens next.

(DONE ⟨ActionExpression⟩) — One of the (sequence of) events described by
   ⟨ActionExpression⟩ has *just* happened.

(AGT ⟨Agent-var⟩ ⟨Action-var⟩) — Agent ⟨Agent-var⟩ is the *only* agent of the
   sequence of events denoted by ⟨Action-var⟩.

∃ ⟨Variable⟩ ⟨Wff⟩ where ⟨Wff⟩ contains a free occurrence of variable ⟨Variable⟩.

⟨Variable⟩$_1$ = ⟨Variable⟩$_2$

True, False

(BEL ⟨Agent-var⟩ ⟨Wff⟩) — ⟨Wff⟩ *follows from* ⟨Agent-var⟩'s beliefs.

(GOAL ⟨Agent-var⟩ ⟨Wff⟩) — ⟨Wff⟩ *follows from* ⟨Agent-var⟩'s goals.

⟨Time-proposition⟩

⟨Time-proposition⟩ ::=   ⟨Numeral⟩^{12}

⟨ActionExpression⟩ ::=   ⟨Action-var⟩ | any of the following:

⟨ActionExpression⟩; ⟨ActionExpression⟩ — sequential action,

⟨ActionExpression⟩ | ⟨ActionExpression⟩ — non-deterministic choice action.

⟨Wff⟩? — test action

⟨ActionExpression⟩* — iterative action.

Semantics

We shall adapt the usual possible-worlds model for belief to deal with goals. Assume there
is a set of possible worlds T, which consist of sequences (or courses) of events, temporally
extended infinitely in past and future. Each possible world characterizes possible ways the
world could have been, and could be. Thus, each world specifies what happens in the future.
Agents usually do not know precisely which world they are in. Instead, some of the worlds
in T are consistent with the agents beliefs, and some with his goals, where the consistency is

---

[12]One could encode amore precise (though discrete) clock time here, but little would be accomplished in doing
so.

specified in the usual way, by means of an accessibility relation on tuples of worlds, agents, and an index, n, into the course of events defining the world (from which one can compute a time point, if need be).

To consider what an agent believes (or has as a goal), one needs to supply a world and an index into the course of events defining that world. As the world evolves, agents' beliefs and goals change. When an agent does an action in some world, he does not bring about a new world, though he can alter the facts of that world at that time. Instead, after an event has happened, we shall say the world is in a new "state" in which new facts hold and the set of accessible worlds has been altered That is, the agent changes the possible ways the world could be, as well as ways he *thinks* the world could be or chooses the world to be.

Model Theory

A model M is a structure $< \Theta, P, E, Agt, T, B, G, \Phi >$, where Θ is a set of things, P is a set of people, E is a set of primitive event types, $Agt \in [E \longrightarrow P]$ specifies the agent of an event, $T \subseteq [Z \longrightarrow E]$ is a set of possible courses of events (or worlds) specified as a function from the integers to elements of E, $B \subseteq T \times P \times Z \times T$ is the belief accessibility relation, $G \subseteq T \times P \times Z \times T$ is the goal accessibility relation, and Φ interprets predicates. Formulas will be evaluated with respect to some possible course of events, hereafter some *possible world*, and an "index" into that possible world. [13]

Definitions

- $D = \Theta \bigcup P \bigcup E^*$, specifying the domain of quantification. Note that quantification over sequences of primitive events is allowed.

- $\Phi \in [Pred^n \times T \longrightarrow 2^{D^n}]$, specifying the interpretation of predicates.

- $AGT \subseteq T \times P$, where $x \in AGT[e_1, \ldots, e_n]$ iff there is an i such that $x = Agt(e_i)$. That is, AGT specifies the partial agents of a sequence of events.

Satisfaction

Assume M is a model, σ a sequence of events, n an integer, v a set of bindings of variables to objects in D, and if $v \in [Vars \longrightarrow D]$, then v_d^x is that function which yields d for x and is the same as v everywhere else. We give the following definition of $\models$:

1. $M, \sigma, v, n \models P(x_1, \ldots, x_n)$ iff $< v(x_1) \ldots v(x_n) > \in \Phi[P, \sigma, n]$. Notice that the interpretation of predicates depends on the world σ and the event index n.

---

[13]For those readers accustomed to specifying possible worlds as real-numbered times and events as denoting intervals over them (e.g., [2]), we remark that we shall not be concerned in this paper about parallel execution of events over the same time interval. Hence, we model possible worlds as courses (i.e., sequences of) events.

2. $M, \sigma, v, n \models \neg\alpha$ iff $M, \sigma, v, n \not\models \alpha$

3. $M, \sigma, v, n \models (\alpha \vee \beta)$ iff $M, \sigma, v, n \models \alpha$ or $M, \sigma, v, n \models \beta$.

4. $M, \sigma, v, n \models (x_1 = x_2)$ iff $v(x_1) = v(x_2)$.

5. $M, \sigma, v, n \models \exists x\alpha$ iff $M, \sigma, v_d^x, n \models \alpha$ for some d in D.

6. $M, \sigma, v, n \models (\text{AGT } x_1 \ e_2)$ iff $AGT[v(e_2)] = \{v(x_1)\}$. AGT thus specifies the *only* agent of event e_2.

7. $M, \sigma, v, n \models \langle\text{Time-Proposition}\rangle$ iff $v(\langle\text{Time-Proposition}\rangle) = n$.

8. $M, \sigma, v, n \models (\text{BEL x } \alpha)$ iff for all σ^* such that $\sigma B[v(x)]\sigma^*$, $M, \sigma^*, v, n \models \alpha$. That is, α *follows from* the agents beliefs iff α is true in all possible worlds accessible via B, at index n.

9. $M, \sigma, v, n \models (\text{GOAL x } \alpha)$ iff for all σ^* such that $\sigma G[v(x)]\sigma^*$, $M, \sigma^*, v, n \models \alpha$. Similarly, α *follows from* the agents goals iff α is true in all possible worlds accessible via G, at index n.

10. $M, \sigma, v, n \models (\text{HAPPENS } a)$ iff $\exists m, m \geq n$, such that $M, \sigma, v, n[\![a]\!]m$. That is, a is a sequence of events that happens "next" (after n).

11. $M, \sigma, v, n \models (\text{DONE } a)$ iff $\exists m, m \leq n$, such that $M, \sigma, v, m[\![a]\!]n$

    That is, the sequence of events denoted by a has *just* happened, where

    $[\![]\!] \subseteq [T \times Z \times D \times ActionExpressions \times Z]$ is an anonymous relation constructor, mutually recursive with $\models$, such that

Event variables:	$M, \sigma, v, n[\![x]\!]n+m$ iff $v(x) = e_1 e_2 \ldots e_m$ and $\sigma(n+i) = e_i, 1 \leq i \leq m$. Intuitively, x denotes some sequence of events of length m which appears next after n in the world σ.
Null actions:	$M, \sigma, v, n[\![NIL]\!]n$
Alternative actions:	$M, \sigma, v, n[\![a \mid b]\!]\sigma_1$ iff $M, \sigma, v, n[\![a]\!]\sigma_2$, or $M, \sigma, v, n[\![b]\!]\sigma_2$.
Sequential Actions:	$M, \sigma, v, n[\![a; b]\!]m$ iff $\exists k, n \leq k \leq m$, such that $M, \sigma, v, n[\![a]\!]k$ and $M, \sigma, v, k[\![b]\!]m$
Test Actions:	$M, \sigma, v, n[\![\alpha?]\!]n$ iff $M, \sigma, v, n \models \alpha$
Iterative Actions:	$M, \sigma, v, n[\![a^*]\!]m$ iff $\exists n_1, \ldots, n_k$ where $n_1 = n$ and $n_k = m$ and $\forall i, 1 \leq i \leq m$ $M, \sigma, v, n_i[\![a]\!]n_{i+1}$

The test action, $\alpha?$, is an action expression that denotes either the action NIL if α holds, or "blocks" (fails), if α is false. The operators HAPPENS and DONE, when applied to test actions $\alpha?$, essentially constrain the possible worlds to be ones where α is true at the requisite time. For example, (HAPPENS a;(POOR x)?) is true iff a sequence of events described by the action expression a happens next after which x is poor. The iterative action a^* denotes a finite sequence of a's. A wff α is *satisfiable* if there is at least one model M, world σ, index n, and value assignment v such that $M, \sigma, v, n \models \alpha$. A wff α is *valid*, iff for every model M, world σ, event index n, and assignment of variables v, $M, \sigma, v, n \models \alpha$.

Abbreviations

It will be convenient to adopt the following:

Conditional action: [IF α THEN a ELSE b] $\stackrel{def}{=} \alpha?;a \mid \sim \alpha?;b$
   That is, as in dynamic logic, an if-then-else action is a disjunctive action of doing action a at a time at which α is true or doing action b at a time at which α is false.

While-loops: [WHILE α DO a] $\stackrel{def}{=} (\alpha?;a)^*; \sim \alpha?$
   While-loops are a sequence of doing action a zero or more times, prior to each of which α is true. After the iterated action stops, α is false.

Eventually: $\diamondsuit\alpha \stackrel{def}{=} \exists x$ (HAPPENS $x;\alpha?$).
   In other words, $\diamondsuit\alpha$ is true if at some point in the future (in a given possible world), some action happens after which α holds.

Always: $\square\alpha \stackrel{def}{=} \forall x$ (HAPPENS x) $\supset$ (HAPPENS $x;\alpha?$).
   $\square\alpha$ means that α is true throughout the course of events.

   A useful application of $\square$ is $\square(p{\supset}q)$, in which no matter what happens, p still implies q. We can now distinguish between p $\supset$ q's being logically valid, its being true in all courses of events, and its merely being true after some event happens.

Constraints on the Model

1. *Consistency:* B is Euclidean, transitive and serial, G is serial. B's being Euclidean essentially means that the worlds the agent thinks are possible form an equivalence relation but do not necessarily include the real world [22]. Seriality implies that beliefs and goals are (separately) consistent. This is enforced by there always being a world that is either B- or G-related to a given world.

2. *Realism:* $\forall\sigma, \sigma^*$, if $\langle\sigma, n\rangle G[p]\sigma^*$, then $\langle\sigma, n\rangle B[p]\sigma^*$ In other words, $B \supset G$. That is, the set of worlds that are consistent with what the agent has chosen are included in those that the agent thinks is possible. Without this constraint, the agent could choose worlds that he takes to be impossible. We believe this constraint to be so strong, and its model theoretical statement so simple, that it deserves to be imposed as a constraint. It validates that an agent does not want the opposite of what he believes to

be unchangeable. For example, assume an agent knows that he will die in two months (and he does not believe in life after death). One would not expect to that agent, if still rational, buying a plane ticket to Miami in order to play golf three months hence. Simply, agents cannot choose such worlds since they are not compatible with what he believes.

Properties of the Model

We begin by exploring the temporal and action-related aspects of the model, describing properties of our modal operators HAPPENS, DONE, and $\diamond$. Next, we discuss belief and relate it to the temporal modalities. Then, we explore the relationships among all these and GOAL. Finally, we characterize an agent's persistence in achieving a goal.

Valid properties of the model are termed "Propositions". Properties that constitute our theory of the interrelationships among agent's beliefs, goals, and actions will be stated as "Assumptions". These are essentially nonlogical axioms that constrain the models that we consider.[14] The term "theorem" is reserved for major results. Although no attempt is made here to develop a proof theory, semantical proofs of the propositions can be found in a forthcoming paper.

Events and Action Expressions

The framework proposed here separates primitive events from action expressions. Examples of primitive events might include moving an arm, grasping, exerting force, and uttering a word or sentence. Action expressions denote sequences of primitive events that satisfy certain properties. For example, a movement of a finger may result in a circuit's being closed, which may result in a light's coming on. We will say that one primitive event happened, which can be characterized by various complex action expressions. This distinction between primitive events and complex action descriptions must be kept in mind when characterizing real world phenomena or natural language expressions.

For example, to say an agent does a particular action, we will use (HAPPENS a). To characterize world states that are brought about, we would use (HAPPENS ~p?;a;p?), saying that event a brings about p. To be a bit more concrete, one would not typically have a primitive event type for closing a circuit. So, to say that John closed the circuit one would say that John did something (perhaps a sequence of primitive events) causing the circuit to be closed — ∃x (DONE JOHN ~(CLOSED c)?;x;(CLOSED c)?).

Another way to characterize actions and events is to have predicates true of them. For example, one could have (WALK e) to say that a given event (type) is a walking event. This way of describing events has the advantage of allowing complex properties (such as running a

---

[14]One also needs to show that there is at least one model that does. That is, the axioms are consistent. We will do this in a longer version of this paper.

race) to hold for an undetermined (and unnamed) sequence of events. However, because the predications are made about the events, not the attendant circumstances, this method does not allow us to describe events performed only in certain circumstances. We will need to use both methods for describing actions.

Properties of Acts/Events under HAPPENS

We adopt the usual axioms characterizing how complex action expressions behave under HAPPENS, as treated in a dynamic logic (e.g., [23,34,37]) — including,

Proposition 1 *Properties of complex acts —*

$\models$(HAPPENS a;b) $\equiv$ (HAPPENS a;(HAPPENS b)?)
$\models$(HAPPENS a|b) $\equiv$ (HAPPENS a) $\vee$ (HAPPENS b)
$\models$(HAPPENS p?; q?) $\equiv$ p $\wedge$ q
$\models$ (HAPPENS a*) $\equiv$ (HAPPENS NIL | a;a*)

That is, action a;b happens next iff a happens next producing a world state in which b then happens next. The "non-deterministic choice" action a|b (read "|" as "or") happens next iff a happens next or b does. The test action p? happens next iff p is currently true. Finally, the iterative action a* happens next iff nothing happens (which always does) or one step of the iteration has been taken followed by the a* again. HAPPENS and DONE have the following additional properties:

After doing action a, a would have just been done:

Proposition 2 $\models \forall$ a (HAPPENS a) $\equiv$ (HAPPENS a;(DONE a)?)

If a has just been done, then just prior to its occurrence, it was going to happen next.

Proposition 3 $\models \forall$a (DONE a) $\equiv$ (DONE (HAPPENS a)?; a)

Although this may seem to say that the unfolding of the world is determined only by what has just happened, and is not random, this determinacy is entirely moot for our purposes. Agents need never know what possible world they are in and hence what will happen next. More serious would be a claim that agents have no "free will" — what happens next is determined without regard to the agent's intentions. However, as we shall see, this is not a property of agents; agents' intentions constrain their future actions. Next, we state that deduction can take place inside the test action.

Proposition 4 $\models p \equiv (DONE\ p?)$

That is, the test action filters out courses of events in which the proposition tested is false. The truth of Proposition 4 follows immediately from the definition of "?". Notice that (DONE *False*?) is false, and (DONE *True*?) is valid. However, *True*? has no agent.

For convenience, let us define versions of DONE and HAPPENS that specifies the agent of the act.

Definition 1 $(DONE\ x\ a) \stackrel{def}{=} (DONE\ a) \wedge (AGT\ x\ a)$

Definition 2 $(HAPPENS\ x\ a) \stackrel{def}{=} (HAPPENS\ a) \wedge (AGT\ x\ a)$

Finally, one distinction is worth pointing out. When action variables are bound by quantifiers, they range over sequences of events (more precisely, event types). When they are left free in a formula, they are schematic and can be instantiated with complex action expressions.

Temporal Modalities: DONE, $\Diamond$, *and* $\Box$

Temporal concepts are introduced with DONE (for past happenings) and $\Diamond$ (read "eventually"). To say that p was true at some point in the past, we use $\exists a\ (DONE\ p?;a)$. $\Diamond$ is to be regarded in the "linear time" sense and is defined above. Essentially, $\Diamond p$ is true iff somewhere in the future, p becomes true. $\Box$ and $\Diamond$ are duals. That is, $\Box p \equiv \sim \Diamond \sim p$. $\Diamond p$ and $\Diamond \sim p$ are jointly satisfiable. Since $\Diamond p$ starts "now", the following property is also true,

Proposition 5 $\models p \supset \Diamond p$

Obviously, $\Box$ is related to $\Diamond$ as follows:

Proposition 6 $\models \Diamond(p \vee q) \wedge \Box \sim q \supset \Diamond p$

Proposition 7 $\models \Box(p \supset q) \wedge \Diamond p \supset \Diamond q$

To talk about propositions that are not true now, but will become true, we define:

Definition 3 (LATER p) $\stackrel{def}{=}$ ~p $\wedge \Diamond$p

Time Propositions

Time propositions are currently just numerals. However, for ease of exposition, we shall write them as if they were time-date expressions such as 2:30PM/3/6/85. These will be true or false in a course of events at a given index iff the index is the same as that denoted by the time proposition (i.e., numeral). Depending on the problem at hand, we may use timeless propositions, such as (AT ROBOT NY). Other problems are more accurately modeled by conjoining a time proposition, such as (AT ROBOT NY) $\wedge$ 2:30PM/3/6/85. Thus, if the above conjunction were a goal, both conjuncts would have to be true simultaneously.

Constraining Courses of Events

We will have occasion to state constraints on courses of events. To do so, we define the following:

Definition 4 (BEFORE p q) $\stackrel{def}{=}$ $\forall$ c (HAPPENS c; q?) $\supset \exists$ a (a $\leq$ c) $\wedge$ (HAPPENS a; p?)

This definition states that p comes before q (starting at index n in the course of events) if, whenever q is true in a course of events, p has been true (after the index n). Obviously,

Proposition 8 $\models \Diamond$q $\wedge$ (BEFORE p q) $\supset \Diamond$p

That is, if q is eventually true, and q's being true requires that p has been true, then eventually p holds. Furthermore, we have

Proposition 9 $\models$ ~p $\supset$ (BEFORE ($\exists$a (DONE ~p?;a;p?)) p)

This basically says that worlds are consistent — no proposition changes truth-value without some event's happening, after which that proposition's truth-value has been changed. One would like to adopt the view that some event *causes* that change, but as yet, there is no primitive relation of causality.

The Attitudes

BEL and GOAL characterize what is *implicit* in an agent's beliefs and goals (chosen desires), rather than what an agent actively or explicitly believes, or has as a goal.[15] That is, these operators characterize what *the world would be like* if the agent's beliefs and goals were true. Importantly, we do not include an operator for wanting, since desires need not be consistent. Although desires certainly play an important role in determining goals and intentions, we assume that once an agent has sorted out his possibly inconsistent desires in deciding what he wishes to achieve, the worlds he will be striving for are consistent.

Belief

For simplicity, we assume the usual Hintikka-style axiom schemata for BEL [22] (corresponding to a "Weak S5" modal logic)

Proposition 10 *Belief Axioms:*
a). $\models \forall x \, (BEL \, x \, p) \wedge (BEL \, x \, (p \supset q)) \supset (BEL \, x \, q)$
b). $\models \forall x \, (BEL \, x \, p) \supset (BEL \, x \, (BEL \, x \, p))$
c). $\models \forall x \sim (BEL \, x \, p) \supset (BEL \, x \sim (BEL \, x \, p))$
c). $\models \forall \, x \sim (BEL \, x \, False)$

And, we have the usual "necessitation" rule

Proposition 11 *If* $\models \alpha$ *then* $\models (BEL \, x \, \alpha)$

If α is a theorem (i.e., is valid), then it follows from the agent's beliefs at all times. For example, all tautologies follow from the agent's beliefs. Clearly, we also have

Proposition 12 *If* $\models \alpha$ *then* $\models (BEL \, x \, \Box \, \alpha)$

That is, theorems are believed to be always true. Also, we introduce KNOW by definition:

Definition 5 $(KNOW \, x \, p) \stackrel{\text{def}}{=} p \wedge (BEL \, x \, p)$

Of course, this characterization of knowledge has many known difficulties, but will suffice for present purposes. Next, we will say an agent is COMPETENT with respect to p if he is correct

---

[15]For an exploration of the issues involved in explicit vs. implicit belief, see [31].

whenever he thinks p is true.

Definition 6 (COMPETENT x p) $\stackrel{\text{def}}{=}$ (BEL x p) ⊃ (KNOW x p)

Agents competent with respect to some proposition p adopt only beliefs about that proposition for which they have good evidence. We will assume all agents are competent with respect to their own beliefs, goals, their having done primitive events.

Belief and Action

Below we provide, as assumptions, a characterization of the interaction of agents' beliefs and primitive actions, patterned, in part, after Moore's analysis [34].

Assumption 1 $\models$ ∀ x, a (AGT x a) ⊃ [(DONE a) ≡ (BEL x (DONE a))]

Assumption 2 $\models$ (BEL x ∃a(DONE x a)) ≡ ∃a (BEL x (DONE x a))

The first assumption states that agents know what they have done. The second says that if an agent believes there is some sequence of primitive acts that he has just done, then (because agents have only done one primitive act at a time, and because of Assumption 1) he knows what sequence it was, and vice versa.

These assumptions characterize agent's retrospective beliefs about their having done their own primitive actions. Also of interest are agent's beliefs regarding actions they are about to do (that are) next. We make the following additional assumptions, and then examine agents' beliefs about their doing actions characterized by action expressions.

First, consider agents beliefs about sequences of actions they are about to do:[16]

Assumption 3 $\models$ (BEL x (HAPPENS x $a_1;a_2$)) ⊃
          (BEL x (HAPPENS x a_1; (BEL x (HAPPENS x a_2)?;a_2)))

In other words, if an agent now believes he is about to do a_1 followed by a_2, then he now believes that he is about to do a_1 bringing about a state of the world in which he believes he is about to do a_2. Of course, in actuality, things could go awry, and he could change his

---

[16]Actually, what counts is that he is about to do something *that is next* in the course of events describing the world. This limitation occurs because we are not considering simultaneous actions. Future versions of this paper should loosen this restriction.

beliefs after doing the first action. But, what this assumption says is that he *now* believes that after doing the first action he will believe he is about to do the second.

Next, we assume if an agent thinks he is about to do *something* there is some initial sequence that he believes he is going to do that is next.

Assumption 4 $\models$ (BEL x $\exists$ e (HAPPENS x e)) $\supset$
(BEL x $\exists$ e (HAPPENS x e) $\wedge$ $\exists$ e' $\leq$ e $\wedge$ (BEL x (HAPPENS x e')))

The antecedent would be true if the agent believes he is about to do a complex action (e.g., one containing a disjunction). So, the agent need not know at the start everything he is about to do. We assume however, that the agent does not have such beliefs there is only some initial sequence that he thinks he is going to do.

We make two additional assumptions to complete our statement that agents are "in control" of their primitive actions. First, agents are not undecided about which, if any, primitive actions they believe they are about to do that are next:

Assumption 5 $\models$ $\forall$ e (AGT x e) $\supset$ (BEL x (HAPPENS x e)) $\vee$ (BEL x $\sim$(HAPPENS s e))

In other words, for each primitive event of which x is the agent, either he believes the next event to happen is his doing that primitive event, or he believes it is not the next event to happen.

Lastly, the only way an agent's primitive action can happen next is if he believes it is about to happen next.

Assumption 6 $\models$ $\forall$ e (HAPPENS x e) $\supset$ (BEL x (HAPPENS x e))

This rules out accidental or unknowing execution of *primitive actions by an agent*. It does not rule out, say, one agent's lifting up the arm of another, or accidental actions. In the former case, the first agent is doing the action, even though the second agent's arm is going up. In the second case, accidental actions are possible, but happen *to* an agent. Notice that the converse of this proposition does not hold. Although an agent may believe he is about to do something that is next, he could be wrong, and another agent acts before he does (and hence acts next). Of course, there are long-standing philosophical problems lurking here about what is an action (e.g., is sneezing an action agents do, or is it something that happens to them.) We do not claim to solve such foundational problems, or even to address them seriously. Rather, we are characterizing what follows from being an agent of an action in our scheme.

With these assumptions, and given the expansion of complex action expressions in terms of the primitives, we can now complete the description of the consequences of an agent's believing he is about to do a complex action. First, consider disjunctive actions:

Proposition 13 *Agents are not non-deterministic*

$$\models \forall e_1, e_2 \ (\text{BEL } x \ (\text{HAPPENS } x \ e_1|e_2) \supset (\text{BEL } x \ (\text{HAPPENS } x \ e_1)) \vee (\text{BEL } x \ (\text{HAPPENS } x \ e_2)) \vee$$
$$\exists z \neq \text{NIL} \wedge (\text{BEL } z \leq e_1 \wedge z \leq e_2 \wedge (\text{HAPPENS } x \ z))$$

That is, if an agent believes he is about to do a disjunction of primitive events, then he must believe he is about to do one, or believe he is about to do the other, or believe he is about to do their non-empty common subpart. For example, if an agent believes the next action in the world is his lifting his arm or his moving his foot, then the agent has an opinion on which act he will do. This Proposition follows from Assumption 4.

As a possible counterexample, imagine two agents, A and B having a fight. A believes he is about to block B's punch by either lifting his right or lifting his left arm. However, in our model, A does not believe that his blocking action is the next action; the next action is B's swinging. Once B swings, whichever act A does next will follow from A's beliefs (albeit quickly, and perhaps unconsciously).

From Assumption 3 and Proposition 13, we can now show that an agent who is about to do an an if-then-else, must believe the condition of if-then-else to be true, or believe it to be false. More generally, if he believes he will do an if-then-else in the future, he believes he will have an opinion on the truth of the condition. More formally, one can show that:

Proposition 14 *If-then-else*
$\models \forall e_1, e_2, e_3, e_2 \neq e_3 \ (\text{BEL } x \ (\text{HAPPENS } x \ e_1;[\text{IF } p \text{ THEN } e_2 \text{ ELSE } e_3])) \supset$
$(\text{BEL } x \ (\text{HAPPENS } x \ e_1;[(\text{BEL } x \ p \wedge (\text{HAPPENS } x \ e_2)) \vee (\text{BEL } x \sim p \wedge (\text{HAPPENS } x \ e_3))]?))$

The proof of this follows from the previous two assumptions and the expansion of an if-then-else action expression into its definition. This proposition says that an agent cannot believe he is about to do an if-then-else without coming to a belief about the condition. This holds true *provided* that the *then* part and the *else* part are disjoint. A case in which that would not be the case would be that of a physical "test", such as testing that a liquid is acidic or basic. [17] An agent who believes he is is about to do

ACID?;Dip;(RED Paper)? | ~ACID?;Dip;(BLUE Paper)?

should not have to know in advance whether the liquid is acidic or basic. The third disjunct in Proposition 13 allows for this possibility.

---

[17]See [34] for another analysis of such tests.

Because of the definition of iterative actions in terms of the '*' operator, one can show:

Proposition 15 *While-loops*
⊨ (BEL x (HAPPENS x [WHILE p DO a])) ⊃
(BEL x ~p) ∨ ((BEL x p) ∧ (BEL x (HAPPENS x a;[WHILE p DO a])))

That is, if an agent believes he is about to do a while-loop, then he either believes the condition is false (and does nothing) or believes it is true and believes he is about to take one step of the loop, after which, of course, he will either believe **p** or believe ~**p**, etc.

At this point, we have characterized the dependencies among an agent's beliefs, the actions he has taken, and the actions he is about to take (that are next). These dependencies will be vital to an understanding of intention. Next, we describe goals and their dependence on all these.

Goals

At a given point in a course of events, agents choose worlds they would like (most) to be in — ones in which their *goals* are true. (GOAL x p) is meant to be read that p follows from the agent's goals, or p is true in all worlds, accessible from the current world, that are compatible with the agent's goals. Since agents choose entire worlds, they choose the logically and physically necessary consequences of their goals. At first glance, this appears troublesome if we interpret the facts that are true in all worlds compatible with an agents goals as intended. However, intention will involve a form of commitment that will rule out such consequences as being intended, although they are chosen.

GOAL has the following properties:

Proposition 16 *Consistency:* ⊨ ~(GOAL x *False*)

What is implicit in someone's goals is closed under consequence:

Proposition 17 ⊨ (GOAL x p) ∧ (GOAL x p⊃q) ⊃ (GOAL x q)

Again, we have a necessitation property:

Proposition 18 *If* ⊨ α *then* ⊨(GOAL x α)

That is, if α is a theorem, it is true in all chosen worlds. However, agents can distinguish such "trivial" goals from others, as explained below.

Achievement Goals

Agents can distinguish between achievement goals and maintenance goals. Achievement goals are those the agent believes to be false; goals of maintenance are those the agent already believes to be true. We shall not be concerned in this paper with maintenance goals. But, to characterize achievement goals, we use:

Definition 7 (A-GOAL x p) $\stackrel{def}{=}$ (GOAL x (LATER p)) $\wedge$ (BEL x $\sim$p)

That is, x's chosen worlds have p's being not currently true, but true later, and x believes p is currently false.

No Persistence/Deferral Forever

Agents are limited in both their persistence and their procrastination. They cannot try forever to achieve their goals; eventually they give up. On the other hand, agents do not forever defer working on their goals. The assumption below captures both of these phenomena.

Assumption 7 $\models \Diamond\sim$(GOAL x (LATER p))

Thus, agents eventually drop all achievement goals. Because one cannot conclude that agents always act on their goals, one needs to guard against infinite procrastination. However, one could have an agent who forever fails to achieve his goals, but believes success is still achievable. The limiting case here is an agent who executes an infinite loop. Another case is that of a compulsive gambler who continually thinks success is just around the corner. Our assumption rules out these pathological cases from consideration, but still allows agents to try hard. Finally, since no one ever said the world is fair (in the computer science sense), an agent who is ready to act in what he believes to be the correct circumstance may never get a chance to execute his action because the world keeps changing. We only require that if faced with such monumental unfairness, the agent reach the conclusion that the act is impossible.

One might object that there are still achievement goals that agents could keep forever. For example, one might argue that the goal expressed by "I always want more money than I have" is kept forever (or at least as long as the agent is alive);[18] but consider a plausible

---

[18]However, we have assumed immortal agents.

logical representation of that sentence in our formal language.

$$\Box \; [\forall \; x \; (\text{KNOW I (HAVE I } x)) \supset \exists \; y \; y > x \land (\text{A-GOAL I (HAVE I } y))]$$

Here, there is no single sentence that the agent always has as a goal; the goal changes because of the quantified variables. Hence, one cannot argue he keeps anything as a goal forever. Instead, the agent forever gets new goals.

Important consequences will follow from Assumption 7 when combined with an agent's commitments. First, we need to examine what, in general, are the consequences of having goals.

Goals and their Consequences

Unlike BEL, GOAL needs to be characterized in terms of all the other modalities. In particular, we need to specify how goals interact with an agent's beliefs about the future.

The semantics of GOAL specifies that worlds compatible with an agent's goals must have a non-empty intersection with those compatible with his beliefs. This is reflected in the following property:

Proposition 19 $\models (\text{BEL } x \; p) \supset (\text{GOAL } x \; p)$

From the semantics of BEL and GOAL, one sees that p will be evaluated at the same point in the *B*- and *G*-accessible worlds. So, if an agent believes p is true now, he cannot not now want it to be currently false; agents do not choose what they cannot change. Conversely, if p is now true in all the agent's chosen worlds, then the agent does not believe it is currently false. For example, if an agent believes she has not just done event e, then she cannot have (DONE x e) as a goal. [19]

This relationship between BEL and GOAL makes more sense when one considers the future. Let p be a proposition of the form $\Box q$. So, if the agent believes q is forever true (an example would be a tautology), the above Proposition says that any worlds that the agent chooses must have q's being true as well. Conversely, let p be of the form $\Diamond q$. From Proposition 19, we derive that if the agent wants q to be true sometime in the future, he does not believe it will be forever false.

Notice that although an agent may have to put up with what he believes is inevitable, he may do so reluctantly, knowing that if he should change his mind about the inevitability of that state-of-affairs, he choices would change. For example, the following is satisfiable:

---

[19]Of course, she *can* have (LATER (DONE x e)) as a goal.

$$(BEL \ x \ \Diamond p \land \Box[\sim(BEL \ x \ \Diamond p) \supset (GOAL \ x \ \Box \sim p)])$$

That is, the agent can believe p is inevitable (and hence is true true in all the agent's chosen worlds, but at the same time believe that if he ever stops believing it is inevitable, he will choose worlds in which it is never true.

Notice also that, as a corollary of Proposition 19, agent's beliefs and goals "line up" with respect to their own primitive actions that happen next.

Proposition 20 $\models \forall x, a \ (BEL \ x \ (HAPPENS \ x \ a)) \supset$
$$(GOAL \ x \ (HAPPENS \ x \ a)))$$

That is, if an agent believes he is about to do something that is next, then its happening next is true in all his chosen worlds. Of course, "successful" agents are ones who choose what they are going to do before believeing they are going to do it; they come to believe they are going to do something because they have made certain choices. We discuss this further in our treatment of intention.

Next, as another simple subcase, consider the *consequences* of facts the agent believes hold in all of that agent's chosen worlds.

Proposition 21 *Expected consequences:* $\models (GOAL \ x \ p) \land (BEL \ x \ p \supset q) \supset (GOAL \ x \ q)$

By Proposition 19, if an agent believes $p \supset q$ true, $p \supset q$ is true in all his chosen worlds. Hence by Proposition 17, q follows from his goals as well.

At this point, we are finished with the foundational level, having described agents' beliefs and goals, events, and time. In so doing, we have characterized agents as not striving for the impossible, and eventually foregoing the contingent. Our agents now need to be committed.

Persistent goals

To capture *one* grade of commitment (fanatical) that an agent might have towards his goals, we define a persistent goal, P-GOAL, to be one that the agent will not give up until he thinks it has been satisfied, or until he thinks it will never be true. The latter case could arise easily if the proposition p is one that specifically mentions a time. Once the agent believes that time is past, he believes the proposition is impossible to achieve. Specifically, we have

Definition 8 $(P\text{-}GOAL \ x \ p) \overset{\text{def}}{=} (GOAL \ x \ (LATER \ p)) \land (BEL \ x \sim p) \land$
$$[BEFORE \ ((BEL \ x \ p) \lor (BEL \ x \ \Box \sim p))$$
$$\sim(GOAL \ x \ (LATER \ p))]$$

Notice the use of LATER, and hence $\diamondsuit$, above. Clearly, P-GOALs are achievement goals; the agent's goal is that p be true in the future, and he believes it is not currently true. As soon as the agent believes it will never be true, we know the agent must drop his goal (by Proposition 19), and hence his persistent goal. Moreover, as soon as an agent believes p is true, the belief conjunct of P-GOAL requires that he drop the persistent goal that p be true. Thus, these conditions are necessary and sufficient for dropping a persistent goal. However, the BEFORE conjunct does *not* say that an agent *must* give up his *simple* goal when he thinks it is satisfied, since agents may have goals of maintenance. Thus, achieving one's persistent goals may convert them into maintenance goals.

The Logic of P-GOAL

The logic of P-GOAL is weaker than one might expect. Unlike GOAL, P-GOAL does not distribute over conjunction or disjunction, and is closed only under logical equivalence. First, we examine conjunction and disjunction. Then, we turn to implication.

Conjunction and Disjunction

Proposition 22 *The Logic of* P-GOAL:

a.) (P-GOAL x p∧q) $\not\supset\atop\not\subset$ (P-GOAL x p)∧(P-GOAL x q)

b.) (P-GOAL x p∨q) $\not\supset\atop\not\subset$ (P-GOAL x p)∨(P-GOAL x q)

c.) (P-GOAL x ~p) ⊃ ~(P-GOAL x p)

First, (P-GOAL x p∧q) does not imply (P-GOAL x p) ∧ (P-GOAL x q) because, although the antecedent is true, the agent might believe q is already true, and thus cannot have q as a P-GOAL. Conversely, (P-GOAL x p) ∧ (P-GOAL x q) does not imply (P-GOAL x p∧q), because (GOAL x (LATER p)) ∧ (GOAL x (LATER q)) does not imply (GOAL x (LATER p∧q)); p and q could be true at different times.

Similarly, (P-GOAL x p∨q) does not imply (P-GOAL x p) ∨ (P-GOAL x q) because (GOAL x (LATER p∨q) does not imply (GOAL x (LATER p)) ∨ (GOAL x (LATER q)); p could hold in some possible worlds compatible with the agent's goals, and q in others. But, neither p nor q is forced to hold in all *G*-accessible worlds. Moreover, the implication does not hold in the other direction either, because of the belief conjunct of P-GOAL; although the agent may believe ~p or he may believe ~q, that does not guarantee he believes ~(p∨q) (i.e., ~p ∧ ~q).

No Consequential Closure of P-GOAL

We demonstrate that P-GOAL is closed only under logical equivalence. Below are listed the possible relationships between a proposition p and a consequence q, which we term a "side-effect". Assume in all cases that (P-GOAL x p). Then, depending on the relationship of p to q, we have the cases shown in Table 1. We will say a "case" fails, indicated by an "N" in the third column, if (P-GOAL x q) does not hold.

Table 1
P-GOAL and progressively stronger relationships
between p and q.

Case	Relationship of p to q	(P-GOAL x q)?
1.	$p \supset q$	N
2.	(BEL x $p \supset q$)	N
3.	(BEL x $\Box(p \supset q)$)	N
4.	$\Box$(BEL x $\Box(p \supset q)$)	N
5.	$\models p \supset q$	N
6.	$\models p \equiv q$	Y

Case 1 fails for a number of reasons, most importantly because the agent's persistent goals depends on his beliefs, not on the facts. However, consider Case 2. Even though the agent may believe p⊃q holds, Case 2 fails because that implication cannot affect the agent's persistent goals, which refer to p's being true *later*. That is, the agent believes p is false and does not have the goal of its currently being true.

Consider Case 3, where the agent believes the implication *always* holds. Although Proposition 19 tells us that the agent has q as a goal, we show that the agent does not have q as a *persistent* goal. Recall that P-GOAL was defined so that the only reason an agent could give up a persistent goal was if it were believed to be satisfied or believed to be impossible. However, side-effects are goals only because of a belief. If the belief changes, the agent need no longer choose worlds in which p ⊃ q holds, and thus need no longer have q has the goal. However, the agent would have dropped the goal for reasons other than those stipulated by the definition of persistent goal, and so does not have it as a persistent goal.

Now, consider Case 4, in which the agent *always* believes the implication. Again, q need not be a persistent goal, but for a different reason. Here, an agent could believe the side-effect already held. Hence, by the second clause in the definition of P-GOAL, the agent would not have a persistent goal. This reason also blocks Case 5, closure under logical consequence. However, instances of Case 4 and Case 5 in which the agent does not believe the side-effect already holds *would* require the agent to have the side-effect as a persistent goal. Finally, in Case 6, where q is logically equivalent to p the agent has q as a persistent goal. Having shown what cannot be deduced from P-GOAL, we now turn to its major consequences.

Persistent Goals Constrain Agents' Future Beliefs and Actions

An important property of agents is that they eventually give up their achievement goals (Assumption 7). Hence, if an agent takes on a P-GOAL, she must give it up subject to the constraints imposed by P-GOAL.

Proposition 23 $\models$ (P-GOAL x q) $\supset \Diamond[$(BEL x q) $\vee$ (BEL x $\Box \sim$q)$]$

Proof: This proposition is a direct consequence of Assumption 7, the definition of P-GOAL, and Proposition 6. In other words, because agents eventually give up their achievement goals, and because the agent has adopted a persistent goal to bring about such a proposition q, eventually the agent must believe q or believe q will never come true. A simple consequence of Proposition 23 is:

Proposition 24 $\models$ (P-GOAL x (DONE x a)) $\supset \Diamond[$(DONE x a) $\vee$ (BEL x $\Box \sim$(DONE x a))$]$,

Proof: Using Proposition 23, the agent eventually believes he has done the act or the act is impossible for him to do. By Assumption 1, if the agent believes he has just done the act, then he has.

We now give a crucial theorem:

Theorem 1 *From persistence to eventualities — If someone has a persistent goal of bringing about* p, p *is within his area of competence, and, before dropping his goal, the agent will not believe* p *will never occur, then eventually* p *becomes true.*

$$\models \forall\ y\ \text{(P-GOAL}\ y\ p) \wedge \Box\ \text{(COMPETENT}\ y\ p) \wedge \sim\text{(BEFORE (BEL}\ y\ \Box \sim p)$$
$$\sim\text{(GOAL}\ x\ \text{(LATER}\ p)) \supset \qquad \Diamond p$$

Proof: By Proposition 23, the agent eventually believes either that p is true, or that p is impossible to achieve. If he eventually thinks p is true, since he is always competent with respect to p, he is correct. The other alternative sanctioned by Proposition 23, that the agent believes p is impossible to achieve, is ruled out by the assumption that (it so happens to be the case that) any belief of the agent that the goal is impossible can come only *after* the agent drops his goal. Hence, by Proposition 6, the goal comes about.

If an agent who is not competent with respect to p adopts p as a persistent goal, we cannot conclude that eventually p will be true, since the agent could forever create incorrect plans. If the goal is not persistent, we also cannot conclude $\Diamond$p since the agent could give up the goal without achieving it. If the goal actually is impossible, but the agent does not know this and commits to achieving it, then we know that eventually, perhaps after trying hard to achieve it, the agent will come to believe it is impossible and give up.

Acting on Persistent Goals

As mentioned earlier, one cannot conclude that, merely by committing to a chosen proposition (set of possible worlds), the agent will act; someone else could bring about the desired state-of-affairs. However, if the agent knows that he is the only one who could bring it about, then, under certain circumstances, we can conclude the agent will act. For example, propositions of the form (DONE x a) can only be brought about by the agent x. So, if an agent always believes the act a is possible (or at least believes that longer than he keeps the persistent goal), the agent will act.

A simple instance of Proposition 23 is one where q is (HAPPENS a) $\land$ (AGT x a). Such a goal is one in which the agent's goal is that eventually the next thing that happens is his doing action a. Eventually, the agent believes either the next action is his, or the agent eventually comes to believe he will never get the chance. We cannot guarantee that the agent will actually do the action next, for someone else could act next. If the agent never believes his act is impossible, then by Proposition 23, the agent will eventually believe (HAPPENS a) $\land$ (AGT x a). By Proposition 20, we know that (GOAL x (HAPPENS a)). *If* the agent acts just when he believes the next act is his, we know that he did so believing it would happen next and having its happening next as his goal. One could say, loosely, that the agent acted "intentionally".

Bratman [9] argues that one applies the term "intentionally" to foreseen consequences as well as to truly intended ones. That is, one intends a subset of what is done intentionally. Proposition 20 requires only that agents have goal, but not a persistent goal, for expected effects. Hence, the agent would in fact bring about intentionally all those forseen consequences of his goal that actually obtain from his doing the act. However, the would not be committed to bringing about the side-effects, and thus did not intend to do so.

If agents adopt *time-limited* goals, such as (BEFORE (DONE x e) 2:30pm/6/24/86), one *cannot* conclude the agent definitely will act *in time*, even if he believes it is possible to act. Simply, the agent might wait too long. However, one *can* conclude (see below) that the agent will not adopt another persistent goal to do a non-NIL act he believes would make the persistent goal impossible to achieve. Still, the agent could unknowingly (and hence, by Proposition 20, accidentally) make his persistent goal impossible. If one makes the further assumption that agents always know what they are going to do just before doing it, then one can conclude agents will not in fact do anything to make their persistent goals impossible for them to achieve.

All these conclusions are, we believe, reasonable. However, they do not indicate what the "normal" case is. Instead, we have characterized the possibilities, and await a theory of default reasoning to further describe the situation.

Intention as a Kind of Persistent Goal

With our foundation laid, we are now in a position to define intention. There will be two defining forms for INTEND, depending on whether the argument is an action or a proposition.

INTEND$_1$

Typically, one intends to do actions. Accordingly, we define INTEND$_1$ to take an action expression as its argument.

Definition 9 (INTEND$_1$ x a) $\overset{def}{=}$ (P-GOAL x (DONE x (BEL x (HAPPENS a))?; a)),
where a *is an action expression.*

Let us examine what this says. First, (fanatically) intending to do an action a is a special kind of commitment (i.e., persistent goal) to have done a. However, it is not a commitment just to doing a, for that would allow the agent to be committed to doing something accidentally or unknowingly. It seems reasonable to require that the agent be committed to believing he is about to do the intended action, and then doing it. Thus, intentions are future-directed, but here directed toward something happening *next*. This is as close as we can come to present-directed intention.

Secondly, it is a commitment to success — to having done the action. As a contrast, consider the following inadequate definition of INTEND$_1$:

$$(\text{INTEND}_1 \text{ x a}) \overset{def?}{=} (\text{P-GOAL x } \exists \text{ e (HAPPENS x e;(DONE x a)?))}$$

This would say that an intention is a commitment to being *on the verge* of doing some event e, after which x would have just done a.[20] Of course, being on the verge of doing something is not the same as doing it; any unforseen obstacle could permanently derail the agent from ever performing the intended act. This would not be much of a commitment.

---

[20]Notice that e could be the last step of a.

Intending act expressions

Let us apply $\mathrm{INTEND_1}$ to each kind of action expression. First, consider intentions to achieve certain states-of-affairs p. ($\mathrm{INTEND_1}$ x p?) expands into

$$\text{(P-GOAL x (DONE x [BEL x (HAPPENS x p?)]:p?)).}$$

By Proposition 1, this is equivalent to (P-GOAL x (DONE x (KNOW x p)?)), which reduces to (P-GOAL x (KNOW x p)). That is, the agent is committed to its being the case that he comes to know p (and he does not know it now). However, the agent is not committed to bringing about p himself.

Second, consider action expressions of the form e;p?. An example would be safe-cracking:[21]

$$\exists e, s \text{ (SAFE s)} \wedge \text{(DIAL e)} \wedge \text{(INTEND}_1 \text{ x e:(OPEN s)?)}$$

That is, there is a dialing event that the agent is committed to doing to open the safe, and he believes just prior to doing it that it opens the safe. Notice that the agent need not know now which dialing event it is — it is not yet quantified into his beliefs, although it *is* quantified into his goals. However, we know that eventually, the agent will believe of that event that it opens the safe. This seems reasonable. To intend to *crack* the safe, rather than merely to hope to open it, or to intend to do something to open it, one should believe that one eventually will know just what to do. An agent would be justified in having such an intention if he knows, for example, that by listening to the tumblers in the lock, he will think that the next turn will open the safe.

However, certain intentions cannot be so characterized — an agent may never come to believe of any given event that it will achieve the intention. This kind of case holds for iterative actions. For example, consider encoding "I intend to chop down tree T" as

$$\exists e \text{ (Chopping e T)} \wedge \text{(Tree T)} \wedge \text{(INTEND}_1 \text{ x [WHILE} \sim\text{(Down T) DO e]).}$$

That is, there is a chopping event (type) e, such that the agent intends to do e until the tree is down. It is important to notice that at no time does the agent need to know precisely which sequence of chopping events (say one of length n) will result in the tree's falling. Instead, the agent is committed solely to executing the chopping event until the tree is down. To give up the commitment (i.e., the persistent goal) constituting the intention, the agent must eventually come to believe he has done the iterative action believing it was about to happen. Also, we know by Proposition 15 that when the agent believes he has done the iterative action, he will believe the condition is false (i.e., here, he will believe that the tree is down).

Lastly, consider intending a conditional action. ($\mathrm{INTEND_1}$ x [IF p THEN a ELSE b]) expands into

---

[21]Notice that because there are no action constants (for now), the event variables in an action expression must be quantified outside of $\mathrm{INTEND_1}$ to form a wff.

(P-GOAL x (DONE x [BEL x (HAPPENS x [IF p THEN a ELSE b])]?;
                    [IF p THEN a ELSE b])))

So, we know that eventually (unless, of course, he comes to believe the conditional is impossible), he will believe he has done the conditional in a state in which he believed he was just about to do it. As we discussed in Assumption 14 the agent cannot believe he is about to do a conditional (more generally, a disjunction) without either believing the condition is true or believing the condition is false. So, if one intends to do a conditional action, one expects (with the usual caveats) not to be forever ignorant about the condition. This seems just right.

In summary, we have defined intending to do an action in w way that captures many reasonable properties, some of which are inherited from the commitments involved in adopting a persistent goal. However, it is often thought that one can intend to achieve states-of-affairs in addition to just actions. Some cases of this are discussed above. But INTEND$_1$ cannot express an agent's intending to do *something* herself to achieve a state-of-affairs, since the event variables are quantified outside INTEND$_1$. To allow for this case, we define another kind of intention, INTEND$_2$.

INTEND$_2$

One might intend to become rich, become happy, or (perhaps controversially) to kill one's uncle,[22] without having any idea how to achieve that state-of-affairs, not even having an enormous disjunction of possible options. In these cases, we shall say the agent x is committed merely to doing something himself to bring about a world state in which (RICH x) or (HAPPY x) or (DEAD u) hold.

Definition 10 (INTEND$_2$ x p) $\overset{def}{=}$ (P-GOAL x
                    $\exists$e (DONE x [(BEL x $\exists$e' (HAPPENS x e';p?)) $\wedge$
                                $\sim$(GOAL x $\sim$(HAPPENS x e;p?))]?; e;p?))

We shall explain this definition in a number of steps. First, notice that to INTEND$_2$ to bring about p, an agent is committed to doing some sequence of events e himself, after which p holds. However, as earlier, to avoid allowing an agent to intend to make p true by committing himself to doing something accidentally or unknowingly, we require the agent to think he is about to do *something* (event sequence e') bringing about p.[23] From Assumption 4 we know that even though the agent believes only that he will do *some* sequence of events achieving p,

---

[22]We are not trying to be morbid here; just setting up a classic example.

[23]The definition does not use e instead of e' because that would quantify e into the agent's beliefs, requiring that he (eventually) have picked out a precise sequence of events that he thinks will bring about p. If we wanted to do that, we could use INTEND$_1$.

the agent will know which initial step he is about to take.

Now, it seems to us that the only way, short of truly wishful thinking, that an agent can believe he is about to do something to bring about p is if the agent in fact has a *plan* (good, bad, or ugly) for bringing it about. In general, it is quite difficult to define what a plan is, or define what it means for an agent to have a plan.[24] The best we can do, and that is not too far off, is to say that the agent has an action expression in mind. That is, we would want to say that eventually, the agent forms a plan to achieve p. However, one cannot express this in our logic since one cannot quantify over action expressions. So, we shall leave it as a problem, both for us and for the agent, to justifiably arrive at the belief that he (the agent) is about to do something bringing about p.

Finally, we require that prior to doing e to bring about p, the agent not have as a goal e's not bringing about p. This condition is required to handle the following example, due to Chisholm [11] and discussed in Searle's book [41]. An agent intends to kill his uncle. On the way to his uncle's house, this intention causes him to become so agitated that he loses control of his car, and runs over a pedestrian, who happens to be his uncle. Although the uncle is dead, we would surely say that the agent did not do what he intended.

Let us cast this problem in terms of $INTEND_2$, but without the condition stating that the agent should not want e not to bring about p. Call this $INTEND_{2weak}$. So, assume the following is true: $(INTEND_{2weak} \ x \ (DEAD \ u))$. The agent thus has a commitment to doing some sequence of events resulting in his uncle's death, and immediately prior to doing it, he has to believe there would be some sequence (e') that he was about to do that would result in the uncle's death. However, the example satisfies these conditions, but the event he in fact does that kills his uncle may not be the one forseen to do so. A jury requiring only the weakened $INTEND_2$ to convict for first-degree murder would find the agent to be guilty. Yet, we clearly have the intuition that the death was accidental.

Searle argues that a prior intention should cause an "intention-in-action" that presents the killing of the uncle as an "Intentional object", and this causation is self-referential. To explain Searle's analysis would take us too far afield. However, we can handle this case by adding the second condition to the agent's mental state that just prior to doing the action that achieves p, the agent not only believes he is about to do some sequence of events to bring about p, he also does not want what he in fact does, e, *not* to bring about p. In the case in question, the agent does not want driving onto the sidewalk to bring about his uncle's death. So, in swerving off the road, the agent may still have believed some sequence e' that he was about to do would kill his uncle (and, by Proposition 19, he wanted e' to kill his uncle), he did not want swerving off the road to kill his uncle. Hence, our analysis predicts that the agent did not do what he intended, even though the end state was achieved, and resulted from his adopting an intention. Let us now see how this analysis stacks up against the problems and related desiderata.

---

[24]See [36] for a discussion of these issues.

Meeting the Desiderata

In this section we show how various properties of the commonsense concept of intention are captured by our analysis based on P-GOAL. In what follows, we shall use $INTEND_1$ or $INTEND_2$ as it bests fits the example. Similar results hold for analogous problems posed with the other form of intention.

We reiterate Bratman's [7,8] analysis of the roles that intentions typically play in the mental life of agents:

1. *Intentions normally pose problems for the agent; the agent needs to determine a way to achieve them.* If the agent intends an action expression, then the agent knows in general terms what to do. However, the action expression may have disjunctions and conditionals in it. Hence, the agent would not know at the time of forming the intention just what will be done. However, eventually, the agent will know which actions should be taken. In the case of nonspecific intentions, such as $(INTEND_2 \ x \ p)$, we can derive that, under the normal circumstances where the agent does not learn that p is impossible for him to achieve, the agent eventually believes he is about to achieve p. Hence, our analysis shows the problem that is posed by adopting a non-specific intention, but does not encode the solution — that the agent will form a plan.

2. *Intentions provide a "screen of admissibility" for adopting other intentions.* If an agent has an intention to do b, and the agent (always) believes that doing a prevents the achievement of b, then the agent cannot have the intention to do a;b, or even the intention to do a before doing b. Thus, the following holds:

Theorem 2 *Screen of Admissibility:*
$\models \forall \ x \ (INTEND_1 \ x \ b) \wedge \Box(BEL \ x \ [(DONE \ x \ a) \supset \Box \sim(DONE \ x \ b)]) \supset \sim(INTEND_1 \ x \ a;b),$
where a and b are arbitrary action expressions, and their free variables have been bound outside.

The proof is simply that there are no possible worlds in which all could hold; in the agent's chosen worlds, if a has just been done, b is impossible to do. Hence, the agent cannot intend to do a before doing b. Similarly, if the agent first intends to do a, and always believes the above relationship between a and b, then the agent cannot adopt the intention (now or later) to do b.[25]

Notice that our agents cannot knowingly (and hence, by Proposition 20, deliberately) act against their own best interests. That is, they cannot intentionally act in order to make their persistent goals impossible. Moreover, if they have adopted a time-limited

---

[25]Notice that the theorem does not require quantification over primitive acts, but allows a and b to be arbitrary action expressions.

intention, they cannot intend to do some other act knowing it would make achieving that time-limited intention impossible.

3. *Agents "track" the success of their attempts to achieve their intentions.* In other words, agents keep their intentions after failure. Assume an agent has an intention to do **a**, and then does something, **e**, thinking it would bring about the doing of **a**, but he believes it does not. If the agent does not think doing **a** is impossible, does the agent still have the intention to do **a**? Yes.

Theorem 3 $\models \forall x \, \exists e \, (\text{DONE } x \, [(\text{INTEND}_1 \, x \, a) \wedge (\text{BEL } x \, (\text{HAPPENS } x \, a))]?;e) \wedge$
$\qquad (\text{BEL } x \sim(\text{DONE } x \, a)) \wedge \sim(\text{BEL } x \, \square \sim(\text{DONE } x \, a)) \supset (\text{INTEND}_1 \, x \, a)$

The proof of this follows immediately from the definition of INTEND_1, which is based on P-GOAL, which states that the intention cannot be given up until it is believed to have been achieved or is believed to be impossible. Here, the agent believes it has not been achieved and does not believe it to be impossible. Hence, the agent keeps the intention.

Other writers have proposed that if an agent intends to do **a**, then

4. *The agent believes doing* **a** *is possible.* We can state, via Proposition 19, that the agent does not believe doing **a** is impossible. This is not precisely the same as the desired property, but surely is close enough for current purposes.

5. *Sometimes, the agent believes he will in fact do* **a**. This is a consequence of Theorem 1, which states the conditions (call them C) under which $\diamondsuit(\text{DONE } x \, a)$ holds, given the intention to do **a**. So, if the agent believes she has the intention, and believes C holds, $\diamondsuit(\text{DONE } x \, a)$ follows from her beliefs as well.

6. *The agent does not believe he will never do* **a**. This principle is embodied directly in Proposition 19, which is validated by the simple model theoretical constraint that worlds that are consistent with one's choices are included in worlds that are consistent with one's beliefs (worlds one thinks one might be in).

7. *Agents need not intend all the expected side-effects of their intentions.*

   Recall that in an earlier problem, an agent intended to have her teeth filled. Not knowing about anaesthetics (one could assume this took place just as they were being first used in dentistry), she believed that it was always the case that if one's teeth are filled, one will feel pain. One could even say that surely the agent *chose* to undergo pain. Nonetheless, one would not like to say that she intended to undergo pain.

   This problem is easily handled in our scheme: Let x be the patient. Assume p is (FILLED-TEETH x), and q is (IN-PAIN x). Now, we know that the agent has surely chosen pain (by Proposition 21).

   Given all this, the following holds (see section 4.1.2, Case 3):

$(INTEND_2 \ x \ p) \land (BEL \ x \ \Box(p \supset q)) \not\supset (INTEND_2 \ x \ q).$

Thus, agents need not intend the expected side-effects of their intentions.

At this point, the formalism captures each of Bratman's principles. Let us now see how it avoids the "Little Nell" problem.

Solving the "Little Nell" Problem: When not to give up goals

Recall that in the "Little Nell" problem, Dudley never saves Nell because he believes he will be successful. This problem will occur (at least) in logics of intention that have the following initially plausible principles:

1. Give up the intention that p when you believe p holds.

2. Under at least some circumstances, an agent's intending that p entails the agent's believing that p will eventually be true.

These principles sound reasonable. One would think that a robot who forms the intention to bring David a beer should drop that intention as soon as he brings David a beer. Not dropping it constrains the adoption of other intentions, and may lead to David's receiving a year's supply of beer. The second principle says that at least in some (perhaps the normal) circumstances, one believes ones intentions will be fulfilled. Both of these principles can be found in our analysis.

One might say these two principles already entail a problem, because if p will be true, the agent might think it need not act (since p is already "in the cards"). However, this is not what Principle 1 says. Rather, the agent will drop his intentions when they are currently satisfied, not when they will be satisfied.

Now, the problem comes when one adopts a temporal or dynamic logic (modal or not, branching or not) that expresses "p will be true" as (FUTURE p) or $\Diamond p$. Apply Principle 2 to a proposition p of the form $\Diamond q$. For example, let p represent "Nell is out of danger" by $\Diamond$(SAVED NELL). Hence, if the agent has the intention to bring about $\Diamond$(SAVED NELL), under the right circumstances ("all other things being equal"), the agent believes $\Diamond\Diamond$(SAVED NELL). But, in most temporal logics, $\Diamond\Diamond$(SAVED NELL) entails $\Diamond$(SAVED NELL). So, it is likely that the agent believes that $\Diamond$(SAVED NELL) holds as well. Now, apply Principle 1. Here, the agent had the intention to achieve $\Diamond$(SAVED NELL) and the agent believes it is already true! So, the agent drops the intention, and Nell gets mashed.

Our theory of intention based on P-GOAL avoids this problem because an agent's having a P-GOAL requires that the goal be true later and that the agent not believe it is currently true. The cases of interest are those in which the agent purportedly adopts the intention and believes he will succeed. Thus, (BEL x $\diamond\diamond$q), and so (BEL x $\diamond$q). However, agents cannot even *form* these intentions since the second conjunct of the defining P-GOAL requires that (BEL x $\sim\diamond$q), so (BEL x $\Box\sim$q). However, from Proposition 19, we see that if (BEL x $\Box\sim$q) then $\sim$(GOAL x $\diamond$q), contradicting the first conjunct of the definition of P-GOAL.

One might argue that this analysis prevents agents from dropping their intentions when they think another agent will achieve the end goal. For example, one might want it to be possible for Dudley to drop the intention to save Nell (himself) because he thinks someone else, Dirk, is going to save her. There are two cases to consider. The first case involves goals that can only be achieved once. The second case concerns goals that can be reachieved. We treat the second case in the next section. Regarding the first, one can easily show the following:

Theorem 4 *Dropping Futile Intentions:*
$\models \forall$ x, y$\neq$x $\land$ (BEL x $\diamond\exists$ e, (DONE y $\sim$p?;e;p?)) $\supset$
$\sim$(INTEND$_2$ x p) $\lor$ $\sim$(BEL x [$\exists$e (DONE y $\sim$p?;e;p?) $\supset$ $\Box$ $\sim$ $\exists$e (DONE x $\sim$p?;e;p?)])

That is, if an agent believes someone else truly is going to achieve p, then either the agent does not intend to achieve p herself, or she does not believe p can be achieved only once. Contrapositively, if an agent intends to achieve p, and always believes p can only be achieved once, the agent cannot simultaneously believe someone else is definitely going to achieve p. Intuitively, the reason is simple. If the agent believes someone else is definitely going to achieve p, then, because the agent believes that after doing so no one else could do so, the agent cannot have the persistent goal of achieving p herself; she cannot consistently believe she will achieve p first, nor can she achieve p later. A more rigorous proof is left to the determined reader.

At this point, we have met the desiderata. Thus, the analysis so far has merit; but we are not finished. The definition of P-GOAL can be extended to make explicit what is only implicit in the commonsense concept of intention — the background of other justifying beliefs and intentions. Doing so will make our agents more reasonable.

The End of Fanaticism

As the formalism stands now, once an agent has adopted a persistent goal, he will not be deterred. For example, if agent *A* receives a request from agent *B*, and decides to cooperate by adopting a persistent goal to do the requested act, *B* cannot "turn *A* off". This is clearly a defect that needs to be remedied. The remedy depends on the following definition.

Definition 11 *Persistent, Relativized Goal:*

$$(\text{P-R-GOAL x p q}) \overset{\text{def}}{=} (\text{GOAL x (LATER p)}) \wedge (\text{BEL x} \sim\!\text{p}) \wedge$$
$$(\text{BEFORE } [(\text{BEL x p}) \vee (\text{BEL x } \square \sim\!\text{p}) \vee (\text{BEL x} \sim\!\text{q})]$$
$$\sim\!(\text{GOAL x (LATER p)}))$$

That is, a necessary condition to giving up a P-R-GOAL is that the agent x believes it is satisfied, or believes it is impossible to achieve, or believes $\sim$q. Such propositions q form a background that justifies the agent's intentions. In many cases, such propositions constitute the agent's *reasons* for adopting the intention. For example, x could adopt the persistent goal to buy an umbrella relative to his belief that it will rain. X could consider dropping his persistent goal should he come to believe that the forecast has changed.

Our analysis supports the observation that intentions can (loosely speaking) be viewed as the contents of plans (e.g., [8,15,36]). Although we have not given a formal analysis of plans here (see [36] for such an analysis), the commitments one undertakes with respect to an action in a plan depend on the other planned actions, as well as the pre- and post-conditions brought about by those actions. If x adopts a persistent goal p relative to (GOAL x q), then necessary conditions for x's dropping his goal include his believing that he no longer has q as a goal. Thus, (P-R-GOAL x p (GOAL x q)) characterizes an agent's having a persistent *subgoal* p relative to the *supergoal* q. An agent's dropping a supergoal is now a necessary (but not sufficient) prerequisite for her dropping a subgoal. [26] Thus, with the change to relativized persistent goals, we open up the possibility of having a complex web of interdependencies among the agent's goals, intentions, and beliefs. We always had the possibility of conditional P-GOALs. Now, we have added background conditions that could lead to a revision of one's persistent goals. The definitions of intention given earlier can now be recast in terms of P-R-GOAL.

Definition 12 $(\text{INTEND}_1 \text{ x a q}) \overset{def}{=} (\text{P-R-GOAL x}$
$$[(\text{DONE x}$$
$$(\text{BEL x (HAPPENS x a;p?)})?;\!a;\!p?))]$$
$$\text{q})$$

Definition 13 $(\text{INTEND}_2 \text{ x p q}) \overset{def}{=} (\text{P-R-GOAL x}$
$$\exists e \ (\text{DONE x } [(\text{BEL x } \exists e' \ (\text{HAPPENS x e';p?})) \wedge$$
$$\sim\!(\text{GOAL x} \sim\!(\text{HAPPENS x e;p?})) \ ]?; e;p?))$$
$$\text{q})$$

With these changes, the dependencies of an agent's intentions on his beliefs, other goals, intentions, and so on, become explicit. For example, we can express an agent's intending to

---

[26]Also, notice that (P-GOAL x p) is now subsumed by (P-R-GOAL x p p).

take an umbrella relative to believing it will rain on March 5, 1986 as:

$$\exists e, u \; (\text{TAKE } u \; e) \wedge [\text{INTEND}_1 \; x \; e{:}3/5/86? \; \Diamond(\text{RAINING} \wedge 3/5/86)]$$

One can now describe agents whose primary concern is with the end result of their intentions, not so much with achieving those results themselves. An agent may first adopt a persistent goal to achieve p, and then (perhaps because he does not know any other agent who will, or can, do so), subsequently decides to achieve p himself, relative to that persistent goal. So, the following is true of the agent: $(\text{P-GOAL } x \; p) \wedge (\text{INTEND}_2 \; x \; p \; (\text{P-GOAL } x \; p))$. If someone else achieves p (and the agent comes to believe is true), the agent must drop $(\text{P-GOAL } x \; p)$, and is therefore free to drop the commitment to achieving p himself. Notice, however, that for goals that can be reachieved, the agent is *not forced* to drop the intention, as the agent may truly be committed to achieve p himself.

Matters get more interesting still when we allow the relativization conditions q to include propositions about other agents. For example, if q is $(\text{GOAL } y \; s)$, then y's goal is an *interpersonal supergoal* for x. The kind of intention that is engendered by a request seems to be a P-R-GOAL. Namely, the speaker tries to bring it about that $(\text{P-R-GOAL hearer } (\text{DONE hearer } a) \; (\text{GOAL speaker } (\text{DONE hearer } a)))$. The hearer can get "off the hook" if he learns the speaker does not want him to do the act after all.

Notice also that given this partial analysis of requesting, a hearer who merely says "OK" and thereby accedes to a request has (made it mutually believed) she has adopted a commitment relative to the speaker's desires. In other words, she is committed *to* the speaker to do the requested action. This helps to explain how social commitments can arise out of communication. However, this is not the place to analyze speech acts (but see [12]).

Finally, interlocking commitments are obtained when two agents are in the following states: $(\text{P-R-GOAL } x \; p \; (\text{GOAL } y \; p))$, and $(\text{P-R-GOAL } y \; p \; (\text{GOAL } x \; p))$. Each agent will keep his intention at least as long as the other keeps it. For example, each might have the intention to lift a table. But each would not bother to try unless the other also had the same intention. This goes partway toward realizing a notion of "joint agency" espoused by Searle [42]. [27]

In summary, persistent relativized goals provide a useful analysis of intention, and extend the commonsense concept by making explicit the conditions under which an agent will revise his intentions.

Conclusion

This paper establishes basic principles governing the rational balance among an agent's beliefs, actions, and intentions. Such principles provide specifications for artificial agents, and

---

[27]Ultimately, one can envision circular interlinkages in which one adopts a persistent goal provided another agent has adopted it relative to your having adopted it relative to his having adopted it, etc. For an analysis of circular propositions that might make such concepts expressible, see [5].

approximate a theory of human action (as philosophers use the term). By making explicit the conditions under which an agent can drop his goals, i.e., by specifying how the agent is *committed* to his goals, the formalism captures a number of important properties of intention. Specifically, the formalism provides analyses for Bratman's three characteristic functional roles played by intentions [7,8], and shows how agents can avoid intending all the forseen side-effects of what they actually intend. Finally, the analysis shows how intentions can be adopted relative to a background of relevant beliefs and other intentions or goals. By relativizing one agent's intentions in terms of beliefs about another agent's intentions (or beliefs), we derive a preliminary account of interpersonal commitments.

The utility of the theory for describing people or artificial agents will depend on the fidelity of the assumptions. It does not seem unreasonable to require that a robot not procrastinate forever. Moreover, we surely would want a robot to be persistent in pursuing its goals, but not fanatically so. Furthermore, we would want a robot to drop goals given to it by other agents when it determines the goals need not be achieved. So, as a coarse description of an artificial agent, the theory seems workable.

The theory is not only useful for describing single agents in dynamic multiagent worlds, it is also useful for describing their interactions, especially via the use of communicative acts. In a companion paper [12], we present a theory of speech acts that builds on the foundations laid here.

Much work remains. The action theory only allowed for possible worlds consisting of single courses of events. Further developments should include basing the analysis on partial worlds/situations [6], and on temporal logics that allow for simultaneous actions [2,30,18]. Undoubtedly, the theory would be strengthened by the use of default and non-monotonic reasoning.

Lastly, we can now allay the reader's fears about the mental state of the rationally unbalanced robot, Willie. If manufactured according to our principles, it is guaranteed that the problems described will not arise again; Willie will act on its intentions, not in spite of them, and will give them up when you say so. Of course, Willie is not yet very smart (as we did not say *how* agents should form plans), but he is determined.

Acknowledgments

Michael Bratman, Joe Halpern, David Israel, Ray Perrault, and Martha Pollack provided many valuable suggestions. Discussions with Doug Appelt, Michael Georgeff, Kurt Konolige, Amy Lansky, Fernando Pereira, Martha Pollack, Stan Rosenschein, and Moshe Vardi have also been quite helpful. Thanks to you all.

References

[1] J. F. Allen. *A Plan-Based Approach to Speech Act Recognition.* Technical Report 131, Department of Computer Science, University of Toronto, Toronto, Canada, January 1979.

[2] J. F. Allen. Towards a general theory of action and time. *Artificial Intelligence*, 23(2):123–154, July 1984.

[3] J. F. Allen and Perrault C. R. Analyzing intention in dialogues. *Artificial Intelligence*, 15(3):143–178, 1980.

[4] D. Appelt. *Planning Natural Language Utterances to Satisfy Multiple Goals.* PhD thesis, Stanford University, Stanford, California, December 1981.

[5] J. Barwise and J. Etchemendy. Truth, the liar, and circular propositions. In preparation.

[6] J. Barwise and J. Perry. *Situations and Attitudes.* MIT Press, Cambridge, Massachusetts, 1983.

[7] M. Bratman. *Casteñda's Theory of Thought and Action*, pages 149–169. Hackett, Indianapolis, Indiana, 1983.

[8] M. Bratman. Intentions, plans, and practical reason. 1986. In preparation.

[9] M. Bratman. Two faces of intention. *The Philosophical Review*, XCIII(3):375–405, 1984.

[10] H. N. Castenada. *Thinking and Doing.* Reidel, Dordrecht, Holland, 1975.

[11] R. M. Chisolm. *Freedom and Action.* Random House, New York, 1966.

[12] P. R. Cohen and H. J. Levesque. Communication as rational interaction. In preparation.

[13] P. R. Cohen and H. J. Levesque. Speech acts and rationality. In *Proceedings of the Twenty-third Annual Meeting*, Association for Computational Linguistics, Chicago, Illinois, July 1985.

[14] P. R. Cohen and H. J. Levesque. Speech acts and the recognition of shared plans. In *Proceedings of the Third Biennial Conference*, pages 263–271, Canadian Society for Computational Studies of Intelligence, Canadian Society for Computational Studies of Intelligence, Victoria, B. C., May 1980.

[15] P. R. Cohen and C. R. Perrault. Elements of a plan-based theory of speech acts. *Cognitive Science*, 3(3):177–212, 1979. Reprinted in *Readings in Artificial Intelligence*, Morgan Kaufman Publishing Co., Los Altos, California, B. Webber and N. Nilsson (eds.), pp. 478-495.

[16] R. Fagin and J. Y. Halpern. Belief, awareness, and limited reasoning: preliminary report. In *Proceedings of the Ninth International Joint Conference on Artificial Intelligence*, pages 491–501, Morgan Kaufman Publishers, Inc., Los Altos, California, August 1985.

[17] R. Fikes and N. J. Nilsson. Strips: a new approach to the application of theorem proving to problem solving. *Artificial Intelligence*, 2:189–208, 1971.

[18] M. P. Georgeff. Actions, processes, and causality. In *Proceedings of the Timberline Workshop on Planning and Reasoning about Action*, Morgan Kaufman Publishers, Inc., Los Alto, California, 1987.

[19] M. P. Georgeff. Communication and interaction in multi-agent planning. In *Proceedings of the National Conference on Artificial Intelligence*, pages 125–129, Morgan Kaufman Publishers, Inc., Los Altos, California, 1983.

[20] M. P. Georgeff and A. L. Lansky. A bdi semantics for the procedural reasoning system. 1986. Technical Note in preparation, Artificial Ingelligence Center, SRI International.

[21] A. Haas. Possible events, actual events, and robots. *Computational Intelligence*, 1(2?):59–70, 1985.

[22] J. Y. Halpern and Y. O. Moses. A guide to the modal logics of knowledge and belief. In *Proceedings of the Ninth International Joint Conference on Artificial Intelligence*, IJCAI, Los Angeles, California, August 1985.

[23] D. Harel. *First-Order Dynamic Logic*. Springer-Verlag, New York City, New York, 1979. Lecture Notes in Computer Science, *68*, edited by G. Goos and J. Hartmanis.

[24] G. Harman. *Change in View*. Bradford Books, MIT Press, Cambridge, Massachusetts, 1986.

[25] K. Konolige. *Experimental Robot Psychology*. Technical Note 363, Artificial Intelligence Center, SRI International, Menlo Park, California, November 1985.

[26] K. Konolige. *A first-order formalization of knowledge and action for a multiagent planning system*. Technical Note 232, Artificial Intelligence Center, SRI International, Menlo Park, California, December 1980. (Appears in *Machine Intelligence*, Volume 10).

[27] K. Konolige and N. J. Nilsson. Multiple-agent planning systems. In *Proceedings of the First Annual National Conference on Artificial Intelligence*, August 1980.

[28] L. Lamport. "sometimes" is sometimes better than "not never". In *Proceedings of the 7th Annual ACM Symposium on Principles of Programming Languages*, pages 174–185, Association for Computing Machinery, 1980.

[29] A. L. Lansky. *Behavioral Specification and Planning for Multiagent Domains*. Technical Note 360, Artificial Intelligence Center, SRI International, 1985.

[30] A. L. Lansky. A representation of parallel activity based on events, structure, and causality. In *Proceedings of the Timberline Workshop on Planning and Reasoning about Action*, Morgan Kaufman Publishers, Inc., Los Alto, California, 1987.

[31] H. J. Levesque. A logic of implicit and explicit belief. In *Proceedings of the National Conference of the American Association for Artificial Intelligence*, Austin, Texas, 1984.

[32] J. McCarthy and P. J. Hayes. Some philosophical problems from the standpoint of artificial intelligence. In *Machine intelligence 4*, American Elsevier, New York, 1969.

[33] D. McDermott. A temporal logic for reasoning about processes and plans. *Cognitive Science*, 6(2):101–155, April-June 1982.

[34] R. C. Moore. *Reasoning about Knowledge and Action*. Technical Note 191, Artificial Intelligence Center, SRI International, Palo Alto, October 1980.

[35] C. R. Perrault. An application of default logic to speech act theory. In preparation.

[36] M. E. Pollack. *Inferring Domain Plans in Question Answering*. PhD thesis, Dept. of Computer Science, University of Pennsylvania, 1986.

[37] V. R. Pratt. *Six Lectures on Dynamic Logic*. Technical Report MIT/LCS/TM-117, Laboratory for Computer Science, MIT, Cambridge, Massachusetts, 1978.

[38] J. S. Rosenschein. *Rational Interaction: Cooperation among Intelligent Agents*. PhD thesis, Dept. of Computer Science, Stanford University, Stanford, California, 1986.

[39] J. S. Rosenschein and M. R. Genesereth. *Communication and Cooperation*. Technical Report 84-5, Heuristic Programming Project, Dept. of Computer Science, Stanford University, Stanford, California, 1984.

[40] S. J. Rosenschein. Plan synthesis: a logical perspective. In *Proceedings of the Seventh International Joint Conference on Artificial Intelligence*, pages 331–337, Vancouver, Canada, August 1981.

[41] J. R. Searle. *Intentionality: An Essay in the Philosophy of Mind*. Cambridge University Press, New York City, New York, 1983.

[42] J. R. Searle. The structure of social facts. Lecture delivered to the Center for the Study of Language and Information, Stanford University, Stanford, California, 1986.

THE CONTEXT-SENSITIVITY OF BELIEF AND DESIRE

Richmond H. Thomason
Linguistics Department
University of Pittsburgh
Pittsburgh, PA 15260

ABSTRACT

Beliefs and desires cannot be attributed to reasoning agents without taking contextual factors into account. Among the factors that serve to determine belief, for instance, are risk, belief-hunger, interest, topic, and supposition management. Among the factors that determine motives are opportunity, the alternatives that are envisaged in deliberation, and entrenchment through commitment.

I present a number of examples, chosen to be as realistic as possible, to illustrate this point. The purpose is in part to undermine accounts of practical reasoning based on oversimplified concepts of belief and desire, and so to develop alternative reasons for the dissatisfaction with Bayesian approaches that has been voiced by many researchers in Artificial Intelligence.

In an attempt to say something positive about the sort of theory that is needed, I discuss a simple model that treats an agent's beliefs as distributed, and suggest that work in Artificial Intelligence may be helpful in providing the materials for a more adequate theory, one that pays some attention to resource limitations in reasoning.

1. INTRODUCTION[1]

In accounting for reasoned decision-making, beliefs and desires are indispensable; you can't begin to construct a model of practical reasoning without taking them into account. And these factors are also critical; the way in which they are represented will shape the resulting theory in fundamental ways.

The main point that I want to communicate in this paper is that our theories of practical reasoning have been oversimplified at the critical stage at which reflection begins to focus on beliefs and desires. Neglecting the process of reasoning and concentrating on the product, these theories represent an agent as containing somehow a system of beliefs and a system of desires that can only be changed in "rational" ways like learning, or in "irrational" ways like motive conversion.

This oversimplification makes the available theories of practical reasoning hard or impossible to apply in real-life situations, even when we allow for the fact that these theories are to be regarded as idealizations. At best, the Bayesian model gives us general criteria for the correctness of decision making under uncertainty only in certain cases: cases in which success can be measured by performance in meeting goals under repeated trials, in which the variables relevant to the decision can be limited to a manageable number, and in which no cost is placed on the time available for reasoning. Most reasoned decisions that we actually find ourselves making in practice are not like this.

The chief purpose of this paper is to deploy a number of examples designed to loosen the grip of oversimplified theories of belief and desire. I will not try here to examine why these theories are inadequate.[2] Nor will I have much to say about how to construct an adequate theory of practical reasoning. The present situation, in fact, seems to call for the construction of local, process-oriented models of reasoning phenomena—models of the sort that are currently being developed by researchers in Artificial Intelligence in order to

---

[1]This paper was first presented at a conference on the philosophy of Donald Davidson, held in March of 1984. A final draft of that version was prepared in May of 1984 and circulated privately. The present version has been much revised, though the paper as it appears here still reflects the philosophical origins of the problem and is largely a philosophical exercise. Since that time, I have come to appreciate the root philosophical problem as ramifying into a number of more specific problems in Artificial Intelligence, and have tried to begin working on some of these problems. That work is not reflected in this version. See, however, Touretzky, Horty and Thomason (1987) and Horty, Thomason, and Touretzky (1987).

[2]I suspect that the ultimate source of the problem is neglect of the fact that practical reasoning utilizes limited reasoning resources, in situations that often involve time pressure. But I know of no proof that an adequate reasoning system subject to these constraints will have the characteristics that I am pointing to in this paper.

explain and design programs that engage in various decision-making tasks. It may be a very long time until we are able to feel comfortable with a more ambitious, global theory that provides general foundations for this work.

2. BELIEF: SOME CASE STUDIES

I am proposing that belief depends on many things other than what we have somehow learned and stored as data. Though I don't have any systematic way of classifying the things on which belief depends, it seems to me that these divide into two chief sorts of factors, which bear on belief in ways that are quite different. A belief should be something that we are in general willing to act on; it should represent information that we are able to retrieve; and we must suppose it to be true.

My primary division separates factors influencing our willingness to act on a proposition from other factors: some of these having to do with representation and storage, others with the maintenance and suspension of suppositions. Among influences of the former sort, I include *risk*, *belief hunger*, and *interest*.

RISK

I believe that the radio is playing Mozart. But now I consider acting on this belief, and it occurs to me that the stakes are high. I would like to impress my audience with my knowledge of music, and am tempted to make a remark like "They're playing that Mozart well." But my audience is knowledgeable about music and critical, and I fear their disapproval. Reflecting on this, I have *second thoughts* about the proposition—after all, I'm not *sure* that it's Mozart. Now, experiencing a certain amount of doubt about the composer, I find that my conviction is shaken and decide to remain silent; although I now think it's likely that Mozart is the composer, I no longer believe it. The risk of appearing ignorant has destroyed a belief that would not have been affected if I had been talking to musical novices.[3]

Here, if I have learned anything at all, I have certainly learned nothing that would lower the probability that the composer is Mozart. But nevertheless I have lost a belief; what passed muster earlier, and would have persisted as a belief if I have been asked about

---

[3]Some readers may notice at this point that I haven't ruled it out that in this example I have cynically decided it is too risky to *say* that the composer is Mozart, while retaining the belief that he is the composer. That is right; but this case is different from the more likely sincere one, and more literary detail would be needed to exclude the cynical interpretation. It is interesting that the examples that are wanted in order to make the points required by the thesis of this paper seem to require a level of detail that is usually not needed in making philosophical points. It is actually necessary to take the time to engage in some creative writing. I have not tried to do that in the examples in this paper.

the music in private by, say, one of my children, is dropped when my credulity is raised because of social risk.

This is a familiar experience, one that we should all be able to recognize. In the course of practical reasoning, we in fact routinely monitor contemplated actions to identify risks, and then reassess beliefs in light of the results. Part of the context, then, that sustains a belief is the current assessment of the risk that attaches to acting on that belief; and by reassessing risk, we are able to undermine beliefs by increasing our threshold of credulity.

BELIEF HUNGER

Beliefs can also be *created* by similar processes; there are cases in which one acquires a belief not by learning anything, but simply by adjusting one's credulity.

As David Lewis pointed out in another connection,[4] skepticism seems to have the dialectical edge: the rules of credulity kinematics make it easier to raise the skeptical threshold than to lower it. But this doesn't prevent us from indulging in intentional credulity; it only means that we often have to achieve a state of relaxed inattention in order to do so. Again, this makes it difficult to find short examples of the phenomenon that are entirely convincing.

But consider the following case. Suppose that you and I are on a committee that is supposed to draw up a budget. I believe in financial responsibility, and am really worried about whether here is a cheaper way to get the photocopying machine. Our committee meeting drags on and on. "Come on," you finally say. "We've looked into this pretty carefully, and this is certainly the least expensive copier we could find. Now we have to come to a decision." I see the force of your point, and I agree with you.[5]

By filling in details such as these, the example can be deployed so that it is clear that I really have come to have a belief. But in persuading me, you said nothing to make me think that the proposition I originally doubted was more plausible. You persuaded me by increasing my belief-hunger, pointing out the committee's need to reach a decision in a reasonable time.

INTEREST

Of course, interest plays a role in determining belief. We needn't concoct an elaborate example to show this; here is a short one.

---

[4] Lewis (1979).

[5] To make this case convincing, this example needs to be fleshed out enough to ensure that I'm not just pretending to agree with you, but really have acquired the conviction that this is the cheapest machine we can find. This can be done by adding appropriate detail.

Like many purchasers of microcomputers, I go to the computer store ignorant and bewildered, but eager to conceal this by appearing decisive. I buy an IBM PC, without believing that this is the best personal computer for me; but it seems safe, given what I've heard of IBM. Later, as I grow attached to my PC, I believe it's the best; in fact, I'm willing to argue this vociferously in discussions with other microcomputer users. But in the meantime, I've learned nothing about rival computers, nothing that is really relevant to the doubts that I had when I went into the store—doubts that concerned the relative merits of various brands. And if I had bought an Apple, I'd have believed that this was the best computer for me, and would have been equally prepared to defend its merits.

The idea that interest can affect beliefs is not exactly new—I learned from van Fraassen (1983) that it goes back to Carneides, the proto-skeptic who used it in his attack on Stoic epistemology. But I want to suggest a contextual mechanism for the process; interests can favor contexts that promote beliefs. I will not be able shed much light on the workings of the mechanism, so I can't really claim to have gotten much further than Carneides; but at least it may be a useful beginning to place interest among the factors that make suppositions count as beliefs.[6]

The most compelling reason for this contextual approach is that reasoning agents are capable of harboring conflicting interests, *both* of which can compel beliefs—opposite beliefs. In such cases, it is misleading to say that the agent has both of the beliefs, and equally misleading to say that he has neither. Rather, one belief is sustained relative to one interest, and the opposite belief is sustained relative to the other.

The main work, then, of showing that dependence on interest can be a form of the context-sensitivity of belief, will consist in showing that interest can be a contextual factor. I will say something about this when I come to desire.

TOPIC

This factor has more to do with belief as information that must be represented and processed, than with its action-guiding role.

When I think about dentist appointments, I believe that I have one on Friday. When I think about things I have to do on Friday, the belief may be absent; in fact, I may believe that I have no appointments that day, and schedule a conflict.[7]

---

[6] This way of looking at things also makes it clear that interest can affect beliefs in other ways as well. For instance, our assessments of risk will depend on our interests, and we have already seen that beliefs depend on risk assessments. Once the general point has been made, it is easy to construct an example; I leave this to the reader.

[7] As it stands the example is not watertight, but I think that it can be defended against objections. For instance, someone may say that this is a case of *forgetting*. I scheduled a meeting at 2:00 on Friday because

Or consider the writer of letters of recommendation, who sincerely feels, as he writes about each student, that this one is the best ever—and says so in each letter. Although this phenomenon may in part be due to interest (conditioned in part by generosity), it is also perhaps a matter of what Bentham called "propinquity"; and this could be subsumed under topic. When the topic is *this* student, the letter-writer has the belief that she is the best one; when it is *that* one, the letter-writer has the belief that he is the best.

To a certain extent, topic-induced effects on belief are unstable; like the case of the dentist appointment, many of them disappear as soon as you become aware of them. We are often capable of subsuming several topics under a wider one, and in doing so we tend to smooth out variations in belief due to topic. Even so, it is important to recognize that widening the topic is not always useful. Too much clutter can make reasoning impracticable, and as John McCarthy has persistently pointed out, we need to approach a problem from a tightly circumscribed standpoint in order to reason effectively.[8] Distortions in belief due to topic are one price we pay for such circumscription.

SUPPOSITION KINEMATICS

Seeing may be believing, but supposing surely is not. The extreme case is that of supposing for the sake of argument. In undertaking a *reductio ad absurdum* argument, we need not believe that our supposition is true. In fact, we usually will *disbelieve* the supposition, since the purpose of the argument will be to betray the supposition by refuting it. But if supposing were an entirely different sort of thing from believing, there would be no reason to *resist* suppositions; and yet in general we are suspicious of suppositions. Entertaining a supposition is often a serious matter; invite a supposition, and very soon it will make itself at home and begin telling you what to do. Try going to a dean and asking

---

I forgot that I had a dentist appointment then. Later, perhaps, I remembered that I had the appointment. This, I think, is either false or provides additional support for the view that I am urging. On the most plausible understanding of 'forget', to forget is simply to come to lack a belief. This is how we should be interpreted when we speak of forgetting something because our attention was distracted, or of forgetting our principles in the face of overpowering temptation. If this is the interpretation we have in mind, forgetting is just as topic-sensitive as believing. In the case of the dentist appointment, I have come to lack the belief because I was searching the things I had to do on Friday, and didn't find the dentist appointment. If I had prompted myself then by asking myself whether I had a dentist appointment that day, or by asking when my next dentist appointment was, I would have had the belief. On the other hand, if we think of forgetting as total erasure of memory—as when I try to remember the first sentence of my high school geometry book—then I have not forgotten the appointment. When the fact that I have an appointment occurs to me, I am painfully aware that the information was *not* totally erased. It was accessible; it just slipped my mind, and when I was reminded of it I did not relearn something that had been totally lost. Rather, it is as if my attention was redirected to something I had misplaced.

[8]See McCarthy (1980).

him to suppose—even for the sake of argument—that your salary should be doubled.

Of course, suppositions are indispensable in contingency planning. If I need to get to the airport and don't know whether my car will start, I need to construct two alternative suppositions for parallel planning. I only have to make sure that when such a contingency plan is carried out, I can find out which supposition is correct in time to implement either plan. (I shouldn't wait to find out whether my car will start till it is too late to call a cab.) Unless we monitor them, however, and stay alert to explicitly posited alternatives, suppositions have a way of becoming entrenched and figuring in serious categorical deliberation: planning that will translate more or less automatically to action.[9]

But there are important differences between suppositions and beliefs, which show up in the mechanisms whereby we can create them: and this, of course, has to do with the fact that beliefs are action-oriented. If we want a supposition we can simply *make* it, by implementing a straightforward intention. If I want to suppose that my landlord is a crook, I can set about doing this quite openly, and perform the act directly, by saying to myself "Let me suppose that my landlord is a crook." I can't proceed this way with belief. Telling myself (even quite forcefully) "Let me believe that my landlord is a crook" is not the way to go about having the belief; in this respect, it's a bit like telling myself not to think about my landlord. So, if my goal is to have the belief, I have to go about achieving this goal in some indirect way. Perhaps I give myself a *reason* for believing that my landlord is a crook. (But the reason can't always be another belief, or we will never be able to create the desired belief in cases in which it doesn't follow from things we already believe.) Or I resort to some other indirect tactic; for instance, I first suppose the target proposition, and then forget to monitor it.[10]

The picture that emerges from this is a little reminiscent of natural deduction. The various systems of natural deduction provide a mechanism for making suppositions, for marking some suppositions as subordinate to others, and for keeping tabs on consequences, so that a definite cluster of suppositions is associated with each consequence. This is exactly what seems to happen in supposition kinematics. But, since suppositions can be practical, we also need some system of monitoring suppositions, of keeping track of how seriously we are willing to take them. Also some way of creating suppositions is needed, and of activating suppositions, so that—to return to the analogy of a natural deduction

---

[9]This discussion assumes a contrast between deliberative planning, and decision making that is done while implementing a plan (which may be partial in many ways) "on the fly," that is, in the course of acting. This is a very natural distinction to make in the theory of planning, and in fact one of the most crucial applications of good judgment in planning is deciding what to plan in deliberative mode and what can be left to work out on the fly. Other papers in this volume touch on this matter.

[10]Of course, I can't directly make myself forget something, either. But when it comes to forgetting, nature can come to my assistance by providing distractions.

proof—I can tell where I am located in the proof. I have suggested that supposition activation is in part contextually determined, that it may not always yield a unique cluster of suppositions, and that beliefs are simply suppositions that are practical with respect to a given context.

3. BELIEF: A TOY MODEL

As I said, I don't think that we are in a position at the moment to attempt a general theory that does justice to the phenomena that I have been discussing. But part of the picture, at least, has to be a picture of deliberating agents as *distributed systems*, capable of harboring different systems of beliefs.

In such a situation there of course are many conceptual problems, but there also are many opportunities for model-building; see, for instance, the overview given in Halpern (1986) and the references given there. The model that I will build is actually a generalization of that of van Fraassen (1973); this does not represent the interplay of beliefs and interests, and it assumes that there is no need for common knowledge among the various components of the system.

According to this model, there will be a space of *supposition indices* associated with each agent, and a function taking each index into a set of suppositions. As an idealization, we can imagine that these sets are closed under logical consequence. This sort of condition is familiar.

So far, we have not distinguished practical suppositions from the rest. So we will have to label a set of indices that the agent takes seriously as alternatives for practical deliberation; these represent competing systems of suppositions which could guide the agent as reasons for action.

But a moment's reflection shows that this is not sufficiently informative; we really need something like a *measure* on the indices, since in general we need to make distinctions that are finer than the simple binary one between practicality and impracticality. For instance, suppose that i_1 differs from i_2 in supporting an additional supposition to the effect that a certain coin will come up heads (and the logical consequences that follow from this). Then i_1 may have half the practical force that i_2 does for me.

A probability measure μ on indices will induce a probability-like measure on individual suppositions.[11] If each supposition set were negation-complete, the measure that is induced

---

[11]The definition would be:

$$P(\phi) = \sum_{\{i:\ \phi \in S(i)\}} \mu(i).$$

would be a probability measure of the familiar sort; in general, though, it will be a relaxed measure, which, for instance, would no longer satisfy the law that $P(\phi) + P(\sim\phi) = 1$.[12]

Whether or not P is a probability measure, it can serve to regulate belief-based choice by measuring our susceptibility to beliefs; we can think of $P(\phi)$ as an indicator of our willingness to act on the supposition that ϕ. Thus, P could be regarded as an indicator of prejudice in favor of a supposition—of the benefit of the doubt that an agent is willing to give the supposition. Imagine, for example, that I face a choice between two plans, one of them depending on the supposition that ϕ and the other on the supposition that $\sim\phi$. Then if I am inhibited from acting in the absence of one supposition or the other, and if time is too short for me to gather any more relevant information, I will be more likely to suppose the alternative that receives the larger measure.

In speaking of "belief-based choice," I am assuming from the outset that certain types of choices call for reasoned decisions—decisions that rest on beliefs which function as reasons. This is the source of the phenomenon that I called "belief hunger." In the case of the budget committee, for instance, I would not have been satisfied with a high probability that this copier is the cheapest—I need the belief that it is the cheapest. Moreover, the belief needs to be *reasoned.* Suppose that I am about to fight a battle. I have only two tactical plans, which are very different. Which plan I should use depends on whether my allies will arrive on the field before dusk. A calculation that the probability that they will arrive is .5 will not enable me to act. Even if I decide in desperation to flip a coin in order to decide my course of action, it is unlikely that this will enable me to act. I need to find some consideration that will enable me to believe that they will arrive before dusk, or one that will enable me to believe the opposite. Acting on a belief can occur even in situations in which there are severe time constraints, and in which there is no gap between forming a plan and acting on it. Athletes, I think, often act in this way—and this is one reason why it is possible to dislocate an opponent through surprise in games like tennis.

Even if the measure P could be used to explain the beliefs on which someone bases a plan, it will not be part of the agent's reasons for the belief. We cannot convince ourselves that something is so by noting that we have a prejudice in favor of it.

Probabilities can guide choice in another way; when a choice doesn't matter to us but nevertheless has to be made (if only because any action that is performed has to be

---

[12]The completeness assumption is, of course, quite unrealistic when the space of propositions is large. When this space is very small, and when the agent is in a state of "belief hunger" with respect to each question that can be stated on the space, it seems to be quite a reasonable condition. In intermediate cases, it is plausible only if some "closed world" mechanism can be specified for forming complete theories from partial information.

definite), then I can choose at random.[13] My recipe for meatloaf calls for an egg, so at the proper point I take an egg from the refrigerator. There are many eggs in the refrigerator, all of them equally good for my purposes. So I choose one of them, for no reason at all. It is natural to use probabilities to account for choices of this sort. But these probabilities would apply to actions rather than beliefs, and would not ordinarily enter into planning or be a part of deliberation.

If we think of the epistemology of an agent as described by a collection of indices and associated theories, together with a practicality measure on the indices, this conception of an instantaneous state will of course affect how we think of epistemic kinematics. In particular, it doesn't follow from the fact that we have synchronic probability measures on suppositions that learning takes place by anything like conditionalization on this function.

Even in the case in which there is just one supposition index, learning may involve a process of *jumping to conclusions*. Although I will not argue the matter here, I don't think that probabilities provide a correct model of such processes. When I conclude that you are in your office because I see that the light is on there, I don't think that this is to be explained by saying that I give probability *1* to the supposition that you are in your office, conditional on the supposition that the light is on, or even probability $1 - \epsilon$.[14]

Moreover, the case in which there is only one supposition index is relatively trivial. In the general case, learning will depend to a great extent on strategic shifts of the practicality measure on indices.[15]

In short, we need models of epistemic kinematics that leave room for all manner of *local* and *rational* constraints capable of guiding belief change. Such constraints seem to play a prominent role in actual learning, and, according to many computer scientists, need to be implemented in nonprobabilistic ways.

Of course, Bayesian conditionalization has many nice properties, which can be seen as arguments in favor of conditionalization as a model of ideal learning. In particular, David Lewis has been developing arguments to the effect that other principles of learning will

---

[13] The best philosophical description known to me of this sort of "surrendering to accident" in decision making is the discussion in Edwards (1957), pp. 195-202, of choice under indifference.

[14] For a discussion of the issues as they concern the epistemology of science, see Chapter III, "Why I am not a Bayesian," of Glymour (1980). Doyle (1983a) provides a theoretical basis for one alternative to the Bayesian approach, with suggestions about how to accommodate probabilities; Doyle (1983b), Szolovits (1978) and Szolovits and Pauker (1978) provide additional background on the issues as they arise in Artificial Intelligence.

[15] The difference between *supposition kinematics*, which involves managing the function taking indices into theories, and maintenance of the practicality measure may have something to do with the distinction between "knowing that" and "knowing how."

fall prey to Dutch bookmakers.[16] The force of such arguments is controversial, even in the synchronic case. But recent work of van Fraassen's[17] shows that if the diachronic version of this approach is taken seriously, it leads to paradoxical results. Of course, it is also controversial whether these paradoxes signal foundational problems for theories that rely on Dutch book arguments. But at least they help to sow the seeds of doubt.

Nor (as Glymour, for instance, has pointed out) do the Dutch book arguments mean that nonBayesian agents will be ripe for plucking by confidence men. A fair way to put the question is this: could you always make book on any mechanical reasoning system designed on nonBayesian principles and capable of making bets? There is no reason to think that you could.

For instance, on the model I am advocating the defenses against being plucked in gambling situations would be built into a system not in the form of a global requirement on reasoning, but by means of a number of *local* rules concerning the adjustment of the practicality measure in the presence of risk. Although such an approach might well lead to modest short-term losses, it could serve as a protection against large short-term losses as well as long-term money siphons. The point is that a healthy suspicion of bookmakers can be an adequate protection in itself. And making the cure local will carry many advantages, the greatest of which will be the ability to jump to conclusions. It is difficult to see how a creature that occasionally needs to act on beliefs can do without this ability.

4. BELIEF: SOME APPLICATIONS

I hope that the cases I have surveyed give some plausibility to the idea that it is possible to acquire a belief without learning anything. The case of the budget meeting, for example, does this in a particularly straightforward way. Turning things around, we can think of such examples as providing ways of putting to work the idea that belief is context-sensitive. But the philosophical literature provides other applications.

THE LOTTERY PARADOX

Kyburg's Paradox of the Lottery[18] shows that it is hard to mix probabilities and belief. Putting it generally, the problem seems to be that we are justified in believing something if its subjective probability is very high, and justified in disbelieving it if its probability is very low. But belief should be closed under conjunction; and so by conjoining believed propositions which all have very high probability, we could obtain a proposition with arbitrarily low probability, which however must be believed.

---

[16]Lewis' work is unpublished. But see Teller (1976).

[17]van Fraassen (1983).

[18]See Kyburg (1961) and Hilpinen (1968).

If belief is context-sensitive, we can say that the context is switched in the course of the paradoxical argument. Suppose that we are dealing with a fair lottery that has 10,000 entries. I have before me a list of entries' names: Bas van Fraassen is the first entry, David Lewis is the second. When I think of van Fraassen, the first entry, I believe that he won't win. When I think of Lewis, I believe that *he* won't win; and the same is true when I think of any other entry. But the proposition that none of the entries will win is not among my beliefs, even though this proposition is equivalent to the conjunction of my beliefs about each entry.

Here, the change of context seems to be determined by topic. Limiting my attention to a single individual provides a circumscribed arena of relevant suppositions and interests that somehow help to condition the belief. One way in which this can happen is that I am thinking of plans that involve one of the entries in particular. Should I make any plans that rest on the expectation that van Fraassen will win? For instance, can I expect him to be in a position to loan me $10,000, or should I worry about his quitting his job at Princeton and buying a villa on the Mediterranean? Obviously not. In fact, for such purposes I can suppose that he *won't* win the lottery. And as I have already argued,[19] supposing is not different in practical contexts from believing.

Whether or not this is a matter of dependence on topic, I think there is no doubt that it involves dependence on context. If I am deciding whether to bother trying to sell a Florida condominium to Lewis, I will suppose that he won't win; there is no point in deciding to convince him to buy on the strength of his one lottery ticket. But if I am wondering whether to send prospectuses on the condominium to all of the 10,000 entries, I will *not* suppose that he won't win. This case is like the ones I discussed above—a change of belief that is not conditioned by any gain or loss of information. And it is precisely the switch of topic accompanying this change that accounts for the paradox. For instance, when we consider the proposition that I will win the lottery, we imagine a context in which I am planning my future, having bought a ticket; this makes it plausible to say that I believe I won't win. But if we imagine that we are planning a mailing list of the possible winners, this plausibility disappears. There is, as far as I can see, no reason to suppose that if a topic T_1 conditions a belief that a set X of entries won't win, and another topic T_2 conditions a belief that a set Y of entries won't win, then there is a way of subsuming these topics under a supertopic $T_1 + T_2$ that conditions the combined belief. Topics certainly needn't be additive in this way. Thus, although for each entry x there may be a single topic sustaining the belief that x won't win, there may be no single topic sustaining the belief that no entry will win.[20]

---

[19] Or, perhaps, as I have supposed.

[20] There is a residual problem here—where to draw the line. But this is a general problem about vagueness,

RATIONALIZATION AND SELF-DECEPTION

Even if some beliefs can be acquired unreflectively, so that we have them without having any reasons for them, reflectively acquired beliefs will in general be accompanied by reasons. And the life of a reflective belief is intimately connected with its reasons. We can't acquire a belief just by gritting our teeth and trying to believe; we must find reasons. And later, if you remove the reasons you undermine the belief.

But reasons are clearly context-dependent; for instance, they fluctuate along with epistemic responsibility. Hearsay evidence may serve as a reason for a belief when I am not responsible for making decisions based on this information. But if I am promoted to a position of responsibility, I may need better reasons. Making belief context-dependent, then, connects it more closely with reasons.

And making reasons context-dependent makes it possible to initiate an account of *rationalization*. In general, rationalization seems to be implemented by manipulating the context so that something makes the grade as a reason which ordinarily would be fishy. Rationalization is reason-giving—a rationalization is a reason. But in calling something a rationalization, we are saying that a flaw of judgment occurred in taking it to be a reason.[21]

The apparatus of context-dependency, both of beliefs and of reasons, helps to explain how by lowering our standards, by circumscription, and by other context-manipulating devices, we can cultivate a reason, and hence a belief, that would not survive in a less favorable environment.

And of course, this has something to do with self-deception. We have provided a model of belief on which it is possible for an agent to harbor contradictory beliefs. (This means that a supposition index can appeal to the agent on which a proposition is true, while at the same time another index, on which it is false, also appeals to the agent.) Also, in manipulation of the context, we have a mechanism that provides techniques of self-deception.

This does not engage many of the most difficult questions about self-deception; in

---

not a particular problem about belief. Formally, the solution is isomorphic to supervaluation treatments of the Sorites Paradox. I think that this method works pretty well on the Lottery Paradox, but I have my doubts about the Sorites.

[21]One way of motivating the general approach I am taking in this paper is to see it as an attempt to develop a theory meeting the conditions outlined in Davidson (1970) for an account of weakness of will. I believe, however, that such a theory must deal simultaneously with beliefs as well as with (all-things-considered) desires, and that weakness of will cannot be considered independently of rationalization and self-deception. Moreover, the mechanisms that make these phenomena possible have to be healthy and necessary components of practical reasoning.

particular, I have provided no model of attention, and no explanation of how it is possible for an agent to distract his own attention. But at least it is a beginning.

5. MOTIVES

A motive is something that *moves* us; something that matters to us. Ordinarily, I will not plan unless I harbor some motive, however weak, for implementing the resulting plan; I won't work out the steps required by making a trip to Puget Sound, for instance, unless the thought of a trip to Puget Sound strikes me as attractive or needful. But even categorical plans—ones that aren't made contingently—needn't be implemented. There are plans that are made idly; plans that are supported by motives we don't have wholeheartedly, or that are counterbalanced by other motives, as my desire to travel may be offset by indolence and fear of change.

Groups harbor motives, as well as individuals. But, since the members of a group may represent different interests, these motives are not in general held homogeneously by the group. Some members of a policy-making committee, for instance, may represent the need to raise faculty salaries, while others represent the need to avoid raising student tuition. We can imagine a homogeneous committee, all of whose members represent identical interests; but, of course, there are many cases to which this idealization does not apply.

If we represent interests by preference rankings among alternatives, it seems that there is no magic formula for constructing the group interest of a heterogeneous committee out of the conflicting interests of its members.[22]   And yet committees are decision-making bodies, and can be charged with the responsibility of shaping a group interest. The moral, it seems to me, is that such tasks call for cooperation and judgment. In many cases, it is good to have a procedure for arriving at a group decision even when there are unresolved differences among the members. But judgment has to be used in applying such procedures, since issues may always arise in which defending an interest is more important to a member of a group than following the procedures. In the best decision-making situations, and especially where the group is small, discussion and willingness to compromise will serve better than a voting procedure.

It would be wrong to think that individual agents are different from small, cooperative decision-making groups, at least as far as homogeneity is concerned. It is easy to imagine a committee consisting of three individuals. Two of them wholeheartedly represent certain interests, which, however, conflict. The third is the swing member: he feels the attractions of both positions. In trying to decide which way to swing, this individual is in much the same position as the committee itself; both points of view speak to him and compel him, just as his fellow committee members do. The two points of view have to be resolved in

---

[22]I have in mind Arrow's Theorem and related results; see Sen (1970), for instance.

coming to a decision, and there is no ready-made formula enabling them to be reconciled or subsumed under some more dominant interest. Obviously, individuals can find themselves in such situations even when the conflicting interests are not represented by others—nor do the interests need to be personified, as in cartoons in which a little angel whispers into one ear, and a little devil into the other.

You might think that the need to resolve conflicting interests will not arise so often in the life of an individual—that it is somehow more characteristic of groups. But to make the comparison fair, you have to imagine a committee that is obliged to decide many routine, day-to-day matters, a committee that does not enjoy the benefit of some executive authority to screen out the cases that can be handled without group deliberation. Also, you might think that the need for resolution of conflict is more compelling in the case of an individual. But there are times, I believe, in which groups feel this need just as keenly as individuals; and individuals can also set their agendas, and so may deal with conflicting motives by dodging or ignoring situations in which these conflicts will make nuisances of themselves.

At any rate, I find the analogy compelling and true-to-life. Motives are not vectors, complete with a direction and a scalar value, and there is no rule for summing them into a single motive. There isn't any way to define a resultant motive, that would act on an individual in much the same way that a resultant force acts on a boat being paddled across a river. It *is* true, of course, that individuals will eventually do something or other, even when they harbor conflicting motives. But this would be true even if motives were not additive.

The argument that since an individual will act in some way there must be a strongest motive to determine this action is simply a special case of the principle that if something is so, then there must be something that makes it have to be so. This is not a particularly compelling principle.

In many cases, it may be true that we can assign strengths to motives, and regard these strengths as statistical determinants of behavior. I may be a conservative poker player, and want to play by the book. But also I see the need not to establish a pattern, so occasionally I stand pat with two pair and bet the limit. The frequency with which I do this is a measure of the strength of my estimate of how important it is for me to be unpredictable.

But many cases of decision making don't succumb to this sort of analysis. A philosopher, say, is interested in being profound, and interested in being clear. The two motives, let's imagine, conflict with each other. But we aren't going to get any very interesting measure of the relative strengths of these motives for our philosopher by, say, counting the relative frequencies of profound sentences to clear ones in his writings. And in any case, there are many instances in which we *can't* consciously succumb to chance in acting:

instances in which it would simply be perverse, or otiose, to flip a coin or to advise some-one to flip a coin, even if the considerations on each side are equally balanced. When the decision matters a great deal to us and we have time to deliberate, we are generally unable to act without giving ourselves a reason. (This is one of the causes of the phenomenon that I called "belief hunger.")

6. MOTIVES: SOME CASE STUDIES

We are accustomed to the idea that people are susceptible to a variety of motives, whose power to influence us depends on circumstances. There is the ebb and flow of appetite; at lunchtime I am hungry, and afterwards I may be regretful about having eaten so much. And *habit* can affect the strength of motives: I hate to answer letters, so I set aside a time for answering them. If I can acquire the habit of sitting down regularly at this time and answering letters, I will have weakened my distaste for correspondence.

But there are other determinants of motives that are more internal to the process of practical reasoning, and that in this respect are similar to some of the factors that influence belief.

OPPORTUNITY

We tend to want only what we think we can get: thus, it would be strange for me to say that I want to own the Grand Canyon, even though it may be true that I would like to own it. Ordinarily, to think of something as unobtainable will extinguish the desire to have it, or at least will suspend the operation of this desire in planning.

But 'can' is a highly contextually sensitive word, whose horizons I can expand or contract by taking more or fewer possibilities into account. By changing the context, I can make it true that I can play squash, even though I may have a broken leg.[23] And, as I widen my possibilities in this way, I can waken dormant motives.

ALTERNATIVES

Almost all of our planning involves deciding among a small number of alternatives. Although whenever we act we have to act in a specific way, many of the details of our actions are not planned, even though we would say that they are intentional. (My choice of a chair on sitting down at a meeting in a strange room may well be like this: unplanned, but intentional.)

It is important that the list of alternatives be small; the larger the menu in a restaurant, the more difficult our decision; and so we go to a restaurant equipped with hasty procedures

---

[23]See Kratzer (1979).

for eliminating many choices from a large menu. This isn't an accident. If in general we are only capable of planning when the number of alternatives is small, and decisions have to be made in a reasonable amount of time, we need to have nonreflective ways of determining what these alternatives are.

But desires depend on the alternatives with which we are presented. When the dentist asks you whether you want novocaine, a situation is created in which you want a needle inserted into the tissue of your mouth. Unless the dentist is unusual, he probably didn't ask you if you wanted your tooth filled.

ENTRENCHMENT THROUGH ACTION

The very act of basing a decision on a motive can strengthen the motive, by making it ours—something we have to cherish and defend. This is particularly evident in more or less portentous decisions, made in situations of extreme conflict.

At the time of the American Revolution, a number of people were forced to decide whether to support the legitimate government or the revolution. Many Colonial citizens, of course, were acutely conscious of the claims of both sides. Imagine such a person trying to decide where his loyalties lie, and finally grasping at his duty to the king as a deciding factor. This choice was perhaps made in desperation—his loyalty to the country in which he was born seems equally compelling to him—but in a moment of attending to the claims of the conservative position, he acts and declares himself publicly. Having done this, he is committed; his pride prevents him from changing his mind. He has put himself in the position of being willing to suffer for a conviction; and this itself strengthens the conviction. He is forced to cherish this motive, and to relinquish motives that conflict with it.

This factor helps to make acute conflict of motives an unstable situation, in cases in which some sort of action is forced. This is perhaps just as well for our peace of mind, though it also tends to foster intolerance.

7. CONCLUSION

Belief is context-sensitive; moreover, it is context-sensitive in such a way that we may be able to put ourselves in the appropriate context. There are many factors that serve to determine belief: risk, belief-hunger, interest, topic, and supposition kinematics are among the most important of these. We can imagine that by specifying enough contextual factors we can determine a single set of beliefs. But real-life situations often do not specify enough to do this; the most we can say in such situations is that we have multiple systems of beliefs, which may even be incompatible. This may or may not prevent us from acting; action depends on desires as well as on beliefs, and it may not be fully determined even by these. Sometimes, for instance, we act more or less unreflectively, without any particular desire or belief seeming to guide the choice.

Context-sensitivity often is accompanied by vagueness, and indeed it often is vague, I think, whether or not we believe something. And there are a number of theoretical considerations suggesting that it is more useful to think of *suppositions* than of beliefs. Suppositions can be idle, but when they are put to practical work, and an agent bases plans and actions on their truth, we are willing to call them beliefs; a belief is a supposition that is obtained in a more or less practical mode.

I have tried to avoid talking about rationality in this paper, though I have presented arguments showing why I feel that this concept, which is so much appealed to in contemporary philosophical discussions of practical reasoning, is not likely to be of much use in finding realistic and implementable foundations for practical reasoning. Though, since the goal is a theory, some idealizations will of course have to be made, we are abandoning all faithfulness to resource limitations in concentrating on rationality. When reasoning must be carried out in a limited time, we have to rely on heuristic reasoning processes that are unreflective and hasty, therefore would fall far short of the standards that are imposed by ideals of rationality. Allocating limited reasoning resources to a practical problem is a problem that calls for good judgment, but not for thorough calculation of every alternative.

At a first approximation, we might limit the role of rationality to reasoning processes that occur once a context has been established. But, if there is anything to what I have been saying, manipulating the context itself is also an important part of practical reasoning. The fact that we do not in general manipulate context reflectively, and that there may even be no specification of ideal correctness for such manipulations, does not mean that these reasoning processes are entirely random and "irrational." In fact, if our motives and beliefs depend to some extent on the context in which we find ourselves, and we are capable of manipulating this context, then it is vital to manipulate it wisely.

ACKNOWLEDGMENTS

A large part of the research that is summarized in this paper was devoted to organizing examples of decision-making, and to developing ways of interpreting them that seemed illuminating. This project was enriched and shaped by discussions with Rebecca Holsen. Her influence runs deeply through the way in which applications are addressed in this paper. The theoretical parts of the project exploit the insights of many people, among whom I would especially like to mention Jon Doyle, Clark Glymour, William Harper, Robert Stalnaker, and Bas van Fraassen. I also owe thanks to the Carnegie Mellon University Computer Science Department, on whose system this document was prepared.

REFERENCES

D. Davidson. "How is Weakness of the Will Possible?" In *Moral Conflicts*, ed. J. Feinberg, Oxford University Press, pp. 93-113 (1970).

J. Doyle. "Some Theories of Reasoned Assumptions." Technical Report, Computer Science Department, Carnegie Mellon University (1983a).

J. Doyle. "Methodological Simplicity in Expert System Construction." Technical Report, Computer Science Department, Carnegie Mellon University (1983b).

J. Edwards. *Freedom of the Will*, Yale University Press (1957). [*Note:* This is a later edition of a work first published in 1754.]

C. Glymour. *Theory and Evidence*, Princeton University Press (1980).

J. Halpern. "Reasoning About Knowledge: an Overview." In *Reasoning About Knowledge*, ed. J. Halpern, Morgan Kaufmann, pp. 1-17 (1986).

R. Hilpinen. *Rules of Acceptance and Inductive Logic*, North-Holland (1968).

J. Horty, R. Thomason, and D. Touretzky. "A skeptical theory of inheritance in non-monotonic semantic nets." Technical Report, Carnegie Mellon University (1987).

Kratzer, A., "What 'Must' and 'Can' Must and Can Mean." *Linguistics and Philosophy 1,*. pp. 337-355 (1979).

H. Kyburg, *Probability and the Logic of Rational Belief*, Wesleyan University Press, (1961).

D. Lewis. "Scorekeeping in a Language Game," *Journal of Philosophical Logic 8*, pp. 339-359 (1979).

J. McCarthy. "Circumscription—a Form of Non-Monotonic Reasoning," *Artificial Intelligence 13*, pp. 27-39 (1980).

A. Sen. *Collective Choice and Social Welfare*, Elsevier (1970).

P. Szolovits. "The Lure of Numbers: How to Live Without Them in Medical Diagnosis." In *Proceedings of a Colloquium on Computer-Assisted Decision Making using Clinical and Paraclinical (Laboratory) Data*, eds. B. Statland and S. Bauer, Technicon Press, pp. 65-76 (1978).

P. Szolovits and S. Pauker "Categorical and Probabilistic Reasoning in Medical Diagnosis," *Artificial Intelligence 11*, pp. 115-144 (1978).

P. Teller. "Conditionalization, Observation, and Change of Preference." In *Foundations and Philosophical Applications of Probability Theory*, eds. W. Harper and C. Hooker, D. Reidel, pp. 205-253 (1976).

D. Touretzky, J. Horty, and R. Thomason. "Issues in the design of nonmonotonic inheritance systems." Technical Report, Carnegie Mellon University (1987).

B. van Fraassen. "Values and the Heart's Command," *Journal of Philosophy 70*, pp. 5-19 (1973).

B. van Fraassen. "Belief and the Will." Unpublished manuscript, Princeton University (1983).

THE DOXASTIC THEORY
OF INTENTION

J. David Velleman
Department of Philosophy
University of Michigan
Ann Arbor, MI 48109

ABSTRACT

The doxastic theory of intention says that an intention to act consists in the belief that one is going to act because of having adopted this very belief. I present a version of the theory and argue that it yields a fruitful conception of free will. I then defend the theory against some of the many objections that have been raised against it.

The doxastic theory of intention says that an intention to act consists in a belief that one is going to act -- more specifically, in a belief that one is going to act because of having adopted this very belief.[1] Gilbert Harman argued for a form of this theory in his article "Practical Reasoning."[2] The theory had previously been discussed, though not endorsed, by H.P. Grice.[3] It has come under attack from Donald Davidson,[4] Michael Bratman,[5] Myles Brand, [6] and others.[7] In this paper I shall defend the theory, but I shall confine my attention to its account of immediate intentions; its account of long-range plans would require more space that I have here.[8] My present goal, then, is to defend the theory that the immediate intention of doing something consists in a belief that one is going to do it because of having adopted this very belief.

---

[1]I am indebted to Dion Scott-Kakures, Paul Boghossian, Nicholas White, George Wilson, Don Regan, and Don Demetriades for discussions on the topics covered in this paper.

[2]29 *Review of Metaphysics* 431 (1976). I say that Harman argued for "a form" of the doxastic theory because he qualified it in various ways -- most notably, by stipulating that intentions must issue from practical rather than theoretical reasoning [pp. 448 ff]. Some have therefore interpreted Harman as rejecting the doxastic theory. (See Hugh J. McCann, "Rationality and the Range of Intention," forthcoming in 10 *Midwest Studies in Philosophy* 186 - 206, p. 191.) In any case, Harman seems to have backed away from the doxastic theory in his recent book *Change in View; principles of reasoning* (Cambridge, MA: MIT Press, 1986). He now says that intentions "involve" beliefs, but are "distinctive attitudes" (p. 95).

[3]"Intention and Uncertainty," 57 *Proceedings of the British Academy* 263 (1971).

[4]"Intending," in *Essays on Actions and Events* (Oxford: Clarendon Press, 1980), 83 - 102.

[5]"Intention and Means-End Reasoning," 90 *Philosophical Review* 252 (1981) and "Two Faces of Intention," 93 *Philosophical Review* 375 - 405.

[6]*Intending and Acting; toward a naturalized action theory* (Cambridge, MA: MIT Press, 1983), especially Chapter Six.

[7]See McCann, "Rationality and the Range of Intention," *op. cit.*

[8]Many issues not covered in this paper, including long-range plans, are discussed in my book-length manuscript entitled *Facing the Mirror: Self-Inquiry as Practical Reasoning*

I shall begin with a few remarks about the logical status of the theory. Then I'll set out my version of the theory. Finally, I'll address myself to two of the objections that have been raised against it.

I
The Logical Status
of the Theory

The doxastic theory asserts an identity between intentions and beliefs. What sort of an identity-statement is this?

A. What the Theory Isn't

To begin with, it is not a piece of conceptual analysis. Our everyday concept of intention contains nothing about self-referring and self-fulfilling beliefs,[9] and so a theory identifying intentions with such beliefs cannot purport to be analyzing our concept. The theory makes an assertion about what intention is, not about what we already conceive it to be.

Nor does the theory give materially necessary and sufficient conditions for the existence of an intention. The reason is that 'intention', being a term of commonsense psychology, is essentially vague.

Some of the vagueness in the term 'intention' can be explained. This vagueness arises because the classic case of intention is distinguished by several features, and mental states sharing some but not all of those features may qualify as intentions in some contexts but not in others. The classic intention has a characteristic content, a characteristic cause, and a characteristic effect. Its characteristic content is that one is going to perform an action, partly because of having opted to

---

[9]When I call a belief self-referring, I mean that it refers to itself -- *i.e.,* to that very belief. My usage of the phrase 'self-referring belief' thus differs from that of some philosophers, who have used it to denote beliefs that refer to the believer. (See, e.g., Myles Brand, *Intending and Acting, op. cit.* , Chapter Four, and "Intending and Believing," in James E. Tomberlin (ed.), *Agent, Language, and the Structure of the World; essays presented to Hector-Neri Castañeda, with his replies* (Indianapolis: Hackett Publishing Co., 1983), 171 - 193.)

form this very intention;[10] its characteristic cause is a desire
that one perform the action; and its characteristic effect is
the action itself.[11]   Sometimes, however, an agent's attitude
has only the content and causes of an intention, but not the effect: he doesn't act.   In that case, we may say that the agent
has an ineffective intention, but we may also say that he didn't
really intend to act.   On other occasions, an agent's attitude
has the causes and effects of an intention, but a slightly different content, since the agent, though acknowledging the action's performance, disavows intending it.   His attitude therefore represents the action, and causes the action, but doesn't
represent itself as causing it.   Here again, we may say either
that the agent has a defective intention or that he has none at
all.

One of the virtues of the doxastic theory, to my mind, is
that it can account for these defective intentions and not just
the classic specimen.   (Unfortunately, I shall not have space in

---

[10]I shall not argue for this assumption here.   It is supported by cases
such as the following:

> Betty intends to kill someone.   She aims her gun and, at the
> crucial moment, a noise startles her, leading her to contract
> her finger so that she shoots and kills him ... .   Although she
> intends to kill him and does kill him, she does not do what she
> intends.   For her intention to kill him is the intention that
> that very intention will lead her to pull the trigger at the
> crucial moment; and that does not happen.   [Gilbert Harman,
> "Practical Reasoning," *op. cit.*, p. 445]

See also John Searle, *Intentionality; an essay in the philosophy of mind*
(Cambridge: Cambridge University Press, 1983), Chapter Three; and David
Pears, "Intention and Belief," in Bruce Vermazen and Merrill B. Hintikka
(eds.), *Essays on Davidson; actions and events* (Oxford: Clarendon Press,
1985) 75 - 88.

In fact, the content of an intention probably includes the manner in
which the intention will cause the intended action.   For as Harman goes on
to say, "If Betty's intention makes her nervous and nervousness causes her
to pull the trigger, her intention leads her to pull the trigger but not in
the intended way; so she does not do what she intends ..." [*ibid.*].   Similar cases are discussed by Searle, *loc. cit.;* Davidson, "Freedom to Act,"
in *Essays on Actions and Events, op. cit.,*   63 - 81, pp. 79 ff.; and R.M.
Chisholm, "Freedom and Action," in K. Lehrer (ed.), *Freedom and Determinism*
(New York: Random House, 1966) 11 - 44.

[11]Compare Alvin Goldman's definition of volitions as "conscious occurrences
which are, or express, propositional attitudes, and ... have the following
property: each has a tendency to cause an event which satisfies or fulfills
its propositional content" ["The Volitional Theory Revisited," in M. Brand
and D. Walton (eds.), *Action Theory* (Dordrecht: D. Reidel, 1976) 67 - 84,
p. 68].

this paper to show how it does so.) What the doxastic theory cannot do, in any case, is to account for our decision, in the face of a defective instance, to confer or withhold the title 'intention'. That decision depends on considerations and interests that are beyond the scope of the present theory.[12] What's more, the doxastic theory doesn't deny that the term 'intention' may be vague in further, less explicable respects. Perhaps we sometimes confer the title 'intention' on attitudes that bear no systematic resemblance to what I have called the classic case; and perhaps we withhold the title from some attitudes that aren't systematically different. In that case, intentions would be a miscellany -- not the only one in commonsense psychology, I'd bet -- and the doxastic theory wouldn't claim to capture every instance.

B.   What the Theory Is

If the doxastic theory doesn't purport to give a conceptual analysis of intention, or even to map the concept's extension, then what's the point?

The point of the theory is to explain the possibility of the will -- that is, the faculty or capacity for intentions -- in some of its most characteristic and puzzling manifestations. As creatures possessing a will, we find that it gives us various occasions for philosophical puzzlement. How is it that we can spontaneously generate knowledge about our future conduct, simply by forming intentions? How can our decisions be motivated and yet seemingly free of motivational predetermination? How can our capacity to form and execute intentions make us self-governing, or free?

These are the questions that the doxastic theory of intention seeks to answer. And in order to answer them, it need only arrive at descriptions that are true of our intentions by and large. Insofar as our intentions are as the theory describes them, their puzzling features can be explained. This much is worth knowing even if the theory's description of intentions doesn't always match the extension of the term in common parlance. Of course, discrepancies between the theory and common parlance will indicate that at least one of them fails to reflect the actual boundaries of the will. But the theory seeks to explain the possibility of the will, not to map its boundaries.

---

[12]For example, Harman has suggested (in "Practical Reasoning" and *Change in View*) that our decision to call something an intention may depend on our interest in blaming or excusing the agent for the resulting action. Perhaps, then, the extension of the term 'intention' cannot be mapped without the help of moral theory.

II
The Possibility
of Intentions[13]

The doxastic theory initially raises two questions, which turn out to be one and the same. The first question is how the intentions that it posits could ever be effective. How could someone bring himself to act by forming an intention to act, if that intention consisted in the mere belief that he was going to act because of having adopted that very belief?[14] The second question is how an agent could ever be correct in holding a belief of the sort that is here identified with an intention. How could he be correct in believing that he was going to act because of having adopted this very belief? As I have said, these two questions are really one. For if an intention to act consists in the belief that one will act because of this belief, then the intention's taking effect is identical with the belief's coming true. The intention just is, if you like, a belief in its own effectiveness as an intention, and so its effectiveness and its truth are inseparable.

A.   Self-fulfilling Beliefs

How, then, could intentions be effective if they consisted in beliefs? How could the beliefs that constituted them be true? I shall answer this two-sided question by making two assumptions, neither of which I shall adequately defend in the course of this paper.

My first assumption is that the ordinary person wants to know what he's doing. Let's take you as an example. I assume that you want roughly the following to be the case: that as soon as you are doing something, you know that you're doing it, under

---

[13]Some of the material in this section is drawn from my "Practical Reflection," 94 *Philosophical Review* 33 (1985). I am grateful to the editors of the *Review* for permission to reprint this material.

[14]Myles Brand denies that a belief could have the requisite motivational force: "A person might believe that he will jump up and touch the ceiling; but no matter the strength of his belief, this attitude by itself will not result in his jumping and touching the ceiling" [*Intending and Acting, op. cit.,* p. 94, and "Intending and Believing," *op. cit.,* p. 177].

some minimally adequate description.[15] My second assumption is
that your desire for concurrent awareness of your actions is not
automatically fulfilled by virtue of some quirk about first-person knowledge. I assume that you aren't necessarily aware of
what you're doing, but that you want to be.

How could you go about fulfilling this desire? Well, you
could simply pay attention to yourself, monitoring your every
move. The problem is that such reflective surveillance would
prove to be too little, too late. Suppose that you want a
breath of fresh air, and that this desire moves you to get up
and leave the room. A moment's observation will tell you that
you're leaving; but a moment's observation will take a moment,
during which you won't yet know what you're doing. As you be-
stir yourself, you won't yet know that you're getting up; as you
get up, you won't know that you're leaving; and so on.

Reflective surveillance would be sufficient, of course, if
you could be content to identify your conduct in minute stages.
As soon as you stir, you'll see that you're stirring; as soon as
you flex your leg, you'll see that you're flexing it; and so on.
But surely such knowledge is not enough to satisfy you. Even as
you stir, you're starting some larger action -- namely, leaving
the room -- which will occupy more than an instant. Surely you
want to know which larger action you're starting, and you want
to know as soon as you start it. Unfortunately, you won't learn
so much so soon simply by watching yourself act.

There is a way of preventing your actions from outrunning
your awareness, however -- namely, to forecast them in advance.
Instead of waiting to see what you'll do next, you can try to
anticipate what you'll do, so that by the time you do something,
you'll already know what it will be. If you thus foresee what
you're going to do, you will never find yourself falling behind
on what you're doing. Your desire to stay abreast of what
you're doing is therefore a motive for ensuring that you foresee
what you're going to do next.

Now, you might try to foresee your actions by looking for
clues that foreshadowed them. Your present thoughts and feel-
ings, your long-established aspirations, the exigencies of your
situation, your past record of behavior, all shed light on your
forthcoming conduct. Unfortunately, the light they shed is often dim or deceptive. If you had to rely on behavioral fore-

---

[15]Note that I do not individuate actions in the manner of Alvin Goldman (*A
Theory of Human Action* (Princeton: Princeton University Press, 1970),
Chapters One and Two). Goldman would say that to know what you're doing
under only one description would be to know only one of the things that
you're doing. I heartily endorse the critique of Goldman offered by G.E.M.
Anscombe in "Under a Description," 13 *Nous* 219 (1979).

casting, in the present state of that art, you'd often expect to do one thing and then find yourself doing another.

Fortunately, you needn't rely on such reflective forecasting. The reason is that you have two coordinate means of ensuring that you will have foreseen your next action. One is to anticipate what you're going to do; the other is to do only what you have already anticipated. You can not only form expectations that are true *of* your forthcoming actions: you can also perform actions that are true *to* your prior expectations.[16] Both of these steps will tend to ensure that you will have foreseen whatever you do, and hence that you know from the outset what you're doing.

The desire to know what you're doing therefore inclines you to perform all and only those actions which you already expect yourself to perform. Until there is something that you expect to do next, the desire to know what you're doing restrains you from so much as stirring. To stir at such a time would be to start an action that you might not identify until it was well underway; and until then you wouldn't know what you were doing. The desire to know what you're doing therefore opposes your doing anything. But once there is something that you expect to do next, you will presume your next move to be the beginning of that action; and so if you begin the expected action, you'll know from the outset what you're doing. At this point, the desire to know what you're doing favors the action that you expect. If you begin a different action, however, you'll first mistake it for the expected one, and then you'll have to identify it from scratch -- not knowing, in the meantime, what you're doing. The desire to know what you're doing therefore favors the expected action only, and continues to oppose any others.

---

[16]G.E.M. Anscombe proposes a similar account of "practical truth" in the last two paragraphs of "Thought and Action in Aristotle" (in R. Bambrough (ed.), *New Essays on Plato and Aristotle* (London: Routledge and Kegan Paul, 1965) 143 - 158). She thereby picks up a theme that was left undeveloped in her book *Intention* (Ithaca, NY: Cornell University Press, 1963), pp. 1 - 5; 56 - 58; 87. In the latter context, she tied this theme to the ancient and medieval notion of "practical knowledge," which is "the cause of what it understands" [Aquinas, *Summa Theologica* Ia IIae, Q3, art. 5, obj. 1]. Anscombe's notion of practical truth is discussed at length by David Pears in Chapter Eight of *Motivated Irrationality, op. cit.* Arthur Danto criticizes Anscombe's views on practical knowledge in "Action, Knowledge, and Representation," in M. Brand and D. Walton (eds.), *Action Theory* (Dordrecht: D. Reidel, 1976) 11- 25. Also relevant here is John Searle's discussion of "direction of fit" [*Intentionality; an essay in the philosophy of mind* (Cambridge: Cambridge University Press, 1983), pp. 7 ff.; and *Expression and Meaning* (Cambridge: Cambridge University Press, 1979), pp. 1 - 27].

Here, then, is a way of explaining how the expectation of doing something can cause you to do it. The reason why your expectation of doing something causes you to do it is that doing what you expect is the best way of ensuring that you know what you're doing, and you want to know what you're doing.

B. The Epistemology of Reflective Expectations

I have now explained how an expectation of acting can have the same effects as an intention of acting, and can therefore be correct in representing itself as having those effects. But why would it represent itself as having those effects? And could it also have an intention's causes? That is: how could your expectation of doing something come to represent itself as causing you to do it, and be occasioned by your desire to do it, rather than by prior evidence that you're going to? In order to answer these questions, I shall have to delve into the epistemology of your reflective expectations.

i.   The evidence. The epistemology of these expectations is odd, because you aren't fully constrained by the antecedent evidence. Within limits, you can predict whichever action you like, since you'll end up performing whichever action you predict.

I am not claiming here that that your inclination to do what you expect entitles you to expect any action whatsoever, regardless of the evidence. For although you are inclined to do what you expect, that inclination isn't irresistible. Your inclination to do as you expect wouldn't make you dance naked on the table, even if you expected to. True, if you expected to dance naked on the table, then the prospect of doing so would have the added attraction that you would know what you were doing from the very first pirouette. But the attraction of knowing what you were doing wouldn't be strong enough to outweigh the deterrent of looking like a fool -- not to mention catching a cold. Hence even if you expected yourself to dance naked on the table, you wouldn't -- and so you had better not expect to.

Generally speaking, then, if you have an aversion to a particular action, your expecting that action may not give you a sufficient motive for taking it. Indeed, merely lacking any other motive for the expected action may prevent your bearing out the expectation, since your motive for bearing out such expectations may not be sufficient, in itself, to make you act in the face of motives that you have for alternative actions. In forming such expectations, then, you must look for evidence of conditions that would prevent you from bearing them out. You may not expect yourself to do something if you find evidence that you won't do it even if you expect to.

Yet to avoid expecting anything that the evidence rules out is not the same as to insist on expecting only what the evidence

rules in.   After you have eliminated the actions that you
wouldn't perform even if you expected to, there will usually remain several alternative actions that you would perform if you
expected to; and the prior evidence doesn't dictate which of
these actions to expect.[17]

The reason is that there are usually several different actions toward which you're somewhat inclined, each inclination
being capable of prevailing over the others if it is reinforced,
while the others are suppressed, by your inclination to do what
you expect.   At any moment you have various sets of motives, favoring various alternative actions.   Which action you take will
of course depend on which one is favored by the strongest set of
motives.   But the way to anticipate which action you'll take is
not to ascertain which set of motives is antecedently the
strongest.   After all, the set that's strongest before you form
an expectation about your next action is not necessarily the one
that will be strongest after you form such an expectation.   If
you expect a different action, you will thereby acquire a new
motive for that action and against all others; and your motives
for the expected action, which were antecedently the weaker set,

---

[17]This statement might seem inaccurate.   Suppose that before you form an
expectation of acting, there is conclusive evidence about which action
you'll expect.   If there is also conclusive evidence that the action you'll
expect is the one that you'd perform if you expected to, then the evidence
prior to your expectation might seem to dictate which action you ought to
expect: you would seem obliged to expect the very action which, according
to the evidence, you're going to expect.

But the evidence in question here is not evidence that you need to
consult in forming your expectation.   You cannot go wrong by forming a different expectation from the one that, according to the evidence, you going
to form, and hence fulfill.   For if you do manage to defy the evidence by
forming a different expectation, you'll fulfill the expectation you form
instead of the one currently indicated by the evidence.

I discuss this issue at greater length below.

may then become the stronger, with the result that you bear out your expectation.[18]

The upshot is that if you have significant motives for various actions, you can expect any one of those actions before you have found evidence that you will in fact perform it. All you need to find, before expecting an action, is evidence that you'll perform it if you expect to. And this is evidence of a sort that you can usually find in reference to many different, mutually incompatible actions. Among these actions, your prior evidence is neutral. It doesn't mark any one of these actions as the action to expect; rather, it marks all of the actions equally as candidates for your expectation, each on a par with the others in its likelihood of being performed if expected.

Yet the neutrality of the evidence doesn't require you to remain neutral in your expectations. Even though your prior evidence doesn't favor expecting one of the actions instead of the others, you can go ahead and form a determinate expectation. For as soon as you expect to perform one of the actions instead of the others, the evidence falls in line behind your expectation. Given the prior evidence that you would perform an action if you expected to, the additional evidence that you now expect to perform it clinches the case for so expecting. Thus, no sooner do you form a determinate expectation than it becomes better justified than the erstwhile alternatives.

ii. Grounds vs. occasion. One might think that you aren't entitled to expect anything in these circumstances, since you cannot obtain the necessary evidence for your expectation until

---

[18]Your antecedently weaker motives would not become the stronger, of course, if their initial disadvantage were too great to be redressed by your motives for doing what you expect. An expectation couldn't alter the balance of your motives if they were initially too far out of balance. But if the motives favoring the available alternatives were all of moderate strength, then any alternative could indeed become the favorite by being anticipated. No matter which action you expected, your motives for it would then gain the advantage and produce the action, thus bearing out your expectation.

My argument here is analogous in some respect to Charles Taylor's claims about self-description. (See "Responsibility for Self," in A.O. Rorty (ed.), *The Identities of Persons* (Berkeley: University of California Press, 1976), 281 - 99, esp. pp. 294 ff.) Taylor says that an agent's description of his motives *alters* his motives. I say that it gives rise to a *new* motive, which helps to determine which of the others takes effect. See also Jon Elster's interpretation of Taylor (*Ulysses and the Sirens; essays on rationality and irrationality* (Cambridge: Cambridge University Press, 1979), p. 106.)

after you've formed it.[19]   How can you come to expect an event
if, so long as you don't yet expect it, it isn't set to happen?

This question betrays a confusion, I think, between the
grounds for a belief an the occasion for it.   Let me illustrate
the confusion I have in mind, by quoting a passage from G.E.M.
Anscombe's *Intention:* [20]

> [W]hen a doctor says to a patient in the presence of a
> nurse 'Nurse will take you to the operating theatre',
> this may function both as an expression of his inten-
> tion ... and as an order, as well as being information
> to the patient; and it is the latter in spite of being
> in no sense an estimate of the future founded on evi-
> dence.

To be sure, the doctor's assertion could not have been elicited
by evidence; for until he said that the nurse was going to take
the patient to the operating theater, the nurse wasn't going to.
Anscombe therefore infers that the doctor isn't giving "an estimate of the future founded on evidence."   But the doctor's assertion is indeed founded on evidence.   His evidence for telling
the patient, "Nurse will take you to the operating theater" is
that the nurse is herewith getting implicit instructions to do
so, and that nurses tend to understand and obey such instructions.

Although the doctor's assertion thus rests on evidence, that
evidence wasn't there to elicit his assertion, since it wasn't
there until the assertion itself was made.   Before the doctor
made the assertion, then, he didn't have evidence that it was

----

[19]See H.P. Grice, "Intention and Uncertainty," *op. cit.,* p. 274:

> If my going to London is to depend causally on my acceptance
> that I shall go, the possession of satisfactory evidence that I
> shall go will involve possession of the information that I ac-
> cept that I shall go.   Obviously, then, I cannot (though others
> can) come to accept that I shall go on the basis of satisfac-
> tory evidence;   For to have such evidence I should have *already*
> to have accepted that I shall go.

My reply to this objection is similar to Harman's: "The problem arises from
supposing that the justification of a belief represents a way that someone
might reach that belief as a conclusion" ["Practical Reasoning," *op. cit.,*
p. 448, n. 8].   Harman expands on this point in "Willing and Intending," in
Grandy and Warner (eds.), *Philosophical Grounds of Rationality; intentions,
categories, eds* (Oxford: Oxford University Press, 1986), 363 - 380.

[20](Ithaca: Cornell University Press, 1957) p. 3.

true: all he had was evidence that it *would* be true if he made it. And he had similar evidence about various other assertions, many of them inconsistent with the one he actually made; for there are many mutually incompatible actions of which any one would have been forthcoming from the nurse if only the doctor had said so. The evidence prior to the doctor's assertion was thus insufficient to dictate what he should assert; and yet whatever he asserted would thereby have come to rest on sufficient evidence. Hence Anscombe would have been right if she had said that the assertion wasn't occasioned by evidence; but she was wrong to infer that it lacks evidential grounds.

A mistake like Anscombe's lies behind the suspicion that an agent can't come to expect that he'll do something if, in fact, he wouldn't do it unless he already expected to. The reasoning behind this suspicion seems to be that if a person wouldn't do something unless he already expected to, then the evidence that he was going to do something would have to include the fact that he expected to; in which case, unless he already expected to do something, he would lack the evidence that he would do it, and could therefore never come to expect so.

This reasoning assumes that a rational person could never come to have a belief unless he had evidence for it in advance. And this assumption contains a confusion like Anscombe's, between the grounds and the occasion for a belief. If rationality required beliefs to have evidence as their occasion, then the only beliefs that one could rationally form would be those for which one had prior evidence. What rationality requires, however, is that beliefs have evidence as grounds, not occasion. As for the ways in which beliefs are occasioned, rationality requires only that they be occasioned in such a way as to ensure that they have adequate evidential grounds. And some beliefs can be ensured of evidential grounds without being occasioned by that evidence. In particular, beliefs whose formation will complete the evidence for them are sure to have adequate grounds, if formed, even though their grounds cannot occasion their formation. Forming such beliefs, in the absence of prior evidence, is therefore consistent with the requirements of rationality.

Another way of analyzing the mistake involved here is to say that it confuses two kinds of evidential warrant. Consider the legal analogy embodied in the empistemological term 'warrant'. What kind of warrant does rationality demand of someone in a state of belief? I contend that rationality requires a warrant for occupying that state, not for entering it. To be in a state of belief without a warrant is irrational; but to enter a state of belief without a warrant may be rational, if a valid warrant of occupancy is to be found within.

Thus doxastic warrant is less like a search warrant than it is like a landholder's right of possession. If the police want to search a house, they must show their warrant at the door; and so if they ever needed to search a house in order to obtain a warrant for searching it, they would never be allowed in. But a prospective landholder may sometimes enter a piece of land for the purpose of obtaining the right to it -- for instance, if he is homesteading.[21]

My view is that an agent stakes a claim, if you will, to a belief about his future conduct. That is, he enters upon such a belief in the confidence of thereby gaining the right to occupy it. The agent may thus form an expectation about his forthcoming action without being prompted by evidence. His expectation is a conclusion to which he jumps before the evidence is complete; but he jumps with the assurance that the evidence will be completed even as he lands.[22]

C. Beliefs Adopted as a Means to Their Fulfillment

This brings me to a third assumption -- also undefended -- which is that you have a rough and ready understanding of how your reflective expectations influence your actions, and hence of your latitude in forming such expectations. That is, you know that you tend to do whatever you expect, and that there are therefore several different actions that you would be equally justified in expecting.

One consequence of this last assumption is that you can be moved to expect an action by the desire to prompt its performance. Since you feel free to expect whichever action you like (among the ones that you would perform if you expected to), which action you expect depends on which one you'd like to ex-

---

[21] I am grateful to Don Loeb for helping me to fill out this legal analogy.

[22] Here I am subscribing to a view put forward, most famously, by William James:

> There are ... cases where a fact cannot come at all unless a preliminary faith exists in its coming. *And where faith in a fact can help create the fact,* that would be an insane logic which should say that faith running ahead of scientific evidence is the 'lowest kind of immorality' into which a thinking being can fall. ["The Will to Believe," in *Essays on Faith and Morals* (New York: New American Library, 1974) 32 - 62, p. 56.]

I would add that forming a self-fulfilling belief isn't merely "running ahead" of the evidence: it's running *toward* the evidence -- that is, toward evidence that will consist in the belief itself. For if faith in a fact can help create the fact, then the faith can constitute decisive evidence in its own favor. To rule out beliefs that would thus be justified as soon as they existed would indeed be an insane logic.

pect. And since you know that expecting an action is way of
getting yourself to perform it, which action you'd like to expect depends which one you'd like to get yourself to perform.
Hence your expectation of performing an action is occasioned by
your desire that you perform it.

Another consequence of my third assumption is that your reflective expectations can represent themselves as bringing about
the expected action, and as having been formed at the instance
of your desire to bring that action about. Because you know
that you'll do whatever you expect, your expectation, though
sometimes expressed simply as "I'm going to do it," can more
accurately be expressed as "I'm hereby causing myself to do it."

The resulting beliefs are the ones that I identify with intentions to act. They have all of the characteristic features.
Like intentions, they both represent a forthcoming action and
tend to bring it about. Like intentions, they are formed, not
at the dictation of antecedent evidence about your forthcoming
action, but rather at the instance of a desire to bring the action about. And like intentions, they represent themselves as
having these first two features -- that is, as tending to bring
about an action at the instance of a desire.[23] In sum, the beliefs in question resemble intentions in that they are self-fulfilling mental representations that are adopted as a means to
their fulfillment and that represent themselves as such.[24]

----

[23]See the works cited in note 10, above.

Harman believes that some intentions do not represent themselves as
bringing about the intended action. He calls these "negative" intentions,
because they are mostly intentions *not* to do things, although the content
of such intentions can of course be rephrased in positive terms. Harman's
example of negative intention is the case in which I intend not to go out
tonight, even though I believe that I wouldn't have gone out anyway. In
this case, according to Harman, my intention doesn't present itself as
causing me not to go out.

The problem here is that Harman doesn't describe the case with sufficient precision. Although he says my intention is not "responsible" for my
staying in tonight, he also says that it "settles that issue," -- i.e., the
issue of whether to go out -- so that I can make plans for my evening at
home [*Change in View,* p. 80]. But surely if I were already certain of not
going out, then there would be no issue to settle, and I could make home-
bound plans without forming an intention of not going out. Just imagine a
prisoner saying, "I intend to stay in tonight." This remark would be iron-
ic: the prisoner isn't in any position to intend on staying in, precisely
because there is no question of his going out, and hence no issue to be
settled by his intention.

(Footnote 23 continued on page 376. Footnote 24 on page 376.)

II
Freedom of the
Doxastic Will

My main reason for identifying intentions with self-consciously optional and self-fulfilling beliefs that this identification provides some insight into the question of free will.

The will, after all, is the capacity to form intentions. And if intentions are self-consciously optional and self-fulfilling beliefs, then the will is the capacity to form those beliefs. In what respects would the will, so conceived, be free?

Well, I think that our capacity to form reflective expectations is free in one rather impressive respect. When we form the expectation of doing something next, we aren't bound by the evidence about what our motives will cause us to do. We aren't bound by this evidence even though it is there -- even though our forthcoming action can be deduced from the antecedent state of our motives. Our motives have the force of conclusive evidence about our next action, and yet our intentions -- which consist in predictions of that action -- are immune to that force.

How could our predictions be immune to the force of conclusive evidence about the events that they predict? Let me explain.

(Continued from page 375)
     The case that Harman seems to have in mind is one in which I think that I am unlikely to go out in any case, but I want to make sure. I form my intention in order to rule out an eventuality that I already regard as unlikely. In this case, however, I regard my intention as reducing the probability of my going out, and hence as raising the probability of my staying in, which is the intended outcome. I may not want to call the intention "responsible" for my staying in; but I do think that I will stay in partly because of the intention -- that is, partly because of its having raised the probability of my staying in. Here I am making a causal judgment of a familiar statistical variety.

[24]These beliefs are somewhat restricted by antecedent evidence, of course, but so are intentions: just as you aren't entitled to expect an action unless you would perform it if you expected to, so (I would claim) you aren't entitled to intend an action unless you would perform it if you intended to. This last point is somewhat controversial, and I shall defend it below.

A. Freedom from the Evidence

I shall begin my explanation by considering the epistemic position of an ideal outside observer who seeks to predict your actions, an observer who obtains all the prior evidence that can
in principle be obtained. Such an observer will learn all there
is to be learned about your motives for acting, their relative
strengths, and their probable consequences. If my theory of
self-knowledge is right, one of the motives he learns about will
be your desire to know what you're doing, a desire that first
discourages you from doing anything until you anticipate what it
will be, and then encourages you to do whatever you anticipate.
He will also find various sets of other motives, favoring various alternative actions, each set being strong enough to prevail
over the others if it is reinforced, while they are opposed, by
your motive for doing what you anticipate. An ideal observer
will therefore conclude that, among the actions toward which
you're predisposed, your next one will be whichever one you expect. In order to predict your next action, then, he will try
to predict your expectation.

Now, your expectation should be predictable -- at least, in
principle. Which action you come to expect will be determined
largely by your current attitudes. One such attitude is your
awareness of several actions as equal candidates, of which you
can expect whichever you prefer; another relevant attitude is
your preference for expecting, and thereby prompting, one of
these actions instead of the others. An ideal observer could
predict that the action you expect will be the one you prefer to
expect, and that you'll prefer to expect whichever action you
most want yourself to perform. The action that you most want
yourself to perform is the one that an outside observer would
predict that you'd expect, and hence perform.

For an outside observer, this prediction would be dictated by
the prior evidence -- evidence about your inclinations toward
various actions; your inclination to perform whichever action
you expect; and your inclination to expect one action rather
than the others. If the evidence about these inclinations dictates which action an outside observer should expect of you, why
doesn't it similarly dictate what you, the agent, should expect?

The answer is that such evidence dictates which action an
observer *should* expect only because it includes information
about which action you, the agent, *will* expect. And this information rules out alternative expectations for outside observers but not for you. The present evidence shows that you are
going to perform a particular action next, and hence that expecting a different action would be incorrect. Yet expecting a
different action would be incorrect, according to the present
evidence, only because, according to that evidence, *you* aren't
going to expect one. If you did expect to perform a different

action, you would thereby prove the present evidence to have
been incorrect about what you were going to expect, and hence
about what you were going to do; and you would thereby create
different evidence, justifying you in expecting a different action. As it happens, this alternative expectation is false, but
only because you won't in fact form it. It would be true if you
formed it, and so its falsity doesn't constitute any reason
against your forming it.

Look at it this way. The evidence about your forthcoming action is compelling to an outside observer because it indicates
that a particular action is going to occur next whether or not
he expects so, and hence that he had better expect so, on pain
of error. But the evidence indicates something different to
you, the agent. To you, it indicates -- not that the action is
going to occur next whether or not you expect so -- but rather
that it's going to occur next because you're about to expect so.
Thus, it doesn't indicate that you had better expect the action,
on pain of error. Quite the reverse: it indicates that if you
didn't expect the action, it wouldn't occur, and hence that you
are immune to error. The evidence therefore doesn't compel you
as it does the outside observer.

In short, there may be conclusive evidence to the effect that
you're going to expect a given action and hence determine yourself to perform it next. That evidence may forbid anyone else
from expecting you to act differently. But it doesn't forbid
you from expecting yourself to act differently; for if you did,
you would.

B. Freedom from the Evidence as Freedom of the Will

In forming intentions, then, we are forming behavioral predictions that are unconstrained by the motivational evidence. Our
motives indicate which action we'll take, and yet we aren't obliged, epistemically speaking, to predict the action they indicate. Therein lies our freedom.

The freedom of our wills thus resides in what we'd be epistemically justified in believing, and hence intending; but it
also has tangible effects on how we actually form the beliefs
constituting our intentions. Because we're entitled to contravene the evidence, we feel free to disregard it, and to let our
desires determine what we believe. The result is that reflective predictions are formed differently from other predictions.
In predicting ordinary events we tend to take our cue from the
evidence, suppressing our desires about what to believe. In
predicting our forthcoming actions, however, we tend to forget
about the evidence and believe what we want. We don't discover
our next action: we invent it.

What's especially odd about this method of reflective forecasting is that it isn't due to any indeterminacy in the events
being forecast. Our next action is predetermined: its nature
has already solidified, as a fact to be discovered. Even so,
that fact never obtrudes itself upon us as we look toward our
future. In foretelling our next action, we can tell it as we
like, without deferring to the present evidence, which already
foreshadows it as it will be. The reason, once again, is that
the present evidence foreshadows our action only by foreshadow-
ing our forecast, and so a different forecast would be self-jus-
tifying.

C. Epistemic vs. Metaphysical Freedom

Now, to say that our intentions, considered as predictions, are
independent of our motives, considered as evidence, is not to
say that our intentions are completely independent of our motives. In forming our intentions, we invent our next action
without regard to what our motives foreshadow, but we don't invent anything unless we have adequate motives for inventing it.
Insofar as we can predict whatever we want, we are liberated
from the motivational evidence; but insofar as we don't predict
anything unless we want to, we are still the slaves of our motives.

In short, epistemic freedom of will is not metaphysical freedom. It's the right to expect, and thereby intend, any action
we like, despite motivational evidence that we'll intend and act
otherwise. Insofar as we exercise this right, we expect what we
like, rather than what prior evidence dictates; but insofar as
we expect what we like, our expectations -- and hence our intentions -- are causally determined. Metaphysical or contracausal
freedom from our motives is wholly absent from my account of intentions. According to my account, we do whatever we most want
to do, which depends partly on what we have intended; and we intend whatever we most want to intend, which depends on what we
most wants ourselves to do. In this respect, our intentions and
our actions are fully determined by our motives.

Unfortunately, we may be tempted to describe our epistemic
freedom in words that can be interpreted metaphysically. We may
say, for instance, that we can form intentions contrary to our
strongest motives. This statement is true so long as it means
that, no matter what our strongest motives indicate that we
shall intend and consequently do, we would be epistemically justified in expecting to do something else. But the same statement may be taken to mean that our intentions or actions can
somehow buck the causal force of our strongest motives. And in
the latter, metaphysical interpretation, the statement is simply
false. An intention is a behavioral prediction that needn't be
derived from our motives, in their capacity as evidence. But
our forming an intention is an event, and this event is caused

by our motives, in their capacity as dispositions. The problem is that the inferential slack between motives-as-evidence and intentions-as-beliefs is mistaken for causal slack between the corresponding dispositions and events. Thus is the epistemic freedom of our wills mistakenly projected onto the world, as metaphysical freedom -- in much the way that Hume described.[25]

One might suspect that I have overstated our epistemic freedom, given our metaphysical bondage. Although we can indeed believe what we like about our forthcoming actions, the reason might seem to be, not that we're entitled to contravene the evidence, but rather that we're predetermined not to contravene it. After all, if the evidence indicates that we're bound to do something because our desires will make us expect to, then it indicates that our desires will make us expect precisely what we're bound to do. Perhaps, then, the reason why we can allow our desires to determine our beliefs is that they can be trusted to keep our beliefs in line with the evidence.

But no. To say that we can believe what we want because it is bound to be congruent with the evidence is to suggest that congruence with the evidence is a desideratum for us -- which it isn't. The idea of relying on our desires to keep us in line with the evidence grossly misrepresents our situation, in which conformity to the evidence is of no concern to us. *Our departing from the evidence would be causally impossible, but it would be epistemically permissible; and precisely because it would be epistemically permissible, its impossibility is unimportant.*

Still, epistemic freedom may seem worthless without its metaphysical counterpart. If we don't have metaphysical freedom, then our right to contravene the motivational evidence is a right that we haven't the power to exercise. For although we're entitled to expect an action other than the one indicated by the evidence, our motives predetermine that we're not going to form that alternative expectation. What good is an epistemic license that we are predetermined not to invoke?

_____

[25]Hume believed that we think of two events as causally connected insofar as we feel constrained to infer the occurrence of one event from that of the other. The concept of causal necessity, according to Hume, is simply the feeling of inferential constraint mistakenly projected onto the event inferred; and the concept of freedom from causality is a similar projection of our freedom from inferential constraint. (For this view about the concept of freedom, see, e.g., *A Treatise of Human Nature,* II iii 2, (Oxford: Clarendon Press, 1978), p. 408.) I don't believe that this confusion can account for our concepts of causal necessity and freedom; but I do believe that a similar confusion can account for our belief in contracausal freedom of the will.

Well, to say that we lack the metaphysical freedom to contravene the evidence is not to say that we never invoke our epistemic license to do so. We invoke our license to contravene the evidence whenever we let our desires determine our beliefs. We believe what we want, and we do so precisely because the evidence has no authority over us. To be sure, we end up believing just what the evidence would have dictated, if given the authority; but we believe it because we want to, not because the evidence would have dictated it. Thus, our stance toward the resulting belief -- which constitutes our intention -- is radically altered by our epistemic freedom, even if the content of that belief is not.

D. Does Epistemic Freedom Entail Metaphyscial Freedom?

Some philosophers have attempted to bridge the gap between epistemic and metaphysical freedom, by showing that the existence of the one entails the existence of the other.[26]

Their argument, in its clearest form, goes something like this.[27] A person cannot predict an action immediately before he

---

[26]Those who make this attempt include Carl Ginet, "Can the Will Be Caused?" 61 *Philosophical Review* 49 - 55 (1962); and Richard Taylor, "Deliberation and Foreknowledge," 1 *American Philosophical Quarterly* 73 - 80 (1964). Related arguments appear in: Stuart Hampshire and H.L.A. Hart, "Decision, Intention and Certainty," 67 *Mind* 1 - 12 (1958); Stuart Hampshire, *Thought and Action* (London: Chatto and Windus, 1965), and *Freedom of the Individual* (Princeton: Princeton University Press, 1975); and D. M. Mackay, "On the Logical Indeterminacy of a Free Choice," 69 *Mind* 31 - 40 (1960). For comments on these works, see David Pears, "Predicting and Deciding," 50 *Proceedings of the British Academy* 193 - 227 (1964); John Canfield, "Knowing about Future Decisions," 22 *Analysis* 127 - 129 (1962) ; Andrew Oldenquist, "Causes, Predictions and Decisions," 24 *Analysis* 55 - 58 (1964); Alvin I. Goldman, *A Theory of Human Action*, *op. cit.*, Chapter Six; and Roy A. Sorensen, "Uncaused Decisions and Pre-Decisional Blindspots," 45 *Philosophical Studies* 51 - 56 (1984).

[27]Here I am using Ginet's argument, as clarified by Sorensen. See Ginet, *op. cit.*, p. 51:

> For a person to claim that he knows what he will decide to do, hence, what he will at least try to do, and *then* to begin the process of making up his mind what he will do -- trying to persuade himself one way or another by offering himself reasons for and against the various alternatives -- would surely be a procedure of which we could make no sense. Either his undertaking to make a decision belies his prior claim to knowledge, or his prior claim makes a farce of his undertaking to make a decision.

decides whether to perform it, since his foreknowledge would reveal that the issue to be decided was moot, thus preempting his decision. If a person's decisions were caused, however, there would be grounds on which he could predict them; and if he could predict the decisions, then he could also predict the resulting actions. But as we have just seen, a person cannot predict actions that he is to decide; and so his decisions must not be caused.

There are several possible objections to this argument, and I shall not consider all of them. My objection is that the argument misconstrues the decider's epistemic freedom. The first premise of the argument says, in effect, that a necessary condition of something's being a decision is that it be epistemically free -- in other words, that it not be preempted by prior evidence about the outcome that one is purporting to decide. The second premise is that if one's decision were caused, then it wouldn't be epistemically free, since its causes would constitute compelling evidence about the outcome that one was purporting to decide. The conclusion is that a decision cannot be caused.

The mistake here is in the assumption that if a decision were caused, then its causes would constitute evidence that would be compelling, for the decider, about the outcome being decided. The argument assumes that if a person knew of causes sufficient to make him decide upon an action, he would be compelled to expect that he'd try to perform that action, and hence could no longer undertake to decide whether to perform it. But as we have seen, an agent cannot be compelled to expect an action by evidence that he's going to decide upon it and consequently try to perform it. The reason is that the agent would be justified in defying such evidence, by expecting a different action, precisely because he would thereby be reaching a different decision. Since the agent is entitled to expect himself to do something other than what prior conditions indicate that he will, he needn't regard those conditions as prempting his decision.

III
Replies to Objections

The doxastic theory of intention has been criticized at two levels. Some philosophers have directly attacked the thesis that intentions consist in beliefs. Others have attacked a weaker thesis, arguing that the intention to act, far from consisting in the belief that one will act, doesn't even entail the presence of that belief. I shall consider one criticism on each level.

A.   Intention Entails Belief

Donald Davidson is foremost among the philosophers who have attempted to refute the thesis that intention entails belief.[28] Davidson offers counterexamples that purport to show an agent intending to perform a difficult task without necessarily believing that he will succeed. For instance, "in writing on this page I may be intending to produce ten legible carbon copies," and yet "I do not know, or believe with any confidence, that I am succeeding."[29] From such examples Davidson concludes that intending to do something doesn't necessarily entail believing that one will do it.

Gilbert Harman offers several persuasive arguments to defeat such examples, and what I shall say here is merely an amplification of Harman's arguments.[30] He points out, for instance, that if we wish to concede the difficulty of a task, we don't say

---

[28]"Intending,"*op. cit.*, p. 92. For a useful discussion of Davidson's theory of intention, seen M. Bratman, "Davidson's Theory of Intention," in B. Vermazen and M.B. Hintikka (eds.), *op. cit.*, pp. 13 - 26. Bratman is among those who have joined Davidson in denying that intention entails belief ("Intention and Means-Ends Reasoning," *op. cit.*, pp. 254 - 256; "Two Faces of Intention," *op. cit.*, pp. 384 - 385). However, Bratman does think that intending to do something while believing that one won't do it is irrational ("Castañeda's Theory of Thought and Action," in James E. Tomberlin (ed.), *op. cit.*, 149 - 169, pp. 159 ff). Others who deny that intention entails belief include: David L. Perry, "Prediction, Explanation and Freedom," 49 *Monist* 234 - 247 (1965); Hector-Neri Castañeda, *Thinking and Doing; the philosophical foundaions of institutions* (Dordrecht: D. Reidel, 1975, pp. 41 - 42; Myles Brand, *Intending and Acting, op. cit.*, Chapter Six; Christopher Peacocke, "Intention and *Akrasia*, " *op. cit.*; and Hugh McCann, "Rationality and the Range of Intention," *op. cit.*

Philosophers who have endorsed the thesis that intention entails belief include not only Harman and Grice but also Stuart Hampshire and H.L.A. Hart in "Decision, Intention and Certainty," *op. cit.*; Stuart Hampshire in *Thought and Action, op. cit.*, and *Freedom of the Individual, op. cit.*; Roderick Chisholm in "The Structure of Intending," 67 *Journal of Philosophy* 633 - 647 (1970), p. 646; Robert Audi in "Intending," 70 *Journal of Philosophy* 387 - 403 (1973); Jaegwon Kim in "Intention and Practical Inference," Juha Manninen and Raimo Tuomela (eds.), *Essays on Explanation and Understanding* (Dordrecht: D. Reidel, 1976), 249 - 269, pp. 259 - 260; Monroe C. Beardsley in "Intending," Alvin Goldman and Jaegwon Kim (eds.), *Values and Morals; essays in honor of William Frankena, Charles Stevenson, and Richard Brandt* (Dordrecht: D. Reidel, 1978) 163 - 184; and David Pears in "Predicting and Deciding," 50 *Proceedings of the British Academy* 193 - 227 (1964), pp. 197 - 198; *Motivated Irrationality, op. cit.*, p. 124; and "Intention and Belief," *op. cit.*, 75 -88.

[29]*Op. cit.*, p. 92.

[30]In "Willing and Intending," *op. cit.*

that we intend to accomplish it; we say that we intend to try.[31]

---

[31]David Pears has argued that the intention of trying to do something is no different in content from the intention of doing it ("Intention and Belief," *op. cit.*, p. 86). Pears's argument is this: "[I]f I were asked whether I had done what I intended to do when I had tried and failed, I would give a negative answer." Hugh McCann has argued, somewhat similarly, that trying to do something entails intending to do it; and hence that an intention to try has, as its object, something that entails the intention to succeed (*op. cit.*, pp. 196 ff.).

The proper response here, I think, is that Pears and McCann are falling prey to an ambiguity in the idiomatic use of the word 'intention'. [Harman notes this ambiguity in *Change in View, op. cit.*, pp. 93 - 94. The existence of any ambiguity is denied by G.E.M. Anscome in *Intention, op. cit.*, p. 1; and by Davidson, *Intending, op. cit.*] In one sense, the word denotes a distinctive mental state, which can be recognized most easily, perhaps, as the state by which a person brings his deliberations to a close. The state is that of *being decided upon* an action, and it gets formed typically, though not only, when a person deliberates about what to do and concludes by making a decision. The word 'intention' is used in another sense, however, when it denotes the intention with which a person acts. To act with the intention of doing something is to act for the sake of doing it -- to have the deed as one's goal. And there is an obvious difference between having a deed as one's goal and being decided upon doing it. [The difference between intention and goal is noted by Annette C. Baier in "Act and Intent," 67 *Journal of Philosophy* 648 - 658 (1970), p. 649 ff. Baier's remarks are endorsed by Hector-Neri Castañeda in "Intentions and Intending," 9 *American Philosophical Quarterly* 139 - 149 (1972), p. 140.]

A person isn't said to be decided upon something if it isn't within his control. An Olympic athlete cannot ordinarily decide to win a gold medal, since whether he wins is not within his control and hence not for him to decide. Yet an outcome needn't be within a person's control in order to be among his goals; indeed, being within the person's immediate control would tend to exclude an outcome from his goals, since a goal is something whose attainment requires intermediate steps. Although an athlete's goals may include winning a gold medal, for example, they do not include taking his next breath, since there's no point in his making a goal out of something that he can accomplish straightaway, without any further ado.

The problem is that we use the word 'intend' equivocally, both for having a goal and for being decided upon an action. No wonder, then, that Pears and McCann cannot imagine intending to try without intending to succeed. If one tries or intends to try, then success is one's goal; and it is therefore what one intends, in one sense of the word. The fact remains, however, that one wouldn't need to speak of trying if one could simply have decided to succeed; and so intending to succeed, in the sense of having success as one's goal, does not entail having an intention of succeeding, in the sense of being decided upon it.

(Footnote 31 continued on page 385)

He argues, further, that in some cases in which an agent is thought to intend an action without expecting to perform it, he doesn't really intend the action, but only seems to, because he ends up performing it intentionally. Yet one can do something intentionally without having an intention of doing it;[33] and so the fact that one can do something intentionally without having expected to do it doesn't prove that intention can exist without belief.

I want to skip over both of these arguments, however, in order to focus on a third, because it is one that Davidson attempts to forestall, in a way that is deeply mistaken. Harman points out that apparent discrepancies between an agent's intentions and his beliefs may be due to differences in the precision with which the attitudes in question are expressed. Just as a person can be said to intend an action even though he concedes that his attempt at it may fail, so he can be said to expect the action despite the same concession. That is, he can admit the possibility of failure and still be said to believe that he'll succeed. Hence Davidson's doubts about whether he'll make ten carbon copies should not prevent him from saying that he still believes he'll make them, any more than they prevent him from saying that he intends to. Davidson can of course reject this characterization of his belief, arguing that if he admits the possibility of failure, then all he believes, strictly speaking, is that he'll he make the copies if he can. But then, Harman argues, equal precision should be introduced into the characterization of his intention. If the claim that Davidson expects

---

(Continued from page 384)
The sense of the word 'intention' that I am defining is the sense that denotes the mental state of being decided. I could have called this state a decision, but that term seems to denote, not the state itself, but the process of forming it. And even when 'decision' denotes a state, it seems to imply that the state in question has closed an actual episode of deliberation; whereas I claim only that the state is of the sort that characteristically closes deliberation, when deliberation occurs and reaches closure. The same state can also be formed without any deliberation at all -- in which case it *fore* closes deliberation rather than closes it.

Now, if Davidson doesn't know whether his attempt to make ten carbon copies will succeed, then he cannot have decided, or be decided, upon making them. He can still intend to make them, in the sense that he can have making them as his goal. But the most that he can intend in my sense -- that is, the most that he can be decided upon -- is to try. Hence Davidson's example is not one in which he intends do something, in my sense of the word, without believing that he will.

[33]Harman defends this claim at length in "Rational Action and the Extent of Intentions," 9 *Social Theory and Practice* 123 - 142 (1983).

to succeed should be qualified, on the grounds that what he
expects, strictly speaking, is to succeed if he can; then the
claim that he intends to succeed should undergo the same qualification. Speaking with equal strictness, what Davidson intends
is to make ten carbon copies if he can; and so his intention
still corresponds to his belief.

Davidson objects to the suggestion that his counterexamples
involve intentions whose precise expression would require such
qualifications. On the one hand, he contends that if intention
did entail belief, then 'I intend to do it if I can' would convey no more or less than 'I intend to do it', since nobody uttering the latter would be thought to believe, and hence to intend, that he would do the thing even if he couldn't. On the
other hand, Davidson would also reject the suggestion that he
should say something more specific, like "I intend to make ten
copies if this paper isn't too thick." For according to
Davidson, if precision required an agent to mention one condition that he considered necessary to the intended outcome, then
it would require him to mention many such conditions -- which it
clearly doesn't. Thus Davidson would argue, for instance, that
if precision required him to say "I intend to make ten copies if
this paper isn't too thick," on the grounds that he doesn't believe he'll succeed if it is, then precision would also require
him to say "I intend to make ten copies if I'm not struck by
lightning, or kidnapped by terrorists," and so on, since he
doesn't believe that he'll succeed in any of those circumstances, either. But the latter statement, having been qualified to
death, would tell us little about what Davidson intended; and so
he concludes that precision doesn't require him to mention any
such conditions. In his view, an agent who states an unqualified intention of doing something, but doesn't expect to do it,
need not be omitting anything from his statement of intention.

One problem with these objections is that even if they were
valid, they would apply not just to statements of intention but
to statements of belief as well, thus frustrating Davidson's attempt to drive a wedge between the two attitudes. Davidson
claims that he intends to make ten carbon copies but that he
doesn't believe he will. But Davidson would surely admit to believing that he'll make the copies if he can; and then his own
objections should persuade him to drop the qualifier "if I can,"
and to admit that he believes simply that he'll make the copies.
For if the qualifying phrase "if I can" would have added nothing
to Davidson's statement of intention, then it would add nothing
to his statement of belief, either, and for the same reason --
namely, that nobody would take him to believe that he'd make the
copies even if he couldn't. And if the phrase "if I can" were
no more necessary to a precise statement of inention than other,
superfluous phrases such as "unless I'm struck by lightning,"
then why would it be more necessary to a precise statement of
belief?   Thus Davidson's reasons for making an unqualified

statement of intention would also favor an unqualified statement of belief, thereby removing the discrepancy between his beliefs and intentions.

Of course, Davidson shouldn't remove the qualifier "if I can" from the expression of his belief. But this just goes to show that there's something wrong with his reasons for removing it from the expression of his intention. Indeed, Davidson's article subsequently provides an example that shows what's wrong.[34] Consider the following passage:[35]

> I intend to eat a hearty breakfast tomorrow. You know, and I know, that I will not eat a hearty breakfast tomorrow if I am not hungry. And I am not certain I will be hungry, I just think I will be. Under these conditions it is not only not more accurate to say, 'I intend to eat a hearty breakfast if I'm hungry', it is *less* accurate. I have the second intention as well as the first, but the first implies the second, and not vice versa, and so the first is a more complete account of my intentions. If you knew only that I intended to eat a hearty breakfast if I was hungry, you would not know that I believe I will be hungry, which is actually the case. But you might figure this out if you knew I intend to eat a hearty breakfast tomorrow.

According to Davidson, if we know that he intends simply to eat breakfast, rather than to eat it if he's hungry, we can then infer that he expects to be hungry. What Davidson doesn't mention is that we might have drawn a different inference -- namely, that he intends to eat breakfast whether he's hungry or not. For all we know, Davidson could be one of those health enthusiasts who force themselves to eat three square meals a day no matter what. But the intention of eating no matter what is not the intention that Davidson professes to have. He implies, on the contrary, that he has no intention of eating if he isn't hungry. But his intention is nevertheless unqualified, because he assumes that he will be hungry -- which is what he expects us to to infer.

The real moral of Davidson's story, then, is that there are two different ways of intending without qualification. An agent

---

[34]For a slightly different, though compatible explanation, see, G.E.M. Anscombe, *Intention, op. cit.*, p. 92 - 93.

[35]p. 100.

can flatly intend to do something either because he intends to do it under any condition or because he intends to do it under particular conditions that he believes will obtain.[36] Davidson's unqualified intention of eating breakfast can arise from either of two underlying states -- an intention of eating whether or not he's hungry; or an intention of eating if he's hungry, together with the belief that he will be.

Because an unqualified intention can arise in two different ways, the implications of qualifying the statement of an intention are doubled. For as Davidson points out, stating a qualified intention is imprecise if one could have stated the same intention unqualified. The result is that if someone says "I intend to eat breakfast if I'm hungry" and purports to be speaking precisely, then he implies that he isn't in a position to form an unqualified intention of eating breakfast. As we have seen, he would have been in a position to form the unqualified intention either if he had intended to eat no matter what, or if, in addition to intending to eat if he was hungry, he assumed that he would be hungry. Hence someone who says "I intend to eat if I'm hungry" implies, not only that he doesn't intend to eat unless he's hungry, but also that he isn't assuming that he will be.

We can now see that Davidson was mistaken to say that, if intention entails belief, then the statement "I intend to do it if I can" says no more or less than "I intend to do it." As we have just seen, the qualified statement implies, not only that one doesn't intend to do the thing unless one can, but also that one isn't assuming that one can do it. The former implication may be trivial, if intention entails belief, but the latter is not. Conversely, the unqualified statement "I intend to do it" implies that one either intends to do the thing even if one can't or is assuming that one can. And although the former implication is absurd, if intention entails belief, the latter is not.

Davidson was equally mistaken when he said that if precision required an agent to mention one condition that he considered necessary to the intended outcome, then it would require him to

---

[36]See Michael Bratman, "Simple Intention," 36 *Philosophical Studies* 245 - 259 (1979), p. 246:

> Ordinary language distinguishes between conditions which are cited in the content of a conditional intention and those conditions whose expectation serves as a background against which one's intentions are held. Though these latter conditions are not cited in the content of one's intention, they constitute circumstances of the intended action whose expectation qualifies one's intention.

mention all such conditions. What precision requires is that the agent mention only those conditions which meet two criteria -- namely, that he considers them necessary to the intended outcome and that he isn't confident of their being satisfied. Hence precision may well require Davidson to say "I intend to make ten copies if this paper isn't too thick," but not "...if I'm not struck by lightning," and so on. For Davidson may assume that he won't be struck by lightning, while suspecting that the paper is, in fact, too thick.

I therefore reject Davidson's reasons against qualifying his statement of intention.[37] The point of saying "I intend to make ten copies if I can" would be -- not to rule out the notion that he intends to make the copies even if he can't, which would be absurd whether or not intention entailed belief -- but rather to express uncertainty about whether he can make the copies, which is precisely what prevents him (so he claims) from believing categorically that he will. The doubts that lead Davidson to qualify his statement of belief should therefore lead him to qualify his statement of intention;[38] and so I stand by my contention that Davidson believes precisely what he intends.

B. Intention Consists in Belief

Thus far I have been considering Davidson's objection to the thesis that intention entails belief. Davidson also objects to the stronger thesis, that intention actually consists in belief. Davidson's argument against identifying intention with belief is that "reasons for intending to do something are in general quite different from reasons for believing one will do it":[39]

---

[37]Davidson offers one further reason, which I find equally unconvincing. He argues that the intention "I'll do it if I can" is not genuinely conditional, as is the intention "I'll leave the picnic if it starts to rain" (p. 94). (The same point is made by Hugh McCann in "Rationality and the Range of Intention," op. cit., p. 197). True enough, the relation between antecedent and consequent in "I'll do it if I can" is different from that in "I'll leave if it rains." But all that this contrast can prove is that intentions can be conditional in more than one way. We place conditions on some intentions in order to make them consistent with conditional desires -- that is, desires to act only under certain conditions. We place conditions on other intentions in order to make them consistent with our beliefs about the conditions under which they can be fulfilled. The fact that the resulting intentions are conditional in different ways doesn't entail that some of them aren't genuinely conditional.

[38]I believe that the same arguments would prevail against a counterexample offered by Michael Bratman in "Two Faces of Intention," 93 *Philosophical Review* 375 - 405, pp. 384 - 385 (1984).

[39]*Op. cit.*, p. 95.

Here is why I intend to reef the main: I see a squall coming, I want to prevent the boat from capsizing, and I believe that reefing the main will prevent the boat from capsizing. I would put my reasons for intending to reef the main this way: a squall is coming, it would be a shame to capsize the boat, and reefing the main will prevent the boat from capsizing. But these reasons for intending to reef the main in themselves give me no reason to believe I will reef the main. Given additional assumptions, for example, that the approach of a squall is a reason to believe I believe a squall is coming, and that the shamefulness of capsizing the boat may be a reason to believe I want to prevent the boat from capsizing; and given that I have these beliefs and desires, it may be reasonable to suppose I intend to reef the main, and will in fact do so. So there may be loose connection between reasons of the two kinds, but they are not at all identical (individual reasons may be the same, but a smallest natural set of reasons that supports the intention to act cannot be set that support the belief that the act will take place).

I find this argument difficult to interpret. For one thing, I can't figure out what Davidson takes himself to be introducing with the words, "Here is why I intend to reef the main ... ." He seems to be introducing the reasons for his intention. Yet the reasons thus introduced have to do with his motivating attitudes -- that is, with his perceptions, desires, and beliefs -- which are later said to provide reasons for believing that he will reef the main. And in the very next sentence, Davidson suggests that his reasons for intending to reef the main have to do, not with his attitudes (e.g., "I see a squall coming"), but rather with the external circumstances that they represent (e.g., "a squall is coming").[40]

Partly because of this inconsistency, I'm not sure what Davidson thinks is the difference between reasons for intending to do something and reasons for believing that one will do it. At the end of the paragraph he concedes that some reasons can serve in both capacities. Hence the difference between reasons for intending and reasons for believing, in Davidson's eyes, cannot be that they consist in items of different kinds or with

---

[40]Davidson introduces the latter formulation with the words "I would put my reasons for intending to reef the main this way ... ." Is he trying to suggest that there's a difference between the reasons why he intends to reef the main and how he would put his reasons for so intending? What would this difference have to do with that between reasons for intending and reasons for believing?

different contents. The closest that Davidson comes to defining the difference is his claim that "a smallest natural set of reasons that supports the intention to act cannot be a set that supports the belief that the act will take place." But he never explains or defends this claim.

Before I can rebut Davidson's argument, then, I first have to guess what it is. My guess is that the argument goes something like this. Davidson assumes that his reasons for believing "I am going to reef the main" must be considerations that induce him to believe it, and that do so by indicating that it's true. Yet he cannot be induced to intend "I am going to reef the main" by considerations indicating that it's true, since the whole point of having an intention with this content is to make it true. That is, the point of Davidson's intending "I'm going to reef the main" is to bring about his reefing the main; and so considerations indicating that he is already going to reef the main would seem to prove the intention superfluous. Davidson therefore concludes that any set of reasons sufficient to support the belief would be sufficient to preempt the intention, while any set of reasons that didn't preempt the intention wouldn't support the belief.

The problem with this argument is that its initial assumption is false in the case of an agent's reflective predictions. For as I have shown, an agent cannot be induced to make reflective predictions by considerations indicating their truth. When an agent believes that he's going to act, he does of course rely on considerations that he regards as indicating the truth of his belief; but these considerations necessarily include the fact that he already holds the belief, and so they couldn't have induced him to form it. And considerations preceding the belief couldn't have induced him to form it, either, since they would have indicated, at most, that the belief was true because he was going to form it -- and hence that it wouldn't be true if he didn't.

What induces the agent to form his reflective prediction, I believe, is the desire to make it true, not his evidence for its truth. Since what induces the agent to form his reflective prediction is different from his evidence for the prediction, the phrase 'reason for believing' cannot in this case mean "belief-inducing evidence." It must mean either what induces the belief or what is taken as evidence of its truth, but not both. And neither reading of the phrase yields any objection to the thesis that the belief constitutes an intention.

If 'reason' means that which induces formation of the belief, then Davidson's reason for believing that he'll reef the main is identical with what we would ordinarily take to be a reason for intending to reef main -- namely, a conscious desire to get him-

self to reef the main.[41]   And if 'reason' means that which is
taken as indicating the belief's truth, then Davidson's reason
for believing that he'll reef the main, though not identical
with a reason for intending to, is identical with a necessary
presupposition of that intention, and hence not capable of preempting it.   For in that case, his reason for believing that
he'll reef the main is the fact that his holding this very belief will make its content true.   And this fact cannot preempt
the coinciding intention; on the contrary, an intention posi-
tively depends on the presupposition that the agent's holding it
will make its content true, since there would otherwise be no
point in holding it at all.   Indeed, preempting the intention
would entail defeating this very presupposition of the intention's efficacy.   Hence evidence that confirms the presupposition can hardly preempt the intention.

Note, here, how epistemological confusions are once again to
blame for the distinction between the theoretical and the practical.   What leads Davidson to distinguish between belief and
intention is his assumption that the former attitude is a passive reflection of antecedent truth.   Davidson reckons that a
passive reflection of antecedent truth cannot constitute an intention, because an intention purports to make its content true
and therefore presupposes that its content was antecedently
false.   But I have argued at length that a belief can present
its content as antecedently false, and as true only because of
being believed; and such an attitude can indeed constitute an
intention, which presents its content as true only because of
being intended.   Once we realize that belief can represent a
truth for which it is responsible, and can represent that truth
as its responsibility, then we come regard belief as no less
practical than theoretical.

There are several other important objections to thesis that
intentions consist in beliefs -- most notably, one from Michael
Bratman.[42]   Bratman argues that intention cannot consist in belief because the intention of doing something, unlike the belief
that one will do it, gives one reason to adopt some means of do-

---

[41]Here I am not in a position to argue that these reasons for the belief
deserve to be called reasons for the coinciding intention.   That argument
must be postponed until Chapter Seven.   All I am claiming here is that they
coincide with what we ordinarily call the reasons for the intention.

[42]"Intention and Means-End Reasoning," *op. cit.*, pp. 252 - 256.   For other
objections, see Brand, *Intending and Acting, op. cit.*, pp. 154 ff., and
"Intending and Believing," *op. cit.*; and Castañeda, *Thinking and Doing, op.
cit.*, pp. 154 - 169.   I discuss these objections in *Facing the Mirror,*
Chapter Five.

ing it. To cite Bratman's example, intending to meet someone uptown gives one a reason for taking the uptown bus, whereas believing in the same uptown rendezvous gives one no reason for bringing it about.

I do not have the space to answer Bratman's objection in detail. An answer to his objection would require, first, a doxastic theory of long-range intentions and, second, a companion theory of reasons acting. Here I can merely issue a promissory note for delivery of those two items on some future occasion. My promissory note bears the claim that a self-fulfilling belief adopted as a means to its fulfillment can indeed provide a reason for acting.

AN ARCHITECTURE FOR INTELLIGENT REACTIVE SYSTEMS

Leslie Pack Kaelbling
Artificial Intelligence Center
SRI International
and
Center for the Study of Language and Information
Stanford University

ABSTRACT

Any intelligent system that operates in a moderately complex or unpredictable environment must be *reactive* — that is, it must respond dynamically to changes in its environment. A robot that blindly follows a program or plan without verifying that its operations are having their intended effects is not reactive. For simple tasks in carefully engineered domains, non-reactive behavior is acceptable; for more intelligent agents in unconstrained domains, it is not.

This paper presents the outline of an architecture for intelligent reactive systems. Much of the discussion will relate to the problem of designing an autonomous mobile robot, but the ideas are independent of the particular system. The architecture is motivated by the desires for modularity, awareness, and robustness.

Any intelligent system that operates in a moderately complex or unpredictable environment must be *reactive* — that is, it must respond dynamically to changes in its environment. A robot that blindly follows a program or plan without verifying that its operations are having their intended effects is not reactive. For simple tasks in carefully engineered domains, non-reactive behavior is acceptable; for more intelligent agents in unconstrained domains, it is not.

This paper presents the outline of an architecture for intelligent reactive systems. Much of the discussion will relate to the problem of designing an autonomous mobile robot, but the ideas are independent of the particular system. The architecture is motivated by three main desiderata:

Modularity: The system should be built incrementally from small components that are easy to implement and understand.

Awareness: At no time should the system be unaware of what is happening; it should always be able to react to unexepected sensory data.

Robustness: The system should continue to behave plausibly in novel situations and when some of its sensors are inoperative or impaired.

Modularity

It is well-established principle of software engineering that the modular design of programs improves modifiability, understandability and reliability [4]. The ability to combine simple behaviors in different ways will facilitate experimentation in the design of a complex, reactive system.

Brooks [5] has proposed a *horizontal* decomposition of a robot's control system, in which the fundamental units of the program are task accomplishing behaviors. Each behavior consists of both an action and a perception component and may, in a structured manner, depend on other behaviors in the system. This is in contrast with the standard approach, which he refers to as *vertical* decomposition — namely, a division into many subsystems, each of which is essential for even the most elementary behavior. Such a vertical decomposition might include the following components: perception, modeling, planning, execution, and effector control.

Horizontal decomposition is attractive because the system can be built and debugged incrementally, allowing the programmer to test simple behaviors, then build more complex ones on top of them. There are some difficulties involved in having perception distributed throughout multiple behavior components, however. The first is that special-purpose perception mechanisms tend to be weak. Raw sensory data is often noisy and open to a variety of interpretations; to make perception robust, it is necessary to exploit the redundancy of different sensor systems and integrate the information from many sources. The second difficulty

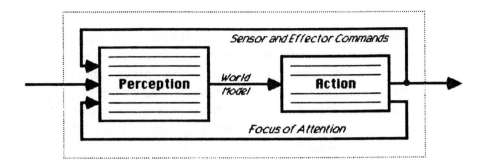

Figure 1: Top-Level Decomposition

stems from the fact that, as behaviors become more sophisticated, they tend to be dependent on conditions in the world, rather than on the particular properties of sensor readings. A general perception mechanism can synthesize information from different sensors into information about the world, which can then be used by many behaviors.

We propose a hybrid architecture with one major vertical division between the perception component and the action component. There is to be a horizontal decomposition within each of these components, but any of the action subcomponents may take advantage of any of the perception component's outputs. This component will be decomposed into layers of abstraction, with uninterpreted sensor readings available at the lowest level and sophisticated world models available at the highest level. The action component will consist of a set of behaviors, each of which may undergo some further structural decomposition.

Figure 1 contains a block diagram of this architecture. The system receives raw data from the sensors, and emits commands to the sensors and effectors. The action component takes the output of the perception component as input and, as in the preceding case, generates commands to both the sensors and effectors. This differs from many other systems, in which control of the sensors is the responsibility of the perception component. In many situations the sensors are a scarce resource; consequently, decisions must be made about where to point the camera or which ultrasonic sensor to fire at a given time. What should be done in such cases depends critically on the action strategy that is being followed at the moment: Is the robot following a wall on the left? Is it trying to locate an object in front of it? Since the action component is deciding on the strategy of the effectors, it is in the best position to do so for the sensors as well. For the same reasons, if the perception component is limited in the amount of processing it can do, the action component generates an attention command to the perception component, indicating where its computing power should be directed. It might focus attention on a particular region of the visual field, or on a certain kind of object. The entire sensory data stream goes directly into the perception component, along with the both the attention command of the action component and the commands that were last sent to the effectors.

Awareness

For a robot to be truly aware of its environment, it must be designed in such a way that there is a constant bound on the interval between the time the sensors get a particular reading and the time the effectors can react to that information. Many robots simply "close their eyes" while a time-consuming system, such as a planner or vision system, is invoked; the penalty for such unawareness is that perceptual inputs are either lost or stacked up for later processing. During this period of dormancy, a truly dynamic world might change to such an extent that the results of the long calculation would no longer be useful. Worse than that, something might happen that requires immediate action on the part of the robot, but the robot would be oblivious of it.

Our approach to this problem is to have a number of processes that work at different rates. We define a tick to be the constant minimum-cycle time for the entire system. During each tick, the inputs are read, some computation is done, and the outputs are set. If a process cannot complete its computation during its portion of a cycle, either because its runtime is inherently non-constant, or has a large constant, it emits a signal indicating that its outputs are not yet available, whereupon its state is saved for resumed execution during the next tick. The Rex language, which is discussed below, allows such a system to be easily constructed.

Robustness

Once again we propose a solution similar to that of Brooks [5]. His system is broken down into *levels of competence* in such a way that, if higher levels break down, the lower levels will still continue to work acceptably. This is especially important for Brooks, since his levels are intended to be built on separate physical devices that can fail independently. Our system, on the other hand, will be implemented on a single piece of hardware, so we will concern ourselves with robustness only in relation to failed sensors or to the possibility of general confusion because of new or unusual situations. We shall refer to these two types of robustness as *perceptual* and *behavioral*.

Perceptual robustness can be achieved by integrating all sensory information into a structure that represents the robot's knowledge or lack of knowledge about the world. If a particular sensor fails and its failure has been detected, the robot's information about the world will be weaker than it would have been if all of the sensors had been working correctly. We say that the information I, carried by an agent is weaker than information I' if and only if the set of possible worlds compatible with I is a superset of the set of possible worlds compatible with I'. Thus, with weaker information, the robot can make fewer discriminations among the states of the world, but it is can still be the case that that information integrated from the remaining sensors will suffice for reasonable but degraded operation. If a particular behavior depended entirely on a single sensor, there would be no room for graceful degradation; it would simply fail. The problem of detecting sensor failure is a difficult one that we shall not be examining here. Eventually, however, work in fault detection mechanisms will have to be integrated into such a system.

Behavioral robustness depends upon the ability to trigger a system's actions in direct accordance with the strength of available information. Consider a behaviorally robust robot with a high-level path-planning module that generates actions based on a strong model of the environment. If the robot's actual information is insufficient for the path planner to produce a plan — perhaps because the robot had just been switched on or had become lost or confused, that module will simply emit a signal indicating its inability to form a plan. In that case, some less sophisticated module that is capable of operating with weaker information will know what to do; its actions might be directed toward gaining sufficient information to enable the first module to work and avoiding coming to any harm in the process. Another example of behavioral robustness concerns the robot's behavior in case any of the necessary action-computing processes, such as planners or visual matching systems, cannot run in real time. The high-level planning module may not know what to do for several ticks until it has finished computing its plan; during this time, however, lower-level, less competent action modules should be in control, attempting to maintain the status quo and to keep the robot out of danger.

Building Real-time Systems

Rex

Rex is a language designed for the implementation of real-time embedded systems with analyzable information properties [12,8]. It is similar to a hardware description language in that the user declaratively specifies the behavior of a synchronous digital machine. Johnson [7], exploring the idea of using purely functional notation and recursion equations for circuit description, found that it was indeed viable and, moreover, in many ways preferable to standard techniques. He presents techniques for synthesizing digital designs manually from recursion equations. In Rex, the programmer can use both recursion and functional style, as well as having the specifications be translated automatically into hardware descriptions. There are, however, many complex recursion equations that are not automatically translatable into Rex. The declarative nature of Rex makes programs amenable to analysis of semantic and behavioral properties. From a Rex specification, the compiler generates a low-level structural description that can then be simulated by sequential code in C or Lisp.

The resulting machine description can be visualized as a large collection of integer variables and code that updates them once per tick. The variables can be divided into *input*, *state*, and *output*. The input variables, conceptually connected directly to the sensors, contain current sensory values at the beginning of each tick. The state variables are updated during each tick as a combined function of the values of the input variables and the old values of the state variables. The output variables, conceptually connected to the effectors, are updated during each tick as a combined function of the inputs and the old values of the state variables. Rex can be thought of as specifying a function $F : I^{i+s} \to I^{s+o}$, where i, s, and o are the numbers of input, state, and output variables, respectively, that maps the values of the inputs and the old values of the state variables into new values of the state variables and outputs. For any machine specified in Rex, the function F is guaranteed to be calculable in constant time. This in turn guarantees that the minimum reaction time (minimum time required for the value of an input to affect the value of an output) also has a constant bound, therey making all machines defined in Rex real-time.

Embedding Slow Processes in Fast Systems

As control systems become more sophisticated, they almost always involve planning of some sort. David Chapman has shown that a general planning problem is undecidable and that many restricted planning problems are intractable [6]; we must therefore consider methods for embedding processes that do not operate in constant time in systems with a constant tick rate. The intractability of planning, as well as other time-consuming problems, usually stems from the need for graph search. There are two methods for implementing search procedures in real-time systems. The first is to exploit the power of parallel processing and devote a large amount of dedicated hardware to doing the search in constant time. The second method is to conserve hardware and to search by using a conventional algorithm, such as backtracking, but to guarantee that the searching process will be "swapped out" in such a way that other processes are assured a chance to react to inputs in real time.

Production systems are often used to perform search and inference in problem solving and planning systems. In many of these systems, the rules are fixed and cannot be changed during execution. If this is the case, an inference net [13] can be explicitly implemented in hardware, allowing all search and inference to take place in parallel in constant time that is proportional to the maximum depth of the net. For many problems, the inference net will require less space than would have been needed to encode a rule interpreter and the production rules implicitly embodied by the net.

In general, any computation can trade time for space. Thus, if sufficient computing hardware is not available to implement large searching processes in parallel, they may be serialized and run on general-purpose hardware. Von Neumann computer architecture is an extreme example of this; it allows huge programs to be run on a very small amount of hardware, trading time for space. We propose a middle ground for embedding processes like planners into real-time systems, using general-purpose searching hardware for the processes that involve search, and iterating the searching process over time, while the other processes continue to run in parallel with it.

Planning

There are two problems that arise when a planner is run in a dynamic environment. The first is that, if the planner takes control of the processor, the robot can no longer respond, even at a reflex level, to events in the environment. The second problem is that, during the process of planning, the environment may have changed to such an extent that the newly created plan is no longer executable in the current situation.

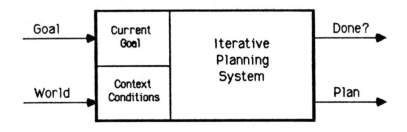

Figure 2: Schematic of an Embedded Planner

A solution to the first problem is for the planner to work incrementally, doing a few computation steps during each state transition, then storing its state until the next tick. Other parts of the system that react more quickly to changes in the environment will be running in parallel with the planner, and will therefore be able to act even if the planner has not finished its computation. This behavior is in contrast to that of a program that "calls" the planner and waits for it to finish executing before doing anything else. When the planner is finished, it issues the plan; until that time, it emits a signal that says it is not ready yet and has no answer. The specification of a planner that works incrementally and saves its state is written easily in Rex. A similar system might also be constructed using an operating system with message passing and a round-robin scheduler. This would make it possible for other processes to respond to external events while the planner is working, although the informational analysis of the Rex version would be much more tractable.

A planner is typically given a description of some initial state and a goal, and then activated. The planner constructs a plan that depends on the truth of some of the conditions in the initial state; we shall call these *context conditions*. The rest of the initial state is either irrelevant to the plan (for instance, the temperature is irrelevant to planning to go down the hall), or can be handled conditionally during plan execution (the robot might assume that it can navigate around local obstacles without planning). A planner embedded in a real-time system must be especially conscious of its context conditions; otherwise it cannot know whether the plan it is working on will be valid when it is done.

In Figure we present a schematic diagram of a planner that works flexibly in dynamic environments. Its inputs are a goal and the output of the world model; its outputs are a plan and a signal as to whether or not the plan is ready. When it is given a new goal, it remembers that goal and the current values of the context conditions in its local state. It begins planning with respect to those values of the goal and context conditions until the plan has been completed or until the goal or context conditions in the world differ from those that are stored in the planner.

If the goal or context conditions change before the completion of the plan, the planner stores their new values and begins planning again. This scheme has the property that the planner will notice at the earliest instant if its plan is no longer valid because of a change in goal or context conditions, and will therefore start working on a new one. The planner might be made more efficient if, when the goal or context is changed, it tried to salvage parts of the plan in progress. It is true that, if the context conditions or goal vary too rapidly, the planner will never succeed in generating a plan. This would happen only if the planner were not written with adequate generality for the environment in which it is embedded. One way to simplify the design of embedded planners, as well as to make the planning process more efficient, is to use many small planners that are domain-dependent, rather than one large, general, domain-independent planner. Much of the domain knowledge can be "procedurally represented" in a domain-dependent planner, eliminating the need for its runtime manipulation.

The Perception Component

As in the domain of actions, perception can be done at many levels of abstraction. Normally, the higher the level of abstraction, the more processing power is required to integrate new information. Thus, we will break the perception component of this architecture down into several levels of abstraction that can be made to work at different speeds, using the techniques that were applied to the planner in the preceding section. At the lowest level, we might simply store the most recent raw perceptual readings. Since this level requires no interpretation or integration, the data are immediately available to highly time-critical behavior components, such as obstacle-avoidance reflexes. More advanced behaviors will require information that is more robust and abstract. Eventually this will culminate in a representation that integrates data from all of the sensors into a coherent world model. The world model itself might exist at various levels of abstraction, from Cartesian locations of obstacles, to a topological map of interconnections of hallways, doors, and rooms.

It is important to note that these levels of perception may have no direct mapping to the levels of competence in the action component. The highest level of action competence will consist of behaviors at many different levels of abstraction; it thus relies on many or all of the layers of the perception component. It is likely however, that the lower action levels will not make use of the higher perception levels, thereby allowing each of the major components to be constructed incrementally.

For a system to be behaviorally robust, the representation of perceptual data must explicitly encode the robot's knowledge and lack of knowledge about the world. If we consider the propositional case, the robot can stand stand in three relations to a proposition φ: it can know that φ holds $(K(\varphi))$, it can know that φ doesn't hold $(K(\neg\varphi))$, or it can be unaware as to whether φ holds $(\neg K(\varphi) \wedge \neg K(\neg\varphi))$. If φ were the proposition "I'm about to run into the wall," we might have the following set of action rules:

$$K(\varphi) \quad \rightarrow \quad stop$$
$$K(\neg\varphi) \quad \rightarrow \quad go$$

$$\neg K(\varphi) \wedge \neg K(\neg\varphi) \quad \rightarrow \quad stop \wedge look\_for\_wall$$

These rules do something reasonable in each case of the robot's knowledge, or lack thereof, guaranteeing that it won't hit the wall but will go forward if it knows that such a collision is not imminent. It also tries to strengthen its information in case of uncertainty. For many applications, this approach may have to be extended to the probabilistic case, substituting $P(\varphi) > a \rightarrow \alpha$ for $K(\varphi) \rightarrow \alpha$, where a is the necessary degree of belief in the proposition φ to make α an appropriate action. We would similarly substutute $P(\varphi) < b$ for $\neg K(\varphi)$ and $b \leq P(\varphi) \leq a$ for $\neg K(\varphi) \wedge \neg K(\neg\varphi)$.

Framework for Adaptive Hierarchical Control

In this section we present a scheme for the hierarchical decomposition of robot control in terms of compositions of behaviors. We define a *behavior* to be a procedure that maps a set of inputs, which in this case are the outputs of the perception module, into a set of outputs to the effectors of the system. Each behavior is has the same input/output structure as the action module in Figure 1, with possibly some additional outputs that are intended to be used internally. To compose behaviors, we use procedures called *mediators*. A mediator's inputs are outputs of several *subbehaviors* and the the perception module. Since it generates outputs of the same type as a behavior, the complex module consisting of the subbehaviors and a mediator is itself a behavior.

Mediating Behaviors

One scheme for mediation between subbehaviors, described by Kurt Konolige [9], is a "bidding" system in which each behavior outputs in the form of sensor effector commands not only what it wants to do, but also some measure of its "desire" to do it. The mediator decides what to do on the basis of some weighted average of the the outputs of the subbehaviors and their respective degrees of urgency. There are two possible difficulties with such a scheme. One is that, when the behaviors are at a higher level than simple motor control, the mediation will have to be more than a simple average; for example, a robot performing the average of going to office A and office B probably won't get far. A logical response to this difficulty is that the two behaviors (the office A behavior and the office B behavior) would have to know something about each other, and so would only request actions that are compatible. But this seems to require mediation again, albeit internal to the behaviors, and it brings us to the second difficulty. One of the greatest advantages of a compositional methodology is that a particular component can be independently designed and tested, then used in more than one place in a system. In Konolige's approach there is something crucially context dependent about each low-level behavior, since its urgency parameters will have to be tuned for each specific application, depending on what other behaviors it is being combined with.

One approach that appears to overcome these difficulties is to move all the intelligence governing behavior selection into the mediator function itself. In this scheme, the mediator would take the outputs of the subbehaviors, as well as the world model and other perceptual data, as inputs. Then, on the basis of these data, the mediator could output some weighted combination of the input behaviors or, alternatively, simply switch through the output of a particular behavior. If there are very different effectors, it might make sense to perform part of one behavior and part of another; for example, a walking and a talking behavior could be mediated by outputting the speech commands of the talker and the motor commands of the walker. Each behavior can be designed and debugged independently, then used without modification as a building block for other, more complex behaviors. Another advantage of this approach is that proofs of correctness of complex behaviors can be done compositionally. A proof involving a complex behavior need only involve the switching behavior of the mediator and those properties of the subbehaviors that can be proved independently.

Hierarchically Mediated Behaviors

We will approach the the design of a robot's action component as a top-down decomposition of behaviors into lower-level behaviors and mediators. At the top level, adopting the scheme of Brooks, we have a number of behaviors that represent different levels of competence at executing the main task of the system. Each behaviors, unlike those of Brooks, computes its outputs independently of the outputs of the other modules. Included in the set of possible outputs of each behavior is no-command, a signal denoting that that behavior doesn't know what to do in the current situation. We have some intuitive idea of what competence is, and, given two modules, can make subjective judgements about which works "better." We hope to formalize the notion of what makes one action or strategy better than another with respect to some goal; since that has not yet been done, however, the balance of this discussion must be based on our intuitive understanding of "better." If the following four properties hold of a system whose top-level mediation function switches through the entire output of the most competent behavior that knows what to do, the system as a whole will always do the best thing of which it is capable, given the available information.

- The lowest level of competence never outputs no-command
- No level emits a command other than no-command unless it is a correct command
- Lower levels of competence require weaker information
- If any two levels both emit commands in the same tick, the output of the higher level is better

Thus, if the more competent levels fail or have insufficient information to act, the robot will be controlled by a less competent level that can work with weak information until the more competent components recover and resume control.

Within each of the levels of competence, decomposition is based on abstraction rather than competence. The highest-level behavior is constructed by mediating among medium-level behaviors. Those behaviors are constructed by mediating among low-level behaviors.

The structure will typically be a graph rather than a tree, since many high-level behaviors will ultimately be constructed from a few low-level ones. In practice, it will also happen occasionally that the hierarchy will not be strict; that is, a certain behavior might be present at two different levels in the graph.

There has been other work exploring the use of a hierarchy of abstraction for reactive control. James Albus [1,2,3] in the RCS (Real-time Control System), employs an abstraction hierarchy of "multivariant servos" for controlling factory automation systems. Although his approach is similar to ours, it does not allow the simultaneous combining of components of more than one behavior, even if they are potentially compatible. This is equivalent to having the mediating functions always switch through one entire behavior. Nils Nilsson has proposed using triangle tables as a robot programming language[11]. They were originally used in the SRI robot *Shakey* [10] for plan execution monitoring, but the formalism can be extended to hierarchical systems that are very much like the one described by Albus.

Example

We shall now present an example that illustrates the methods of hierarchical decomposition discussed in the preceding section. After sketching the top-level decomposition of a complex behavior into levels of competence, we will show how the most competent module is broken down into levels of abstraction. A block diagram of this example is presented in Figure 3.

The task of this robot is to traverse a very long hall without crashing into anything. It is more important to avoid crashes than to get to the end of the hall. The robot's construction is such as to make it highly unlikely that it can roll straight down the hall without veering into the sides unless it corrects its course along the way. The robot has distance sensors pointing forward and to each side. We decompose this problem into three behaviors at different levels of competence, as follows:

Level 1 This behavior looks at accumulated raw sensor data. If any of the measurements in taken from the front of the robot too short, or a significant interval has elapsed since the last measurement was made by the front sensor, it stops; otherwise it moves forward.

Level 2 This behavior also looks at accumulated raw sensor data. As in the preceding behavior, it stops if the measurements are too short or too old. If it has stopped and cannot move forward, but the sensor data imply that it is safe to turn, the robot turns until the sensor data are no longer too short, then moves. If it isn't save to turn, it emits no-command.

Level 3 This behavior looks at data that has been combined at a higher level of abstraction. It can tell whether there is a wall to the front or side, how far away it is, and how tight the bounds on its knowledge of its position are. If it knows that there is no wall too

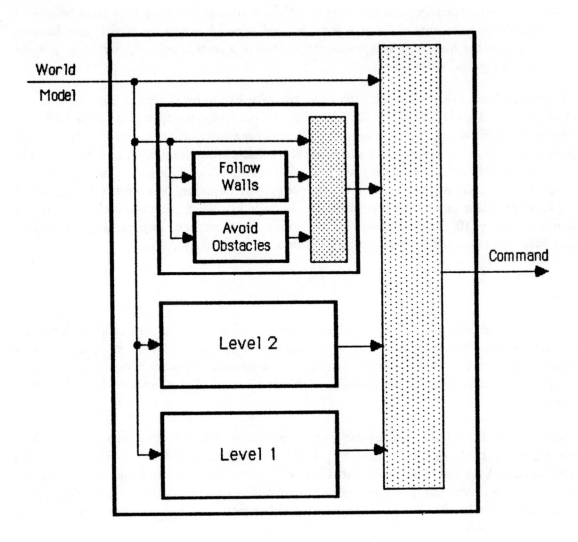

Figure 3: Example of Hierarchies of Competence and Abstraction. (The shaded boxes are mediators).

close to it,[1] and knows fairly tight bounds on the locations of the walls on either side, it moves in such a way as to go forward in the middle of the hall, staying parallel to the walls. If it doesn't know this, it emits no-command.

This set of behaviors satisfies the rules given above for a correct decomposition. The lowest level always either moves or stops. Each level acts only when it knows the particular action is safe — that is, when executing it will not cause the robot to crash into something. The lowest level requires only sensor readings, which, although weak, are available instantly. The second level requires information about whether it is safe to turn; this information, stronger than that needed by the first level, must be synthesized from the raw sensor readings. The highest level requires very strong wall-location data that must be derived from the aggregation of many sensor readings and knowledge about the world. If each level knows what to do, it is intuitively obvious that the highest-level behavior is "best." It is better to proceed along a hall by staying parallel to the walls than by zig-zagging from side to side (which is what the second behavior is likely to do), or just by going to one side of the hall and stopping when obstructed.

The highest level of competence can be divided into subbehaviors at different levels of abstraction, as shown in Figure 3. The first division is into a behavior that stays parallel to the walls on the sides and one that causes the robot to slow down linearly as a function of its distance to an obstacle in front of it. Each of these behaviors is composed of subbehaviors that cause the robot to move at certain velocities and request certain sensor measurements. Let us assume that each behavior consists of a motor command and sensor command (the robot can poll only one sensor at a time).

Then, in pseudocode, the follow-walls behavior is

```
sensor-command := if left-info-weak then left-sensor
                  else if right-info-weak then right-sensor
                  else *noop*
motor-command  := if K-location-of-left-wall and
                     K-location-of-right-wall then servo-to-midline
                  else *no-command*
```

This behavior requests a sensor measurement if it has weak information about one side or the other, and returns *noop* if it has no immediate need for sensor information. If it knows the location of the left and right walls to a close enough tolerance, it performs the behavior that servos to the middle line of the hallway; otherwise, it emits *no-command*, indicating that it does not know what to do.

The no-crash behavior is described by

---

[1] A wall is too close to the robot if it will crash into the wall unless it begins its stopping action immediately.

```
sensor-command := if front-info-weak then front-sensor
                  else *noop*
motor-command := if K-location-of-front-obstacle then linear-speed-limit
                  else *no-command*
```

This behavior requests a sensor measurement from the front sensor if it needs it and, if it knows the location of the nearest obstacle in front to sufficient tolerance, it performs the behavior that causes the robot slow down in proportion its distance from the obstacle. If it does not know that location, we emit *no-command*.

Now it remains only to combine these two behaviors. The mediator is

```
sensor-command := if no-crash-sensor-command = *noop*
                  then follow-wall-sensor-command
                  else no-crash-sensor-command
motor-command  := if (follow-wall-motor-command = *no-command*) or
                     (no-crash-motor-command = *no-command*)
                  then *no-command*
                  else rescale (follow-wall-motor-command, no-crash-motor-command)
```

If the no-crash behavior does not request a sensor command, the mediator does what the follow-wall behavior wants to do; otherwise it does what the no-crash behavior wants to do. This gives priority to acquiring information that is relevant to the more important goal of avoiding obstacles. If either motor command is *no-command*, the motor command of the mediator will be the same. If both motor commands are defined, the wall-following motor command defines a set of differential velocities for maintaining the heading of the robot down the center of the hall and the crash-avoidance motor command defines a limit for safe speed, given the knowledge of the distance to obstacles in front of the robot. These values are input to the function rescale which performs a ratiometric scaling of the servo velocities. This is done so that neither velocity will them exceed the speed limit, but their ratio will maintained.

Future Work

This methodology has been applied to simple tasks, such as the one described above, with a large degree of success. As well as expanding the implemented example, we will continue research on the formal specification of goals and the ranking of the "goodness" of behaviors with respect to particular sets of goals. The problem of perceptual organization also requires more attention, with the aim of devising algorithms that use predictions about the environment from old information to facilitate analysis of new information.

Acknowledgments

This work was supported in part by a gift from the Systems Development Foundation, in part by FMC Corporation under contract 147466 (SRI Project 7390), in part by the office of Naval Research under contract N00014-85-C-0251, and in part by General Motors Research Laboratories under contract 50-13 (SRI Project 8662). It was done in the context of programming the SRI Artificial Intelligence Center's mobile robot to perform hallway navigation tasks. Many of these ideas arose from discussions with Stan Rosenschein, and debugging sessions with Stan Reifel and Sandy Wells.

References

[1] Albus, James S., 1981: *Brains, Behavior, and Robotics* (BYTE Books, Subsidiary of McGraw-Hill, Peterborough, New Hampshire).

[2] Albus, James S., Anthony J. Barbera, and Roger N. Nagel, 1981: "Theory and Practice of Hierarchical Control," *Proc. 23rd IEEE Computer Society International Conference* (September).

[3] Barbera, Anthony J., M. L. Fitzgerald, James S. Albus, and Leonard S. Haynes, 1984: "RCS: The NBS Real-time Control System," *Proc. Robots 8 Conference and Exposition, Detroit, Michigan* (June).

[4] Booch, Grady, 1983: *Software Engineering with Ada* (The Benjamin/Cummings Publishing Company, Menlo Park, California).

[5] Brooks, Rodney, A., 1985: *A Robust Layered Control System for a Mobile Robot* (A. I. Memo 864, MIT Artificial Intelligence Laboratory, Cambridge, Massachusetts).

[6] Chapman, David, 1985: *Planning for Conjunctive Goals* (Technical Report 802, MIT Artificial Intelligence Laboratory, Cambridge, Massachusetts).

[7] Johnson, Steven D., 1983: *Synthesis of Digital Designs from Recursion Equations* (The MIT Press, Cambridge, Massachusetts).

[8] Kaelbling, Leslie Pack, 1986: *Rex Programmer's Manual* (Technical Note 381, Artificial Intelligence Center, SRI International, Menlo Park, California).

[9] Konolige, Kurt, 1986: personal communication.

[10] Nilsson, Nils J., 1984: *Shakey the Robot* (Technical Note 323, Artificial Intelligence Center, SRI International, Menlo Park, California).

[11] Nilsson, Nils J., 1985: *Triangle Tables: A Proposal For A Robot Programming Language* (Technical Note 347, Artificial Intelligence Center, SRI International, Menlo Park, California).

[12] Rosenschein, Stanley J. and Leslie Pack Kaelbling, 1986: "The Synthesis of Digital Machines with Provable Epistemic Properties," *Proc. Conference on Theoretical Aspects of Reasoning About Knowledge, Asilomar, California*, pp. 83-98.

[13] Winston, Patrick Henry, 1984: *Artificial Intelligence*, second edition (Addison Wesley, Reading, Massachusetts), pp. 181-187.

ABSTRACT REASONING AS EMERGENT
FROM CONCRETE ACTIVITY

David Chapman
Philip E. Agre

Artificial Intelligence Laboratory
Massachusetts Institute of Technology
545 Technology Square
Cambridge, MA 02139
Zvona@AI.AI.MIT.EDU; Agre@AI.AI.MIT.EDU
(617)253-8827; (617)253-8826

ABSTRACT

We believe that *abstract reasoning* is not primitive, but derived phenomenologically, developmentally, and implementationally from *concrete activity*. We summarize recent advances in the understanding of the mechanisms of concrete activity which suggest paths for exploring the emergence of abstract reasoning therefrom.

We argue that abstract reasoning is made from the same building blocks as concrete activity, and consists of techniques for alleviating the limitations of innate hardware. These techniques are formed by the internalization of patterns of interaction between an agent and the world. Internalization makes it possible to represent the self, and so to reflect upon the relationship between the self and the world. Most patterns of abstract thought originate in the culture. We believe that ideas such as plans, knowledge, complexity, understanding, order, search, and forgetting are learned. We present examples of everyday planning and analyze them in this framework. Finally, we describe cognitive cliches, which we take to be the most abstract mental structures.

Agre has been supported by a fellowship from the Hertz foundation.

This report describes research done at the Artificial Intelligence Laboratory of the Massachusetts Institute of Technology. Support for the laboratory's artificial intelligence research has been provided in part by the Advanced Research Projects Agency of the Department of Defense under Office of Naval Research contract N00014-80-C-0505, in part by National Science Foundation grant MCS-8117633, and in part by the IBM Corporation.

The views and conclusions contained in this document are those of the authors, and should not be interpreted as representing the policies, neither expressed nor implied, of the Department of Defense, of the National Science Foundation, nor of the IBM Corporation.

We want to understand the emergence of abstract reasoning from concrete activity. We believe that abstract reasoning is not innate, but derived from concrete activity, in three senses: phenomenologically, developmentally, and implementationally. We hope that an understanding of the first two senses can guide the development of an understanding of the third.

Heidegger [9,10] argues that the *phenomenologically* primordial way of being is involvement in a concrete activity. Everyday activity consists in the use of equipment for a specific reason. When this activity is going well, it is "transparent." An experienced driver does not have to think about driving, he just does it; and he can be doing something else, possibly requiring abstract thought, at the same time. It is only when there is a breakdown in the activity that abstract thought is needed. Only when I have too many things to do do I need to make a plan or schedule, to wonder what order to do them in, how they can be most efficiently combined. And it is only when that too fails that I might give up, become curious, and reflect theoretically about scheduling algorithms.

Several branches of psychology suggest that abstract reasoning appears *developmentally* later in individuals than involvement in concrete activity. Jean Piaget's stage theory of cognitive development [13,14] traces development from the beginning of infancy, in which there are only blind stimulus/response reflexes with no abstraction, representation, or reasoning. "Formal operations"—fully abstract reasoning—appear only around puberty. Psychoanalytic developmental psychology (particularly object-relations theory as found in D. W. Winnicott [20]) sees the infant as a chaotic mass of impulses and fantasies leading directly to action. The infant has no self-representation and so is undifferentiated from the world. Gradually, scattered mental elements are integrated to produce adult rational thought. Crucial to the process of integration is *internalization*: getting control over interactions with the environment by bringing them inside yourself. Internalization leads to decreased egocentricity. By representing the relationship between his self and the world, a person is better able to be detached from it. Detachment is never complete; the ability to distinguish self from other, fantasy from reality, continues to develop throughout life.

The third sense in which we believe abstract reasoning is derived is *implementationally*. *Constructivism* is the position, held by many developmental psychologists, that human development occurs roughly in stages, and that each stage is built upon the previous one. We believe that abstract reasoning appears late because it is emergent from or parasitic upon concrete activity. We want to understand the nature of this emergence relationship. How, even in principle, can abstract thought be mechanistically derived from simple action?

CONCRETE ACTIVITY

Study of the emergence of abstract reasoning must begin with an understanding of concrete activity. We believe that the beginnings of such an understanding are found in Gary Drescher's work on the machinery to implement infant sensorimotor learning and in Agre's work on that needed to implement adult routine activity.

Agre's theory of routine activity [1,2,3] describes adult action when everything is going well: the fluent, regular, practiced, unproblematic activity that makes up most of everyday life. The theory includes an account of the innate hardware, which we believe is, loosely, connectionist. It also includes a description of the sorts of cognition and activity that are most appropriate to that hardware. It turns out that the sort of computation most appropriate to the hardware is also the primary sort of computation that actually transpires in everyday life, namely concrete activity.

Routine activity is *situated*: it makes extensive use of the immediate surrounds and their accessibility for observation and interaction. Rather than using internal datastructures to model the world, the world is immediately accessed through perception. Much of the theory is concerned with the emergence of *routines*, which are dynamics of interaction: patterns of activity that occur not as a result of their representation in the head of the agent, but due to a Simon's-ant relationship to a complex environment. The world and the mind interpenetrate. Routine activity is conducted in a society of other people, who provide a variety of types of support, from helping when asked to transmitting cultural techniques for solving classes of problems. Routine activity is concerned with the here-and-now; it rarely requires planning into the future, reflection upon the past, or consideration of spatially distant causes. It rarely involves thinking new thoughts; for the most part existing patterns of activity suffice to cope with the situation. Finally, routine activity takes the forms most natural to the hardware: those that can be implemented efficiently on a connectionist architecture.

The architecture we propose to support routine activity consists of a very large number of simple processors. The connectivity of the processors is quasi-static, meaning that the cost of creating a new connection between processors is very high relative to that of using an existing connection. The connections pass tokens from a small set of values, rather than real-valued weights, as in most connectionist learning schemes.

Such an architecture can represent abstract propositions, if at all, only by adding a layer of interpretation which is very computationally expensive. We think that *indexical-functional* representations are used instead. These are fully indexical representations which can be evaluated relative to the current situation very cheaply by virtue of their grounding in sensorimotor primitives. They can be thought of as definite noun phrases: an indexical-functional representation picks out, for example, *the cereal box* or *the tea strainer* from the visual field. The indexicality of such representations is mostly a matter of egocentricity. *The cereal box* implicitly means the cereal box in front of *me*. Compare developmental psychology's description of child thought as egocentric.

Indexical-functional representations can't involve logical individuals or variables; the hardware can not reason about identity. Traditional AI representations use variables which are bound to constants which in turn are somehow connected by the sensory system to objects in the real world. Each constant is connected to a distinct real world object. So, for example, we can say that *all bowls are containers*, and instantiate this on bowl-259. If the bowl-259 is seen later, it will be recognized as the same one. For indexical-functional representations, things that look the same *are* the same. All you can do is see if there is a bowl there or not. There is no way to represent permanent objects in Piaget's sense.

Another consequence of quasi-static connectivity is that introspection is very expensive: you can't examine your own datastructures unless you built them with extra connections and processing elements for the purpose.

The theory of routines is incomplete; it describes adult mental architecture without explaining how that architecture came about. Drescher [8,7] gives a theory of sensorimotor development motivated to fine levels of detail by Piaget's observations of the early stages of infant development. He proposes hardware to support the emergence of the necessary software to account for the first five stages.

Drescher's architecture, the Schema Mechanism, is quasi-static. It consists of very large numbers of *items* and *schemas*, which respectively represent properties of the world and the effects of actions in situations. Items are boolean-valued representations of conditions in the world. Schemas are indexical assertions that if certain items hold, after a given action other items will hold. The architecture initially has only sensory primitives as items and no schemas. Various learning techniques create new schemas to represent observed regularities, compound procedures for achieving states of items, and synthetic items, which represent conditions in the world which are not immediately observable. Some of these techniques collect empirical statistics to discover correlations. Implementation of the architecture is in progress.

Drescher presents a hypothetical scenario of his architecture progressing through the first five stages of infant development. Initially, all the representations constructed are purely indexical, but eventually these are partly deindexicalized, so that there develop representations of objects independent of the sensory mode in which they are perceived and then of objects independent of *whether* they are seen. Similarly, actions are initially represented egocentrically, but come to be represented independent of the actor who performs them.

THE EMERGENCE OF ABSTRACT REASONING

Abstract reasoning uses abstract representations and performs detached search-like computations.

Abstract representations differ from concrete indexical-functional representations along several dimensions, and intermediates are possible. They are *universally quantified* and so capture eternal truths, independent of the current situation. They are *general purpose*: a very broad range of sorts of knowledge can be encoded in a uniform framework. They can involve *variables* which must be instantiated in use; this requires notions of identity and difference. They are *compositional*: sentence-like, in that the meaning of the whole depends on the meanings of the parts. Natural language spans the range from indexical-functional to abstract. Utterances such as "the big one!" (requesting a coworker to pass a hammer) encode indexical-functional representations; those such as "Everyone hates the phone company" are abstract.

By detached computation, we mean that the agent, presented with a situation and a goal, thinks hard about how to achieve the goal, develops a plan, and then executes the plan without much additional thought. Because the agent is detached from the world, he can not depend on clues in the world to tell him what to do, and he must reason about hypothetical future situations, rather than simply inspecting the current state of the world. Any sort of search in an internally represented state-space is a detached computation.

We believe that abstract reasoning uses the same hardware as concrete activity. It is computationally expensive (in general, and particularly on quasi-static hardware), and since it is not necessary for routine activity, it is resorted to only when routines break down, when reflection or problem-solving are required. Thus, we believe that abstract reasoning is *perforated*: it is not a coherent module that systematically accounts for all or even a class of mental phenomena. It is not a general-purpose reasoning machine, as it appears to be, but only a patchwork of special cases. (Later in the paper, we sketch a general theory of special cases.) It appears seamless because people are good at giving post-hoc rationalizations for their actions, but those rationalizations are not causally connected to the activity they purport to explain. Techniques are often abstract by virtue of depending only on the form, not the content, of the concrete problems they apply to.

We believe that abstract reasoning consists of a set of techniques, mostly culturally transmitted, for alleviating the limitations of quasi-static hardware to constrain the ways one organizes one's activity. These techniques are implemented with the same building blocks used in routine activity, but interconnected in different ways, which generally run slowly and consume much hardware. The techniques mostly act to build static networks to routinely cope with some new type of situation: they compile abstract knowledge into machinery for concrete activity. This is similar to chunking in Soar [11], the use of a dependency network in Agre's running arguments [2], the instantiation of virtual structures in the Schema Mechanism, and Jeff Shrager's mediation theory [15].

INTERNALIZATION

The content of routine activity is not innate; it must be learned. The Schema Mechanism provides one account of this development; we don't know if it is sufficient. But apart from the hardware required, we can study the dynamics of skill acquisition: *in what way* is it learned?

The problem is in a way more difficult than earlier approaches such as Sussman's [17] suggest, because most interesting activity arises not from the execution of plans, which are accessible datastructures, but from interactional routines, which do not derive from explicit representations. You can, and typically do, participate in a routine without being aware of it. So the first step of improving a routine is to make some aspect of it explicit. As each new aspect of a routine is represented, it can be modified. This process rarely terminates in a complete procedural representation.

The making explicit of routines is a good candidate for the mechanistic correlate of the psychoanalytic concept of internalization. [2] gives this example of internalizing a routine:

> An everyday example is provided by the myopic vacuumer of dining rooms who hasn't thought to describe the process as one of alternating between vacuuming and furniture-moving. Explicitly representing that aspect of the vacuuming process should make one think to move all the furniture before getting started. ...Vacuuming is often best characterized as interleaving the processes of moving the furniture, running the vacuum around, and returning the furniture. Sometimes it is better to deinterleave these processes.

We don't know how internalization happens in general. For lack of a better idea, we reluctantly suspect that a brute-force statistical induction engine is involved. However, something like Weld's *aggregation* [19] would be very useful in detecting loops such as the vacuuming one. Unfortunately, known aggregation algorithms do not scale well with the complexity of the input, and probably will fail in the face of the richness of the real world.

A strong clue that a cyclic process is occurring is a rhythm. The Schema Mechanism can be extended with hardware for rhythm detection. Add to each item hardware which keeps a history of the last several changes in value of the item and computes the variance of the Δt. If the variance is small, a synthetic item can be created to represent the rhythmicity of the given one, and the state of the synthetic item can be maintained in hardware. These synthetic rhythm items themselves can have rhythm detectors, so that more complex rhythms can be detected. How useful such hardware would be remains to be seen.

One result of internalization is the construction of the *mind's eye*. Imagine that parts of the central system can gain write access to the wires on which the outputs of sensory systems, at various levels of abstraction, are delivered to the central system. Then one part of the central system can induce hallucinations, and another part will do something based on what it implicitly supposes are inputs from the world. In order to avoid actually acting in the imaginary situation, it must also be possible to short-circuit outputs to the motor system. In this way, the ability to consider hypothetical situations begins. If the situation is well-enough understood, the results of imaginary actions can be hallucinated. Iterated, this permits the internalization of routines. The resulting internal representation of a routine is another routine which simulates it, interacting with the sensorimotor interface, rather than the real world. This is, we think, the mechanistic correlate of the introspective phenomenon of visual imagery. The mind's eye extends to all sensory modalities and to motor actions. Constructed similarly is the internal dialog, the sentences we say to ourselves silently. Computation in this internal world is just like computation in the real one; it is just as concrete and situated, except that the situation is imaginary.

We suspect that early language acquisition is intimately tied up with the first development of abstract thought. Natural language provides a bridge between indexical-functional and abstract representations. Children's first utterances are single words: "ball!" "Mummy!" "hungry!" The production of these highly-indexical "observatives" might very well be directly driven by indexical-functional representations. There follows a long two-word stage, producing utterances like "give ball," "more cookie," and "bad kitty." There is no real syntax to these utterances, but there are a dozen or so different kinds of semantic relationships between the two words to be mastered [12]. The compositionality makes even such simple less than fully indexical. Production of such utterances both requires and drives the development of abstract thought.

REFLECTION AND THE SELF

Brian Smith [16] makes a useful distinction between *introspection* (thinking about yourself by virtue of having access to your own datastructures) and *reflection* (thinking about the relationship between yourself and the world). Introspection has traditionally been thought necessary for reflection.

The construction of the mind's eye gives you partial introspective access in a systematic way. You can observe what you would do in hypothetical situations, but without access to the machinery that engenders the action, you won't know quite how or why. By varying the imaginary situation, you can induce a model of your own reasoning. This model, however, can only be as good as your ability to simulate the world's responses to your actions, and so must constantly be checked against experience.

Routine activity does not require reflection; the necessary computation just runs. Moreover, quasi-static hardware makes introspection very expensive. We suspect, therefore, that reflection is not only not used in concrete activity, but also is little used in problem solving. It is primarily useful in long-term development: a relatively crude self-model may be good enough to base long-term planning on. This is compatible with the psychoanalytic understanding of self-models, used in determining basic values and orientations, incomplete, inexact, and in pathological cases completely unlike the self that is modeled.

We believe that reflection, rather than being based on introspection, primarily "goes out through the world." Just as concrete activity generally uses the real world as the model of the world, so reflection uses the world's mirroring of the self as a model of the self. Smith gives the example of realizing that he is being foolishly repetitive at a dinner party and shutting up. Such a realization might possibly be made by examining one's own actions, but might much more likely be cued by signs of boredom on the part of the audience. This again is consonant with psychoanalytic emphasis on the role of the mother in mirroring the infant's facial expressions and gestures and, in later life, the role of the reactions of others in maintaining self-esteem. [20]

Smith is concerned in [16] with translation between the indexical representations needed for concrete activity and the abstract representations needed for reflection. He proposes the use of the self-model as a pivot in this translation. Deindexicalization consists in part in filling in implicit extra arguments to relations with the self. Thus, to take Smith's example, the sensory item **hungry!** can be used concretely to activate eating goals. But to reason about other people's hunger, it must be deindexicalized to (**hungry me**), generalized to (**hungry x**), and perhaps instantiated as (**hungry bear**). Similarly, only by deindexicalizing the cereal box representation can cereal boxes in general, or cereal boxes remote in time or space, be considered.

COGNITIVE IDEOLOGY; PLANNING

The nature of abstract thought, unlike that of concrete activity, is determined by your culture. (The *content* of concrete activity is of course also culturally determined, but its form is determined by the innate hardware.) We use the term *cognitive ideology* to refer to culturally transmitted ways of organizing activity that involve ideas such as plans, knowledge, complexity, understanding, order, search, and forgetting.

We would like to provide an account of planning, an item of cognitive ideology, as a paradigm form of the sort of abstract reasoning we have sketched above. [3] argues that very little planning is done in daily life, and that such plans as are constructed are only skeletal, never more than a dozen steps. The latter is a good thing, because [4] shows that planning, even in the trivial sorts of domains considered in the AI literature, is computationally intractable.

The remainder of this section presents first-person anecdotes from the daily life of one of us (Chapman). These anecdotes illustrate sorts of activity that are not well accounted for by current AI planning theories and which must be explained either in giving a psychologically realistic account of human activity or in building a robot that acts in real-world domains. Our partial analyses hint at the form an account of planning in the framework of this paper might take.

Classical planning emphasized the means-ends relationship between plan steps and the discovery of order constraints among them based on interactions between pre- and postconditions. Observation of everyday planning leads us to believe that these sorts of reasoning are unusual.

In general, the right way to achieve a goal is obvious. Pre- and postconditions are unknown, variable, too hard to represent accurately, or out of the agent's control. Ordering decisions are generally made for quite other reasons.

When [4] was printed, I sent about sixty copies out to people who had asked for them. I set up an assembly line for putting copies in envelopes and addressing them. The Tyvek envelopes I use have gummed flaps with waxpaper over them; to make them sticky, you pull off the waxpaper, rather than licking the glue. So I pulled the waxpaper off an envelope, shoved a copy of the report in, and sealed the flap. The second time I tried, the glue stuck to the back of the report as it slid half-way in. I had to tear the report away from the flap, damaging both somewhat, and seal the envelope with tape. From then on, I put the reports in before pulling off the waxpaper. In this example, the two steps must be ordered, but it is hard to give an account of the reason in terms of preconditions. You could say that it's a precondition for putting reports in envelopes that the flap not be sticky, but that isn't really true; you can still do it if you're lucky or careful. Such a precondition seems artificial, because it doesn't tell you *why* you have to put the report in first. In any case, if there were such a precondition, I didn't know about it when I started, though I think I had a pretty complete understanding of envelopes and tech reports. The problem was not in the static configuration of the pieces, but a dynamic emergent of their interaction.

Bicycle repair manuals tell you that when you disassemble some complex subassembly like a freewheel, put all the little pieces down on the ground in a row *in the order you disassembled them*. That's because (if you know as much about freewheels as I do) the only available representation of the pieces is "weird little widgets." They are indistinguishable from each other under this representation. Because quasi-static hardware can't represent logical individuals, you can't remember (much less reason about) which is which and what's connected to what.

This story illustrates several themes of the paper. The manual's advice is a piece of culturally transmitted metaknowledge that allows you to work around the limitations of your hardware in order to perform activity in a partly planned way. The plan—the order in which the freewheel should be reassembled—is not sufficient to completely determine the activity; you still have to be responsive to the situation to see just how each piece should be put back on. In fact, the plan is not even represented in your head, but externally, as a physical row of objects on the floor. Internalization of such an external representation may be the basis of our ability to remember lists of things to do.

I have a very large spice shelf, which until recently was total chaos. It occurred to me one day while fruitlessly searching for a jar of tarragon to alphabetize the shelf. In the course of doing so, I discovered a number of amazing things, among them that I had fourteen bottles of galangal. Galangal is not an easy spice to come by. I realized that every time I went to an oriental food store, as I do every few months, I would remember that difficulty and pick up a bottle. Using the culturally-given idea of alphabetizing, I was able to overcome my inability to introspect about my spice-buying routines. Since this routine (buying a jar of galangal every time) was certainly nowhere explicitly represented, introspection would not have helped even had my hardware supported it. Only if I thought to simulate several cycles of oriental-food-store shopping and could do so accurately (both unlikely) could I have discovered the bug.

Finding a spice jar on an alphabetized shelf is a search *in the world*, rather than in the head. Internalization of such searches produces the internal searches of which AI currently posits so many.

Sometimes planned action is fluid and routine. I have observed in more detail than belongs here the way I cope with the routine situation of coming through the front door of my house with a load of groceries on my bicycle, while wearing heavy winter clothing. Immediately after opening the door a dozen actions occur to me. This may seem like a lot; because we know how to cope with it, we underestimate the complexity of daily life. These actions for the most part do not stand in a means-ends relationship to each other; they satisfy the many different goals which are activated as I come through the door.

I can not do all these things at once. However, this situation is routine in the sense that it happens often and I know how to cope with it without breakdown: it is not routine in that it is sufficiently complex and sufficiently variable that I have to plan to deal with it; I don't have a stored macrop (canned action sequence) for it.

I can plan routinely to deal with this situation because about twenty arguments about how to proceed immediately occur to me. These are just at the fringe of consciousness. I can make them conscious effortlessly, but typically they flash by many per second, so they aren't fully verbalized in the internal dialog. The arguments concern the order in which the actions should be done. If we were to encode these arguments in a dialectical interpreter, nonlinear planning would fall out automatically. A set of arguments about action orderings effectively constitute a partial order on plan steps. The argument that A should be before B can simply be phrased as objecting to B, non-monotonically dependent on A's not having been done; then nonlinear planning and execution fall out directly.

Of the arguments, roughly half are what might be called *necessity orderings*. They are arguments about what order things must be done in in order to work at all. They don't say, action A has prerequisite p, which is clobbered by action B, so do A first; like the envelope example, they are at a higher level. You have to take off your coat before putting it away because... well, because that's just the way it is. I must have known the reason once; it just seems self-evident now; and certainly doesn't have anything to do with preconditions.

Besides necessity orderings, there are optimization arguments. Some of these are orderings; some are in the vocabulary of quasiquantitative time intervals. For example, I should lock the door before leaving the front hall, or I will forget to do it once I'm out of that context. Similarly,

I should sign up for grocery money spent as soon as possible, because I often forget to do so, but remember now. Here I am working to overcome my own future immersion in a concrete situation. The door should be closed (as opposed to locked) within about ten seconds, because it's freezing cold out. Again, I need to take off my coat within about a minute, or I will get hot and sweaty.

In fact, it so happens that the set of orderings is cyclic: there is an argument that I should put my keys (which I am holding) in my pocket first thing, to make it possible to grasp my bicycle and push it through the door; but there is also an argument that I shouldn't put the keys away until I've locked the door, which can't happen until I've closed it, which can't happen until I've pushed the cycle through. This registers phenomenologically as a minor hassle; I feel slightly annoyed. Like cycles in planning generally, it must be resolved by adding another step (a white knight): in this case, it was to put the keys in my pocket now and take them out again later.

These arguments don't take into account the number of available manipulators. For example, I could take off my coat before putting the bicycle up against the wall where it belongs. There is in fact an argument for that: I want to get out of my coat as soon as possible, while it doesn't matter just when the cycle gets put away. However, I need about one and a half hands to hold up the bike (with its destabilizing load of groceries), so it would be difficult to take off my coat first. Introspectively, I *don't* reason about hand allocation as I build the plan; and when I went to set it down on paper, it became obvious why. It's absurdly difficult. It's a pain even for a linear plan; you have to keep track of what's in each hand at every instant. In a nonlinear plan, it seems to be just about impossible.

So I don't plan manipulator allocation ahead of time; it's very easy to deal with during execution, because I can just sense what is in my hands at any given instant. This is another example of the immediacy of the world making reasoning easy. Part of the reason this planning is routine and breakdown-free is that it happens that I never run out of hands. This is a contingent, emergent fact about the structure of the world and my ability to plan and our interactions. I couldn't make the optimal decision in all cases, but I can do well enough in this one. To prove the former point, on the couple of occasions on which the phone has rung as I came in through the door, I experienced a breakdown. I left the door open and it got real cold in the front hall and my bicycle ended up on the floor with groceries spilling out of it and I left my coat on and I ended up feeling upset.

CLICHES

Cognitive cliches [5] are Chapman's theory of the most abstract structures in the adult mind. These structures are substantially less general than, for example, predicate calculus formulae with a theorem prover. Cognitive cliches support only *intermediate methods*, which are moderately general purpose, in that a few of them will probably be applicable to any given task; efficient; and not individually particularly powerful. These structures are useful in representation, learning, and reasoning of various sorts. Together they form a general theory of special cases.

A cognitive cliche is a pattern that is commonly found in the world and, when recognized, can be exploited by applying the intermediate methods attached to it. The flavor of the idea is perhaps best conveyed by some examples: *transitivity, cross products, successive approximation, containment, enablement, paths, resources,* and *propagation* are all cognitive cliches. In general, a cognitive cliche is a class of structures which are components of mental models, occur in many unrelated domains, can be recognized in several kinds of input data, and for which several sorts of reasoning can be performed efficiently. [4] describes the possible application of cliches to classical planning. If a problem can be characterized in terms of certain cliches, otherwise intractable planning problems can be solved by polynomial intermediate methods.

Developmentally, cliches are abstracted from concrete competences in specific domains. Ideally, instances of, say, *cross-product* in many domains would be analogically related and the commonalities abstracted into a single coherent, explicitly represented intermediate-competence module. In fact, it seems likely that not all instances of cross-products are recognized as such, and that several clusters of them might join together, creating subtly different intermediate competence. This competence might not be as general in application as ideally it could be, yet still be useful.

What sort of routine activity might cognitive cliches be abstracted from? We suspect that the most basic, central cliches, the naive mathematical ones such as cross-product and ordering, are abstracted principally from the *visual routines* described by Shimon Ullman [18]. In thinking about naive-mathematical cliches, we have a strong sense of visual processing being involved. When we think about cross products, we think of a square array or grid; when we think of an ordering, we think of a series of objects laid out along a line. We suspect that these cliches have been abstracted from *visual routines* for parsing just such images. There is a specific visual competence involved in looking at a plaid fabric, which is the ability to follow a horizontal line, then change to the vertical, and scan up or down, thus reifying the cross point. The internalization of this visual routine and others like it is the ability to see an array in the mind's eye and similarly to scan either axis. This ability may serve as the nucleus for the development of all the naive-mathematical competence surrounding the idea of cross-products.

Visual routines are procedures for parsing images that are dynamically-assembled from a fixed set of visual primitives. By Ullman's account, visual routines are compiled from explicitly represented procedures, but they might also be non-represented routines in our sense. We also suppose that oculomotor actions, as well as early vision computations, might be primitives in visual routines. Visual routines are used for intermediate-level vision: the primitives are too expensive to be computed locally over an entire image (as early vision computations are). The routines are executed in response to requirements of a late-vision object-recognition competence, which are too various to build into hardware. The internalization of visual routines results in a mind's eye that is very far from an array of pixels, but rather consists of just enough machinery to simulate outputs from the visual routine primitives.

CONCLUSION

This paper summarizes portions of a paper [3] we are writing about an emerging view of human activity. The new view starts from the concrete and uses an understanding of it to approach the traditional problems of abstract reasoning. This view is shared, at least in part, by many researchers who have come to it independently from very different perspectives. This gives us more confidence in its necessity. In most cases, researchers have reluctantly given up the traditional primacy of the abstract only in the face of some driving problem. Among these problems are programming a mobile robot, writing reflexive interpreters, deriving an ethnomethodological account of human-machine interaction, programming quasi-static computers, encoding complex concrete real-world problems, working around the computational intractability of classical planning, and developing a computational account of what is known in psychology about human development. We believe that finding coherence among such diverse problems will provide a broad base for work in the new view.

ACKNOWLEDGMENTS

Gary Drescher, Roger Hurwitz, David Kirsh, Jim Mahoney, Chuck Rich, and Ramin Zabih read drafts of this paper and provided useful comments.

We would like to thank Mike Brady, Stan Rosenschein, and Chuck Rich for the several sorts of support they have provided this research in spite of its manifest flakiness.

References

[1] Philip E. Agre, "The Structures of Everyday Life." MIT Working Paper 267, February 1985.

[2] Philip E. Agre, "Routines." MIT AI Memo 828, May 1985.

[3] Philip E. Agre and David Chapman, "AI and Everyday Life: The Concrete-Situated View of Human Activity." In preparation.

[4] David Chapman, *Planning for Conjunctive Goals*. MIT AI Technical Report 802, November, 1985. Revised version to appear in *Artificial Intelligence*.

[5] David Chapman, *Cognitive Cliches*. MIT AI Working Paper 286, February, 1986.

[6] Jon Doyle, *A Model for Deliberation, Action, and Introspection.* MIT AI Technical Report 581.

[7] Gary L. Drescher, *The Schema Mechanism: A Conception of Constructivist Intelligence.* Unpublished Master's thesis, MIT Department of EE and CS, February, 1985.

[8] Gary L. Drescher, "Genetic AI: Translating Piaget into LISP." MIT AI Memo 890, February 1986.

[9] Hubert Dreyfus, *Being-in-the-world: A Commentary on Heidegger's* Being and Time, *Division I.* MIT Press, Cambridge, Massachussetts, forthcoming.

[10] Martin Heidegger, *Being and Time.* Harper and Row, New York, 1962.

[11] John E. Laird, Paul S. Rosenbloom, and Allen Newell, "Chunking in Soar: the Anatomy of a General Learning Mechanism." To appear, *AI Journal.*

[12] Paula Menyuk, *Sentences Children Use.* MIT Press, Cambridge.

[13] Jean Piaget, *The Origins of Intelligence in Children.* Norton, New York, 1952.

[14] Jean Piaget, *Structuralism.* Basic Books, New York, 1970.

[15] Jeff Shrager, "(Cognitive) Mediation Theory." Unpublished manuscript.

[16] Brian Cantwell Smith, "Varieties of Self-Reference." *Proceedings of the Conference on Theoretical Aspects of Reasoning About Knowledge,* Monterey, California, March 1986.

[17] Gerald Jay Sussman, *A Computational Model of Skill Acquisition.* American Elsevier, New York, 1975. Also MIT AI Technical Report 297, August 1973.

[18] Shimon Ullman, "Visual Routines." MIT AI Memo 723, June, 1983.

[19] Daniel Sabey Weld, "The Use of Aggregation in Causal Simulation." To appear in *Artificial Intelligence,* Volume 29, Number 3, August 1986.

[20] D. W. Winnicott, *Through Paediatrics to Psycho-Analysis.* Basic Books, New York, 1975.

AUTHOR INDEX